A Dialogical Concept of Minority Rights

Studies in International Minority and Group Rights

Editors-in-Chief

Gudmundur Alfredsson and Kristin Henrard

Advisory Board

Han Entzinger, *Professor of Migration and Integration Studies (Sociology), Erasmus University, Rotterdam, The Netherlands;* Baladas Ghoshal, *Jawaharlal Nehru University (Peace and Conflict Studies, South and Southeast Asian Studies), New Delhi, India;* Michelo Hansungule, *Professor of Human Rights Law, University of Pretoria, South Africa;* Baogang He, *Professor in International Studies (Politics and International Studies), Deakin University, Australia;* Joost Herman, *Director, Network on Humanitarian Assistance The Netherlands, The Netherlands;* Will Kymlicka, *Professor of Political Philosophy, Queen's University, Kingston, Canada;* Ranabir Samaddar, *Director, Mahanirban Calcutta Research Group, Kolkata, India;* Prakash Shah, *Senior Lecturer in Law (Legal Pluralism), Queen Mary, University of London, the United Kingdom;* Tove Skutnabb-Kangas, *Åbo Akademi University, Dept. of Education, Vasa, Finland;* Siep Stuurman, *Professor of History, Erasmus University, Rotterdam, The Netherlands;* Stefan Wolff, *Professor in Security Studies, University of Birmingham, the United Kingdom.*

VOLUME 11

The titles published in this series are listed at *brill.com/imgr*

A Dialogical Concept of Minority Rights

By

Hanna H. Wei

BRILL
NIJHOFF

LEIDEN | BOSTON

Library of Congress Cataloging-in-Publication Data

Names: Wei, Hanna Hua
Title: A dialogical concept of minority rights / by Hanna H. Wei.
Description: Leiden ; Boston : Brill Nijhoff, 2016. | Series: Studies in
   international minority and group rights ; volume 11 | Based on author's
   thesis (doctoral - University of Bristol, 2012). | Includes
   bibliographical references and index.
Identifiers: LCCN 2016010595 (print) | LCCN 2016010771 (ebook) (print) |
   LCCN 2016010772 (ebook) | ISBN 9789004312036 (hardback : alk. paper) |
   ISBN 9789004312043 (E-book)
Subjects: LCSH: Minorities--Legal status, laws, etc. | Group rights.
Classification: LCC K3242 .W4495 2016 (print) | LCC K3242 (ebook) | DDC
   342.08/7--dc23
LC record available at http://lccn.loc.gov/2016010595

Want or need Open Access? Brill Open offers you the choice to make your research freely accessible online in exchange for a publication charge. Review your various options on brill.com/brill-open.

Typeface for the Latin, Greek, and Cyrillic scripts: "Brill." See and download: brill.com/brill-typeface.

ISSN 2210-2132
ISBN 978-90-04-31203-6 (hardback)
ISBN 978-90-04-31204-3 (e-book)

Copyright 2016 by Koninklijke Brill NV, Leiden, The Netherlands.
Koninklijke Brill NV incorporates the imprints Brill, Brill Hes & De Graaf, Brill Nijhoff, Brill Rodopi and Hotei Publishing.
All rights reserved. No part of this publication may be reproduced, translated, stored in a retrieval system, or transmitted in any form or by any means, electronic, mechanical, photocopying, recording or otherwise, without prior written permission from the publisher.
Authorization to photocopy items for internal or personal use is granted by Koninklijke Brill NV provided that the appropriate fees are paid directly to The Copyright Clearance Center, 222 Rosewood Drive, Suite 910, Danvers, MA 01923, USA.
Fees are subject to change.

This book is printed on acid-free paper and produced in a sustainable manner.

For my grandfather

Contents

Preface XI
Introduction XII

1 **Group Rights: Laws, Concepts, Contestations** 1
   1 Historical Evolution of Group Rights 1
   2 Laws: International, Regional, National 7
      2.1 *The United Nations and Minority Protection* 7
      2.2 *The Council of Europe and Minority Protection* 21
      2.3 *The OSCE and Minority Protection* 27
      2.4 *The European Union and Minority Protection* 31
      2.5 *Minority Rights Protection in Other Regions of the World* 41
      2.6 *What's Wrong, What's Right, What to Expect?* 65
   3 Concepts: Legal, Political, Social 67

2 **Liberal Ideals, the Nature of Identity, Minority Rights**
   Towards a Fusion of Group Rights and Individual Rights 74
   1 Taxonomies of Group Rights (Claims) 75
   2 Necessity of Group Rights 81
   3 Theoretical Validity and Moral Defensibility of Group Rights 84
   4 Group Interests, *Illiberal* Group Rights, the Principle of Toleration 90
   5 The Dialogical Nature of Identity, of Minority Rights 100
   6 'Proximity' and a Dialogical Concept of Minority Rights 102

3 **A Dialogical Translation of the Concept of Minority Rights** 105
   1 Substantive, Procedural, Dialogical: What's In a Name? 105
   2 Legitimacy of Law and Dialogical Minority Rights 106
   3 A Dialogical Concept of Minority Rights 112
      (1) *Rights against the State and Rights against the Group* 112
      (2) *Rights to External and Internal Dialogue vs. Freedom of Expression* 115
      (3) *Substantive Collective Minority Rights with a Dialogical Dimension* 121
   4 Minority Rights and their Prioritisation 123
   5 Conclusion: Contextualising Dialogic Processes in Law and Society 124

4 Minority Rights against the State   126
1.   Minority Rights Held by the *Group* against the *State*   126
    (1)   *Rights to Self-determination and Autonomy*   126
    (2)   *The Limits of Toleration and the Boundaries of Autonomy*   130
    (3)   *Rights to State Assistance and Appropriate Intervention*   138
    (4)   *The Collective Right to External Dialogue*   139
2.   Minority Rights Held by *Members* of the Group against the *State*   155
    (1)   *Individually Held Rights to Cultural Belonging*   155
    (2)   *Rights to State Assistance and Appropriate Intervention*   157
    (3)   *Individual Right to External Dialogue*   158
3.   Conclusion   159

5 Rights against the Minority Group   161
1.   Why is this Limb of Minority Rights Necessary?   161
2.   The Right to Equal Concern   163
3.   Well-being, Happiness, and the Right to Internal Dialogue   165
    (1)   *Objective Well-being and the Right to Internal Dialogue*   166
    (2)   *Subjective Well-being and the Right to Internal Dialogue*   167
4.   Theory in Practice: Cases   171
    Group 1: Cultural Dissidents' Right to Internal Dialogue   172
    Group 2: Minority Children, the Mentally Incapacitated and the Elderly   175
    Group 3: Minority Women's Right to Internal Dialogue   182
5.   The Right of Exit   185

6 Group Agency and the Capacity to Self-govern
From Dependency, through Assisted Capacity-Building, to Meaningful Autonomy   187
1.   Moral Agency, Capacity, and Group Rights   187
2.   The Practical Necessity of Internal Decision-Making Bodies   190
3.   Upgrading Self-governing Capacities   190
    (1)   *Self-determination and Self-governance in International Law*   190
    (2)   *Interpretations of the Right to Self-determination: Three Approaches*   192
    (3)   *From Dependency, through Assisted Capacity-Building, to Autonomy*   196
4.   Conclusion   207

7 **The Rights Culture vs. A Dialogical Rights Culture**
   The Conclusion 209
   1   Minority Rights in the Human Rights System: Pros and Cons   210
   2   Minority Rights and Dialogue: Limits, Challenges, Possibilities   218
   3   Conclusion: The Rights Culture vs. A Dialogical Rights Culture   228

Diagram   230

Bibliography   231
Index   247

Preface

This book is partly based on my doctoral thesis completed at the University of Bristol. My gratitude and thanks are owed to those who made this possible. I am greatly indebted to Professor Julian Rivers, who oversaw the first half of my doctoral research, for introducing me to the deeply sophisticated but wildly exciting world of Jurisprudence. I am very grateful also to Professor Steven Greer, who supervised the second half of my thesis. It was from him that I gained much of my interest in and knowledge of human rights. My sincere appreciation also goes to Professor Stephen Tierney of the University of Edinburgh, Professor Patrick Capps of the University of Bristol and Dr Gabriel Faimau of the University of Botswana for their insights and ever engaging discussions. A special thank you goes to Julián Simón Gómez for never failing to give me a hard time whenever I wanted to give up on this manuscript. I thank my parents for their endless supply of support, advice and freedom over many years. Thanks also to Lindy Melman, Bea Timmer, Wilma de Weert and the team at Brill | Nijhoff for their kind advice, patience and impeccable technical assistance. Most importantly, I thank my colleagues at the Law School of Shandong University, who I have had the great honour to know and respect in a very short period of time. Their friendship and kindness are deeply felt and for which I am profoundly thankful. They know who they are.

During the course of my doctoral research, my grandfather lost his long battle with Parkinson's disease. It has been my most painful regret that during his last remaining years, I, his only grandchild, was absent in every sense of the word. Widely known as a man of principle, dignity, and above all kindness, he would appreciate some of the ideas presented in this work yet remain very critical of many others. It is to him that I dedicate this book.

Hanna H. Wei
Jinan, April 2016

Introduction

The primary objective of *A Dialogical Concept of Minority Rights* is to clarify and re-conceptualise the notion of minority rights, with the specific aim of challenging the generalisations and presuppositions on which much of the ongoing and heated debate on multiculturalism and minority protection has been based, which have generated profound confusions, irrational fears, and worsening minority-state relations in some parts of the world. This will involve a critical analysis of competing theories and conceptions of minority rights as well as current international minority rights law. There are three main aims. The first is to demonstrate that a more plausible and more realistic concept of minority rights should consist of not only *rights against the state* but also *rights against the group*, and that the notion of *group rights* must and can be formally endorsed in order to accurately reflect the interests and needs of minority groups.

The second aim is to call for a decisive departure from the determinist understanding of *rights* (both group rights and individual rights) and seeks to build dialogue into the notion and regime of minority rights by formulating and defending three separate but related *rights to dialogue: the group's collective right to external dialogue, individual members' individual right to external dialogue, and individual members' right to internal dialogue*. The book will show how these three dialogical rights can operate to maintain a healthy balance between the minorities' need to be culturally distinct and their need to relate to, to communicate with, and to belong in, the wider society.

The third aim is to argue that the focus of attention in the field of minority rights protection should shift from drawing fixed boundaries to conflict resolution and interaction management – conflict and interaction between group rights and individual rights, between short-term aims and long-term goals, and between ethno-cultural justice, social unity and geo-political security. Particular attention is paid to the interplay between legal, non-legal, social, cultural and political factors in the recognition and effective protection of minority rights.

The book is divided into 7 chapters. In the *opening chapter*, I examine key legal and political concepts of group rights. Particular attention is paid to the controversies surrounding the notion as it stands. An examination of the historical evolution of the relevant laws, concepts and theories will be followed by a discussion of the contestations and objections to the notion and its formal recognition. The aims are two-fold. The first is to identify the moral dilemmas and political complexities, and to provide a historical and theoretical background against which further analysis can be intelligible and meaningful. The second is to demonstrate why matters concerning minority group interests

INTRODUCTION   XIII

and cultural belonging are matters of 'rights' and nothing less. It is not a call for new rights, but a clarification of existing concepts and laws. Through examining the generalisations and presuppositions on which much of the debate is based, I hope to show that the concept of group rights as it stands is flawed, which has rendered proper understanding and implementation impossible.

Chapter 2 constitutes the first step in the process of rethinking the causes of conflict and confusion in the field of minority rights, and of rediscovering alternatives and possibilities. It begins with an examination of the various taxonomies of group rights, which are widely understood to be collective and substantive in nature, before moving on to examine the necessity, theoretical validity, and moral defensibility of these rights. While critical evaluation of the current approaches will be carried out, it is not my aim to adjudicate between opposing views; rather, I aim to discover common grounds, to work out how these opposing approaches relate to each other in theory and in practice, with the specific aims of, firstly, further identifying and challenging underlying assumptions; secondly, exploring what it is that group rights should aim to protect; thirdly, establishing a theoretical basis for a *dialogical* concept of minority rights through exploring the *dialogical nature of cultural identity*, replacing the basis of *conflict* with a basis of *consensus*.

Building on these discussions, Chapters 3, 4 and 5 flesh out the dialogical account of minority rights. *Chapter 3* aims to show why a plausible account of minority rights should be *dialogical* rather than *substantive* in nature, and why these rights should be more adequately seen as *initially and essentially rights to certain dialogues (and/or procedures) rather than rights to certain ends*. Close attention is paid to minority rights instruments in explaining the differences between the existing notion of minority rights and the *dialogical* one presented here. I will also demonstrate why a plausible dialogical account of minority rights should consist of two broad categories of rights: *rights against the state* (Chapter 4), and *rights against the group* (Chapter 5). This chapter is written with two things in mind. First, the importance of continuity of law; second, a law concerning cultural minorities must accurately identify and reflect their concerns and needs.

Chapter 4 looks at the first limb of the dialogical concept of minority rights: *rights against the state*. These rights are held against the state by *both* the group in question as a collectivity and by the members of the group as individuals. In the case of the group, the rights in question take the form of the group's *collective rights to autonomy and self-determination, collective rights to state assistance and appropriate intervention*, and a *collective right to external dialogue*. In the case of the group members, such rights take the form of the member's *individual rights to cultural belonging, individual rights to state assistance and intervention,* and *individual rights to external dialogue*. I will demonstrate that on this dialogical account of minority rights, the group's collective rights and the members' individually held rights are not incompatible; they are two necessary internal components of the same concept (of minority rights), and that they can and must co-exist in order to bring about just and effective protection of minorities. Relevant case-law will be examined. Against the background of international and regional minority rights instruments, particular attention is paid to the notion of 'national interests' and its role in the (lack of) recognition of group rights and in actions of state intervention.

Chapter 5 examines the second limb of minority rights of this dialogical account: *rights against the group*. These rights are held only by the members of the group and not by the group as a collectivity. There are three separate but related rights: *the right to internal equality, the right to internal dialogue*, and *the right of exit*. Discussions of legitimate state intervention will continue here but in a different context, focusing largely on the position and treatment of the so-called 'minorities within minorities.' The aim is to adequately address the troubling connections between internal oppression and group autonomy, between restrictions on human freedom and cultural belonging, between gender and culture. Relevant case-law will be examined. Attention will inevitably focus on illiberal groups, which, for the sake of analytical clarity, are further divided into two sub-categories: *non*-liberal groups, and *anti*-liberal groups. Particular attention is paid to the so-called *'right to stay'* proposed by some theorists, and why, I argue, it must be re-formulated as *'the right to internal dialogue.'*

Chapter 6 focuses on one persistent argument against the recognition of group rights – groups' lack of moral agency to hold and exercise rights. Particular attention is paid to how the law currently constructs moral agency as compared to how political theorists construct it. The aims are three-fold. The first is to re-examine and challenge the assumption that autonomy is a precondition for holding and exercising rights, and also the assumption that group autonomy and moral agency are the preconditions for a group's exercise of group rights. The second aim is to examine nevertheless the *practical necessity* of groups having internal decision-making bodies in order to be able to hold and exercise group rights, the reasons for and the means and purposes of the creation of these internal bodies, their maintenance and functioning, and whether the state owes a *duty* to certain groups to establish them. The last and most important aim of this chapter is to examine closely minorities,' especially indigenous minorities,' *capacity to self-govern*, in the light of the UN Declaration on the Rights of Indigenous Peoples. Without denouncing the right to self-determination, this chapter suggests a necessary shift of focus to *assisted capacity building*, which requires integrating minority rights and development.

The *concluding Chapter 7* aims to provide a definitive statement of the necessity, justification as well as limits of this dialogical account of minority rights. Attention will focus on the promotion and implementation of the dialogical account, especially the foreseeable administrative difficulties. The ideas which form the background of this chapter is Kymlicka's arguments that the current standard-setting approach in international human rights system is unhelpful, and that we ought to develop a model that builds *progression* into rights documents to allow *progressive implementation*. Developing such a model and successful implementing it require, on the one hand, stable concepts and consistent attitudes, and on the other, highly complex and responsive organisations to monitor progresses along the way. Whilst I wish to emphasise the importance of effective international supervision in the structural and operational protection of minority rights, I will argue that the ultimate aim should be to generate local support and to build up local capacity for implementation in order to reduce if not yet eliminate rights dependency. Particular attention is paid to the interplay between legal, non-legal, social and political factors in the recognition and protection of minority rights, especially the interplay of the legal system, the educational system, and the media in the shaping of public opinions regarding minority groups. I wish strongly to emphasise – firstly, the need to continue to challenge the generalisations and assumptions on which much of the debate has been based and which have resulted in profound confusions and irrational fears; secondly, that international minority rights documents alone can only ever offer minimal protection to minorities, and that it is dialogue, formal as well as informal, inter-cultural as well as inter-disciplinary, that should be the focus of attention from now on; lastly, the vital importance of *social unity* in society, which a *clarification* and *reformulation* of the concept of minority rights will help reinforce, rather than undermine.

CHAPTER 1

Group Rights: Laws, Concepts, Contestations

In this chapter I examine key legal and political concepts and ideas of group rights as well as the controversies surrounding the notion. An examination of the historical evolution of the relevant concepts, theories and laws will be followed by a discussion of the contestations and objections to the notion and its formal recognition. The focus of this chapter is the historical evolution of the notion and especially the changing contexts and backgrounds from which different conceptions of group rights, different formulations, instruments and mechanisms of minority protection have emerged at different stages in history. It is hoped that a historical account of the development of minority rights coupled with a detailed analysis of the instruments and mechanisms can help us make better sense of the current shift in attitude and policy, and will enable us to work out new options in the light of historical experience. To this end, Part 1 provides an overview of the historical development of the idea of group rights; Part 2 examines existing human rights documents on minority protection and the attempts made by the international community, in Europe, and in other parts of the globe, to achieve the same end. Part 3 considers the relevant concepts. The aims are three-fold. The first is to simply provide a historical and theoretical background against which further analysis can be intelligible and meaningful; the second is to identify the moral dilemmas and political complexities; the last is to demonstrate why matters concerning group interests and cultural belonging are matters of 'rights' and nothing less, and to emphasise that the chapter is *not* a call for new rights, but a *clarification* and *re-formulation* of existing concepts.

1   Historical Evolution of Group Rights

The sound of the term 'group rights' is so familiar that its meaning is often taken for granted. The matter is further complicated as terms like 'group-differentiated minority rights,' 'group rights,' 'collective rights,' and 'minority cultural rights' are often used interchangeably. The international community has never been unaware of the so-called '*minority problem*,' which first became a primary international concern during the first few decades of the 20th Century after the Russian, Habsburg and Ottoman empires collapsed into several independent states, and, particularly after the first World War, it focused on those ethnic groups who found themselves living on the other side of the new international border.[1] Initially, bilateral treaties were drawn up, for example, Germany accorded certain special rights and privileges to the Poles living in Germany as long as Poland provided reciprocal rights and privileges to ethnic Germans living in Poland. This treaty system of minority protection existed without an established international framework of human rights, and was later extended and given a more secure legal basis under the League of Nations.[2] But this consensual formula was quickly rejected after the Second World War, and the very idea of 'minority rights' became widely criticised and rapidly discredited. The main reason was that the bilateral treaties were seen as not only unnecessary but also destabilising and partially responsible for the outbreak of war itself. Not only did they protect only minorities who had a 'kin-state' nearby, but also that where such kin-states existed, these treaties could be called upon to justify invasion and intervention in weaker states – for instance, Nazi Germany invaded Poland and Czechoslovakia on the grounds that the treaty rights and privileges of ethnic Germans living there had been violated.[3]

Consequently, the *group-differentiated minority rights* were replaced with a system of universal, generic human rights, which, in theory, aimed to guarantee basic rights to *all* individuals irrespective of their ethnic background, and hence would protect minorities only indirectly. It was universally believed at the time that as long as universal individual human rights were guaranteed, no group-differentiated minority rights would be necessary, as all minorities were covered under the system, not as *minorities* or members of a particular ethnic group, but as *human beings*. It was thus not surprising that there was no mention of 'minority rights' in either the Charter of the United Nations or the Universal Declaration of Human Rights.[4] For almost 40 years, minority rights issues were essentially invisible within the international community, and the very notion of minority rights was substituted with that of universal

---

1 See Malcolm Evans, *Religious Liberty and International Law in Europe* (Cambridge University Press, 1997), Chapter 2; Will Kymlicka, *Multicultural Odysseys: Navigating the New International Politics of Diversity* (Oxford University Press, 2007), Chapter 2.
2 *Ibid.*
3 Will Kymlicka, *Multicultural Odysseys: Navigating the New International Politics of Diversity* (Oxford University Press, 2007), p. 29.
4 See Michael Freeman, *Human Rights* (Polity Press, 2002), p. 114; Will Kymlicka, *Multicultural Odysseys: Navigating the New International Politics of Diversity* (Oxford University Press, 2007), pp. 28–31; as will be shown later in this chapter, the same individualism, as manifested in the absence of minority clauses or group-specific provisions, exists to varying extents in all regional systems, with the European system being the only one that specifically addresses the protection of minorities.

international human rights, the result of which was the removal of cultural and ethnic particularism[5] from the language of rights.

However, as Pentassuglia observes, this movement advancing 'human rights without minority rights' has never been complete as it has been caught between constant battles between universalistic ideals on the theoretical level and the pressing need to address particularistic minority issues on the ground.[6] In the early 1980s, attitudes to minorities in general and indigenous peoples in particular started to shift once again – most visibly in Europe – from the focus on universal human rights *back* to the promotion of group-differentiated minority rights,[7] which notably gained an urgency as the Cold War ended.[8] The major reason was undoubtedly a regional fear of the spread of ethnic violence following the collapse of Communism in Central and Eastern Europe, which would be likely to cause a flood of refugees into Western Europe. It must be noted though that, as Kymlicka observes, this shift of focus from universal rights to minority rights must *not* be viewed as a 'divergence' from universal values; rather, it was believed at the time that minority rights would support, rather than inhibit, the achievements of the aspirations underlying the UN Charter.[9]

This change of attitude marked the era of minority rights related standard-setting. Special measures were also endorsed to recognise indigenous peoples as self-governing communities and to accommodate and protect their own political, cultural and legal systems. A good example was the International Labour Organisation's 1989 Convention (No.169), which was the first truly multiculturalist norm in the post-war era.[10] It decisively departed from the basic principles of the 1957 Convention (which aimed to encourage and enable assimilation and adaptation of indigenous peoples) and moved to assign specific, group-differentiated rights.[11] There were also the UN's International Covenant on Civil and Political Rights 1966 (ICCPR), and the Declaration on

---

5   See Inis Claude, *National Minorities: An International Problem* (Harvard University Press, 1955), p. 211.
6   Gaetano Pentassuglia, *Minority Groups and Judicial Discourse in International Law: A Comparative Perspective* (Martinus Nijhoff Publishers, 2009), p. 3.
7   See Will Kymlicka, *Multicultural Odysseys: Navigating the New International Politics of Diversity* (Oxford University Press, 2007), Chapter 7.
8   David Galbreath &. Joanne McEvoy, *The European Minority Rights Regime: Towards a Theory of Regime Effectiveness* (Palgrave Macmillan, 2012), pp. 17–18.
9   Will Kymlicka, *Multicultural Odysseys: Navigating the New International Politics of Diversity* (Oxford University Press, 2007), p. 47.
10 *Ibid.*, p. 32.
11 *Ibid.*

the Rights of Persons Belonging to National or Ethnic, Religious and Linguistic Minorities 1992 – both documents have been interpreted (and re-interpreted) to encompass not simply weak *negative freedoms* but also *positive rights* against the state.[12] These were followed by the Draft Declaration on the Rights of Indigenous Peoples 1993, which was adopted by the General Assembly in 2007, and re-affirmed the rights protected under Convention No.169 and further asserted that indigenous peoples had a right to *internal self-determination*. These instruments will be examined in detail in Part 2 below.

During the early 1990s, significant changes were taking place in Europe. The three major European intergovernmental organisations – the Council of Europe, the European Union, and the Organisation for Security and Cooperation in Europe (OSCE) – had all taken positive measures to make minority rights protection a top priority. The network of cooperation between these three organisations constitutes the 'European minority rights regime.'[13] Their respective approaches as well as cooperation will be the focus in the next section, but suffice it to say for the time being that, during this period, Europe witnessed a decisive modification of the older norms and perhaps the most active regional developments of minority protection to date.[14] The change of global and European climates inevitably led to developments in other regions of the international community. For instance, there was, among others, the Proposed Declaration on the Rights of Indigenous Peoples 1997 drafted by the Inter-American Commission on Human Rights. There were also regional versions of ideas and norms on the protection of indigenous peoples in Africa and Asia.[15] These changes can be said to have marked the official re-birth of the idea of minority rights as an international concern as well as of a profound optimism during this period (in the West at least) about ethnic relations and ethnic politics.

Unfortunately (and inevitably), it did not last long enough. In the most recent decade, group-differentiated rights have once again come under intense scrutiny and dropped down the list of international priorities; optimism has been fading rapidly. There are various reasons for this yet another

---

12   See Part 2 of this Chapter.
13   David Galbreath &. Joanne McEvoy, *The European Minority Rights Regime: Towards a Theory of Regime Effectiveness* (Palgrave Macmillan, 2012), p. 2.
14   Will Kymlicka, *Multicultural Odysseys: Navigating the New International Politics of Diversity* (Oxford University Press, 2007), pp. 36–39; Steven C. Greer, *The European Convention on Human Rights: Achievements, Problems and Prospects* (Cambridge University Press, 2006), pp. 30–33.
15   See Will Kymlicka, *Multicultural Odysseys: Navigating the New International Politics of Diversity* (Oxford University Press, 2007), p. 38.

transition from intense involvement to rapid withdrawal. Firstly, many have come to believe that widespread ethnic violence is no longer a possibility or at least not a serious threat to world peace and regional security, thus the philosophical exploration of the relevant issues and accompanying contextual research are considered to be no longer urgently necessary. Secondly, greater concerns and more pressing matters such as terrorism and economic crisis have become the new focus of international attention. Thirdly and very importantly, there has newly emerged in the Western world a widespread belief that multiculturalism and the associated group rights ideals have gone too far. One result has been the rise of the far-right in various countries, a widespread reassertion of assimilationist and anti-immigration policies, and a slow-down in international efforts to adequately address pending minority rights issues and to formulate new rules and policies where necessary. As Kymlicka observes, activists and advocates have very much given up their hopes of turning the 1992 UN Declaration on Minority Rights into a binding Convention, or of turning the Council of Europe's Framework Convention on minority rights into a judiciable part of the European Convention on Human Rights, or of further expanding the activities of the OSCE's High Commissioner on National Minorities.[16] Group-differentiated minority rights – once seen as 'a precondition for lasting peace and security,'[17] 'an integral and inseparable part of human rights,'[18] 'of central importance in the reduction of poverty'[19] – are once again, predominantly but not only in the context of Muslim immigrants, and in practice if not in theory, considered somewhat a threat to democratisation and international security. This may be too strong and too general a statement to make, especially considering, for instance, that the EU demands all aspirant member states to pay particular attention to minority rights protection and ratify the Framework Convention for the Protection of National Minorities. But the reality is that implementation in practice is very complicated, and formal adoption of legal instruments does not necessarily reflect genuine acceptance of their values or those of minorities.

At least three key conclusions can be drawn from this brief examination of the historical development of the notion of group-differentiated rights. First, it has always been in a weak, *reactive, defensive,* position – it carries little independent weight of its own, and its profile is determined by the wider

---

16 *Ibid.*, p. 53.
17 The OSCE's 'Lund Recommendations on Effective Participation of National Minorities' 1999.
18 The UNESCO's Universal Declaration on Cultural Diversity 2001.
19 The UNDP, *Overcoming Poverty* (UN Development Program, 2000), pp. 86–88.

constantly and frequently changing, context – hence the extreme highs and extreme lows. This says something about the nature of the notion: it is more of a political ideal than a concrete legal right; its scope and recognition is more a matter of political negotiation than legal determination. The notion as it stands is not a notion of a type of human right in the classical sense. Secondly, although the notion has experienced ups and downs, the international community has always been acutely aware of the so-called 'minority problem.' What keeps changing is the way the 'minority problem' is conceptualised and presented, the international context in which minority issues situate and are analysed, and the assumptions and expectations about the impact of minority rights on longer-term goals of individual nations and of the international community as a whole. Thirdly, a persistent element in the life and death of the notion – is *'fear,' 'anxiety,'* or *'concerns.'* There are new concerns and fears at different stages, but fortunately there are always renewed defences and remedies generated by new hopes. The question is whether we have found a balance between concerns and reliefs, between fears and hopes, and whether we have brought them into a coherent framework to enable creative interpretation and further development.[20] The answer, for the time being, is: *no*.

We can distinguish two levels at which group-differentiated rights are treated with scepticism, and, in some cases, feared: the *conceptual* level and the *practical* level. Stating the obvious, group rights are group-differentiated by definition. There is thus a mismatch between group rights and the traditional understanding of human rights, which sees human rights as by definition universal and individualistic. People are protected by the human rights system as individuals, not as collectivities or members of collectivities. Such a mismatch has understandably generated discomforts and criticisms regarding the correctness, necessity and workability of group-differentiated rights. In other words, such a category of rights does not fit in well with a system that is predominantly individualistic, except as a category of exceptions. But fit in, accepted, liked or not, such a category does exist, and there is a good reason why it exists: there are claims that the individualistic human rights system simply cannot accommodate. But it remains a category of *exceptions*. The insecurity and scepticism at the conceptual level are reflected at the practical level in a form of *paradoxical weariness/fear*: of group rights *being granted*, and of group rights *not being granted,* simultaneously. This is clearly illustrated in almost all of the major international and regional instruments, where the urgency and force of the *message* conflicts hugely with the *means* adopted to

---

20   See, for instance, Will Kymlicka, *Multicultural Odysseys: Navigating the New International Politics of Diversity* (Oxford University Press, 2007).

see it implemented. While the 'means' will be examined in later chapters, the 'message' will be looked at here in Part 2, through a detailed examination of the major international and regional instruments. It should become clear by the end of Part 2 that the international community has never stopped *announcing* protection of minorities, but could do a lot more to make protection *reality*.

2   Laws: International, Regional, National

The international legal basis of minority rights protection can be found in a considerable range of complex international and regional legislation, declarations and conventions. Most states in the world have been and continue to be confronted with the so-called 'minority problem' in their respective domestic contexts, and most have taken steps to recognise and promote the interests of their minorities. The current retreat from minority rights and multiculturalism should not been seen as indicating that the disadvantages and ill treatment of minorities around the globe have in any way become viewed as unimportant or irrelevant. Minority rights, like most rights, are subject to legitimate limitations and must be balanced against each other as well as other issues of public concern. What has changed over time is the contexts, international as well as regional, in which minority rights are considered and applied, thereby causing significant changes (and confusions) in the conceptualisation of 'minority rights' and minority protection. New issues (especially those concerning international and regional security) against which minority rights must be balanced have emerged in great quantity, and minority protection as theory and policy has become increasingly commonly seen as the source of these problems. Despite many similarities, the developments of the ideas and norms of minority protection within the UN framework are in many ways different from those within the frameworks of the European organisations and organisations in other parts of the globe. They need to be considered separately.[21]

2.1   *The United Nations and Minority Protection*
The words 'minority rights' are contained in quite a few international conventions and human rights documents, but they are not a classic type of human right and cannot be understood in quite the same way. They are much more

---

21   Not all instruments are covered – only the ones relevant to the analyses presented in this book.

controversial and frequently come into conflict with the more classical types of rights provided for in these documents. As already mentioned in the first part of this chapter, the League of Nations had a kind of minority protection system based on consensual bilateral treaties and declarations, but it is now universally seen as a complete failure. Some have argued that it is inappropriate to even call it a 'system' at all due to its 'lack of consistency of application, lack of a uniform system of obligations, and lack of a consistent overall purpose.'[22] Indeed, as Jackson-Preece observes, not only did minority obligations under the League system apply only to Central and Eastern European states, which generated a great deal of resentment, but also that the League Council would ultimately become 'an instrument for fomenting international rivalry and discontent,' and would limit their intervention only to areas deemed a national interest.[23]

The Universal Declaration of Human Rights, which in article 1 states that 'all human beings are born equal in rights,' does not contain any mention of 'minority rights.'[24] The omission was deliberate: the UN at the time took the view that individual human rights in the forms of the right to enjoy and freely practise one's culture and the right to non-discrimination would be enough to sufficiently protect minorities, albeit indirectly. Similarly, another UN instrument that emphasised *equality* rather than *difference* was the 1965 International Convention on the Elimination of All Forms of Racial Discrimination (ICERD). Although it makes no direct reference to minority rights, the very nature of its mandate, its emphasis on *equality*, and its stress on the need for states to take *positive measures* in ensuring adequate development and protection of certain racial groups (but *'for the purpose of guaranteeing them the full and equal enjoyment of human rights and fundamental freedoms'*),[25] have won it a unique place in the modern international minority rights regime.[26] It is clear that, at this early stage, the UN believed in *formal equality*, not *difference*; and it was not until the adoption of the International Covenant on Civil and Political Rights (ICCPR) in 1966 that an international instrument of a universal nature contained a provision that was specifically intended to protect minorities.

---

22   Malcolm Evans, *Religious Liberty and International Law in Europe* (Cambridge University Press, 1997), p. 143.
23   Jackson-Preece, 'Minority Rights in Europe: From Westphalia to Helsinki,' *Review of International Studies*, 23:1, pp. 75–93 (1997), pp. 82–83.
24   Michael Freeman, *Human Rights* (Polity Press, 2002), Chapter 6.
25   Article 2(2).
26   Joshua Castellino &. Elvira Domínguez Redondo, *Minority Rights in Asia* (Oxford University Press, 2006), p. 7.

Article 27 of the ICCPR 1966

In addition to creating the UN Human Rights Committee, the ICCPR provides a basis for protection of minorities against discrimination, minority self-determination, and the rights to access civil and political institutions. Article 27, the so-called 'Minority Clause,' states as follows:

> In those states in which ethnic, religious or linguistic minorities exist, persons belonging to such minorities shall not be denied the right, in community with other members of their group, to enjoy their own culture, to profess and practise their own religion, or use their own language.[27]

This clause has three main characteristics. The first is that minority protection as stated is bound up with the concept of *individual* human rights ('..."*persons*" belong to such minorities...'), i.e. the clause is assigning rights to *individual* members of minority groups, not to *minority groups as collectivities*. But of course individuals will only qualify for these specific rights if they are members of minority groups. It is worth noting that from the text of article 27, it seems that only traditional religious, ethnic and linguistic minorities fall within the clause; but from practice, it is clear that indigenous communities are also included (despite the fact that indigenous peoples themselves often reject the 'minority' label). A more controversial issue is whether *citizenship* is a pre-condition for article 27 protection. The mainstream juristic view seems to be that, in order to qualify as a 'minority' for the purpose of article 27, the group and its members must demonstrate a certain degree of stability and permanence in being resident in the state.[28] This view would exclude new arrivals, and especially immigrant workers and temporary visitors. In contrast, the Human Rights Committee has adopted a much more liberal view on the matter in its General Comment 27(50), asserting that citizenship is *not* a pre-condition for protection under article 27,[29] and that minority membership in a

---

27 A very similar (both in wording and mandate) provision is article 30 of the UN Convention on the Rights of the Child 1989, which reads: 'In those states in which ethnic, religious or linguistic minorities or persons of indigenous origin exist, a child belonging to such a minority or who is indigenous shall not be denied the right, in community with other members of his or her group, to enjoy his or her own culture, to profess and practise his or her own religion, or to use his or her own language.' The discussions and criticisms of article 27 of the ICCPR equally apply to this provision.

28 See, for example, Manfred Nowak, *U.N. Covenant on Civil and Political Rights: CCPR Commentary* (N P Engel Pub, 1993), p. 483.

29 A/50/40 (1995), paras. 322, 384, 401.

cultural, religious or linguistic group is the only relevant criterion.[30] It even went so far as to say that not only migrant workers but also visitors to a member state should not be denied the right to exercise their article 27 rights, if they are recognised minorities.[31] As will be shown in later chapters, this radical departure from the old interpretations has brought benefits as well as caused new problems.

The second characteristic is that the rights assigned here are *universal, generic* in nature and cover *all* types of ethno-cultural minority groups. But they are not universal in the sense that these rights are available to *all*; but only to *members of minority groups*. The third characteristic is that the obligation on states is negative ('…such minorities shall not be denied the right…'), but as will be shown in greater detail later, the practice of the Human Rights Committee has clearly established that this article entails positive state duties. This is reflected not only in the framing of questions posed by the Human Rights Committee experts to representatives of member states inquiring about positive steps taken to promote minority cultures,[32] but also in the wording of the Committee's comments on specific countries (including countries that deny the existence of minorities and therefore also the relevance of minority rights), urging them to adopt positive measures to promote and protect minority rights.[33]

This clause has five main problems. First, the fact that this clause applies only to those states in which minorities exist[34] might encourage states to deny the existence of minorities in their jurisdictions. Secondly, the Covenant does not provide definitions of minority, culture, religion, or language. Neither does it specify the meaning of 'profess and practice' or the precise entailments of having these rights. Though lack of precision could facilitate subsequent creative developments, it also creates room for confusion, inconsistency of interpretation and application. Thirdly, it has been widely argued (though with little practical effect) that the system of *individual* human rights needs to be integrated with positive minority protection on a collective basis. Language, for instance, cannot be reduced to an individual right since the exercise of that right depends on an institutional framework based on a collectivity which shares that language. Culture and its various components are products and

---

30   General Comment 27(50), para. 5.1.
31   *Ibid.*, para. 5.2.
32   For instance, see CCPR/C/SR.502 (1984), 3, para. 8.
33   For instance, see A/48/40 (1993), para. 509; Li-ann Thio, *Managing Babel: The International Legal Protection of Minorities in the Twentieth Century* (Martinus Nijhoff Publishers, 2005), p. 220.
34   Michael Freeman, *Human Rights* (Polity Press, 2002), p. 115.

part of the heritage of a collectivity, and thus can only be effectively protected and developed collectively in order to guarantee protection of any language right based on it. Fourthly, the clause does not seem to have gone far enough as it imposes on states only negative duties of non-interference, but no obligations to *assist*, to actively *promote* minorities' interests.[35] But as discussed above, the Human Rights Committee has established that this article should entail positive state duties in practice. Lastly, the generic nature of the clause has caused enormous difficulties in dealing with distinctive claims raised by different types of minority group. It is too vague, too broad.

In response to these problems and in order to strengthen these generic rights, the UN tried to introduce some more solid minority rights giving rise to positive state obligations, and adopted, in 1994, the UN Human Rights Committee's General Comment on article 27.[36] The Human Rights Committee, the monitoring body to the ICCPR, published their interpretation of article 27 of the ICCPR in their General Comment No.23 on 8 April 1994. It is significant in many respects. Firstly, it makes a clear distinction (in para. 4) between the rights protected under article 27 and the *non-discrimination rights* provided under article 2.1 and the *right to equality* under article 26. It also states in the same paragraph that 'some States parties who claim that they do not discriminate on grounds of ethnicity, language or religion, wrongly contend, on that basis alone, that they have no minorities.'[37] This paragraph liberates the minority rights provided in article 27 from the broad, ambiguous, concepts of 'discrimination' and 'equality.' Also, it does seem that the UN had begun to move away from *formal equality* towards *difference* in the field of minority protection. Such a move would have been much more convincing had we been told what exactly the article 27 rights embraced and thereby making the ideas of a minority and its rights more concrete.[38]

Secondly, the Human Rights Committee (in paragraphs 6.1 and 6.2) reinterpreted article 27 of the ICCPR as encompassing not just a duty of *non-interference* in the protection of civil liberties of minorities, but *positive* minority rights in the sense that states are required to take '*positive measures*' to enable and accommodate minorities' exercise of those rights. Again, the significance of these clarifications and re-affirmations should not be over-stated.

---

35 *Ibid.*; Malcolm Evans, *Religious Liberty and International Law in Europe* (Cambridge University Press, 1997), Chapter 8.
36 Will Kymlicka, *Multicultural Odysseys: Navigating the New International Politics of Diversity* (Oxford University Press, 2007), p. 265.
37 http://www2.ohchr.org/english/bodies/hrc/comments.htm.
38 Para. 7 provides some examples of 'cultural manifestation.' But no definition has been given.

Although they do seemingly move beyond article 27 by explicitly including positive rights, these positive rights are very modest and are essentially variations on 'the right to enjoy one's culture, to profess and practise one's own religion, and to use one's own language' – whatever that means and requires. The generic and universal nature of article 27 remains unchanged; so does its inability to deal with diverse claims from diverse groups; so does its paper guarantee status.

The International Covenant on Economic, Social and Cultural Rights

The International Covenant on Economic, Social and Cultural Rights (ICESCR) is a multilateral treaty adopted by the UN General Assembly in December 1966 and came into force in January 1976. It is monitored by the UN Committee on Economic, Social and Cultural Rights, and commits its parties to the granting of economic, social and cultural rights to individuals. The Covenant contains a number of significant provisions. For instance, the joint article 1 of the ICESCR and the ICCPR states that:

> 1. All peoples have the right of self-determination. By virtue of that right they freely determine their political status and freely pursue their economic, social and cultural development.
> 2. All peoples may, for their own ends, freely dispose of their natural wealth and resources without prejudice to any obligations arising out of international economic co-operation, based upon the principle of mutual benefit, and international law. In no case may a people be deprived of its own means of subsistence.
> 3. The States Parties to the present Covenant [...] shall promote the realization of the right of self-determination, and shall respect that right, in conformity with the provisions of the Charter of the United Nations.

This provision is controversial not least because it has been seen as a political tenet into law.[39] Minorities have on various occasions tried to claim the right to self-determination contained in this joint provision, but the Human Rights Committee (commenting on the ICCPR) has firmly rebutted this, and instead asserts that the self-determination right here is enjoyed by colonial peoples only, not by minorities in the general sense; and in the case where 'colonial peoples' and 'minorities' coincide, the granting of a self-determination right is

---

39 See Joshua Castellino &. Elvira Domínguez Redondo, *Minority Rights in Asia* (Oxford University Press, 2006), p. 8.

only permissible in very exceptional cases and must not be seen as creating precedents for all.[40] Clearly, here the Human Rights Committee has made a sharp distinction between self-determination and the general concept of minority rights, which was clearly reflected by its early jurisprudence. Self-determination for minorities was non-existent at this stage. In recent years, this position has shifted most visibly in the context of indigenous peoples, which will be examined in detail in Chapter 6. It can be argued that with the entry into force of the Optional Protocol to the Covenant on 5 May 2013,[41] which has established complaint and enquiry mechanisms for the instrument, the status of economic, social, and cultural rights is now almost identical to that of the classical civil and political rights under the UN system,[42] despite, of course, differences of degree in terms of justiciability, methods of implementation and associated obligations.

The United Nations' 1992 Minority Declaration

Attempts at minority protection based on human rights norms at the international level can also be found in a few other, more specific, recommendatory, documents, e.g. the United Nations' 1992 Declaration on the Rights of Persons Belonging to National or Ethnic, Religious and Linguistic Minorities. This document was yet another response to the problems of article 27 of the ICCPR and yet another attempt to introduce solid, positive, minority rights. Article 1 of the Declaration provides:

> States shall protect the existence and the national or ethnic, cultural, religious and linguistic identity of minorities within their respective territories, and shall encourage conditions for the promotion of that identity.

This clearly goes further than article 27 of the ICCPR (which only assigns negative rights of non-interference) in imposing on states the obligation to take positive measures to protect and promote minorities' identities. However, the significance of this seemingly new inclusion must not be over-stated. It involves no real significant changes to the basic principles of article 27 and also fails to respond to its major limitation – namely, its inability, due to its generic and universal nature, to adequately deal with distinctive claims raised by

---

40 *Ibid.*, p. 9.
41 It was signed by 40 parties and ratified by 10 and therefore passed the threshold of required ratifications (article 18).
42 See Wiktor Osiatyński, *Human Rights and Their Limits* (Cambridge University Press, 2009), p. 120.

different groups. Of course, minority problems are diverse and it is impossible for one single declaration or legislation to contain cure-all solutions to all problems. What is needed is not a list of pre-designed *solutions* and *standards* as such, but some *detailed guidelines* which take into account national differences and specify realistic short-term expectations as well as long-term aims as to how states should interpret and apply universal human rights norms and principles in *cultural-specific ways* but without *undermining* human rights *universalism*.[43] Article 1 as it is constitutes not much more than yet another paper guarantee. In fact, since a declaration strictly speaking is only recommendatory and not a source of binding legal obligation, even its paper *guarantee* status is questionable.

Furthermore, just like the ICCPR, this Declaration does not contain definitions of 'national minority,' 'culture,' 'religion' or 'language,' which has once again left us wondering what exactly these rights embrace or who exactly should benefit. In defence of the ICCPR, it can be argued that the purpose of article 27 was to make a general statement concerning minority rights in a document that would act as a source of legal inspiration and obligation – it did not seek to define its terminology. Thus it should not be criticised for not having done something it never sought to do.[44] Whereas the UN's 1992 Declaration, a declaration concerned *specifically* with national, ethnic, religious and linguistic minorities, ought to have done so. Even if these terms may be clarified through jurisprudence, jurisprudential reasoning often gives rise to definitions that are more embracive and broader than the legal definitions realistically adoptable by international instruments, as while legal theory and ideals aim to protect all, law, as only one of the means of rights protection, can only ever protect a selected number of people and interests in a selected number of ways. The reality is that, in Europe at least, it is up to states' domestic laws on minorities to determine exactly what minority rights to protect and to whom they should be granted.[45]

---

43   See, for instance, *Ibid.*, p. 160; Will Kymlicka, *Multicultural Odysseys: Navigating the New International Politics of Diversity* (Oxford University Press, 2007), Chapter 5; Riahard Falk's '*Cultural Foundations of International Protection of Human Rights*' in Abdullahi Ahmed An-Na'im (ed.), *Human Rights in Cross-Cultural Perspectives* (University of Pennsylvania Press, 1992), Chapter 2, p. 44.

44   Though it could still be criticised for not seeing to do something it probably ought to have done.

45   Eniko Horvath's '*Cultural Identity and Legal Status: Or, the Return of the Right to Have (Particular) Rights*' in Francesco Francioni &. Martin Scheinin (eds.), *Cultural Human Rights* (Martinus Nijhoff Publishers, 2008), p. 171.

The UN Declaration on the Rights of Indigenous Peoples 2007

Many see the 1993 UN Draft Declaration on the Rights of Indigenous Peoples as one very ambitious attempt made by the UN to integrate generic rights with group rights. It originated in 1982 when the UN Economic and Social Council established its Working Group on Indigenous Peoples to develop norms and rules that would protect the world's then 370 million indigenous population. It took the Working Group eight years to complete the draft, which was submitted to the Sub-Commission on the Prevention of Discrimination and Protection of Minorities in 1993. The draft was then referred to the Human Rights Commission, whose newly set-up Working Group met on eleven occasions to fine-tune the document, the final version of which was adopted in June 2006 and then referred to the UN General Assembly. On 13 September 2007, after a long and difficult journey, a revised version of the original Declaration was finally adopted by the General Assembly, with only four states opposing: the US, Canada, Australia and New Zealand.[46]

Besides individual rights, the Declaration also contains a series of *group rights*, including, among others, the right to autonomy or self-determination (articles 3 and 4); the right to maintain and strengthen their distinct political, legal, economic, social and cultural institutions and to participate fully, *if they so choose*, in the political, economic, social and cultural life of the State (article 5); the right to live in freedom, peace and security as distinct peoples (article 7); the right to practise and revitalise their cultural traditions and customs (article 11); the right to manifest, practise, develop, and teach their spiritual and religious traditions, customs and ceremonies (article 12); the right to revitalise, use, develop and transmit to future generations their histories, languages, oral traditions, philosophies, writing systems and literatures, and to designate and retain their own names for communities, places and persons (article 13(1)); the right to establish their own media in their own languages (article 16(1)); the right to participate in decision-making in matters which would affect their rights, through representatives chosen by themselves in accordance with their own procedures, as well as to maintain and develop their own indigenous decision-making institutions (article 18); the right to determine their own identity or membership in accordance with their customs and traditions (article 33(1)); the right to determine the responsibilities of

---

46 All four countries have since signed up to the Declaration. Australia formally endorsed the Declaration on 3 April 2009; New Zealand officially adopted the instrument on 19 April 2010; Canada officially endorsed it on 12 November 2010. President Obama declared on 16 December 2010 that the United States would also sign the Declaration, making the country the last nation in the world to endorse the instrument.

individuals to their communities (article 35); the right to maintain and develop contacts, relations and cooperation with their own members as well as other peoples across borders (article 36(1)). The Declaration also states in article 22(1) that particular attention shall be paid to the rights and special needs of indigenous elders, women, youth, children and persons with disabilities in the implementation of this Declaration; and, in article 27, that the state should give due recognition to indigenous peoples' laws, traditions, customs and land tenure systems.

Although clearly written in the language of law, the Declaration is not legally binding like a treaty, but its political and moral significance must not be under-stated. Firstly, it reaffirms the 1989 International Labour Organization Convention's provisions of indigenous rights regarding land and resource rights, language rights and customary law; secondly, it goes beyond that Convention and provides indigenous peoples with a right to autonomy and *internal self-determination*, i.e. a right to extensive self-government within the boundaries of the larger state;[47] thirdly, the landslide affirmative votes of 144 states in the UN General assembly also seemed to suggest a global consensus on indigenous issues. It should be noted that the four opposing states (the US, Canada, Australia and New Zealand) opposed only specific components of the Declaration, *not* the principle itself. Having said that, the significance of the Declaration must not be overstated either – it is far from a remarkable success as some have generously claimed.

Firstly, although there was a mixture of reasons why indigenous peoples were targeted, as Kymlicka observes, the main ones were moral and humanitarian.[48] As a result, the proposed rights based largely on humanitarian motivations have willingly and naively ignored geo-political security issues. The reference to self-determination probably does address the needs of indigenous peoples, but it is perhaps also the main reason why the draft document had to remain a draft for two decades. This line of criticism may seem unfair at first sight, as the Declaration does have geo-political security issues in mind. It clearly states in article 46(1) that 'nothing in this Declaration may be interpreted as implying for any State, people, group or person any right to engage in any activity or to perform any act contrary to the Charter of the United Nations or construed as authorizing or encouraging any action which would dismember or impair, totally or in part, the territorial integrity or political unity of sovereign and independent States.' This provision has likely been thrown in to

---

47 Will Kymlicka, *Multicultural Odysseys: Navigating the New International Politics of Diversity* (Oxford University Press, 2007), pp. 32–34.
48 *Ibid.*, p. 270.

overtly condition the right to collective autonomy. Reasonable as it looks, in the absence of a definition of what constitutes 'action which would dismember or impair the territorial integrity or political unity of sovereign and independent States,' and given the complex reality of varied natures of indigenous groups around the globe, the simultaneous presence of *both* the right to self-determination *and* the principle of territorial integrity have returned us all to square one, and the latter can be expected to become a card frequently played in the justification of failure to fulfil the state duties generated by the Declaration.

Indeed, we might be able to agree on the general principles of indigenous protection, but we cannot agree on what indigenous action might damage territorial integrity and political unity, and how. The impairment of territorial integrity is more likely to be a gradual, complex and long process than a one-off event. It can be a whole chain of one-off events. A one-off action warranted by the Declaration might have no *immediate* damaging effect on the territorial integrity and political unity of the state, and might not have been intended to ever have such an effect, and therefore ought to be tolerated, accommodated or supported by the state; but such a damaging effect might become apparent in the longer term, intended or not, once or if the chain of events is complete. What article 46(1) does not tell us is what the determining factor is – *intention* to impair the territorial integrity of the sovereign state, or *actual consequences*. Even if article 46(1) was absolutely clear on this, intention would always be hard to determine in international affairs, and damaging consequences on something as broad and as vague as 'integrity' would always be hard to measure.

Article 36(1) of the Declaration grants indigenous peoples, particularly those divided by international borders, the right to establish and maintain 'contacts, relations, and cooperation' with group members across the borders. Consider this provision in conjunction with the ethnic uprisings in recent years will lead us to conclude that its effective implementation is unlikely especially in the parts of the world where it is most relevant. Many national minorities, who are also 'indigenous peoples' for the purposes of the Declaration, often have much closer cultural, religious and linguistic ties with the neighbouring states than with the larger state in which they reside, and have historically felt a sense of distrust or hatred towards the larger state. In such situations there is no exaggeration in the state's claim that matters concerning such minorities may be issues of national security, and hence it is quite understandable, though not desirable, that the larger state would not be happy with such groups 'establishing and maintaining contacts with members across the borders,' and would take whatever measure possible to prevent them from ever gaining anything close to a right of self-determination. Insofar as the larger state could not *guarantee* protection against these real and potential security risks, it is neither wise nor realistic to grant strong rights, especially rights to *self-determination* as so granted by the Declaration, to the minorities in question. Of course, much depends on the type of 'contact.' It appears that the 'indigenous self-determination' that the Declaration aims to protect seems to be of a largely *cultural* and *spiritual* nature, not *comprehensive* or *political*. However, article 36(1) seems to have gone beyond *cultural* and *spiritual* as it expressively states that 'contacts, relations and cooperation' across borders not only include activities for spiritual, cultural, economic and social purposes, but also activities for *political purposes*. But of course, this still falls short of turning indigenous groups into independent political entities.

The second defect in the Declaration is, as already touched on, the lack of necessary definitions of 'autonomy,' 'self-government,' 'indigenous peoples,' 'culture,' 'nationality,' and the list goes on. The academic debate over the necessity of definitions in such documents has been ongoing and is unlikely to end soon.[49] Many favour the flexibility retained by a lack of definitions, whilst others would want to see clearer definitional boundaries being drawn which will enable unambiguous interpretation and clear-cut implementation. How clearer definitional boundaries can bring about fair implementation is the subject of later chapters. While it is understandable why international and regional human rights documents of a more general nature – e.g. the International Covenant on Civil and Political Rights 1966 – do not contain precise definitions, a document that specifically deals with indigenous peoples ought to have been unequivocally clear as to who exactly it aims to protect and what exactly it aims to guarantee. This is more than just a technical defect; it inevitably subjects the implementation of the warranted rights to endless debate and the future development of minority rights protection to numerous dilemmas. One might well speculate why no definitions have been given in the document. A friend of the Declaration would simply say that flexibility was favoured, or perhaps it was generally presumed that universally accepted definitions of 'indigenous peoples' and their rights already existed, and there would be no need to expressly state them. Whilst someone less sympathetic might interpret the lack of effort as a lack of commitment and/or a sense of direction.

The lack of definitions leads us to the third problem with the Declaration: the possibility of manipulations. Since the international generic rights

---

49   See, for instance, Li-ann Thio, *Managing Babel: The International Legal Protection of Minorities in the Twentieth Century* (Martinus Nijhoff Publishers, 2005), pp. 1–16.

framework provides no special, group-differentiated, rights for *'national minorities,'* it would be politically very advantageous for *national minorities* to adopt the label of *'indigenous peoples'* in order to gain concrete group-differentiated rights and the accompanying benefits and privileges. This has indeed been happening. Lennox in her work identifies an increasing tendency for national minorities in Africa, the Middle East and Asia to re-label themselves as indigenous peoples in order to gain the protection available only to indigenous peoples.[50] What national minority would not want the rights (especially the rights to autonomy and self-determination) available to indigenous peoples? If this tendency is allowed to continue, it is likely not only to destabilise the international system of indigenous rights but also lead to the collapse of the minority rights system.[51] There are two potential solutions to this problem: one, to introduce a carefully-formulated, restrictive definition of 'indigenous peoples;' two, to set up an international system of *group-differentiated* rights for *clearly defined* 'national minorities.'

The fourth defect of the Declaration is that it falsely sees indigenous groups as homogeneous collectivities, and has failed to introduce measures to accommodate internal diversity and to tackle internal oppression. This omission is rather surprising considering how forcefully and consistently political theorists, especially feminist theorists, have been voicing their concerns for the troubling connection between cultural protection and internal oppression and inequality.[52] The only article in the Declaration which indicates that internal oppression might have crossed the mind of the General Assembly is article 44, which states that *'all the rights and freedoms recognised herein are equally guaranteed to male and female indigenous individuals.'* However, consider this article in conjunction with article 18, which gives indigenous peoples the right to be represented in decision-making by 'representatives chosen by themselves in accordance with their own procedures,' and article 27, which requires states to give due recognition to indigenous peoples' laws and traditions, and

---

50   Corinne Lennox, *'The Changing International Protection Regimes for Minorities and Indigenous Peoples'* (presented to Annual Conference of International Studies Association, San Diego, March 2006), p. 18.

51   Will Kymlicka, *Multicultural Odysseys: Navigating the New International Politics of Diversity* (Oxford University Press, 2007), p. 287.

52   See, for instance, Anne Phillips, *Multiculturalism Without Culture* (Princeton University Press, 2007), Chapters 1 and 4; Brian Barry, *Culture and Equality* (Polity Press, 2001), Chapters 5 and 7; Michael I. Blake, *'Rights for People, Not for Cultures,' Civilization,* August/September (2000), p. 50; Susan Moller Okin, *'Mistresses of their Own Destiny: Group Rights, Gender, and Realistic Rights of Exit,' Ethics* 112(2) (2002): pp. 205–230; Peter Jones (ed.), *Group Rights* (Ashgate, 2009), Part IV.

article 35, which states that 'indigenous peoples have the right to determine the responsibilities of individuals to their communities,' one would naturally want to ask the following questions: what if the indigenous group's internal procedures produce 'representatives' who are not actually representative because the procedures favour certain members over others? What if the group's internal decision-making bodies are not competent or sophisticated enough to give rise to meaningful self-determination and autonomy? Should the state accommodate indigenous groups that discriminate against and mistreat some of its own members? What if the indigenous laws and traditions require men and women to be treated differently (which many of them do)? Under what circumstances is the state allowed, legally and/or morally, to interfere in the internal affairs of a protected indigenous group when mistreatment of its own members takes place?

These are not simple questions, thus there are no simple answers. The process of answering these questions is the process of working out the key components of a sophisticated model of group-differentiated minority rights, which should include: first, among others, a layer which specifically deals with internal oppression of the so-called 'minorities within minorities'; second, a shift of focus from the single-minded determination to realise a deterministic absolute right to self-govern to *developing and enhancing capacity to self-governance*; third, a sound accompanying theory of state intervention, which inspires and provides the foundation for realistic, legitimate and effective means of protection. Chapter 5 of this book deals with the first component; Chapter 6 deals with the second; and Chapter 4 with the third.

Apart from the UN system, there are currently three functioning regional human rights systems in Europe, the Americas, and Africa respectively. And as will be shown below, of these three established systems, only the European system specifically addresses minority issues. The Arab Charter on Human Rights, which has been in force since 15 March 2008, affirms the principles contained in major international human rights documents, but its institutional practice is largely missing. Similarly, despite having formally recognised the importance of guaranteeing the rights of all as well as vulnerable minority groups, there is not yet any regional human rights mechanism in Asia.[53] I shall look at each region in turn.

---

53   See para. 11, *Final Declaration of the Regional Meeting for Asia of the World Conference on Human Rights, Report of the Regional Meeting for Asia*, A/CONF.157/ASRM/8A/CONF.157/PC/59(1993).

2.2 The Council of Europe and Minority Protection

The Council of Europe has always seen the protection and development of the European cultural heritage as one of its principal functions. And as the main body for promoting and protecting human rights in Europe, it has made firm minority rights commitments since the very beginning. While the United Nations has been targeting indigenous peoples, the Council of Europe has chosen 'national minorities.' Not surprisingly, there is no universally accepted definition of 'national minority,' and neither of the Council of Europe documents contains such a definition, though it most commonly refers to 'sub-state national groups,' 'territorial minorities,' or 'historically settled homeland groups.'[54]

Article 14 of the European Convention on Human Rights

The European Convention on Human Rights (ECHR) does not *directly* touch upon the protection of minorities, though it contains a generic *anti-discrimination* clause which applies to all. Article 14 states that:

> [T]he enjoyment of the rights and freedoms set forth in this Convention shall be secured without discrimination on any ground such as sex, race, colour, language, religion, political or other opinion, national or social origin, association with a national minority, property, birth or other status.

If this provision can be interpreted as a minority provision at all, it is very modest and indirect. It interprets minority rights as rights to formal equal treatment, which seems to distract attention from the very purpose of minority rights. Experience has shown that formal equal treatment based on non-discrimination alone is not enough to solve the so-called 'minority problem.' Studies have demonstrated that in the absence of effective positive measures for the protection of minorities as *groups* and of their societal and institutional structures, the formal equality approach often encourages and promotes *forced* adaptation and assimilation,[55] which can take place quietly and gently. Adaptation and assimilation involve the renewal and gradual transformation of one's conception of the wider world as well as of oneself. If an individual sees himself/herself as having an inferior status in society, he/she is likely to become hypersensitive, defensive, and aggressively assertive about his/her ethnic identity and/or social status; he/she may also develop what some

---

54 See Will Kymlicka, *Multicultural Odysseys: Navigating the New International Politics of Diversity* (Oxford University Press, 2007), p. 203.

55 See, for example, Peter Kivisto, *Incorporating Diversity: Rethinking Assimilation in a Multicultural Age* (Paradigm Publishers, 2005), Chapters 2, 4 and 6.

psychologists call *'minority group self-hatred.'*⁵⁶ Such people deny to various extents their connections with their ethnic and cultural ancestry, detach themselves from their own group, despise and reject the values and practices traditionally associated with their background, and speedily if not blindly adopt the values and cultural practices of the mainstream society. They might prefer to speak the language of the dominant group; they might refuse to wear the traditional clothing associated with their own ethnic or cultural group; they might pretend to belong to a different ethnic group than their own. And so on. Some describe such people as having selfish motives and who shamelessly trade traditional values and ancestry for social advancement; a more sympathetic person will describe them as *culturally displaced,* whose *forced,* yet seemingly gentle and gradual, assimilation merely reflects a natural need to belong, which we all possess. This is not to say that *all* cases of assimilation are *forced* assimilation – there is often an extremely fine line between an action that is *forced* and one that is *voluntary.* Neither is this to claim that *all* assimilation is bad; but merely that *forced* assimilation is bad. This is a problem that an anti-discrimination approach as advocated by article 14 of the ECHR cannot solve.

The European Charter of Regional and Minority Languages 1992
The European Charter of Regional and Minority Languages was adopted as a Convention by the Committee of Ministers on 25 June 1992, with the main purpose of protecting and promoting regional minority languages as a threatened element of Europe's cultural heritage. Instead of assigning individual or collective language rights to recognised individuals, languages or groups, the Charter sets out the obligations of states and seeks to ensure the use of minority languages in education, the mass media, and also in administrative, judicial and economic fields. In more detail: Part I of the Language Charter defines its terms of reference, and states that the purpose of the Charter is to develop the use of the languages traditionally spoken on the continent, regardless of their current official status. Part II contains a list of objectives and principles which must be implemented with respect to all the languages concerned; whilst Part III contains a list of specific measures to promote the use of regional or minority languages in public life, allowing the states to decide for themselves whether or which provision to adopt. Finally, the Charter sets out in Part IV measures concerning the application of the Charter.

---

56   Kurt Lewin, *Resolving Social Conflicts: Selected Papers on Group Dynamics* (Harper &. Brothers, 1st edition, 1948), pp. 186–200; C.f. Jean-Paul Sartre, *Anti-Semite and Jew* (Grove Press, 1960), pp. 92–100.

It can be argued that since the main aim of the Charter has been to promote minority languages and preserve minority cultures, it protects linguistic minorities only in an indirect way. The Charter does not establish specific individual or collective rights for the *language users* but instead sets out obligations for the states with regard to the use of the languages. Arguably, the cultural preservationist nature of the Charter might be the main reason that it has proven unpopular and ineffective: protecting languages is not always the same as protecting language users, sometimes quite the contrary; and protecting languages is not always the same as preserving languages and precluding change and adaptation, sometimes quite the contrary.[57] Furthermore, although the Charter has taken into account the variable situations of different linguistic groups and offers a menu of 67 measures from which a minimum of 35 must be adopted, nothing in the Charter either compels the states to tailor the chosen measures to match the specific situations of different linguistic groups or to adopt more robust language rights. It is perhaps unlikely that international law will ever be able to do more than specify the most minimal of standards with regard to language rights. Universal language rights seem unable to address the local policy questions, which always centre on more extensive rights-claims, by linguistic minorities as well as majorities, which are always conditional on size, history, culture, and politics.[58]

The Framework Convention for the Protection of National Minorities

The Council of Europe's best effort at minority protection has been the Framework Convention for the Protection of National Minorities, which was partly based on the ideas and norms expressed in Recommendation 1134 (1990) of the Assembly of the Council of Europe,[59] and was adopted by the Committee of Ministers on 10 November 1994 and came into force on 1 February 1998. Being the first multilateral binding instrument devoted to the protection of European national minorities within the respective territories of the member states, it undertakes to combat discrimination, promote equality, preserve and develop the culture and identity of national minorities, guarantee freedoms in relation to the manifestation of religion, access to the media, minority

---

57 See, for instance, Will Kymlicka &. Alan Patten, *Language Rights and Political Theory* (Oxford University Press, 2003), Chapter 5.

58 T. Skutnabb-Kangas &. R. Phillipson, *Linguistic Human Rights: Overcoming Linguistic Discrimination* (Mouton de Gruyter, 1995).

59 Will Kymlicka, *Multicultural Odysseys: Navigating the New International Politics of Diversity* (Oxford University Press, 2007), p. 37.

language use, education, and participation in public life.⁶⁰ Although the Framework Convention is not legally enforceable, article 25 nevertheless binds the signatory states to submit periodic reports to the Council of Europe containing 'full information on the legislative and other measures taken to give effect to the principles set out in this Framework Convention.'⁶¹

The Framework Convention has a number of problems. Firstly, to a large extent, the provisions have merely restated the norms and principles that already exist in international treaties, and maintain an individualistic approach to minority protection with no reference to group-differentiated rights. Secondly, the instrument has not yet become the source of universally accepted standards throughout Europe. Despite the fact that acceptance of the Framework Convention has been a condition for EU membership, not all have signed or ratified it, and those who have signed or ratified it may not have done so whole-heartedly. This apparent lack of political will to fully commit to minority rights may be due to the fact that the Framework Convention is legally binding and obliges member states to introduce legal and political measures to implement the document.⁶² Having said that, so far 39 of the 47 member states of the Council of Europe have both signed and ratified the document – hardly a bad start; Belgium, Greece, Iceland and Luxembourg have signed but not ratified; Andorra, Monaco, Turkey and France have done neither.⁶³ It is necessary to note that, despite the presence of significant minority populations, France denies the existence of 'national minorities' on French soil and thereby denies the applicability of the document.

Thirdly, it contains no definition of 'national minorities' or of any other relevant terms (which may in fact be the chief reason for its relatively successful ratification process). This leaves the door wide open to all sorts of interpretations depending on the interests and attitudes of the member states, and thereby raises and will continue to raise profound confusions and dilemmas for future development. Apparently, an attempt to introduce a definition was rejected on the basis that it would be impossible to reach a general consensus

---

60   Articles 4 and 5.
61   See also Steven C. Greer, *The European Convention on Human Rights: Achievements, Problems and Prospects* (Cambridge University Press, 2006), p. 32.
62   An alternative view is that it is not the awareness of the instrument's significance that has caused the apparent reluctance to sign and ratify, but the lack f it, '[...] the apparent, widespread and erroneous perception that the Convention is a political declaration rather than a human rights treaty legally binding under international law' (NGO Declaration on the Framework Convention, 2008, para. 13).
63   See the website of the Council of Europe: http://www.coe.int/t/dghl/monitoring/minorities/1_AtGlance/PDF_MapMinorities_bil.pdf.

on a definition. While ratifying it, several states, such as Denmark, Germany, Switzerland and Macedonia, made declarations introducing restrictive interpretations of the term 'national minorities,' which were denounced by other states. Indeed, in many instances a sharp distinction cannot be made between national minorities and other minorities. But in the absence of a definition, it would be impossible to reach a general consensus on a universally accepted interpretation of the depositions of the Framework Convention. However, there is an argument that the lack of a definition in the Framework Convention (and similarly in other international and regional instruments) is a positive thing. In a declaration submitted by a coalition of minority rights NGOs at a Strasbourg conference organised by the Council of Europe in October 2008, the following view was put forward:

> While some minorities would benefit from a clear definition, the risk persists that any such definition would be exclusive, thereby unduly limiting the scope of protection. The interpretation and the application of the Framework Convention should be based on the principle that the existence of minorities is a matter of fact and not of law. In the light of this well-established principle in minority rights law, minority NGOs feel that the Advisory Committee should continue to embrace a broad view on which groups are to be covered by its monitoring and offer this view for adoption by the Committee of Ministers. Accordingly, States Parties should unconditionally extend the application of the Framework Convention to all minority groups which self-identify as such.[64]

If the lack of a definition offers flexibility, this huge scope for flexibility is further widened by the frequent appearance of '*as far as possible*' in the Framework Convention.[65] See article 14.2 for example:

> In areas inhabited by persons belonging to national minorities traditionally or in substantial numbers, *if there is sufficient demand* (emphasis added), the Parties shall endeavor to ensure, *as far as possible* (emphasis added) and within the framework of their education systems, that persons

---

64 'Assessing the impact 10 years on: NGO Declaration on the Framework Convention for the Protection of National Minorities,' para. 8: https://www.coe.int/t/dghl/monitoring/minorities/6_resources/PDF_IAConf_NGO_Declaration_en.pdf.
65 Some argue that it is precisely the flexibility of the document that has allowed a large number of member states to ratify it quickly, and that it is likely to attract more new comers.

belonging to those minorities have adequate opportunities for being taught the minority language or for receiving instruction in this language.

This clause does not generate a clear *positive right* to education in one's own language. It is merely inviting states to *contemplate the possibility* of providing education in minority languages, and thereby gives the states a great deal of discretion. Having said that, the document might be weak, it is not useless. Section IV requires member states to submit periodical reports every five years which will be examined by an Advisory Committee as well as the Committee of Ministers. This does indicate a certain level of moral dedication and a minimum level of practical protection. And more importantly, it has helped create a political culture of appreciating national minorities across the European continent. But again, it seems that the control mechanisms function entirely on the basis of member states' reports.

One of the major problems that have arisen out of the reports concerns the political representation of the minorities and their right to autonomy and self-government. This is the fourth problem with the Framework Convention. As Kymlicka observes, the idea that national minorities 'should have *guarantees* regarding participation in decisions affecting regions where they live' was part of the original text of article 15 of the Framework Convention, but was deleted from the final text.[66] Thus, again, although the Framework Convention apparently goes beyond article 27 of the ICCPR by providing for some albeit minor positive rights, the changes are hardly significant. It is yet another very modest instrument containing a weak set of norms. Yet, it has played its role in the protection of national minorities in Europe and brought about interesting results. Among others, its implementation has caused divergence in both the choice of the goals and the choice of the means to achieve those goals, due to the differing interests of the member states and their attitudes towards national minorities.[67] Some states, such as Finland, have focused on engaging with their minorities and seeking to reach a consensus; whilst others, such as France, which has neither signed nor ratified the instrument, are not remotely interested in reaching an agreement of any kind. It does appear that many minorities in Europe have not yet become technically capable or politically organised enough to elaborate and negotiate objectives for their own protection. This inability to self-represent will be explored in greater detail in Chapters 6 and 7.

---

66 Will Kymlicka, *Multicultural Odysseys: Navigating the New International Politics of Diversity* (Oxford University Press, 2007), p. 217.

67 *Ibid.*, Chapter 6.

2.3 The OSCE and Minority Protection

With 56 participating States from Central Asia, Europe, and North America, the Organisation for Security and Cooperation in Europe (OSCE) is the largest regional security organisation in the world, with the primary tasks of conflict prevention, early warning, crisis management and post-conflict rehabilitation under Charter VIII of the UN Charter.[68] It addresses a wide range of security-related issues including counter-terrorism, arms control, human rights, and economic activities. The organisation evolved dramatically following the fall of Communism in Central and Eastern Europe, and issues of minority protection quickly came to the forefront of its agenda.[69] Its work in the field of minority protection, more specifically the protection of linguistic and educational rights of members of national minorities, stems from the so-called 'human dimension' of security, which is one of the three dimensions of security that it deals with and has overtime become the most prominent aspect of the OSCE.[70] Fearing the spread of ethnic conflicts following the collapse of Communism in 1989, which might generate large-scale refugee movements into Western Europe,[71] the Western democracies decided to 'internationalise' the treatment of minorities in post-communist Europe. The OSCE declared that the status and treatment of national minorities did not constitute exclusively internal affairs of the respective State but rather were matters of legitimate regional and international concern.[72]

Although it has been argued that the emphasis of the OSCE has shifted since the early days from standard-setting to monitoring implementation of those standards,[73] its main efforts still seem to be predominantly directed to standard-setting. This started with the signing of the Helsinki Final Act in 1975, and reached its peak in the Copenhagen Document of 1990, in which the OSCE made the first ever European official declaration on the protection of minority rights, containing a comprehensive set of norms and standards concerning the rights of persons belonging to *national minorities*, including the right to use of the mother tongue, the right to education in one's mother tongue, and the right

---

68 See Jane Wright, 'The OSCE and the Protection of Minority Rights,' *Human Rights Quarterly*, Volume 18, Number 1, February (1996), p. 190.
69 *Ibid.*
70 The other two dimensions are the 'politico-military' dimension and the 'economic and environmental' dimension.
71 Will Kymlicka, *Multicultural Odysseys: Navigating the New International Politics of Diversity* (Oxford University Press, 2007), p. 174.
72 *Ibid.*, p. 173.
73 Jane Wright, 'The OSCE and the Protection of Minority Rights,' *Human Rights Quarterly*, Volume 18, Number 1, February (1996), p. 192.

to non-discrimination. The significance of the Copenhagen Document lies mainly in the fact that the OSCE member states accepted that the protection of national minorities was a *fundamental goal* of the OSCE and an integral part of the protection of human rights, fundamental freedoms, democracy and the rule of law;[74] and they declared that 'persons belonging to national minorities can exercise and enjoy their rights individually as well as in community with other members of their groups.'[75] This together with article 35, which notes the use of 'appropriate local or autonomous administrations corresponding to the specific historical and territorial circumstances as a way of protecting or promoting its identity,' seem to point to autonomy, self-determination, and group rights – a very unusual move at the time.[76]

The Charter of Paris for a New Europe, signed on 21 November 1990, took the 'human dimension' further. It not only reiterated the determination of the then 34 participant states to promote the rights of minorities but also moved towards creating institutional structures to enable internal reform. A High Commissioner on National Minorities (HCNM) was appointed at a follow-up meeting in Helsinki in 1992 with the main task of providing early warning and seeking early resolution of ethnic tensions involving national minorities that seemed likely to threaten peace and security between OSCE States.[77] It aims to promote dialogue, engages in preventive diplomacy, collects information regarding minority issues and assesses the nature and degree of tensions, and produces reports when member states depart from recognised norms and standards.[78] Clearly, the HCNM is essentially a security instrument with a predominant emphasis on conflict *prevention*, *not* a vehicle through which minority rights abuses can be efficiently addressed.[79] It concerns only with tensions that *could potentially* develop into conflicts in the OSCE area, not with tensions *within participant states* unless they have the potential to spiral into *regional* conflicts.[80] For this

---

74 Will Kymlicka, *Multicultural Odysseys: Navigating the New International Politics of Diversity* (Oxford University Press, 2007), p. 37.
75 Article 32(6).
76 See Jane Wright, '*The OSCE and the Protection of Minority Rights*,' Human Rights Quarterly, Volume 18, Number 1, February (1996), p. 197; and Geoff Gilbert, '*The Council of Europe and Minority Rights,*' Human Rights Quarterly, Volume 18, Number 1, February (1996).
77 Charter of Paris for a New Europe: http://www.hri.org/docs/Paris90.html; the Helsinki Document.
78 See also 'The Challenges of Change' of 1992, in which the mandate of the HCNM is laid down: http://www.osce.org/hcnm/107878.
79 See Jane Wright, '*The OSCE and the Protection of Minority Rights*,' Human Rights Quarterly, Volume 18, Number 1, February (1996), p. 200.
80 The Helsinki Document.

reason, as Bloed observes, national minorities are not dealt with even-handedly under this instrument: 'Even if such violations would result in "tensions," it might well be that such tensions are not tensions which have the potential to develop into a conflict within the OSCE area, affecting peace, stability or relations between participating States, requiring the attention of the OSCE, as laid down in the HCNM's mandate.'[81] In other words, in order to be paid serious attention, the tensions must be perceived as capable of spreading. Security, not minority rights, is the goal.[82] Yet, despite the organisation's focus on security over rights, some have argued that it in fact offers the most developed and complete approach to minority protection in the world by combing three approaches of implementation: visits to affected areas and discussions with affected parties, recommendations following visitations, and using geo-political connections to influence affected parties and encourage dialogue and cooperation.[83]

Over the years, independent experts had developed a number of important thematic recommendations and guidelines for the protection of minority rights, which were later endorsed by the High Commissioner on National Minorities. These include the Hague Recommendations Regarding the Education Rights of National Minorities (1996); the Oslo Recommendations Regarding the Linguistic Rights of National Minorities (1998); the Lund Recommendations on the Effective Participation of National Minorities in Public Life (1999); Guidelines on the Use of Minority Languages in the Broadcast Media (2003); Recommendations on Policing in Multi-Ethnic Societies (2006); The Bolzano/Bozen Recommendations on National Minorities in Inter-State Relations (2008); and the Ljubljana Guidelines on Integration of Diverse Societies (2012).[84] Scholarly studies have closely examined the impact of the OSCE on minority protection, and have focused particularly on the earlier three recommendations (Hague, Oslo and Lund), mostly concluding that they have had a substantial impact on minority rights standard-setting in the region, some even concluding that these earlier recommendations have come close to the status of politically binding documents, qualify as 'soft law' and are frequently referred to by other

---

81   Arie Bloed, *'Monitoring the CSCE Human Dimension: In Search of its Effectiveness'* in Arie Bloed et al (eds.), *Monitoring Human Rights in Europe – Comparing International Procedures and Mechanisms* (Martinus Nijhoff, 1993), p. 68.

82   The distinction between security/conflict prevention and minority rights was first made by the then High Commissioner Rolf Ekeus. See David Galbreath &. Joanne McEvoy, *The European Minority Rights Regime: Towards a Theory of Regime Effectiveness* (Palgrave Macmillan, 2012), pp. 71–72.

83   *Ibid.*, p. 74.

84   All available at http://www.osce.org/hcnm/66209; Will Kymlicka, *Multicultural Odysseys. Navigating the New International Politics of Diversity* (Oxford University Press, 2007), p. 37

international instruments such as the UN Working Group on Minorities in their reports and opinions.⁸⁵

In *Synergies in Minority Protection,* Henrard and Dunbar evaluate the 2006 Recommendations on Policing in Multi-Ethnic Societies in terms of whether they contribute to the interpretation and development of existing minority rights standards, and conclude that the recommendations constitute 'a missed opportunity' to strengthen existing norms and further develop previous efforts by other expert groups and organisations, and even go as far as to call the recommendations 'a duplication of another document,' namely the 1996 Rotterdam Charter 'Policing for a Multi-Ethnic Society.'⁸⁶ However, de Graaf and Verstichel disagree and argue that the recommendations significantly differ from the Rotterdam Charter in that the former was the only written guidelines at the time that focused on transitional states and post-conflict situations, while the latter concentrated on Western Europe and relations between police and migrant minorities in urban areas.⁸⁷ Neither does the latter address issues of prevention and conflict management, which the recommendations do.⁸⁸ The 2008 Bolzano/Bozen Recommendations on National Minorities in Inter-State Relations have also generated similar debates. Since they concern directly with the relationship between national minorities and their kin states, they immediately bring up questions concerning national sovereignty and interference in states' domestic affairs.⁸⁹

---

85   See, for instance, J. Packer &. G. Siemienski, *'Integration through education: the origin and development of the Hague Recommendations,'* 4(2) *International Journal on Minority and Group Rights* (1996–7), pp. 187–198; A. Eide, *'The Oslo Recommendations Regarding the Linguistic Rights of National Minorities: An Overview,'* 6(3) International Journal on Minority and Group Rights (1999), pp. 319–328; M. Weller (ed.), *The Rights of Minorities in Europe: A Commentary on European Framework Convention for the Protection of National Minorities* (Oxford Univeristy Press, 2005); Kristin Henrard &. Robert Dunbar, *Synergies in Minority Protection: European and International Law Perspectives* (Cambridge University Press, 2008), p. 105.

86   Kirstin Henrard &. Robert Dunbar, *Synergies in Minority Protection: European and International Law Perspectives* (Cambridge University Press, 2008), pp. 111–112; The 1996 Rotterdam Charter 'Policing for a Multi-Ethnic Society' is legally non-binding, jointly produced by representatives of the police, municipal authorities as well as NGOs across Europe. At: http://www.rotterdamcharter.nl/.

87   Vincent de Graaf &. Annelies Verstichel, *'Recommendations on Policing in Multi-Ethnic Societies,'* in: IFSH (ed.), OSCE Yearbook 2006, pp. 317–330 (2007), p. 320.

88   *Ibid.*

89   Hans-Joachim Heintze, *'The Significance of the Thematic Recommendations of the OSCE High Commissioner on National Minorities,'* in: IFSH (ed.), OSCE Yearbook 2012 (2013), pp. 249–265, p. 266.

These are merely some examples of the many commentaries on the work of the OSCE in the field of minority protection. For the purposes of this book, it is unnecessary to repeat in greater detail the various arguments made by different scholars. It should be noted though that the nature of the newer recommendations and guidelines is rather different from that of the earliest three recommendations, in that they are much more technical and operational, without a strong link to existing normative principles and standards. It does seem that, by adopting this new style, the OSCE has lost some of the momentum that it generated in the 1990s with the earlier recommendations,[90] though its combination of conflict prevention strategies and emphasis on compliance with minority rights standards has provided useful guidance for governments and is a source of inspiration for other international organisations working in the field.

2.4   The European Union and Minority Protection

While the United Nations, the Organisation for Security and Cooperation in Europe and the Council of Europe have all introduced measures on minority protection, the European Union appears the least bothered by the issue. This is understandable considering that, although the Treaty of Maastricht of 1992 gave the European integration process a clear trans-economic dimension by establishing a *political* union, EU integration has been a largely *economic* process. As a supranational organisation, it sets forth binding laws in a wide range of sectors. Thus any commitment to minority issues would legally bind all member states. It is perhaps (partly?) for this reason that the EU has been reluctant to consider minority rights protection properly at the European level, but to carry on treating it as internal affair of the sovereign states.

Just because the EU was not established specifically to address minority rights issues does not mean that it can turn a blind eye to such troubles – to do so would undermine its motto 'United in Diversity' and pose considerable threat to its goal of maintaining regional peace and security. The Europa website explains the EU motto as signifying 'how Europeans have come together [...] to work for peace and prosperity, while at the same time being enriched by the continent's many different cultures, traditions and languages.'[91] Indeed the EU is a diverse community, in terms not only of membership but also of institutional arrangements, responsibilities and competences, with a broad range of complex mandates, bodies, and goals. While minority protection is not the EU's main objective, it would be wrong to say that it has either turned a blind

---

90   Cf. *ibid.*
91   http://europa.eu/about-eu/basic-information/symbols/motto/index_en.htm.

eye to it or is unfamiliar with cultural diversity. Rather, it has adopted a negative, indirect, approach to such issues, and has taken steps to ensure that national laws aimed at protecting minorities are compatible with EU norms, by, for instance, since 1993, demanding that countries applying to accede to the EU achieve certain standards of minority protection before being allowed to join; and by checking whether specific linguistic provisions are compatible with the basic freedom of residence of EU citizens and freedom of movement of workers within the EU. Nevertheless, the activities of the EU concerning minority protection remain very limited. It has also been argued that certain aspects of EU minority rights law fall short of international standards, and that the entitlement to a cultural right in the EU framework is very weak.[92]

It was with the adoption of the 1993 Maastricht Treaty (subsequently amended by the treaties of Amsterdam, Nice, and Lisbon) that EU cultural policy finally got its legal basis. The 2009 Treaty of Lisbon (the Reform Treaty) gives greater significance to culture, and states that the EU shall aim to 'respect its rich cultural and linguistic diversity, and shall ensure that Europe's cultural heritage is safeguarded and enhanced.'[93] Article 167 of the Treaty on the Functioning of the European Union (TFEU),[94] formerly article 151 of the Treaty Establishing the European Community (TEC), establishes both the material content of the principles as well as the decision-making procedures. It provides:

> 1. The Union shall contribute to the flowering of the cultures of the Member States, while respecting their national and regional diversity and at the same time bringing the common cultural heritage to the fore.
> 2. Action by the Union shall be aimed at encouraging cooperation between Member States and, if necessary, supporting and supplementing their action in the following areas: improvement of the knowledge and dissemination of the culture and history of the European peoples; conservation and safeguarding of cultural heritage of European significance; non-commercial cultural exchanges; artistic and literary creation, including in the audiovisual sector.

---

92 Tawhida Ahmed, *The Impact of EU Law on Minority Rights* (Hart Publishing, 2011), p. 121.
93 Article 3 TEU (Treaty on European Union). It should also be noted that with the coming into force of the Lisbon Treaty, the Charter of Fundamental Rights of the EU becomes legally binding. Article 22 of the Charter states that 'the EU shall respect cultural, religious and linguistic diversity.'
94 'Treaty on the Functioning of the European Union,' previously named the 'Treaty Establishing the European Community' (TEC; also known as the Treaty of Rome), renamed by the 2009 Treaty of Lisbon. The word 'Community' has been replaced by the word 'Union' throughout the treaties.

3. The Union and the Member States shall foster cooperation with third countries and the competent international organisations in the sphere of culture, in particular the Council of Europe.

4. The Union shall take cultural aspects into account in its action under other provisions of this Treaty, in particular in order to respect and to promote the diversity of its cultures. [...][95]

This provision clearly requires the EU to play a more active role in the cultural field – by way of 'encouraging,' 'supporting,' and 'supplementing.' This relatively weak 'enabler' role means that the EU may not place formal constraints on national constructions of cultural identity or national protection of cultural rights.[96] In other words, article 167 confirms that protection of cultural diversity is largely a matter for the Member States,[97] and that the EU is there to supplement the cultural policies of the States.[98] It is very important to note that article 167 does not specify whether the culture it seeks to promote and protect includes also minority cultures, though nothing in the provision suggests a restricted interpretation of 'culture' limiting to mainstream European identities. To the contrary, the requirement in paragraph 1 to respect 'regional diversity' is a strong indication that the article concerns much more than national identities of the Member States. Indeed, as will be shown in the paragraphs below, activities, schemes and projects of the EU (especially those of the Commission) indicate that a broad interpretation of the provision has been adopted. Rightly so.

So far, among all EU institutions, the European Parliament has shown the most intensive interest in minority rights issues. The evidence lies in a wide range of resolutions dealing with ethnic, cultural and linguistic minorities: Resolution on a Community Charter of Regional Languages and Cultures and on a Charter of Rights of Ethnic Minorities 1981; Resolution on the Multilingualism of the European Community 1982; Resolution on Measures in Favour of Minority Languages and Cultures 1983; Resolution on the Languages and Cultures of Regional and Ethnic Minorities in the European Community 1987; Resolution on the Situation of Languages in the Community and the Catalan

---

95 See the Official Journal of the European Union, C 83/47, 30.3.2010: http://eur-lex.europa .eu/legal-content/EN/TXT/PDF/?uri=CELEX:12010E/TXT&qid=1458210200185&from=EN.
96 Tawhida Ahmed, *The Impact of EU Law on Minority Rights* (Hart Publishing, 2011), p. 126.
97 *Ibid.*
98 Article 6 TFEU provides that 'The Union shall have competence to carry out actions to support, coordinate, and supplement the actions of the Member States.' One of the seven key areas of such actions identified is 'culture' (c).

Language 1990; Resolution on Linguistic Minorities in the European Community 1994; Resolution on the Right to Use One's Own Language 1994; Resolution on the Use of the Official Languages in the Institutions of the European Union 1995; and Resolution on Regional and Lesser-Used European Languages 2001. The Resolution on Racism, Xenophobia and Anti-Semitism and on Further Steps to Combat Racial Discrimination 1999, which states that 'combating discrimination against immigrants and religious minorities is integral to any comprehensive policy against racism and xenophobia,' is another example of the European Parliament's approach to minority rights protection. It also reiterated its fundamental approach to human rights in establishing the respect for the rights of minorities as prerequisites for accession negotiations. However, it should be noted that these are political measures and are not legally binding as directives and regulations – which the European Parliament cannot create. A significant move by the European Parliament was the re-establishment of the Intergroup for Traditional Minorities, National Communities and Languages in December 2009 (around the same time the Lisbon Treaty came into force). It has set itself the task of bringing together the European institutions, international organisations, NGOs and academics to work on issues of national and linguistic minorities.[99] The aim is to make the Intergroup the chief forum for national and linguistic minority issues at the EU level.[100]

Compared to the measures adopted by the European Parliament, those adopted by the Commission and the Council are of a more technical nature. Much of the meaning of the undefined 'culture' can be deduced from the activities of the Commission, who implements the programmes and schemes undertaken on the EU's legal bases, and who clearly does not regard the phraseology of article 151 as a barrier to adopting a broad interpretation of 'culture.' For instance, the European Bureau for Lesser Used Languages (EBLUL) (which was closed by a decision of its Board of Directors on 27 January 2010[101]) acted as an activities coordinator for the 30 million EU citizens who spoke over 30 minority languages. Partly through the EBLUL, the EU commissioned a large number of studies and publications relating to minority protection. The Eastern enlargement process has provided a fresh impulse to go even further in this direction as even greater linguistic diversity would be embraced as the process continues. Thus the cultural dimension of European integration has been acknowledged.

The Stability Pact, adopted in Paris in 1995 by 52 member states of the OSCE, clearly showed that minority issues were of crucial importance in European

---

99   See http://poliglotti4.eu/docs/Publis/2255.pdf.
100 *Ibid.*
101 The official reason given in the Closing Statement of the EBLUL was that 'the funding mechanism of such an organisational model [was] not suitable in current circumstances.'

politics.[102] In 1993, the Council approved a set of criteria which every state interested in accession had to meet. One of which, besides democracy, rule of law and human rights, was that the candidate state must demonstrate respect for and protection of the rights of minorities.[103] Subsequently, the Commission analysed and discussed in detail the situation of ethnic minorities, commented on various discrimination situations in some candidate states, and set out short-term priorities as well as longer-term goals. It was in this way that the Copenhagen criteria became the preconditions and a founding principle of the enlargement process, which must be complied with if any state was to apply for membership.

Further in recognition of linguistic and cultural diversity, the post of the Commissioner for Education, Culture, Multilingualism and Youth was created in 2004 to be responsible for policies in the fields of education, culture, training, youth, translation, interpretation, sport, and civil society, with the specific aim of preserving multilingual heritage. The Commissioner for Justice, Fundamental Rights and Citizenship was also created in 2010 to be the guardian of the Charter of Fundamental Rights and responsible for issues of justice and gender equality. Neither of these commissioners has developed targeted minority policies yet, though all their working areas are of great importance to minorities, who are likely to experience their impact by being in the framework.

There is also a wide range of other policy developments and action programmes that the Commission and the Council have undertaken in the cultural field. For instance, in 2007, the Commission proposed a cultural agenda founded on three sets of objectives: cultural diversity and intercultural dialogue, culture as a catalyst for creativity, and culture as a vital component in international relations.[104] Through this agenda, the EU aims to better understand, promote and protect not only cultural diversity but also intercultural dialogue, and to play a more active cultural role on the international stage.[105] The objective that is most relevant to this book is 'intercultural dialogue,' which, according to the Europa website, 'is an ongoing priority of the EU,' and with the coming into force of the Lisbon Treaty, this dimension of EU cultural policy has become even more significant and there have emerged a wide range of initiatives promoting cultural exchange and dialogue.[106] Various action

---

102 http://www.stabilitypact.org/.
103 See Will Kymlicka, *Multicultural Odysseys: Navigating the New International Politics of Diversity* (Oxford University Press, 2007), p. 37; see also the Convention for the Protection of National Minorities, Council of Europe, 1995.
104 See http://www.europarl.europa.eu/ftu/pdf/en/FTU_4.17.4.pdf.
105 *Ibid.*
106 *Ibid.*

programmes and prizes (e.g. the Cultural Programme (2007–2013), the European Capitals of Culture, and transnational mobility for cultural professionals) have also been introduced in order to celebrate Europe's cultural heritage, reward creativity, and further encourage diversity.[107]

This wide range of programmes and continuous developments are indicative of a broad interpretation of article 167 TFEU, the open quality of which provides the EU with the legal basis and potential to affect minority cultural rights to a much greater extent. It is important to note that projects based on article 167 TFEU as well as in other policy areas that concern specifically with minority groups already exist, though not in great numbers.[108] It is increasingly recognised that the so-called 'European culture' is rapidly and dramatically changing as a result of globalisation which has increased the presence of immigrant populations on the continent who practise a wide range of cultures and religions – hence the renewed focus on the necessity of intercultural dialogue. However, it is important to consider whether these activities actually guarantee any 'minority rights' as such, or merely provide assistance, exposure and opportunities.[109] While official recognition of cultural diversity is undoubtedly beneficial to minorities, promotion and protection of 'minority cultural rights' require more than acknowledgement of presence and expression of interest – they require a sustained systemic commitment to policies and activities that aim at promoting and protecting specific minority rights, e.g. religious rights, linguistic rights, etc. The 2009 Lisbon Treaty is a significant watershed in this regard, if only in a symbolic sense.

Before the Lisbon Treaty, there were no *binding* provisions on minority protection in EU law, only declarations and accession criteria. In other words, although standards had been set before, they remained inspirational with very limited legal significance if any at all. Neither was there any formal enforcement mechanism to compel member states to inject European minority norms into their internal legal systems. With the entry into force of the Lisbon Treaty in December 2009, minorities are now expressly mentioned in two important documents of EU primary law: the Treaty on European Union (TEU), and the Charter of Fundamental Rights (CFR). Article 2 TEU states:

> The Union is founded on the values of respect for human dignity, freedom, democracy, equality, the rule of law and respect for human rights, including the rights of persons belonging to minorities. These values are

---

107　*Ibid.*
108　Tawhida Ahmed, *The Impact of EU Law on Minority Rights* (Hart Publishing, 2011), p. 131.
109　*Ibid.*, p. 133.

common to the Member States in a society in which pluralism, non-discrimination, tolerance, justice, solidarity and equality between women and men prevail.

This provision has two significant features. The first is that it is clearly a statement in favour of *individually*-held minority rights, as it speaks of '*persons belonging to minorities.*' Thus no collective rights can be derived from it. The second feature that must be noted is the fact that the term 'minorities' is not qualified in anyway (i.e. without 'national,' 'linguistic,' 'cultural,' 'ethnic' in front, which often exist in other human and minority rights documents). This naturally leads to the question: who qualifies as a minority under article 2 TEU? Or indeed – who does not? Some may argue that once article 2 TEU is considered in the larger context – i.e. in conjunction with article 21 CFR which speaks specifically of 'national minorities' – it becomes clear that article 2 TEU should also be referring to 'national minorities.' But if this was indeed the case, why were two different terms used in the first place? All things considered, this omission was more likely to have been deliberate than unconscious, and the reason could have been that the EU intended to take a general and flexible approach to the definition of 'minorities' in order for the provision to be very inclusive. It is also possible that it was a deliberate tactic of the EU to get all Member States on-board – by employing a broad term which renders article 2 TEU very much an unenforceable empty promise, the EU has made a formal commitment to minorities by adding them to EU primary law but at very little cost if any at all. Indeed, since the entry into force of the Lisbon Treaty, there has been no clear evidence of improvements in the field of minority protection that can be clearly attributed to the positive impact of article 2 TEU.

Another significant feature of the Lisbon Treaty in relation to minority protection was that it made the EU's bill of rights, the Charter of Fundamental Right (CFR), legally binding.[110] Article 21 CFR explicitly prohibits discrimination on the basis of 'membership of a national minority.' A number of other terms in the provision are also applicable to minorities, e.g. 'race,' 'colour,' 'ethnic or social origin,' 'language,' 'religion or belief.' This wide range of possible bases of claims means that minorities are fairly well-covered by this provision, on paper. Although article 21 CFR is the only provision that explicitly mentions 'minority,' there are a number of other provisions that are of importance to minority protection. For instance, article 22 stipulates that 'the EU shall respect cultural, religious and linguistic diversity.' There are of course also those general human rights provisions which are equally applicable to all people

---

110 Article 6(1) TEU states that the CFR 'shall have the same legal value as the Treaties.'

including members of minority groups. These articles include article 10 CFR (the right to freedom of religion), article 11 CFR (the right to freedom of expression and information), and article 12 CFR (the right to freedom of assembly).

Clearly, the elevation of the CFR's legal status is of some benefit to minorities, in at least four ways. Firstly, it addresses the issue of double standards. As discussed previously, the EU's 'minority condition' and the lack of minority rights provisions *within* the EU legal framework had given rise to the concern that member states on the one hand and candidate states on the other could be measured with different yardsticks, which was a likely possibility, as it gave the impression that once accession into the EU was completed, respect for minority rights could be disregarded and standards would be dropped. The new legal status of the Charter corrects this misimpression.

Secondly, the Charter's wide application is also of practical benefit to minorities. Article 51 CFR specifies that the Charter is addressed to 'the institutions and bodies of the Union with due regard for the principle of subsidiarity and to the Member States only when they are implementing Union law.' In this way, article 51 CFR establishes a link between the Charter and article 2 TEU which requires the EU to respect human rights. It should be noted that the Explanation on article 51 CFR explicitly states that the article 'applies to central authorities as well as to regional and local bodies, and to public organisations, when they are implementing Union law.'[111] This is of particular importance to minorities as their day-to-day protection often directly concerns regional and local authorities and public organisations rather than central authorities.

Thirdly, the CFR is consistent with the ECHR. The Explanations relating to the CFR contain a useful list which specifies which CFR rights correspond to which ECHR rights and therefore have the same meaning and scope of application, and where the meaning and scope are slightly different.[112] Thus, coherent and consistent standards are ensured. Some subtle differences in wording between the two documents should be noted though. For example, while the ECHR speaks of 'association with a national minority,' the CFR refers to 'membership of a national minority.' The significance of the difference is unclear and unaddressed in the Explanations. But the Explanations do expressly state that the CFR article should be applied in compliance with the ECHR article.[113]

---

111   Explanations Relating to the Charter of Fundamental Rights, Explanation on Article 51, para. 2: http://eur-lex.europa.eu/LexUriServ/LexUriServ.do?uri=OJ:C:2007:303:0017:0035:en:PDF.
112   *Ibid.*, Explanation on article 52.
113   *Ibid.*, Explanation on article 21, para. 1.

Fourthly and related, one probable effect of the change of the Charter's legal status is that more actions of EU institutions and member states will be challenged before the European Court of Justice (ECJ). Though it should be noted that even before the elevation of the Charter's status, the ECJ already referred to the instrument, not as a binding source of law, but as one of many sources of legal reasoning.[114] Furthermore, with the entry into force of the Lisbon Treaty, the EU is now obliged to accede to the European Convention on Human Rights (ECHR). In other words, the powers of the EU will be subject to external judicial review when it happens.[115] What this means for minorities is that they can, in theory at least, benefit from *two* legal documents with enforcement mechanisms attached (the ECJ and the ECtHR respectively).[116] Having said that, whether or not this accession will be of real practical benefit to minorities is difficult to say, as it is still unclear in what form this accession will take place. While the merging of the two systems may be beneficial for establishing an unified European human and minority rights system and thus securing a common space for human and minority rights across the continent, it can also create many problems,[117] one of which being the relationship between the two courts (the ECJ and the ECtHR).

If EU institutions are to be subject to the jurisdiction of the ECtHR, as an EU institution, the ECJ will also be subject to the jurisdiction of the ECtHR. This could mean that the ECtHR could rule upon ECJ rulings on rights covered by the ECHR. Indeed, para. 4 of the Explanations on article 52 states clearly that the reference to the Convention and Protocols not only refers to the text of the documents but also the case-law of the ECtHR and the ECJ. This seems to be saying that the ECJ is bound by the case-law of the ECtHR in those areas where

---

114 See, for instance, Case C-540/03 European Parliament v. Council of the European Union, paras. 35–39.

115 Note that Opinion 2/13 of the Court of Justice of the European Union has rejected the draft agreement of EU accession to the ECHR and postponed the accession indefinitely. Opinion available at: http://curia.europa.eu/jcms/upload/docs/application/pdf/2014-12/cp140180en.pdf.

116 Owing to the fact that all EU member states are also members of the Council of Europe and parties to the ECHR, it can be argued that, even before the accession of the EU to the ECHR, minorities could already bring their claims before an international court (as long as all national remedies had been exhausted). Indeed, in the past years, cases concerning minorities have become a regular occurrence. See, for example, Leto Cariolou, 'Recent Case Law of the European Court of Human Rights Concerning the Protection of Minorities' in *European Yearbook of Minority Issues*, Volume 7, 2007/2008, p. 513. Yet, an official link between the EU and the ECHR will elevate judicial possibilities to a whole new level.

117 Hence the troubling negotiation process since July 2010.

the rights overlap, or at least that it should consider it highly relevant and take it into account. It is also important to note that the EU Committee on Constitutional Affairs has expressly stated that 'the Court of Human Rights must be regarded not as a higher court but rather as having special jurisdiction in exercising external supervision over the Union's compliance with obligations under international law arising from its accession to the ECHR.'[118] But how it is possible for the ECtHR to exercise powers of external supervision without acquiring a higher status remains to be explained.

Anyhow, it is likely and logical to expect that the ECJ has perceived accession to the ECHR as a threat to its own jurisdiction. This is clearly reflected in the defensive tone of the ECJ in its discussion document on accession, emphasising its own competence and role in safeguarding human rights in the EU and indicating that accession to the ECHR is unnecessary:

> With respect more specifically to the Convention, the institutions and bodies of the Union have for a long time been seeking to ensure, under the supervision of the Court of Justice, that human rights as guaranteed by the Convention are observed, even in the absence of an express obligation to that effect. As its case-law bears witness, the Court of Justice regularly applies the Convention and refers in that connection, more and more precisely in recent years, to the case-law of the European Court of Human Rights.[119]

It goes on to say in the same document that:

> The Court of Justice has the task of ensuring that in the interpretation and application of the Treaties, the law is observed and it alone has the jurisdiction [...] to declare if appropriate that an act of the Union is invalid.[120]

The ECJ claims that granting the ECtHR the power to invalidate acts of the EU must be avoided wherever possible. It is likely that it will voice strong

---

118   See the Committee on Constitutional Affairs, '*Draft Report on the Institutional Aspects of the Accession of the European Union to the European Convention for the Protection of Human Rights and Fundamental Freedoms,*' p. 4: http://www.europarl.europa.eu/meetdocs/2009_2014/documents/afco/pr/803/803011/803011en.pdf.

119   See http://curia.europa.eu/jcms/upload/docs/application/pdf/2010-05/convention_en_2010-05-21_12-10-16_272.pdf, p. 2.

120   *Ibid.*, p. 3.

opposition when and where it feels that the arrangements made or mechanisms set up as a result of the accession will challenge its own authority over EU law. These views and input of the ECJ are undoubtedly a significant consideration for the negotiators. On the part of the ECtHR, it will also need considerable time and effort to make the necessary adjustments. The end result is hopefully a closer connection and better cooperation between the ECJ and the ECtHR rather than the latter acting as a superior even on issues covered by the ECHR. Again, the precise details remain to be seen.

By way of concluding this part, it is necessary to recognise that the entry into force of the Lisbon Treaty and the future accession of the EU to the ECHR offer new opportunities for minority rights protection in Europe. Minorities now have more legal opportunities, which are likely to lead to an increase in the number of activities in the field. Having said that, while there is a good possibility of moving the minority rights agenda forward in the EU context, going the judicial way is going to be a long and slow process. Since enforcing EU minority rights standards will remain a matter for the states, there are good reasons for us to remain sceptical of how far the EU will be willing and able to enforce minority rights in its member states.[121] Persistent issues of new international attention (e.g. terrorism, economic crisis) mean that it is unlikely that minority protection will come to play a much more significant role on the EU stage in the foreseeable future, thus a restricted development in the field should be expected. In particular, while the Charter of Fundamental Rights and the future possibility of the EU's accession to the ECHR appear to have raised the standards of minority protection, standard-setting is only meaningful if successful implementation follows, which will remain unlikely for the reasons given above.

2.5 Minority Rights Protection in Other Regions of the World
The Americas

Regional human and minority rights obligations on the American continents may arise through membership of the Organisation of American States (OAS), which was founded in 1948 and has a membership of 35 states.[122] All of the OAS member states are bound by the OAS Charter and by the 1948 American Declaration on the Rights and Duties of Man.[123] Although the latter document is only a declaration and not a treaty, the OAS nevertheless deems that all of its members are politically bound to observe its provisions. In addition to the

---

121   More details in Chapter 7.
122   It arose out of the older regional system of the International Union of American Republics.
123   The American Declaration was the first international human rights instrument, preceding the Universal Declaration of Human Rights by a few months.

Charter and the Declaration, a number of more specific human rights treaties have also been adopted since 1969, which include the American Convention on Human Rights (1969) and its Additional Protocols in the Area of Economic, Social and Cultural Rights (1988); the Inter-American Convention to Prevent and Punish Torture (1985); the Inter-American Convention on Forced Disappearance of Persons (1994); and the Inter-American Convention on the Prevention, Punishment and Eradication of Violence against Women (1994). While all these documents are relevant to the protection of minorities, the most important instruments for minority protection in this region are undoubtedly the American Declaration on the Rights and Duties of Man and the American Convention on Human Rights. While the Declaration is applicable to all OAS member states, the Convention is binding only on those states that have ratified it. And while the Declaration addresses a broad range of human rights issues, the Convention is concerned primarily with civil and political rights, and, as noted above, has since been expanded by an additional protocol on economic, social, and cultural rights. Neither document contains any group-specific protective provisions. Minorities are entitled to all of the rights set forth in these documents, but among the rights of the greatest interest to them are the following:

> *Article 2 of the Declaration*: 'All persons are equal before the law and have the rights and duties established in this Declaration, without distinction as to race, sex, language, creed or any other factor.' Similarly, *article 1 of the Convention* requires states parties 'to respect the rights and freedoms recognized herein and to ensure to all persons subject to their jurisdiction the free and full exercise of those rights and freedoms, without any discrimination for reasons of race, color, sex, language, religion, political or other opinion, national or social origin, economic status, birth, or any other social condition.'
> *Article 3 of the Declaration* provides that 'Every person has the right freely to profess a religious faith, and to manifest and practice it both in public and in private.' Similarly, *article 12 of the Convention* also guarantees freedom of conscience and religion, which includes 'freedom to maintain or to change one's religion or beliefs, and freedom to profess or disseminate one's religion or beliefs, either individually or together with others, in public or in private.' Article 12 also provides that parents or guardians have the right to provide for the religious and moral education of their children or wards that is in accord with their own convictions.
> *Article 4 of the Declaration* guarantees freedom of expression. Similarly, *article 13 of the Convention* also guarantees freedom of thought and

expression, and provides in sub-section 5 that 'Any propaganda for war and any advocacy of national, racial, or religious hatred that constitute incitements to lawless violence or to any other similar action against any person or group of persons on any grounds including those of race, color, religion, language, or national origin shall be considered as offenses punishable by law.'

Article 5 of the Declaration provides that 'Every person has the right to the protection of the law against abusive attacks upon his honor, his reputation, and his private and family life.' Similarly, *articles 11 and 14 of the Convention* also guarantee the right to privacy and the right to have one's honor respected and dignity recognised.

Article 12 of the Declaration guarantees the right to education. While the Convention itself contains no reference to the right to education, it is important to note that *article 13 of the Additional Protocol to the Convention* provides that 'education should be directed towards the full development of the human personality and human dignity and should strengthen respect for human rights, ideological pluralism, fundamental freedoms, justice and peace' and that 'education ought to enable everyone to participate effectively in a democratic and pluralistic society and achieve a decent existence and should foster understanding, tolerance and friendship among all nations and all racial, ethnic or religious groups and promote activities for the maintenance of peace.'

Article 13 of the Declaration provides for 'the right to take part in the cultural life of the community, to enjoy the arts, and to participate in the benefits that result from intellectual progress [...].' A similar provision is *article 14 of the Additional Protocol to the Convention* which sets forth 'the right to take part in cultural and artistic life of the community' and 'to enjoy the benefits of scientific and technological progress.'

Article 18 of the Declaration sets forth the right to a fair trial. So does *article 8 of the Convention* which guarantees, among others, the right to a translator or interpreter.

Article 22 of the Declaration provides that 'Every person has the right to associate with others to promote, exercise and protect his legitimate interests of a political, economic, religious, social, cultural, professional, labor union or other nature.' A similar provision is *article 16 of the Convention* which guarantees 'the right to associate freely for ideological, religious, political, economic, labor, social, cultural, sports, or other purposes.'

The two OAS bodies directly concerned with human and minority rights under the Inter-American human rights system are the Inter-American Commission on Human Rights and the Inter-American Court of Human Rights, which play distinct but complementary roles.[124] All 35 members of the OAS fall under the broad jurisdiction of the Commission, which fulfils its mandate mainly by carrying out activities in three main areas: firstly, it may initiate investigations into any human and minority rights situation in any member state of the OAS in any way it sees fit, and to produce country-specific reports; secondly, it receives and considers individual complaints of rights violations in member states; and thirdly, it assists the Court in identifying and handling cases.

In contrast, the Court plays a much narrower role and functions as a forum of last resort for complaints of human rights abuses that are not adequately addressed by member states. To date, it has resolved over 100 cases. Apart from deciding on cases, the Court has two other useful tools to promote and protect human and minority rights in the region. The first is to issue advisory opinions interpreting state obligations under the American Convention and other human rights instruments in the region, either at the request of states parties or an OAS body such as the Commission.[125] States parties may also ask the Court to issue advisory opinions to determine the compatibility of their national laws with the human rights instruments in the region.[126] So far, the Court has issued 20 such opinions, mostly at the request of states parties. The second useful tool is that the Court may order 'provisional measures' in 'cases of extreme gravity and urgency'[127] such as to stop an execution. These may be issued at the request of the Commission even in the absence of a case before the Court.[128] To date, the Court has ordered over 80 provisional measures.

It must be noted, however, that, despite continuous efforts, the Commission and the Court continue to lack sufficient institutional resources to address the vast majority of the allegations and complaints that they receive, and compliance with their recommendations and decisions have mostly been partial and slow.[129] This means that the Inter-American system continues to experience significant difficulties on the way to achieve its full potential. The system also seems ill-equipped to address newly emerged challenges – for instance, it has barely begun to address economic, social and cultural rights matters in the region. Yet, it cannot be denied that the last three decades have witnessed a tremendous shift in attitude towards human and minority rights in the

---

124   See Part II of the American Convention on Human Rights.
125   American Convention, article 64(1).
126   *Ibid.*, article 64(2).
127   *Ibid.*, article 63(2).
128   Commission Procedures, article 25(2).
129   Non-compliance with the Court's provisional orders has resulted in deaths in several cases.

Americas; though it is unclear how much of this shift can be credited to the activities and efforts of the Inter-American system. Having said that, there should be no doubt that the most significant function of the system has been to serve as a sustained source of moral and political inspiration and support for human rights, and a constant reminder of state responsibilities. In this regard, it has been successful.

When examining human and minority rights conditions in the Americas, it is necessary to look at north and south Americas separately. It is North America that has powerfully influenced international thinking on minority rights protection through positive support for anti-discrimination and multicultural policies with the protection of minorities secured by constitutional and sub-constitutional law. The United States in particular deals with minority issues through embracing the concept of universal human rights. The American Declaration of Independence of 1776 states that 'all men are created equal; that they are endowed by their Creator with certain inalienable rights; that among these are life, liberty and the pursuit of happiness.' Although the Civil Rights Act of 1964 outlawed discrimination in voting, employment, federally assisted programmes and public facilities, the United States' courts have in reality equivocated on affirmative action as a remedy for historical discrimination and inherited disadvantage.[130] The favoured approach has been one of integration or assimilation of minority groups into the American way of life, though recent movements, for example, bilingual education for Hispanic groups, seem to demonstrate movement towards a multicultural approach and a more genuine equality of opportunity for different ethnic groups.

Being the very first country to adopt an official multicultural policy, Canada has played a significant role in the development of international minority rights norms and standards. The way Canadian law defines minority rights and multiculturalism makes it very clear that the two notions exist and operate within the framework of human rights and liberal constitutionalism, and that multiculturalism ought to be understood as a policy inspired and restricted by liberal norms.[131] This is clearly demonstrated in the Multiculturalism Act of 1988, the preamble of which states that Canada is adopting an official multicultural policy because of its commitment to civil liberties, to the freedom of individuals 'to make the life that the individual is able and wishes to have,' also

---

[130] Affirmative action is controversial especially in the context of access to education, in particular admission to universities and other forms of higher education. The intense racial preferences debate in this context reflects competing interpretations of the meaning, entailments and purposes of affirmative action as a general policy.

[131] Will Kymlicka, *Multicultural Odysseys: Navigating the New International Politics of Diversity* (Oxford University Press, 2007), p. 106.

to racial and gender equality and international human rights norms and obligations.[132] The Canadian Charter of Rights and Freedoms provides for linguistic and educational rights and basic rights of non-discrimination, as well as demonstrating a commitment to affirmative action. It also refers to the aboriginal peoples of Canada. Section 35 of the 1982 Constitution of Canada states that '[t]he existing aboriginal and treaty rights of the aboriginal peoples of Canada are hereby recognized and affirmed,' making Canada the only major 'settler society' to have recognised indigenous rights in its constitution.[133] Furthermore, through a firm commitment to multiculturalism, which is considered to be strengthening federalism, Canada has attempted to transcend a narrow conception of its own nature and history. Section 27 of the Canadian Constitution expressly states that the document should be 'interpreted in a manner consistent with the preservation and enhancement of the multicultural heritage of Canadians.' That said, as partly demonstrated by Canada's initial objection to the 2007 UN Declaration on the Rights of Indigenous Peoples, the 'minority rights movement' is subject to doubts, inconsistencies, official political motivations as well as practical constraints.[134]

In the most recent decades, Latin America has presented a rather bright picture of minority protection especially in relation to indigenous peoples. The replacement of military dictatorships by democracies has seen the rise of what Donna Lee Van Cott calls 'multicultural constitutionalism' throughout the continent, which has brought about a commitment to group-differentiated rights for indigenous peoples, including rights to self-government and recognition of customary laws.[135] However, the multicultural movement has received mixed reviews. In the case of indigenous peoples, some argue that by providing indigenous peoples with tangible benefits and privileges, the peoples who do not qualify as 'indigenous peoples' are excluded, thereby creating new ethnic

---

132 *Ibid.*
133 Avril Bell, *Relating Indigenous and Settler Identities: Beyond Domination* (Palgrave Macmillan, 2014), p. 151.
134 The Canadian government said that while it supported the 'spirit' of the UN Declaration on the Rights of Indigenous Peoples, it had to vote against it as it contained provisions that were 'fundamentally incompatible with Canada's constitutional framework.' A joint statement from the Canadian ministries of Indian and Foreign Affairs said also that the Declaration did not 'recognise Canada's need to balance indigenous rights to lands and resources with the rights of others.'
135 Donna Lee Van Cott, *The Friendly Liquidation of the Past: The Politics of Diversity in Latin America* (University of Pittsburgh Press, 2000), Chapter 9; Will Kymlicka, *Multicultural Odysseys: Navigating the New International Politics of Diversity* (Oxford University Press, 2007), p. 249.

hierarchies in society.¹³⁶ Others argue that the policies have little more than symbolic significance, as they have been introduced by neo-liberal elites to direct attention away from underlying power structures and problems. This argument is enhanced by the fact that many indigenous political movements in Latin America have entered into tactical alliances with neo-liberal political parties.¹³⁷ It has also been argued that the recognition of self-government rights and customary laws reflects a determinist understanding of cultural identity, thereby creating and enhancing inflexible cultural expectations and locking cultural minorities within fixed boundaries.¹³⁸

Africa

When speaking of regional instruments of human and minority rights protection in Africa, one looks to the Constitutive Act of the African Union,¹³⁹ the African Charter on Human and Peoples' Rights (ACHPR) and some other regional human rights instruments. The notion of 'minority' is a difficult one in the African context, and the issue of minorities and their rights controversial, not least because post-colonial African states were more an arbitrary amalgamation of a multitude of different ethnic groups rather than coherent nations, within which the seeds of dissension and conflict were imbedded. States are often made up of a large number of different ethno-linguistic groups, none of which constitutes a majority. In those states where dominant groups do exist, struggle for power and control often takes priority over concerns for human rights and minority protection. Poor governance, corruption and widespread poverty seem to have disproportionately affected minority peoples,

---

136   Juliet Hooker, 'Indigenous Inclusion/Black Exclusion: Race, Ethnicity and Multicultura‹ Citizenship in Contemporary Latin America,' Journal of Latin American Studies, 37/2 (2005): pp. 285–310; Will Kymlicka, *Multicultural Odysseys: Navigating the New International Politics of Diversity* (Oxford University Press, 2007), p. 250.

137   Xavier Albó's 'And from Kataristas to MNRistas?: The Surprising and Bold Alliance between Aymaras and Neo-liberals in Bolivia,' in Donna Lee Van Cott, *Indigenous Peoples and Democracy in Latin America* (St Martin's Press, 1994), pp. 55–82; Charles R. Hale, *Engaging Contradictions: Theory, Politics, and Methods of Activist Scholarship* (University of California Press, 2008); Will Kymlicka, *Multicultural Odysseys: Navigating the New International Politics of Diversity* (Oxford University Press, 2007), p. 250.

138   Virginia Tilley, 'New Help or New Hegemony? The Transnational Indigenous Peoples' Movement and "Being Indian" in El Salvador,' Journal of Latin American Studies, 34 (2002): pp. 525–554; Will Kymlicka, *Multicultural Odysseys: Navigating the New International Politics of Diversity* (Oxford University Press, 2007), p. 250.

139   Adopted in 2000 to replace the Charter of the Organisation of African Unity (OAU); see Rachel Murray, *Human Rights in Africa* (Cambridge University Press, 2004).

especially indigenous groups such as the Berber in North Africa and the Batwa of Central Africa.

It is important to note that pan-African case-law in general and the ACHPR in particular (as well as subsequent African human rights documents) do not consider ethnic and cultural minorities a legal category recognised in African human rights law and thus have no specific reference to 'minority rights.' The same generic rights as contained in the UN treaties are on offer to all individuals irrespective of ethnic and cultural backgrounds. For instance, the ACHPR recognises the right to *non-discrimination* on grounds including racial, ethnic, language and religion (article 2), their right to equality and equal protection under the law (article 3), the right to respect of human dignity (article 5), the right to freely practise one's religion (article 8), the right to participate in the government of one's country, and the right to equal access of public property and public services (article 13), and the right to freely take part in the cultural life of the community (article 17). Article 12(5) states that mass expulsion of non-nationals 'which is aimed at national, racial, ethnic and religious groups' shall be prohibited.

However, despite lacking specific reference to minority rights, the seemingly non-minority-specific ACHPR refers to the rights of *peoples*. Whether, and if so to what extent, the notion of 'peoples' encompasses 'minorities' remains contested. Whilst we cannot automatically equate 'peoples' with 'minorities,' as long as we accept the working definition of minorities as 'national, ethnic, religious and linguistic groups within a state,' then inevitably there is a high degree of complementarity between the ACHPR's term 'peoples' and the general notion of 'minority.' In this light, one may argue that the ACHPR provides not only for individual human rights, but also for *collective rights* – 'peoples' rights' – based on the assumption that 'fundamental *human rights* stem from the attitudes of human beings […] and the reality and respect of *peoples' rights* should necessarily guarantee human rights' (preamble, para. 5). It guarantees, among others, minorities' collective rights to non-discrimination and equality (article 19), to existence and self-determination (article 20), to freely determine their political status (article 20(1)), to 'dispose of their wealth and natural resources' (article 21), the right to economic, social and cultural development with due regard to freedom and identity (article 22(1)), and the right to a satisfactory environment favourable to their development (article 24).

Furthermore, another significant feature of the Charter is that it not only provides for *rights*, but also lays down *duties*, and considers the two inseparable. Among others, every individual has the duty to exercise rights and freedoms with due regard to the rights of others (article 27(2)); should respect and consider his fellow beings without discrimination (article 28); everyone has the duty to serve his national community (article 29(2)), not to compromise state security (article 29(3)), to preserve and strengthen social and national solidarity (article 29(4)) and the territorial integrity of the state (article 29(5)). Every individual also has the duty to preserve and strengthen positive African cultural values (article 29(7)) and to promote and achieve African unity (article 29(8)). It seems that the focus has been on standard-setting. While this is certainly important, it has not been backed up with effective enforcement mechanisms.

Asia

A full examination of minority rights protection in Asia cannot bypass the 'Asian Values' debate. What is presented here, however, is an empirical overview of the continent's participation in minority rights protection. Just as it remains difficult to arrive at a consensus on the precise meaning and content of 'Asian Values,' it is notoriously difficult if not impossible, and wrong, to look at Asia as one single entity, considering the multi-political, multi-cultural, multi-lingual and multi-religious characters of the enormous continent. There is currently no functioning regional human rights mechanism in Asia, and the state of human and minority rights protection varies from nation to nation. Not all Asian countries challenge the universality of human rights; and not all, if any, Asian countries rely exclusively on 'Asian Values' in their critique of the mainstream Western conceptions of human and minority rights.[140]

However, there are great similarities in the ways different Asian states understand and deal with human rights issues. Firstly, largely due to their colonial pasts, many Asian states firmly adhere to the principle of state sovereignty both when dealing with internal ethnic tensions and especially when responding to criticisms from the outside world. Secondly, due to the continuous influence of Confucian values, some Asian states clearly prefer to deal with human rights issues through internal and external cooperation instead of confrontation (which is seen as excessively favoured by the West), and expect the ethnic and cultural minorities within their borders to voice and advance their claims on the same principles.[141] Thirdly, it seems that no Asian country has taken steps to suggest developing regional systems of human and minority rights protection. The emphasis on sovereignty and the immense diversity of geography, culture and politics, are among the primary reasons.[142] Intensifying rivalries between neighbouring states (e.g. China and Japan, India and

---

140   Joshua Castellino &. Elvira Domínguez Redondo, *Minority Rights in Asia* (Oxford University Press, 2006), p. 22.
141   See Wm. Theodore de Bary &. Tu Weiming (eds.), *Confucianism and Human Rights* (Columbia University Press, 1998).
142   See S. Yee, 'The Role of Law in the Formation of Regional Perspectives in Human Rights and Regional Systems for the Protection of Human Rights: The European and Asian Models as Illustrations,' 8 SYBIL (2004), pp. 157–164.

Pakistan) also make meaningful cooperation, not only in the field of minority rights, very difficult.

Asian states' varying attitudes to *human rights* are reflected in their varying degrees of participation in the international treaty system. In terms of rate of ratification, Eastern Asian countries are most engaged in the international system; South Asia comes second; and the least engaged appears to be the Southeast sub-region.[143] In the case of *minority rights,* none of the Asian states that signed and ratified the ICCPR objected to article 27,[144] suggesting a near universal consensus on the existence of minorities in Asian states and the necessity of their recognition and protection.[145] Information on this subject is not readily available, and state reports under different mechanisms are not always appropriate for comparison. Castellino and Domínguez Redondo have studied Asian state reports on minorities under articles 18 and 27 of the ICCPR and the International Covenant on the Elimination of All Forms of Racial Discrimination (ICERD), which require states to report on minority treatments within their borders periodically. They find that in the three sub-regions indicated, South Asia appears to have the most organised mechanisms for minority protection. Southeast Asian countries also have a wide range of minority rights provisions in their domestic laws, although they are least engaged in the UN mechanisms. States in the Far East, however, with the exception of China, tend to claim to be homogenous, and therefore minority rights regimes are either in their infancy or non-existent.[146]

While there is a variety of political systems in South Asia, and all states are dominated by a large ethnic majority, most states in this sub-region have legal provisions for the identification of minorities, which may or may not have been defined in the state's domestic law.[147] Pakistan and India, according to Castellino and Domínguez Redondo's study, have the highest awareness of minority rights enshrined in law and the largest number of institutions

---

143 Joshua Castellino & Elvira Domínguez Redondo, *Minority Rights in Asia* (Oxford University Press, 2006), p. 31.

144 'In those states in which ethnic, religious or linguistic minorities exist, persons belonging to such minorities shall not be denied the right, in community with other members of their group, to enjoy their own culture, to profess and practise their own religion, or use their own language.'

145 Joshua Castellino & Elvira Domínguez Redondo, *Minority Rights in Asia* (Oxford University Press, 2006), p. 6; note that China has signed the ICCPR but never ratified it.

146 *Ibid.*, pp. 42–57.

147 *Ibid.*, p. 45; see also T.K. Oommen, *'New Nationalisms and Collective Rights: The Case of South Asia,'* pp. 121–143, in Stephen May, Tariq Modood &. Judith Squires (eds.), *Ethnicity, Nationalism and Minority Rights* (Cambridge University Press, 2004).

dedicated to the protection of religious, cultural and linguistic minorities.[148] Yet, Bangladesh and Nepal are the only two countries in the region that accept the concept of 'indigenous peoples.'[149] The measures adopted in Bangladesh to protect the Chittagong Hill Tribes range from economic and developmental aid to guaranteed representation and autonomy.[150] Nepal, on the other hand, has recognised 59 ethnic groups as 'nationalities of Nepal.'[151] Being overwhelmingly Hindu, however, certain degrees of discrimination in society have been inevitable, and the protection measures adopted tend to centre on linguistic rights and guaranteed access to the media only.[152]

The Far East, by contrast, with the notable exception of China, is the most homogenous in Asia. In reporting under article 27 of the ICCPR, both North and South Koreas deny the existence of minorities within their borders, although the latter does admit to having a large number of religious groups and insists that the country's law allows all to freely practise their own culture and religion.[153] Japan is also largely homogenous; its indigenous Ainu people are said to be 'continuing to maintain their ethnic identity with continuous efforts to pass on their own language and culture.'[154] The Committee on the Elimination of Racial Discrimination has recommended special protection measures for two communities, the Burakumin and the Okinawa – the former falls within the concept of descent-based discrimination, and the latter falls within the scope of the rules governing self-identification.[155]

China is undoubtedly the least homogenous in the region and thus has the most urgent need for a sophisticated minority rights regime. Castellino and Domínguez Redondo's 2006 study on minority rights protection in Asia sees the country in a rather positive light and as the exception in the region with its large variety of mechanisms and institutions specifically for the research, protection

---

148 Ibid., p. 46; see also Gurpreet Mahajan, 'Indian Exceptionalism or Indian Model: Negotiating Cultural Diversity and Minority Rights in a Democratic Nation-State,' pp. 288–313, in Will Kymlicka &. Baogang He (eds.), *Multiculturalism in Asia* (Oxford University Press, 2005).

149 See Will Kymlicka, 'Liberal Multiculturalism: Western Models, Global Trends, and Asian Debates,' pp. 46–52, in Will Kymlicka &. Baogang He (eds.), *Multiculturalism in Asia* (Oxford University Press, 2005).

150 Joshua Castellino & Elvira Domínguez Redondo, *Minority Rights in Asia* (Oxford University Press, 2006)., p. 46.

151 Ibid., p. 48.

152 Ibid.

153 Ibid., pp. 49–50.

154 Ibid., p. 51; see also Lam Peng-Er, 'At the Margins of a Liberal-Democratic State: Ethnic Minorities in Japan,' pp. 223–243, in Will Kymlicka &. Baogang He (eds.), *Multiculturalism in Asia* (Oxford University Press, 2005).

155 Ibid.

and promotion of minority rights.[156] But the key challenge confronting minority rights (and human rights) protection in China is not one of lack of laws, but one of implementation, which is largely determined, among others, by the lack of a rights tradition in traditional Chinese thought, the official Chinese attitude to human and minority rights, and the lack of an independent judiciary. The single-minded determination of the Chinese government to develop the western regions – a minority-occupied land mass equivalent to 60 percent of Chinese territory and rich in natural resources – has also increasingly caused minorities to choose between continuous economic gains and greater cultural autonomy, between the right to development and the right to one's own culture and traditional ways of life. The country's vastly expensive Western Development Strategy[157] (with the specific goals of developing infrastructure, promoting education and increasing efforts on ecological protection in the western regions), from which minorities in the regions have undoubtedly benefited, has also been proven to be a threat to the minorities' land rights, especially the right to manage their own natural resources, and the right to cultural integrity.[158]

Southeast Asia is the sub-region that participates least willingly in the UN minority rights regime, and as a result the UN has much less interaction with it than with other parts of the world. That said, Southeast Asia does have a variety of approaches to minority rights protection. What is presented here is a brief overview of the domestic experiences of minority protection of individual states. Out of all the nations in the sub-region, the Philippines is perhaps the most open to international human rights mechanisms and has introduced the Indigenous Peoples' Act in 1997, which provides indigenous populations with a wide range of land and resource rights.[159] However, the country has

---

156 *Ibid.*, p. 45. A great number of laws, resolutions, government white papers, and decisions of the Standing Committee of the National People's Congress contain minority rights content. The most prominent are the Constitution of the People's Republic of China, Government White Paper on National Minorities Policy and its Practice in China (1999), Government White Paper on Freedom of Religious Belief in China (1997), the Law of the People's Republic of China on the Commonly Used Oral and Written Languages of the State, and the 1984 Regional Ethnic Autonomy Law.

157 It formally commenced in 2000.

158 It must be noted that China is not alone in failing to protect the rights of national/indigenous minorities living on resource-rich lands. The challenge is global. A detailed examination of the issue will be carried out in Chapter 6. This example also brings our attention to the fact that rights conflict with each other, the protection of one is often necessarily at the cost of another. This matter will be examined in detail in the concluding chapter.

159 Joshua Castellino & Elvira Domínguez Redondo, *Minority Rights in Asia* (Oxford University Press, 2006), p. 54.

been struggling to cope with the various Muslim Filipino groups, whose use of violence and terrorism has been a constant source of instability in the country.[160] Nearly 46 ethnic groups of Mindanao were classified as 'national cultural minorities' by the Commission of National Integration in 1957, but were excluded from recognition in 1997 as 'indigenous cultural communities.'[161]

While both Vietnam and Laos place great emphasis on national unity, and both, in the development of their minority rights regimes, focus predominantly on equality and non-discrimination, Thailand adopts a very different attitude. In reporting on minorities under article 27 of the ICCPR, the country appears to view minorities as 'problems' and threats to national security, and not surprisingly the 'solutions' the government provides reflect this attitude rather than the need to provide cultural and socio-economic rights as mandated by article 27 of the ICCPR.[162] None of the other states in the sub-region is bound by the ICCPR, or the ICESCR,[163] and they thus do not report to the international regime on issues of minority rights.[164] Nevertheless, some of them have taken positive steps to promote and protect the rights of their minorities. For instance, wide-ranging affirmative action measures in Malaysia have resulted in greater equality and better relations among groups.[165]

Yet, despite increasing efforts in individual countries to promote and protect human and minority rights, Asia-Pacific is the last remaining UN defined region without a regional human rights mechanism. Consistent efforts since the 1960s, mostly through engagement with the UN, to establish a regional human rights framework with corresponding enforcement mechanisms have all failed, resulting in a shift of focus to regional co-operation and development of *sub-regional* instruments and mechanisms.[166] Thus here I shall focus on efforts at the sub-regional level to promote and protect human and minority rights, which are reflected mainly in the work of four intergovernmental bodies: the Association of Southeast Asian Nations ('ASEAN'), the ASEAN Regional

---

160 *Ibid.*; Christine Bell, *Peace Agreements and Human Rights* (Oxford University Press, 2003).
161 Working Group on Minorities, Sub-regional Seminar in Southeast Asia, December 2002, Paras. 16–18, UN Doc. E/CN.4/Sub.2/AC.5/2003/WP.14.
162 See CCPR/C/THA/2004/1 August 2004; Joshua Castellino & Elvira Domínguez Redondo, *Minority Rights in Asia* (Oxford University Press, 2006), p. 55.
163 International Covenant on Economic, Social and Cultural Rights.
164 Joshua Castellino & Elvira Domínguez Redondo, *Minority Rights in Asia* (Oxford University Press, 2006), p. 55.
165 Kirstin Henrard &. Robert Dunbar, *Synergies in Minority Protection: European and International Law Perspectives* (Cambridge University Press, 2008), p. 419.
166 See 'The Role of Regional Human Rights Mechanisms,' Policy Department, Directorate-General for External Policies of the Union, European Parliament, November 2010, p. 82.

Forum ('ARF'), the Pacific Islands Forum ('PIF'), and the Asia Pacific Forum of National Human Rights Institutions ('APF').

ASEAN

The primary goal of ASEAN has never been to promote and protect human and minority rights. Rather, continuous economic growth, social advancement, cultural development and regional peace and security have been its paramount objectives. In fact, the ASEAN has always insisted on a strict separation between human rights matters and economic issues, and has consistently employed a quiet, diplomatic and consensus-based approach to human rights protection, and places strong emphasis on cooperation and friendly relations among member states as well as on the norm of non-interference in internal affairs.[167] It was not until 1998, in the Hanoi Plan of Action, that ASEAN member states for the first time jointly and formally committed themselves to various human rights ideals and activities.[168]

And a range of developments followed. The ASEAN Charter which came into force in December 2008 called for the establishment of a human rights body within the ASEAN framework, though the precise characteristics and functions of such a body remain undetermined.[169] The ASEAN Intergovernmental Commission on Human Rights ('AICHR') was inaugurated in September 2009 as a consultative body of ASEAN to protect human rights and fundamental freedoms, as well as to promote regional dialogue and cooperation in this regard.[170] Observers have criticised the AICHR for lack of a clear mandate, emphasis on consensual decision-making, non-interference in internal affairs of member states, and its silence on the rights of indigenous peoples. The establishment of the AICHR has not challenged the traditional consensus-based approach of ASEAN and has thus been predicted to remain toothless. Yet, its however insignificant role brought about a major achievement of ASEAN in 2012: the ASEAN Human Rights Declaration ('AHRD').

Developed by the AICHR with the purpose of establishing a framework for human rights protection and cooperation among various ASEAN instruments, the AHRD is meant to ensure rights for over 600 million people across Southeast Asia, which renders it the most significant document drafted by ASEAN since

---

167 Kirstin Henrard &. Robert Dunbar, *Synergies in Minority Protection: European and International Law Perspectives* (Cambridge University Press, 2008), p. 404.
168 *Ibid.*
169 Available at: http://www.asean.org/asean/asean-charter.
170 See http://aichr.org/.

the ASEAN Charter.[171] Although it does not directly concern minorities, its articles 26, 32 and 33 are of relevance, which affirm all the economic, social and cultural rights in the UDHR (article 26), guarantee 'the right, individually or in association with others, to freely take part in cultural life, to enjoy the arts and the benefits of scientific progress and its applications and to benefit from the protection of the moral and material interests resulting from any scientific, literary or appropriate artistic production of which one is the author' (article 32), and require member states to take positive steps to progressively realise these rights (article 33).

The document has, however, attracted a great deal of criticism from civil society organisations and other observers. Firstly, concerns have been expressed that the document contains a reference to balancing rights with duties in article 6: 'The enjoyment of human rights and fundamental freedoms must be balanced with the performance of corresponding duties as every person has responsibilities to all other individuals, the community and the society where one lives. It is ultimately the primary responsibility of all ASEAN Member States to promote and protect all human rights and fundamental freedoms.' These concerns are comprehensible considering that the many authoritarian states in ASEAN have traditionally employed a particular conception of 'duty' that aims to constrain individual freedoms and liberties, and sees rights as contingent upon individuals' performance of duties towards the state and society at large. Yet, the last sentence of the article does seem to provide some reassurance regarding the provision's good intention. It can perhaps be argued that the reference to balancing rights with duties is merely a reminder that all rights correlate to certain duties – for instance, the right to life correlates to a duty not to kill.[172]

Secondly, the AHRD has also been criticised for containing a reference to realising rights in 'national and regional contexts,' which is said to have injected cultural relativism into the instrument and revived the 'Asian Values' debate. Article 7 provides that 'All human rights are universal, indivisible, interdependent and interrelated. All human rights and fundamental freedoms in this declaration must be treated in a fair and equal manner, on the same footing and with the same emphasis. At the same time, the realisation of human rights must be considered in the regional and national context bearing in mind different political, economic, legal, social, cultural, historical and religious

---

171 Available at: http://www.asean.org/news/asean-statement-communiques/item/asean-human-rights-declaration.
172 See Matthew H. Kramer's discussion on the Hohfeldian Table in Matthew H. Kramer, N.E. Simmonds &. Hillel Steiner, *A Debate Over Rights* (Oxford University Press, 1998), p. 7 ff.

backgrounds.' It can be argued though that this statement is no more than a mere statement of fact, as long as one accepts that human rights are universal and that there are globally accepted basic standards in the way rights are understood and interpreted. Successful realisation of rights *requires* that local conditions be taken into account; the question is not *whether* they should be taken into account, but rather *how* they should be taken into account.

Thirdly, the AHRD has also been criticised for its limitations provision. Article 8 provides that '[...] The exercise of human rights and fundamental freedoms shall be subject only to such limitations as are determined by law solely for the purpose of securing due recognition for the human rights and fundamental freedoms of others, and to meet the just requirements of national security, public order, public health, public safety, public morality, as well as the general welfare of the peoples in a democratic society.' Some critics have interpreted this as laying down prerequisites to *all* rights listed in the declaration. It should be noted though that this provision is along the exact same line as article 29(2) of the UDHR, yet article 29(2) has not attracted the same criticism. This is because international human rights law is clear that while some rights are subject to just limitations, other are non-negotiable, such as the right to life. There is no reason why article 8 should not be interpreted in the same way. A more valid line of criticism, and one that is relevant to minorities especially the 'minorities within minorities,' is that 'public morality' should not be a presumed limitation on the exercise of rights and freedoms. Since 'public morality' always reflects the dominant and mainstream interpretations of cultural, social and religious values, it inevitably favours some at the expense of others. In Southeast Asia where political, social and religious hierarchies are strong, having 'public morality' as a limitation on rights and freedoms is likely to further marginalise and exclude minorities, be they political, cultural, religious, or social.

A related, fourth, line of criticism is that the AHRD seems to have stipulated that national laws may determine the scope and exercise of some of the rights and freedoms listed in the document – for instance, articles 16, 18, 19, 25 and 27. Such qualification is problematic if it is interpreted as saying that national laws will always prevail, however unjust and discriminatory they may be, and are immune from criticism and scrutiny. If so understood, the inclusion of such provisions seems to be contrary to the very purpose of international and regional human rights instruments, which is to subject nations and national laws and policies to international/regional scrutiny in order to better protect and further promote rights. Yet, the inclusion of such provisions becomes less problematic if understood in the context of a regional document with a specific aim of advancing human rights – while it is understandable that ASEAN states wish to preserve a domain within which national laws prevail, but bearing in mind the purpose and goal of the ADHR, member states should accept that these laws need to be contested and justified.[173]

On the whole, it should be acknowledged that while the ADHR is not perfect (which human rights instrument is?), it is not useless. It should be applauded for having affirmed the general standards of international human rights while at the same time respecting values of the region. It remains to be seen though how the relevant parties interpret and implement the provisions. It is, however, a pity that the instrument contains no specific reference to minority rights. Fortunately though, the region has over the years developed a number of single issue-based instruments which are directly relevant to minorities. For instance, the ASEAN Declaration on Cultural Heritage, adopted in 2000, protects the right to non-discrimination by recognising the 'deep respect for the diversity of cultures and identities in ASEAN, without distinction as to grounds of nationality, race, ethnicity, sex, language or religion.'[174] Some provisions specifically refer to 'traditional communities' and urge ASEAN member states 'to sustain and preserve worthy living traditions and folkways and protect their living bearers in recognition of peoples' right to their own culture,'[175] to 'ensure that traditional communities have access, protection and rights of ownership to their own heritage,'[176] and to 'ensure the effectiveness of cultural policies and laws for the preservation of cultural heritage, and the protection of communal intellectual property'[177] and that these laws and policies 'empower all peoples and communities to harness their own creativity towards human development.'[178] Clearly, this declaration is of particular relevance to the types of minorities we are concerned with in this book. However, it is unclear that when assessing the 'worthiness' of cultures and traditions, who would be in a position to decide, and by what standards and through what processes. It is also unclear whether the provisions entail positive obligations on member states, or how they are to be monitored. Neither is it clear whether the provisions imply a citizenship requirement, and if so, how this may affect members of minority groups who are stateless.

---

173 It should be noted that while international human rights instruments do not contain similar references to national laws, a number of regional documents do – e.g. article 13 of the African Charter on Human and Peoples' Rights, article 22(7) of the American Declaration on the Rights and Duties of Man, and article 25 of the Arab Charter on Human Rights.
174 ASEAN Declaration on Cultural Heritage, the preamble.
175 *Ibid.*, 3.
176 *Ibid.*, 8.
177 *Ibid.*, 9.
178 *Ibid.*

There have also been other encouraging issue-based developments in the region which are not minority-specific but all directly or indirectly concern minorities – for instance, the 2001 Declaration on the Commitments for Children in ASEAN, the 2004 ASEAN Declaration Against Trafficking in Persons Particularly Women and Children, the 2004 Declaration on the Elimination of Violence against Women in the ASEAN Region, and the 2007 Declaration on the Protection and Promotion of the Rights of Migrant Workers. The ASEAN Commission on the Promotion and Protection of the Rights of Women and Children ('ACWC') was inaugurated in April 2010 with the specific aim of protecting the rights and fundamental freedoms of women and children in the region, and promoting their well-being, empowerment and meaningful participation in their own communities and the larger society. Such instruments and bodies are particularly relevant to the protection of the rights of the 'minorities within minorities,' which will be examined in detail in Chapter 5. It should be noted though that these instruments are not complemented by any advisory procedures or monitoring mechanisms. In other words, despite continuous and tentative moves towards addressing human and minority rights issues, the institutional capacities of the ASEAN to enforce those rights are lacking. But the increase of single-issue instruments could gradually lead to the development of more solid texts with monitoring procedures and mechanisms attached.

The ASEAN Regional Forum (ARF) & the Pacific Islands Forum (PIF)

The ARF is the primary forum in Asia-Pacific for political and security dialogue. Its membership includes all ASEAN states as well as China, Japan, South Korea, North Korea, Russia, the United States, and the European Union. As a regional dialogue forum, the ARF has not developed any normative standards or official mechanisms for minority rights protection, though some commentators have called for the establishment of a Regional Commissioner on National Minorities, operating in a non-coercive, assistance-based, friendly 'ASEAN manner.'[179] It makes sense for the ARF to pay greater attention to minority rights issues, as ethnic tension is one of the main causes of violent communal conflicts in Southeast Asian countries, the effects of which are felt not only in the countries of origin but also in the entire wider region. Thus adequately

---

179   G. Evans, *'Conflict prevention with regard to inter-ethnic issues, including the role of third parties: Experiences and challenges from the Asian-Pacific region,'* 8 International Journal on Minority and Group Rights (2001), p. 38; Kirstin Henrard &. Robert Dunbar, *Synergies in Minority Protection: European and International Law Perspectives* (Cambridge University Press, 2008), p. 410.

addressing the so-called 'minority problem' is key to achieving ARF's goal of preserving regional peace and security.

In contrast, the Pacific Islands Forum (PIF) has focused primarily on economic development and regional trade, although security, law enforcement and environmental issues have become increasingly central to its agenda. Recognising the importance of developing a coordinated regional approach to conflict prevention and resolution, and of constructively addressing sensitive issues in a cooperative manner, the PIF has on a number of occasions referred to issues related to minority rights protection. For instance, in 2000, the Forum Regional Security Committee identified that 'ethnic differences [...] and a lack of confidence in governments' ability to resolve these differences' were key factors threatening regional peace and security.[180] The Biketawa Declaration, adopted in October 2000, contains a list of principles that guide the actions of the Forum which include 'recognising the importance of respecting and protecting indigenous rights and cultural values, traditions and customs.'[181] The Pacific Plan, endorsed in the April 2004 Auckland Declaration, outlines a revised mandate for the PIF which has a minority dimension: 'We treasure the diversity of the Pacific and seek a future in which its cultures, traditions and religious beliefs are valued, honoured and developed.'[182] It also calls for the establishment of regional human rights mechanisms and an ombudsman to enable implementation of the PIF's principles. A regional support mechanism will also be set up to help draft, harmonise and promote awareness of domestic human and minority rights instruments in the region.[183]

The Asia Pacific Forum of National Human Rights Institutions

As opposed to the slow evolution of a regional framework, a promising institutional development in rights protection in the region has been the rapid growth of national human rights institutions (NHRIs) and the emergence of regional networks of NHRIs. The most significant of them is the Asia Pacific Forum of National Human Rights Institutions ('APF'), which is perhaps the closest the region has come to a regional arrangement for human rights protection.[184] With 15 full members and 6 associate members, it directs its efforts

---

180 Kirstin Henrard &. Robert Dunbar, *Synergies in Minority Protection: European and International Law Perspectives* (Cambridge University Press, 2008), p. 412.
181 See www.forumsec.org.fj/news/2000/octo6.htm.
182 Pacific Islands Forum Secretariat, *'A Pacific Plan for Strengthening Regional Cooperation and Integration,'* October 2005, p. 3.
183 *Ibid.*, p. 18.
184 APF: http://www.asiapacificforum.net/support/establishment-of-nhris/.

mainly towards providing practical assistance and support to enable members to better promote and protect rights at the national level, aiding governments and civil societies to establish independent NHRIs, and promoting cooperation on human rights issues at all levels. It is actively involved in the work of the UN and has developed working relationships with a number of UN agencies, including the OHCHR, the HRC, UNDP, UNCSW, UNESCO and UNHCR, which is a reflection of its international standing and impact. One aspect of the APF's functions that is particularly relevant to this book is its institutional capacity-building activities, which include training programmes and partnerships to build knowledge and practical skills to enhance member institutions' capacities, be they general institutional capacities or ones with a specific thematic focus.

An important body of the APF is the Advisory Council of Jurists (ACJ), which, since its establishment in 1998, has been advising the APF in the interpretation and application of international human rights law and assisting member institutions to deal with specific human rights situations and problems in their respective national contexts. A number of its reports have played a key role in bringing about positive changes in domestic legislation, including the abolishment of capital punishment in the Fiji Penal Code. Of particular relevance to minority protection is ACJ's recent focus on sexual orientation and gender identity. Having assessed the consistency of national laws and policies with international standards and highlighted problematic areas, the ACJ made a series of recommendations to help NHRIs address identified shortcomings, including strengthening anti-discrimination legislation and re-interpreting religious and customary laws, which caused great divergence and strong opposition among member institutions. This is hardly surprising considering the region's strong cultural traditions and widespread religious practices, which draw our attention to the underlying factors of effective rights protection, and direct us carefully to address and understand the role of local norms in the interpretation of supposedly universal standards.[185] It is worth noting that the ASEAN Declaration on Human Rights contains no mention of the rights of lesbian, gay, bisexual and transgender people in the region who are often subject to frequent and systemic discrimination – especially in minority groups.

In concluding this section on Asia, to date, none of the regional or sub-regional intergovernmental bodies in the region has developed a cohesive framework for minority rights protection, and there is no indication that any solid conceptual understanding of minority rights has been acquired.

---

185   Indeed, this also reminds us of the reference to realising rights in 'national and regional contexts' in the ASEAN Declaration on Human Rights and causes us to rethink its reasonableness.

So far, efforts have been directed more towards implementing international rights standards rather than developing a regional approach. This is perhaps not as big a problem as some have suggested, especially considering that there have been promising national developments in the absence of regional standards and effective monitoring mechanisms.[186] Particularly encouraging is the growth, both in number and capacity, of NHRIs in a short period of time, largely thanks to the efforts of the APF. By ensuring compliance with the Paris Principles before a NHRI can become a member, APF-sponsored NHRIs are well-positioned to ensure their compliance with international rights standards. And as a network of NHRIs rather than a club of sovereign states, the APF is well-placed to be conversant with local conditions and to translate local concerns into practical and realistic strategies of rights protection and promotion, respecting ethnic, cultural, religious and linguistic realities and diversities.[187] Thus, we have reason to believe that a continuous focus on the establishment and strengthening of NHRIs rather than a dedication to develop a comprehensive regional mechanism will perhaps allow for a more realistic and sustainable advancement of rights protection in the region. It is for this reason that the APF is likely to remain the most effective rights mechanism in the region, and one that is most likely to bring about development in the field of minority rights.

It should also be noted that, given their common focus on regional security, there exists promising scope for cross-regional exchange between ASEAN instruments and the OSCE,[188] especially the OSCE High Commission on National Minorities (HCNM). And by examining the OSCE approach, it is also possible to predict, to a certain extent, the limitations and problems that ASEAN instruments are likely to encounter, especially if the latter subscribe to a comprehensive security-oriented approach to minority rights and become more like the HCNM. As already examined earlier, in the OSCE context, in order for a minority issue to be paid serious attention, the tensions caused must be perceived as capable of spreading and turning into regional conflicts, as regional security, not minority protection, is the ultimate goal. This is likely to be the case also in the ASEAN context. But if the last decade of the 20th Century

---

186 Kirstin Henrard &. Robert Dunbar, *Synergies in Minority Protection: European and International Law Perspectives* (Cambridge University Press, 2008), p. 418.
187 Mary Robinson, Opening Address to the 6th Workshop on Regional Human Rights Arrangements in the Asia Pacific Region, Tehran, 28 February 1998, pp. 211–238; Durbach, Renshaw & Byrnes, 'A tongue but no teeth?': *The emergence of a regional human rights mechanism in the Asia Pacific region,* Sydney Law Review, Volume 31:211 (2009), p. 237.
188 Durbach, Renshaw & Byrnes, 'A tongue but no teeth?': *The emergence of a regional human rights mechanism in the Asia Pacific region,* Sydney Law Review, Volume 31:211 (2009), p. 417.

has taught us anything (especially the 1994 Rwandan Genocide and the 1997–1998 repression of ethnic Albanians in Kosovo), it is that there is a close link between minority rights and conflict prevention, and that the latter cannot be achieved without adequately tackling the former.

The Middle East

Although most states in the Middle East claim to be homogenous, the region is in fact home to many ethnic and cultural groups as well as indigenous peoples, who, through geographic, linguistic and religious continuity, have adapted to changing circumstances while at the same time struggling to maintain their own identities.[189] Many have fought for greater freedom since the 20th Century, but successes have been rare or temporary. As Arab nationalism and Sunni Islam continue to occupy ideological and political high ground,[190] the denial of strong group rights (e.g. rights to autonomy and self-determination) is rooted in the historical and doctrinal rejection of non-Muslim people-hood and sovereignty. Jews and Christians have faced varying degrees and types of discrimination, but have found some protection through Islam's classification of their adherents as 'people of the book.'[191] Followers of smaller religions, including smaller Muslim sects, also face high degrees of harassment and discrimination.[192]

It should be noted that many states in the region fail to identify groups that could be considered minorities, and many do not report on minorities under article 27 ('the Minority Clause') of the ICCPR.[193] The Arab Charter on Human Rights, which has been in force since 15 March 2008, supposedly affirms the principles and standards contained in the United Nations Charter, the Universal Declaration of Human Rights, the International Covenant on Civil and Political Rights (with its two Optional Protocols), the International Covenant on Economic, Social and Cultural Rights, and the Cairo Declaration on Human Rights in Islam. Although this 2004 Charter and the establishment of the Arab Committee of Human Rights in 2009 are two significant steps forward in the Arab world, it has been observed that some aspects of the Charter are inconsistent with international human rights standards, and that it is

---

189   See Mordechai Nisan, *'The Minority Plight,' The Middle East Quarterly,* September 1996, Volume III: Number 3.
190   *Ibid.*
191   See 'World Directory of Minorities and Indigenous Peoples: Middle East Overview' online: http://www.refworld.org/cgi-bin/texis/vtx/rwmain?page=publisher&skip=0&publisher=MRGI.
192   *Ibid.*
193   Joshua Castellino & Elvira Domínguez Redondo, *Minority Rights in Asia* (Oxford University Press, 2006), p. 43.

doubtful whether the Committee is sufficiently independent to address human rights issues effectively.[194]

The state of human and minority rights varies from nation to nation in this region. For instance, there are nations such as Saudi Arabia and Iran which are well known for their ultra-repressive regime with little respect for basic human and minority rights; whilst other countries such as Jordan have a relatively progressive record. Transitional countries such as Syria, Egypt, Afghanistan and Libya face unique challenges of promoting and protecting human and minority rights which tend to emerge whenever a formerly authoritarian country begins to move towards some form of democracy (in however small steps). There are also rights issues that are unique to this region due to its common Islamic tradition, such as freedoms of religion and association, and the rights of women.

A well-known example of oppression of minorities in the Middle East is the prolonged Palestinian-Israeli conflict.[195] Israel's significant Muslim minority, including most indigenous Palestinians, has faced systematic discrimination in citizenship, property, education, and other rights. In reaction to attacks on Jewish targets over the years, Israel has imposed drastic security measures on the occupied territories, launched frequent military raids, and stifled Palestine's economy. The two sides remain firmly locked in endless violence fed by the politicisation of religious intolerance. However, the case of the Palestinian Muslims is perhaps a special one, as the Palestinian Arabs may be a demographic minority in Israel, they belong to the dominant Sunni Arab group. This means that they do not need to confront Arab nationalism or Sunni Islam in their struggle and have won considerable political and moral support through this connection.[196] Furthermore, in this region, the restrictions and discriminations vis-à-vis minorities are often presented and justified through a security prism. Israel is a classic example for this security-oriented approach.[197]

---

194 See, for instance, 'The Role of Regional Human Rights Mechanisms,' Policy Department, Directorate-General for External Policies of the Union, European Parliament, November 2010.

195 Note that Rabinowitz, an Israeli sociologist, considers the Palestinians as distinct from other ethnic and national minorities and refers to them separately as a 'trapped minority' to put emphasis on the effects of re-territorialisation on their identity and political and social status. See Dan Rabinowitz, 'The Palestinian Citizens of Israel, the Concept of Trapped Minority and the Discourse of Transnationalism in Anthropology,' 24(1) Ethnic and Racial Studies (2001), pp. 64–85.

196 Mordechai Nisan, 'The Minority Plight,' The Middle East Quarterly, September 1996, Volume III: Number 3.

197 Joshua Castellino &. Kathleen A. Cavanaugh, Minority Rights in the Middle East (Oxford University Press, 2013), pp. 17–29.

The problem with studying minorities in the Middle East is that discussions on minorities are often politically and emotionally loaded. This is the case all over the world in fact, but emotions seem particularly intense in the Middle East. Middle Eastern states are often very sensitive towards outside criticisms over their treatment of minorities. They also do not hesitate to, in self-defence, point to cases of ill treatment of Muslims in some Western countries. Nisan has identified three what he calls 'energizing elements' that may 'help arouse [an awakening] in what appeared as a previously nonexistent or dormant community': social changes, repression and conflict, and foreign involvement and assistance.[198] It still remains to be seen precisely what long-term effects the Arab Spring, in which all three elements were present, would have on the protection of minorities in the region, though, sadly, so far, the short-term effects have been mostly negative.

While it initially appeared to have opened a welcoming door to a great number of Arabs of minority religions (most noticeably, Christians), who, after years of feeling marginalised, eagerly joined the call for democracy, rule of law, and human rights. But a surge of sectarian violence in Cairo turned Christian-Muslim tensions into one of the gravest threats to the 'revolution's stability and credibility. In countries such as Egypt and Syria, where the effects of the Arab Spring have been most profound, the Christian population, along with other minorities, has been subject to increasing attacks and is under constant pressure to determine their relationship with the nation state. We must not forget that all revolutions, at initial stages, empower *the majority*, which, as the authoritarian state falls, tend to allow long-simmering tensions to explode and spread. Though, at later stages, *if* meaningful discourse on the rule of law and human rights is able to take place, new questions about pluralism, tolerance and the protection of minorities are likely to open, and hopefully be answered. Thus the key question is whether such a meaningful discourse on the rule of law and human rights is likely to take place. Some had high hopes for the Egyptian Bill of Rights proposed by Mohamed ElBaradei in June 2011 in a bid to bridge the widening rift between Egypt's Islamists and liberals. But reaching a meaningful consensus on basic principles and rights had been impossible. A controversial provision of the proposed document was article 2, which stated that Islam shall be the religion of the state and that Sharia shall be the main source of legislation. It seems that, while the proposed bill aimed to guarantee political rights without discrimination, it would formally declare

---

198   Mordechai Nisan, *'The Minority Plight,'* The Middle East Quarterly, September 1996, Volume III: Number 3, p. 16.

Egypt an Islamic state whose rules and principles of governance and legislation would stem from Islamic Sharia.[199]

It does seem that one should remain cautious and conservative when predicting the impact of the Arab Spring on the development of human and minority rights in the Muslim world, for two particular reasons. First, it has always been hard if at all possible to predict the outcome of what is likely to transpire in many Middle Eastern states in terms of political climate, security situation as well as overall socio-economic conditions, which all have enormous impact on the treatment of minorities. Second, while events of the Arab Spring share common demands for the rule of law and basic human and minority rights, so far attention has been focussed on searching for governance alternatives and establishing accountability of leaders. Minority rights have not yet been a priority, if they ever will be.

2.6   What's Wrong, What's Right, What to Expect?

Clearly, minorities are treated differently in different parts of the world. Although there remain heated and unresolved debates in all regions, the Western democracies, especially European countries, having previously flirted with the ideals and policies of multiculturalism, have now begun to move in the opposite direction. Asia, Africa and the Middle East (until the recent uprisings) continue to firmly cling to centralised governments and homogenous nation-states and consider self-government of minorities a topic off-limit.[200] Despite significant progresses in all regions, minority groups of considerable magnitude are facing ongoing and new difficulties, including but not limited to that of survival as identifiable and distinct entities. Although in most situations the greatest historical injustices already belong in history, the effects of which have endured and mutated into more covert, but no less damaging, injustices in the contemporary world. It is very easy to fall into a defensive position regarding the effectiveness of the international and regional minority rights systems. Three lines of defence are most commonly used. First, it is unreasonable to

---

199   For discussions on Sharia and the human rights discourse, see, for example, Khaled Abou El Fadl's *'The Human Rights Commitment in Modern Islam'* in Joseph Runzo, Nancy M. Martin & Arvind Sharma, *Human Rights and Responsibilities in the World Religions* (Oneworld Publications, 2003), Chapter 21; Katerina Dalacoura, *Islam, Liberalism and Human Rights* (I.B. Tauris & Co Ltd, 1998), Chapters 2 and 6; and Abudulaziz Sachedina, *Islam and the Challenge of Human Rights* (Oxford University Press, 2009).

200   See, for example, Joshua Castellino &. Kathleen A. Cavanaugh, *Minority Rights in the Middle East* (Oxford University Press, 2013), pp. 318–320; Will Kymlicka, *Multicultural Odysseys: Navigating the New International Politics of Diversity* (Oxford University Press, 2007), Chapter 7; Chapter 6 of this book will examine this issue in greater detail.

expect the international and regional regimes to do any more than provide the most minimal standards. Second, all that *should be* protected *is* protected (– what more do you want?). And third, in the face of continuing challenges to the universal applicability of certain rights norms, a frequently employed defensive and dismissive response is that 'we must not start making different rules for different peoples,' which neither explains the problems nor offers solutions.

The increase in international and regional documents on minority protection in the past few decades is a phenomenon to be applauded. But it is one thing to announce protection and entirely another to make protection reality. As already demonstrated, the effectiveness and applicability of many of the international and regional documents must not be over-stated, and one significant obstacle to universal applicability and effective enforcement of many of the provisions, I argue, is the lack of essential, clear, definitions. John Packer has noted that defining the term 'minority' has been avoided whenever possible.[201] This raises fundamental questions about who the instruments are intended to protect and subjects the provisions to endless debates thereby rendering them inapplicable and unenforceable, as it is impossible to accord real rights to vague, presumed, concepts. Whether or not the international and regional regimes can do more than provide basic standards depends on what these basic standards are. If they are a list of substantive, fixed, norms and rules generated by ambiguous concepts and Western ideals, then providing such a list *is* the ceiling beyond which the international system cannot reach. The problem, in my view, is inherent in the concepts. Good laws and policies require good concepts. Unstable and ambiguous concepts produce unenforceable laws and unrealistic expectations and policies. This is not to deny that the international minority rights regime has made remarkable progress since it first came into being. Rather, new challenges have emerged in recent decades which necessitate new strategies and solutions. But the concepts on which the regime is currently based are flawed in ways that do not necessarily reflect the real needs of minorities or the changing global context in which minority rights issues are situated, perceived and analysed. This prevents a progressive understanding and effective enforcement of minority rights. The turbulent history of the development of minority rights clearly reveals that the system is far from settled but constantly evolving. However, the development so far appears to lack a clear sense of direction as it periodically and reactively tries to escape from the (recent) past without really knowing where its future lies.

---

201   John Packer, '*On the Definition of Minorities,*' in John Packer &. Kristian Myntti (eds.), *The Protection of Ethnic and Linguistic Minorities in Europe* (Institute for Human Rights, Åbo Akademi University, 1993), p. 24.

GROUP RIGHTS   67

Thus it seems impossible to escape from one 'wrong' place and not end up in another. I will argue that in the search for a 'future,' we must dig deep into 'the past' by returning to the very basics, *concepts*, and then move from *concepts* to *re-conceptualisation*.

3   Concepts: Legal, Political, Social

When one considers issues concerning minority rights in general and group rights in particular, one is typically seeking answers to the following questions: who are the minorities? Are the rights individually or collectively held? What does such a right consist of? What does it mean to have such a right? When and how do we know such rights exist, and how do they correlate with duties, if at all? What exactly is one *claiming* when he/she claims such a right, and against whom? What is the relationship between minority/group rights on one hand, and norms, principles and standards, on the other? And so on. Contrary to common belief, it is *not* beyond doubt that certain rights exist whilst others do not, or that the concepts of these rights *per se* do not require close scrutiny. Many concepts and ideas about minority rights do not have realistic and workable implications as they lack the sensitivity as well as the flexibility necessary to reflect the needs and lived experiences of minorities. There has been much debate on contestable generalisations and assumptions, as a result of which meaningful critical analysis is beyond reach, resulting in confusions and fears – some rational and some irrational. As demonstrated in earlier sections, there are no *universally* accepted definitions of minority rights or group rights (which are often used interchangeably); but they are *most commonly* defined, or *perceived*, as follows.

'*Minority rights*' commonly refer to rights of individuals who are members of a recognised minority group. Most of such rights are typically seen as individualistic in nature as they intend to benefit and are exercised by individual members of the minority group. '*Group rights*,' or '*collective rights*,' on the other hand, are commonly seen as rights held and exercised by a group collectively rather than by its members individually. The line between '*minority rights*' and '*group rights*' begins to blur when the minority group in question is a cultural or linguistic group, as cultures and languages are necessarily *collective* phenomena, thus arguably rights that relate to protecting such phenomena or respecting such cultural differences make more sense as '*group rights*' than as 'individualistic *minority rights*.'[202] Therefore some, but not all, minority rights

---

202   Peter Jones (ed.), *Group Rights* (Ashgate, 2009), introduction, xii.

are group rights; some, but not all, group rights are minority rights. There has been a great deal of debate over whether what Kymlicka describes as *'group-differentiated rights'* and *'group-specific rights'* are just two senses of 'group rights.'[203] Kymlicka uses these terms to describe rights accorded to an ethnic, cultural or linguistic minority group that are not available to other members of the larger society. Some argue that since they are accorded on the basis of cultural membership, they are group rights; whilst others say that since it is the individual members of the group who hold and exercise the rights, they are individual rights. This gives the impression that whether or not a right in question is individualistic or collective depends solely on who the right-holder is.

This is not so. As will be shown in Chapter 5 'Rights against the Group,' the right-holder is not the only criterion by which the nature of a right can be determined, and just because the right in question is exercised by the individual members of the group does not mean the right is individualistic in nature. Nevertheless, suffice it to say, for the purpose of this part, that this apparent lack of patience and attention to detail is to a large extent understandable and to a smaller extent inevitable: minority rights are what Neil MacCormick calls 'complex rights:' they are either rights to 'certain *states of being*' (e.g. rights to being free to express one's own views; rights to being free to speak one's own language or dialect; rights to being free to practise one's own religion), or rights to 'certain *states of affairs*' (e.g. rights to a fair trial and fair proceedings).[204] What makes such rights complex and distinguishes them from the simpler 'positive rights' and 'negative rights' is that the former can only ever be stated in vague and much less specific terms, which renders them much more likely than the simpler rights to be subject to conflicting interpretations and confusions – in Hart's terms, they are much more 'open-textured.'[205]

One reason for this complexity is that these more complex rights typically involve several simpler rights (positive rights and negative rights).[206] MacCormick uses the example of the 'right to an effective remedy and to a fair trial' provided in the Charter of Fundamental Rights of the European Union to demonstrate that a whole *set* of complex legal provisions is needed in order to

---

203 See Will Kymlicka, *Multicultural Citizenship* (Oxford University Press, 1995), where Kymlicka himself uses the terms 'group rights,' 'collective rights,' 'group-differentiated rights' and 'group-specific rights' interchangeably.
204 Neil MacCormick, *Institutions of Law: An Essay in Legal Theory* (Oxford University Press, 2007), pp. 130–133.
205 H.L.A. Hart, *The Concept of Law* (Oxford University Press, 1994), Chapter VII.
206 Neil MacCormick, *Institutions of Law: An Essay in Legal Theory* (Oxford University Press, 2007), pp. 131–132.

GROUP RIGHTS 69

make just *one* complex right meaningful and effective. Thus, in order to make sense of the *complex* right, one must first make sense of each and every single one of the meaning and implication of the *simpler* rights, which is hard if not impossible. What MacCormick has not touched on, however, are the so-called *cultural rights for minorities,* or *minority rights to culture.* Employing MacCormick's technical terms and methods in the inspection of the so-called cultural rights, it seems that such rights are much more complex even than what he calls 'complex rights' – as it is possible for cultural rights to consist of a whole *set* of *complex rights* rather than a whole *set* of *simpler rights*. For instance, article 27 of the International Covenant of Civil and Political Rights states that:

> In those states in which ethnic, religious or linguistic minorities exist, persons belonging to such minorities shall not be denied the rights, in community with the other members of their group, to enjoy their own culture, to profess and practise their own religion, or to use their own language.

It is obvious that article 27 lends support to multicultural policies, albeit only symbolically, through providing an encompassing right to one's own *culture*.[207] It is clear that the complex *cultural* right the article provides consists of a whole set of *sub*-complex rights – i.e. the 'right to enjoy their own culture' (culture in a narrower sense), the 'right to profess and practise their own religion,' the 'right to use their own language' – each and every single one of which is vague and open-textured. A meaningful and full specification of the broad article 27 right must specify what each of the *sub*-complex rights means and entails in any given set of circumstances and context, by perhaps breaking these complex rights down into simpler positive and negative rights. This is obviously not an easy task. Consequently, the precise content of the general right to culture is not self-evident.

In ascertaining the scope of the right, both the Human Rights Committee and the Committee on Economic, Social and Cultural Rights have laid down guidelines. The former, without enumerating a fixed list of rights, accepts that culture exists and is practised in many forms.[208] As a result, it goes beyond traditional practices and institutions and includes within the ambit of culture a wide range of interests and practices, from fishing and hunting to extensive

---

207 The word 'culture' here is used in the broadest possible sense to include languages, religions, customs and traditions, and so on.
208 General Comment 23(50), para. 7.

indigenous land rights.[209] In particular, it finds that certain rights seemingly not guaranteed by article 27 might attract article 27 protection if they are an integral aspect of a minority group's cultural identity.[210] The latter also considers a wide range of activities and practices to fall within 'culture' and is particularly concerned for the situations of minorities and indigenous peoples who are particularly disadvantaged in their enjoyment of economic, social and cultural rights.[211] I shall look at this in greater detail in later chapters.

Another factor which renders conceptualising 'minority rights' difficult is the indeterminacy of the meaning of the word 'minority,' as already highlighted in Part 2 above. Many are uncomfortable about drawing a clear line between the 'majority' and the 'minorities,' and argue that such a move underplays similarities and exaggerates differences, which reinforces cultural stereotypes and causes adverse effects on minority protection. This issue will be discussed in more detail later. For the time being, it is sufficient to say that there should be no doubt that minorities exist in all modern societies, be they linguistic, religious, or ethnic minorities, who cannot and must not be imagined away. There is also no doubt that the meaning of the word 'minority' has a significant degree of vagueness, which explains the lack of a universally accepted definition. An example of a definition of 'minority' goes:

> [Minorities are] groups of individuals that, without being necessarily less in number than others [...], are for historical, economic, political or other reasons in a position of disadvantage (of subordination, inferiority in power, etc.) compared to other groups of the same society.[212]

The problem with this definition is its *over-inclusiveness*. Who *isn't* a minority according to this definition? Almost *everyone* in any given society could find a way to make themselves answer to this description and thereby qualify as a 'minority,' as a result of which there will hardly be any 'majority' left. It is simply wrong and impossible that *all* minorities, by the mere fact of *being* minorities, in however vague a sense, should qualify for protection under some sort of minority rights protection scheme. And indeed, not all *minorities* are worthy of protection (murderers are 'minorities' under this description). This leads us to conclude

---

209 Li-ann Thio, *Managing Babel: The International Legal Protection of Minorities in the Twentieth Century* (Martinus Nijhoff Publishers, 2005), p. 229.
210 Ibid.
211 See Annex IV, Economic, Social and Cultural Rights Committee Report (5th Session, 1990), E/1991/23.
212 See Neus Torbisco Casals, *Group Rights as Human Rights* (Springer, 2006), p. 22.

that a plausible concept of minority rights must not be formulated in terms of inferiority and disadvantage and must somehow sophisticatedly and justly distinguish between *minorities* that qualify for protection and *minorities* that do not. This is one of the main aims of this book and will be dealt with later in detail.

It is worth mentioning in passing that many use the term '*social minorities*' to refer to groups or people suffering from discrimination or unequal treatment as a result of deep-rooted historical and social prejudices, stereotypes, traditions or beliefs in society. Thus, women, disabled people, gays and foreigners and so on fall into this category. Members of this group might suffer discrimination as a result of their numerical inferiority, but not necessarily (e.g. women). The *social minority* category and the *cultural minority* category share many common features, especially that members of both categories suffer various degrees of structural and systematic exclusion, be they intentional or unintentional. However, what clearly distinguishes *social minorities* from *cultural minorities* is the fact that the former do not (need to) appeal to *culture* or *multiculturalism* in order to justify their demands.[213] Furthermore, unlike the vast majority of *cultural minorities* which often demand *differential treatment* reflecting cultural differences, *social minorities* often demand to be treated as *equals, the same*, as members of the mainstream society, through effective and fair application of existing legal rules and protection schemes. It is for this reason that the concept developed in this book cannot accurately reflect their demands. As a result they are not covered. This is in no way suggesting turning a blind eye to the on-going discrimination suffered by these disadvantaged social groups; but that corrective justice should be and can be done through effective application of existing human rights laws and affirmative action programmes, and also simultaneously through challenging deep-rooted prejudices. *Cultural minorities*, on the other hand, need something of a different nature.

Thus, since the concept being developed here applies only to *cultural minorities* and no other, and since the rights claimed by *cultural authorities* are commonly associated with rights to sustain or enjoy their own culture or aspects of culture, in order to make sense of the concept of minority rights, it is necessary to clarify what exactly one is referring to when he/she uses the term 'culture.' Anthropologists and philosophers disagree profoundly as to what exactly

---

213 Cf. Martha C. Nussbaum, *Women and Human Development: A Capabilities Approach* (Cambridge University Press, 2000), in which Nussbaum, in Chapter Two, argues that culture *is* a barrier and that it is important for international projects to attune to cultural variety and particularity in the protection and advancement of women's welfare and interests.

culture is. Are they things? Are they traditions? Are they learned habits? Or are they something else? Edward Tylor's much quoted concept of culture states as follows:

> Culture or civilisation, taken in its wide ethnographic sense, is that complex whole which includes knowledge, belief, art, morals, law, custom, and any other capabilities and habits required by man as a member of society.[214]

This concept equates culture with civilisation. It has said everything and nothing and thus not exactly helpful for analytical purposes, as the question that needs to be asked now is: what *isn't* culture? It is unclear if this concept *actually* conceptualises culture. If it is to be taken as a *concept* of culture, then this concept depends on a whole series of *other* concepts for its analysis and explanation – the concepts of 'knowledge,' 'belief,' 'art,' 'moral,' 'law,' and so on – which are all themselves open-textured and each depends on a further series of other concepts for its explanation; it goes on endlessly. It can be argued that this concept of culture has merely provided *examples* of *culture*, or has specified the *content* of *culture*. It is clear though that 'culture' so formulated refers to certain forms of *durable collective experience*. Joseph Raz, for instance, describes cultures as 'encompassing' and having far-reaching influence on individual identities.[215] Kymlicka, by contrast, goes beyond *collective experience and memories* and places greater emphasis on common *institutional structures* and practices. He prefers the term '*societal cultures*' and describes 'culture' as providing its members 'with meaningful ways of life across the full range of human activities, including social, educational, religious, recreational, and economic life, encompassing both public and private spheres.'[216] In this view, an analysis of culture should be more about its institutions and less about the shared experience and memories from which it derives.

Seeing culture as encompassing and shaping individual identities has both pros and cons, which will be examined in detail below. For the time being, suffice it to say simply that a culture is 'a *complex whole* which provides its members with meaningful ways for understanding, interpreting and behaving in the world, which is both enabling and limiting.'[217] The difficulty in defining

---

214   See Edward Tylor, *Primitive Culture* (John Murray, 1871).
215   Neus Torbisco Casals, *Group Rights as Human Rights* (Springer, 2006), p. 73.
216   Will Kymlicka, *Multicultural Citizenship* (Oxford University Press, 1995), p. 76.
217   *Ibid.*, Chapter 5.

'culture' is obvious and profound, and as already seen in Part 2, the lack of clear definitions in international and regional instruments has caused a great deal of trouble and confusion. However, this definitional difficulty is in fact *beneficial* to our analysis, as it clearly demonstrates that cultures are neither fixed nor tightly codified; they are constructed through historical evolution and constant change, which casts significant light on how one may formulate a right that aims to reflect and protect such a fluid being/thing, and how one should understand the concept and protection of *cultural identity*.

What is '*cultural identity*?' What does it mean to '*belong* to a culture?' If 'culture' cannot be properly defined, what does it mean to have a right to it? What does it mean to have a right to something that cannot be defined? What exactly is one claiming when he/she claims that he/she has a right to his/her culture? To say that cultures are all constructed through evolution and change is not to deny the existence of common practices; it is simply intended to avoid misrepresenting and oversimplifying matters. Tariq Modood is right in adopting an anti-essentialist approach and conceiving cultural identity in *relational* terms:

> In individuating cultures and peoples, our most basic and helpful guide is not the idea of an essence, but the possibility of making historical connections, of being able to see change and resemblance. If we trace a historical connection between the language of Shakespeare, Charles Dickens, and Winston Churchill, we call that language by a single name. We say that it is the same language, though we may be aware of the differences between the three languages and of how the changes are due to various influences.[218]

This, and all that has been said so far, lead us to conclude for the time being that a good concept of minority cultural rights must not be one that aims at protecting and sustaining *elements* of *minority cultures* at any given moment in time; rather it should aim at protecting and allowing sufficient *space* for *continuity*, but also for *development* and *change*, which often result from clashes. This is not to deny that certain elements of culture ought to be simply sustained – e.g. historical sites, valuable works of art – but this is not the job of the minority rights system. How can the minority rights system sufficiently protect '*space*?' This, in my view, naturally points to a system that specifies input rather than output, based on a dialogical notion of minority rights. It is the aim of the remaining chapters to develop such an approach, through *re-conceptualisation*.

---

218 Tariq Modood, '*Anti-Essentialism, Multiculturalism, and the 'Recognition' of Religious Groups*,' *The Journal of Political Philosophy* 6 (4) (1998): 378, at p. 382.

CHAPTER 2

Liberal Ideals, the Nature of Identity, Minority Rights

Towards a Fusion of Group Rights and Individual Rights

Having considered some key concepts and ideas of minority rights in the previous chapter, we now know that instead of encouraging flexibility and promoting attentiveness and greater understanding, the elasticity of the concept of culture has had counterproductive and paradoxical effects on the protection of the rights of cultural minorities. This chapter aims to show that successful legal and political interpretation of minority rights requires more than remaining faithful to accepted norms and standard interpretations. First and foremost, it requires one to abandon the essentialist, narrow vision of culture and cultural belonging, be sensitive to one's own cultural standpoint and be willing to subject one's own views to criticism, revision and re-statement.[1] To do so is to challenge underlying presuppositions, the presence of which is inevitable in the process of reasoning, but the acknowledgement and recognition of which might make all the difference and point us in a brand new direction.

There are four main aims. The first is to continue with the conceptual analysis started in the previous chapter and consider a few examples of taxonomies of group rights introduced by modern theorists, which is followed by an examination of the necessity of group rights. The second is to draw on recent scholarship on multiculturalism and minority rights and explore various constructions and justifications of group rights. The focus of attention is on the necessity, theoretical validity and moral defensibility of the notion as it stands. The third, related, aim is to evaluate competing interpretations of the principle of *toleration* and its limits, and especially its application to illiberal groups, which is central to the justification of group rights. The fourth and ultimate aim of this chapter is to indicate a move towards a fusion of group rights and individual rights in both the *concept* and *international legal framework* of minority rights.

---

1 In other words, it is necessary to have a dialogue with oneself.

1 Taxonomies of Group Rights (Claims)

There already exists a large body of literature on classifications of group rights.[2] The specific content and nature of the claims advanced under the term 'group rights' can of course vary enormously, depending on the type and nature of the minority group in question, the group's historical and present circumstances as well as its future prospects.[3] There are therefore many ways of categorising group rights claims – soft-multiculturalist v. hard-multiculturalist, types of groups v. types of demands, formal v. procedural, and so on. The line between different categories is not always easy to draw. Since *cultural minorities* are the focus of attention, it is the rights claims relevant to *them* I will be looking at here.

Thomas Pogge has provided us with a straight-forward classification of cultural group rights. He sees 'group rights' as including at least three types of legal rights, each of which contains both positive and negative rights: first, '*group rights proper*' – rights collectively exercised through internal decision-making bodies; second, '*group-specific rights*' – rights which are enjoyed only by certain groups rather than all, e.g. no-one except the Sikhs have the right to ride bikes without helmets; and finally, '*group-statistical rights*' – rights granted to ensure the representation of certain groups in certain public institutions and procedures, e.g. guaranteed representation in Parliament.[4] Pogge calls this third type of group rights '*funny rights,*' in that they are not exactly group rights in the classical sense as they are clearly exercised by individuals, and yet they are not exactly individual rights either as no individual member of the group is entitled to anything at all – what happens is that an agreed number of the rights objects go to an agreed number of the group members; each individual member gets nothing directly or individually.[5]

In *Multicultural Citizenship*, Will Kymlicka argues that what matters the most is not whether the right in question is *collective* or *individual* in nature, but whether it is *group-differentiated* or not.[6] He therefore offers his own taxonomy of collective cultural rights, which he calls *group-specific rights*, which divides such rights into three broad categories: first, '*self-government rights,*'

---

2 See, for example, Peter Jones (ed.), *Group Rights* (Ashgate, 2009) and Neus Torbisco Casals, *Group Rights as Human Rights* (Springer, 2006).
3 Neus Torbisco Casals, *Group Rights as Human Rights* (Springer, 2006), p. 75.
4 Pogge's '*Group Rights and Ethnicity*' in Ian Shapiro &. Will Kymlicka (eds.), *Ethnicity and Group Rights* (New York University Press, 1997), p. 191 ff.
5 *Ibid.*, p. 192.
6 Will Kymlicka, *Multicultural Citizenship* (Oxford University Press, 1995), pp. 26–33.

which are rights of national minorities to be in charge of their own internal affairs; second, *'poly-ethnic rights,'* which are intended to promote integration, not self-government or autonomy, by helping ethnic and religious minorities express their cultural particularity without hampering their success in the economic and political institutions of the mainstream society – e.g. anti-racism education and policies, public funding of minority cultural practices, and exemptions from state laws and regulations in appropriate cases; and third, *'special representation rights,'* which are a form of temporary political affirmative action intended to guarantee political representation of minorities in response to systemic disadvantage and historic injustice and oppression.[7]

Clearly, anything could potentially fall into Kymlicka's categories as they are very broad. In particular, as Levy criticises, such a classification divides up largely similar claims and group together claims which might well 'be made together but must be justified separately.'[8] In contrast, the taxonomy of minority cultural rights that Jacob Levy provides us with is significantly narrower and more specific, and based on *types of demands* (which do not automatically translate into *rights*) rather than *types of groups*.[9] Each of the eight categories contains rights that Levy sees as 'morally and institutionally similar.'[10] In the first category are *total exemptions*, which aim at allowing cultural traditions and practices that contrast with those of the majority or even infringe upon the majority's legal rules or social norms – e.g. using illegal substances in traditional cultural or religious ceremonies. In the second category are *self-government rights*, which are usually claimed by national minorities and cover a broad range of claims including partial or total control of the group's public and cultural affairs. In the third category are the so-called *assistance rights*, which are contrary to the purposes of the previous two categories and instead request state assistance in overcoming obstacles to engage in the majority's culture and practices, with the specific aim of integration, if not assimilation. A classic example is preferential policies in education for members of certain cultural and linguistic minorities.

In the fourth category are *enforcement, or recognition rights*, a common claim of which is for certain religious or cultural legal codes to be recognised as valid law, even if they conflict with aspects of state law. This type of demand is

---

7   Ibid.
8   Jacob Levy's *'Classifying Cultural Rights,'* in Ian Shapiro &. Will Kymlicka (eds.), *Ethnicity and Group Rights* (New York University Press, 1997), p. 50.
9   *Ibid.*, pp. 22–66.
10 *Ibid.*, pp. 22–24.

sometimes referred to as *'hard multiculturalist demands.'*[11] In the fifth category are certain *external rules* aimed at restricting the liberty of *non-members* so that inherent characteristics of the minority culture in question can be preserved. This type of approach is part and parcel of *'cultural preservationism.'* In the sixth category are certain *internal rules* aimed at restricting the freedom of *members* of a minority group for the purpose of keeping things as they are and preserve the group's distinct identity. In the seventh category are *guaranteed representation demands*, which aim at guaranteeing presence and participation of cultural minorities in national, regional and international decision-making bodies and procedures. And in the eighth category are the so-called *symbolic demands*, which commonly aim at gaining permission to display minority cultural symbols in public, which are seemingly the mildest possible demands but are by no means less significant.[12]

The strengths of Levy's classification are obvious. Firstly, it has great explanatory power as it is sufficiently precise. Secondly, being based on types of *demands* rather than types of *groups*, it successfully avoids unnecessarily distinguishing between largely similar claims made by different groups. Indeed this was Levy's main aim, which he has achieved. Thirdly, although the list is not exhaustive but as Levy claims includes only the most disputable claims, it clearly demonstrates that under the umbrella term *'group rights'* there are many different kinds of claim. It is thus impossible to either condemn or praise 'group rights' *as one single notion, or a class*. Different types of claims require different evaluation and approach, different forms of communication, different means of recognition and corresponding policies. While this greatly complicates matters in practice, it also tells us where we stand and which direction we should be heading in. Yet, Levy's classification also has great limitations, especially that some types of rights significantly overlap, for example, categories 2 and 4, categories 4 and 6, categories 5 and 8. In real life situations it might be impossible to decide in which category the claim should be placed. The analytical usefulness of the model is therefore compromised.

There exist still other classifications which have not been considered. But drawing conclusions from the three above, it is clear that each type of classification has its own focus, strengths and limitations, and it is hard to adjudicate between them. But on the whole, Levy's tentative classification is analytically most useful, though it is subject to further development. We can draw a number

---

11   See Brian Barry, *Culture and Equality* (Polity Press, 2001), for criticisms of hard multiculturalism.
12   Jacob Levy's *'Classifying Cultural Rights,'* in Ian Shapiro &. Will Kymlicka (eds.), *Ethnicity and Group Rights* (New York University Press, 1997), pp. 25–48.

of definite conclusions from the discussion so far. First, the diversity of the types and claims of group rights is so vast that it is absolutely impossible to develop a single attitude towards them, and it is most certainly unwise and irresponsible to attempt to do so. One may be in favour of some group rights but condemns others; one may be in favour of some group rights *individually and separately* but opposes the stacking of them;[13] one can be in favour of group rights granted to groups which one somehow favours, while opposes exactly the same rights granted to other groups of very similar nature but which one does not favour; one can be in favour of some group rights in certain circumstances and opposes exactly the same group rights in other circumstances, say, due to the need to protect certain compelling individual or state interests in those circumstances; one may be in favour of group rights in theory, but is unsure regarding their practical implications. And so on. The rule is to be aware of not only the rich variety of group rights demands but also the uncertainty in our own attitudes and judgments.

The second related conclusion is that, while such categories, classifications or taxonomies are useful as analytical tools in scholarly studies, it is important to realise that they are also simplistic and divisive in their own ways in the sense that once they are employed to define and categorise a rights claim, the claim itself becomes associated with a particular fixed interpretation and understanding, as normally assigned to that particular taxonomy. Such designated associations may provoke expression, confirmation, distribution and reproduction of mainstream, dominant, interpretations as well as prejudices.

The third conclusion we can draw is that we are in need of a universal language to express particularity and difference, a general, sophisticated framework with detailed sub-divisions and categories of group rights based on *types of claims*, and with the varying natures of groups in mind and enough flexibility built in.[14] What this means is that, some universal, general criteria must be applied when sorting cultural group rights into categories, and each category must be attached with its own corresponding policies which are well thought out and specifically designed to deal with that particular category of claims.

The fourth and last conclusion is that, group rights, contrary to common belief and depending on one's own conception, *already exist*. A state is a group which possesses extensive *group rights*, including and not limited to rights to restrict the freedom of its own members, rights to restrict the liberty of non-members, and indeed rights to extensive self-government (or 'state sovereignty'). In other words, while the liberal states almost universally reject the

---

13   *Ibid.*, p. 51.
14   *Ibid.*, pp. 52–53.

notion of group rights and firmly oppose the formal recognition of these rights, they presume and persistently emphasise the strongest type of group rights – self-determination. Furthermore, there also already exist the group rights of indigenous peoples to *internal self-determination* provided in the 2007 UN Declaration on the Rights of Indigenous Peoples and a series of regional documents. Of course, the existence of these group rights does not automatically validate others. Can and should this existing list of recipients of group rights be extended? Are there significant similarities between a state and a cultural group, between indigenous peoples and other types of cultural and ethnic groups? If so, are they sufficient justifications for a more widely spread, more even distribution of group rights? The practical aspect of these questions will be the subject of later chapters; the theoretical aspect will be looked at here.

Sovereign State vs. Cultural Group

The difference between a sovereign state and a cultural group, broadly speaking, is obvious. According to article 1 of the 1933 Montevideo Convention on the Rights and Duties of States, from which the internationally recognised definition of 'sovereign state' derives, a sovereign state should have a permanent population, a defined territory, a government, and the capacity to enter into relations with other sovereign states – hence the capacity to gain formal recognition by other sovereign states and the international community.[15] By contrast, the nature of cultural groups varies; they may or may not possess any of the first three characteristics of a state (i.e. a permanent population, a defined territory, a government), but they most certainly do not have the fourth – they lack the capacity to enter into foreign relations with sovereign states. As already considered in Chapter 1, a cultural group is most commonly defined as a group which has certain distinct ways of life including cultural practices, codes of religious belief and rituals, language, dress, arts and so on which have been passed down and carried on from generation to generation over a long period of time. A cultural group most closely resembling a state is probably a historical national group, such as Wales and Scotland in the United Kingdom. They have a permanent population, a defined territory, a government, but *no* capacity to enter into foreign diplomatic relations with other states.

One conclusion we can draw from this discussion is that, in order to be able to claim strong group rights, e.g. rights to autonomy and self-determination, a cultural group should perhaps in theory have fixed territorial boundaries, a

---

15   Available at: http://www.oas.org/juridico/english/treaties/a-40.html.

determinable population, competent internal decision-making bodies that are capable of governing, and of course a distinct live culture. This is a useful first step in determining in what direction the categories of stronger group rights (in the form of self-determination and autonomy) might be expanded, *if* they should be expanded, and who might qualify for what. The theoretical and practical implications will be spelt out in the next chapter.

Cultural Group vs. Indigenous Community

As already indicated in the first chapter, the difference between a cultural group and an indigenous group is not always clear. An indigenous group is commonly defined as an ethnic or cultural group which inhabits a geographic region (within a state) with which it has the earliest possible historical connections; such a group has maintained distinct historical, cultural and social characteristics and remains largely isolated, culturally and institutionally, from the larger state. It has a clearly defined territory, a largely fixed population, some form of internal governance, but no capacity to enter into foreign relations with other states.[16] Clearly, an indigenous group is always a cultural group, but a cultural group is only an indigenous group if it has the earliest possible historical connections with the region in which it lives and that it is largely isolated from the influence of the larger state, culturally, socially and politically. In real life situations it should not be too difficult to tell which groups are 'indigenous' and which ones are 'cultural' – the former should (in theory) benefit from strong group rights which the latter should not.

The conclusion we can draw from this is that the notion of *distance*, or *remoteness*, or *lack of proximity*, is central to the notion of group rights as it stands. In other words, how strong the granted rights ought to be, how much independence and self-control a group ought to have, should depend on how historically and culturally independent and self-sufficient it already is, which in part depends on how distinct their culture is, how detached they already are from the rest of the state. That said, even if all these requirements are fulfilled, there are still political reasons why some groups should not be granted in reality what they qualify for in theory, to which we will return in later chapters. It should also be borne in mind that, as demonstrated in Chapter 1, international minority rights law on self-determination and autonomy as it is over-emphasises a group's cultural independence and tends to be silent on its self-sufficiency and capacity to self-govern. This will be the sole focus of Chapter 6.

---

16   See, for instance, Will Kymlicka, *Multicultural Citizenship* (Oxford University Press, 1995), pp. 22–23; Brian Barry, *Culture and Equality* (Polity Press, 2001), p. 308.

2 Necessity of Group Rights

Group rights can be deemed necessary if five requirements can be satisfied. First, the notion of group rights is *theoretically valid*. Second, group rights are *morally defensible*. Third, the current individual rights system is insufficient to protect the interests of cultural minorities – i.e. group rights are a *necessity*. Fourth, the formal recognition of group rights will not endanger those *compelling interests* which are often permitted to override *rights*. And fifth, it is practicable to either have two systems of rights in force simultaneously (one of individual rights and one of group rights), or for one system to accommodate and contain a fusion of the two types of rights, and that the administrative difficulties are not too great to overcome.

There are many questions one can ask about group rights. What exactly are they? Do we need them at all? Are they (or, which particular types are) *required, optional,* or *permissible* in various circumstances? What do group rights aim to protect that are not already and cannot be protected by a system of individual rights? How can we assess the correctness of our judgments, by what standards, and who decides? While there are lots of ambiguities, contradictions and unsolved dilemmas in this field, it is very clear that international and regional organisations are committed to the protection of *individual rights*. As shown previously, whilst the group rights approach has gained some ground in the past decades, with the UN targeting indigenous peoples and Europe targeting national historical minorities, the individual rights approach is still mainstream and seen as sufficient and granting all individuals the same right to be equal *and* different. Most recently, we have witnessed a rapid retreat from the targeted group rights approach and the idea of multiculturalism.[17] This must not be seen as a retreat from an international commitment to *minority protection* – such a commitment is present and strong – rather, it is a retreat from a particular understanding of minority rights protection, a retreat from the recognition of *group-differentiated* minority rights. Those in the legal field can say with a fair amount of confidence that in the foreseeable future it is unlikely that either the UN or the European organisations would commit themselves whole-heartedly and formally to a group rights approach in the accommodation of minority claims, as there will always be institutional disagreements and geo-political security risks that such an approach would almost inevitably cause.

A different trend, however, has been emerging in the field of political theory. Political theorists often seem much more optimistic and passionate than

---

17 Will Kymlicka, *Multicultural Odysseys: Navigating the New International Politics of Diversity* (Oxford University Press, 2007), p. 52.

lawyers about the possibility and necessity of a group rights approach. Many argue, with increasing intensity, but in different ways (as will be demonstrated below), that group rights are a necessary corrective to the nation state, an essential tool to protect the minorities against the tyranny of the majority. One question naturally springs to mind: why is the trend in political theory not reflected in international law?

There are several possible explanations. The most obvious one is that lawyers and political theorists approach group rights differently. The former seem to be more pragmatic and tend to over-emphasise the administrative impossibilities of a group rights approach. The latter, by contrast, tend to focus on the normative and positive side of the notion of group rights, but often stop at issues of practical workability and implementation. Secondly, political theorists have conducted thorough studies of culture and are much more successful than lawyers in analysing the notion of group rights in conjunction with, or in the wider context of, culture. Lastly and interestingly, while lawyers often attack the notion of group rights 'as it is,' as it is conventionally understood, political theorists tend to defend the notion 'as it could become,' once it is correctly and properly interpreted or reformulated. Thus, to a certain extent exponents and opponents of group rights have been talking past each other – what is being defended is not what was under attack. This, of course, is an oversimplification of the differences (and similarities) between the two camps (if it is indeed appropriate to so divide people according to their profession alone). But one fact remains unchallenged: the notion of group rights has attracted significantly more supporters from the field of political theory than from the field of law.

This observation is very significant and tells us several things: firstly, a successful project on group rights and minority rights ought to be interdisciplinary. Secondly, a natural and strategic approach is to take a middle path, which may be revealed partly through studying the divergence between political theory and law on group rights: we must not attack the notion of group rights without attentive observation and calm analysis, without studying the full picture and placing the notion in its rightful place within the cultural framework; we must not, on the one hand, over-simplify issues of cultural belonging and their relationship with the notion, and, on the other, over-complicate issues of recognition and implementation of group rights.

There are good reasons why a group rights approach should be adopted, not to *replace* the individual rights system, but to build upon or into it, and supplement it. Firstly, it has been argued that the existing framework of minority rights protection is politically ineffective, not least in that the norms do not solve the problems *they were originally intended* to solve.[18] To use Europe as an example: one of the original reasons for developing minority protection norms and principles were the violent ethnic conflicts in the post-communist states. None of these conflicts revolved around the rights of *individuals* to be treated equally and to freely enjoy their culture. The cause of these violent conflicts was not the violation of some *individual* human rights of members of minorities, and hence respect for and protection of *individual* rights would not resolve these conflicts.[19] Although violent conflicts in parts of the world today have taken new forms, their cause is still *not* exclusively violation of individual human rights. Thus it is unreasonable to continue to expect the current individual rights system alone to adequately respond to these conflicts.

Secondly, although the current individual rights-based human rights system on the whole seemingly guarantees equality for all irrespective of ethnic, cultural, religious and social backgrounds, and that the liberal principles of neutrality and individual freedom on which the system is based do seem to guarantee maximum tolerance and equal protection for all; in reality, *neutrality* plus *freedom* often equals imposition of the dominant values, as it is impossible to decouple the majority culture from the larger political culture, and thus the majority culture was in a much stronger position to begin with than the minority cultures. In the case of cultural and religious practices, *neutrality* plus *freedom* have often led to *cultural privatisation* and *indifference* on all except the most disagreeable or 'rebellious' dissenters. These results are far from desirable. To a large extent, cultural differences have not been properly addressed, understood and accommodated; they have merely been suppressed into the private sphere and shielded from the public view. Those minority cultural practices which are most likely to be categorised as 'private' are precisely those ones that are most controversial.[20] By deleting them from the public arena, their controversial status is merely confirmed, and their real nature remains unexplored, un-debated, and misunderstood. Indifference or even hostility towards them remains unchallenged as the masses remain insufficiently informed.

Thus, to sum up, when debating whether or not we should supplement the existing generic rights, which aim to provide *equal rights* to all irrespective of ethnic, cultural and religious background, with more group-differentiated rights, I propose that we keep one question in mind: are we alike enough to be treated equally? Since human and cultural diversity seems to be at the very

---

18   *Ibid.*, Chapter 6.
19   *Ibid.*
20   See, for example, Brian Barry, *Culture and Equality* (Polity Press, 2001), pp. 24–32.

centre of persistent conflicts around the world, it is perhaps time for us to take a brave step towards diversifying the rights regime by formally accommodating group rights.

3 Theoretical Validity and Moral Defensibility of Group Rights

There seem to be two plausible ways to argue that the notion of group rights is theoretically valid and morally defensible. The first is currently the most fashionable approach which aims to reconcile liberal principles and group rights and formulates the latter as rights protecting *individual* interests, and then justifies the protection of such interests. The second is the more conventional approach which sees no such need to reconcile seemingly irreconcilable principles, and considers group rights as typically protecting *group* interests, and justifies the protection of such interests. I shall consider each in turn.

1st Approach

It is widely believed that group rights and individual rights are deeply incompatible, and that a new category of rights is unnecessary since the liberal doctrines of *tolerance* and *neutrality* already provide a proper framework for ensuring equal status of different groups and peoples.[21] The mainstream liberal approach argues that the recognition of group rights will establish a preference for the community in question over the interests of individual members of that community; while advocates of group rights criticise the dominant liberal approach as being *difference-blind* and claim that nothing less than the formal endorsement of group rights – in some form of differentiated rights and citizenship – can provide an effective means of dealing with identity conflicts and group inequalities in an increasingly multicultural society.

It can be argued that the correlation between liberalism and individual rights on the one hand, and communitarianism and group rights on the other, is over-simplistic and problematic, not only does it ignore the fact that there is no such thing as *the* communitarian theory as the communitarian tradition is diverse and complex, and that the communitarian critiques of liberalism have had a huge impact on the development and self-correction of contemporary liberal theories; it also, by focusing mainly on the formal problems and practical difficulties of recognising group rights, diverts our attention from the numerous *normative* questions arising out of the theories and practices of multiculturalism. As Kymlicka rightly claims, debates about minority rights

---

21 Neus Torbisco Casals, *Group Rights as Human Rights* (Springer, 2006), p. 7.

are *not* 'debates between a liberal majority and communitarian minorities, but rather debates amongst *liberals* about the meaning of liberalism';[22] thus any disagreements arising out of such debates are disagreements about the interpretation and application of *liberal* values and principles, the boundaries and limits of *liberalism*, with far-reaching and long-lasting consequences.

Torbisco Casals has made an attempt to overcome these problems by combining the theories of Joseph Raz and Will Kymlicka on group rights.[23] The strategy has two major elements: the character of *the public good*, and a rationale that defines group rights as '*special rights* that *individuals* have by virtue of their belonging to particular cultural groups.'[24] In general terms, this theory sees group rights as rights to some *public goods* that are not only of vital importance to the *group of individuals* and their *personal well-being*, but also provide benefits to the *society at large*. The interests protected by group rights are *shared* among the members of the group and cannot be simply reduced to a series of individual goods.[25] Raz sees *well-being* as being determined by our *conscious choices* about what is worth pursuing in our lives. He believes that any cultural option can potentially lead to personal well-being as long as we consciously and wholeheartedly believe it is worthwhile, and a good and just society is one that guarantees equally to everyone the chance of finding out for ourselves and the *possibility* of success in this enterprise.[26]

A number of questions arise. Firstly, what constitutes a *conscious choice*? What enables and produces conscious choices? Do we need to be presented with a complete set of options in order to be able to make conscious choices? If yes, should we then recognise those group rights which might have the consequence of limiting options and restricting freedoms?[27] These issues will be best examined in relation to *illiberal groups*, which are the focus of Part 4 below. It is sufficient to say for the time being that although theorists disagree passionately with each other, the dominant approach is one that strongly opposes *illiberal group rights*. Secondly, Raz says that a good society is one that can guarantee equally to everyone *the possibility* of success in one's conscious

---

22 Will Kymlicka, *Politics in the Vernacular: Nationalism, Multiculturalism and Citizenship* (Oxford University Press, 2001), p. 21.
23 Neus Torbisco Casals, *Group Rights as Human Rights* (Springer, 2006).
24 *Ibid.*, p. 43.
25 *Ibid.*, pp. 54–55.
26 Joseph Raz, *The Morality of Freedom* (Oxford University Press, 1986), p. 316; Neus Torbisco Casals, *Group Rights as Human Rights* (Springer, 2006), p. 51.
27 For example, Jacob Levy's Categories 5 and 6 of group rights demands: external rules restricting the liberty of non-members, and internal rules limiting the freedoms of members of a minority group.

cultural pursuit. What are the implications of guaranteeing *the possibility of success* instead of actual *success itself*? Are there any reliable criteria of *equal possibility of success* independent of *equal success*? And indeed, what may constitute 'success' as opposed to 'failure' in cultural pursuits? How may it be measured? Is it not a matter of degree, and varies from person to person, situation to situation? And what light does it shed on a liberal notion of group rights?

Clearly, Raz's statement constitutes his interpretation of the liberal doctrine of *neutrality*. He does not interpret it in a classical liberal sense as to mean *indifference* or *hands-off*. He interprets it as a *'neutral political concern,'* and acting neutrally means *'to do one's best to help or to hinder the various parties in an equal degree.'*[28] Thus, it seems that, far from hands-off, in Raz's view, to maintain neutrality not only *permits*, but also *requires*, intervention.

Thirdly, it can also be argued that it is misleading to speak about *group* rights when we are in fact concerned with *individual* interests and *personal* well-being. Raz's discussion on the right to self-determination responds to this concern:

> [It] is not merely a public good but *a collective one* (italics added), and people's interest in it arises out of the fact that they are members of the group. [T]hough many individuals have an interest in the self-determination of their community, *the interest of any one of them is an inadequate ground for holding others to be duty-bound to satisfy that interest* (italics added). The right rests on the *cumulative interests of many individuals* (italics added).[29]

But if such *group* rights in all but name protect *individual* interests, instead of granting *group rights*, can we not just grant *additional individual rights*? Raz might argue in response that, we might well do exactly that, but any such *additional individual rights* will be granted on the basis of *group membership*. In other words, they might *take the form* of *individual rights* in the sense that they benefit individual members and protect individual interests; they are in essence *group rights*, or *group-differentiated rights* to be precise, as no-one outside the group can ever be granted such *additional rights* even if they have certain, very similar, interests that equally deserve *additional* protection. The key criterion here is not the value of interests, but rather *cultural membership*.

---

28 Joseph Raz, *The Morality of Freedom* (Oxford University Press, 1986), p. 113; Raz calls this 'principled neutrality,' 'the primary sense of neutrality.'

29 *Ibid.*, p. 209.

Further questions arise. How may this general analysis apply to particular types of rights, for instance, language rights, religious rights, the right to self-determination, and so on? In particular, firstly, are all cultural group rights *'rights to public goods'*? Secondly, even if group rights can be shown to protect *individual* interests, advance *personal* well-being, and therefore are compatible with liberal values, does it necessarily mean that they *generate positive obligations*? Furthermore, the phrase *'cumulative interests of many individuals'* in the above quote seems to assume internal homogeneity within minority groups, which is both naive and dangerous.[30] Thirdly, how, if at all, should the state intervene in internal group conflicts, appropriately respond to and accommodate demands voiced by the so-called 'minorities within minorities'? This last question will be the focus of Chapter 5, but it is necessary to consider the first two questions here.

First, must all potential group rights be 'rights to public goods'? It depends on one's definition of 'public good' and from whose points of view one looks at them. There exist various definitions of 'public goods' and they vary greatly. For the purposes of the analysis of cultural rights, a narrow conception such as the one put forward by Boran should suffice: a public good should have the following features: (1) *jointness* in supply and consumption: a public good is available for and can be consumed by *all* members of the society; (2) *non-excludability:* a public good benefits anyone and everyone; no-one is prevented from doing so; (3) *indivisibility:* the good cannot be divided into private goods; and (4) *compulsoriness:* it would be unfeasible to avoid benefiting from the good.[31] There are two ways of applying this conception to minority group rights: one is to see *individual cultures* as public goods; the other is to regard the *diversity of cultures* as a public good.

Cultures are valuable as collective human accomplishments and ongoing manifestations of human creativity. Among other things, having many different cultures means having many different ways and means of human expression, of advancing sciences, creating art and music, and expressing and interpreting human experiences. It has been forcefully put forward by sociologists and political theorists that cultural diversity, just like biodiversity, is a collectively produced public good that people *in general* can enjoy even if they have not contributed to its production or maintenance. People may not be

---

30   See Avigail Eisenberg &. Jeff Spinner-Halev (eds.), *Minorities within Minorities: Equality, Rights and Diversity* (Cambridge University Press, 2005).

31   Idil Boran's *'Global Linguistic Diversity, Public Goods, and the Principle of Fairness'* in Will Kymlicka &. Alan Patten, *Language Rights and Political Theory* (Oxford University Press, 2003), Chapter 8.

conscious of benefiting from it, but neither can they stop themselves from benefiting from it.³² In other words, cultures' *aesthetic value* benefits not just the cultural group members but the entire human community.

While this cannot be denied in most circumstances, one must critically review the ability of *aesthetic value* to provide an adequate basis for *rights*, for *minority rights*, for *group rights*. Firstly, a large number of cultural claims have come from cultures that do not meet the 'public good' and 'aesthetic value' requirements. Does it mean there should never be 'rights' attached to these cultures, their beliefs and practices? But there already exist certain internationally recognised group rights attached to cultures that do not meet the 'aesthetic value' requirements – most noticeably 'indigenous rights.' Secondly, it seems that aesthetic values and needs are not strong enough to make a moral claim for formal legal protection. Consider the difference between a culture and a valuable piece of art: while all states distribute a large amount of resources to protect valuable art, and they should; it would be absurd to say that all members of any given society are obligated to protect them and failure to do so constitutes violations of certain rights. In other words, just because cultures and cultural diversity have aesthetic values and are public goods, they do not necessarily generate legal and political obligations.

This leads to the *second* question asked above – *do group rights necessarily generate positive obligations*? One response to this question is that it depends on what values and interests these rights are intended to protect, how fundamental these values and interests are, and how urgent it is to protect them. Kymlicka's liberal conception of group rights establishes an essential connection between cultural belonging and the meaningful exercise of individual autonomy. He argues that, autonomy – i.e. the individual's ability to exercise his moral capacities to not only discover and choose among different conceptions of the good life but also *to revise and change these choices* in the light of other values or rules of reason – is culturally dependent and enabled, in that individual choices are always formed, shaped and changed within a *'societal culture'*:

> Whether or not a course of action has any significance for us depends on whether, and how, our language renders vivid to us the point of that activity. And the way in which language renders vivid these activities is shaped by our history, traditions and conventions. Understanding these cultural narratives is a precondition of making intelligent judgments about how to lead our lives. In this sense, our culture not only provides

32   *Ibid.*

options, it also provides the spectacles through which we identify experiences as valuable.³³

What this means is that having a rich cultural structure is vital for individuals to be aware of the options available, to assess their values intelligently, and to form reasonable expectations. This line of reasoning does not assume that the cultural community in question is more important than its individual members, or that the state should promote one particular conception of the good life or preserve the purity of one particular culture. Rather, it is the *structure* of a culture or cultural community and the 'context of choice' that it provides that really matter, not the precise *cultural characteristics* at a particular moment in time.³⁴ In this way, minority group rights are justified, on the grounds of enabling and preserving *individual* autonomy, *not* of guaranteeing cultural survival.

Kymlicka's approach has a number of strengths. Firstly, it shows that cultural belonging is a fundamental interest which should generate positive obligations. Secondly, it expressly tells us what group rights should *not* aim to protect – cultural survival. That said, this approach has left many questions unaddressed. Firstly, even if it can be established that these rights do generate obligations, questions remain to be asked as to who holds the rights and who bears the duties. In order to benefit from a right, the person in question does not have to be the right-holder as he/she can benefit from it indirectly. It is also unclear against whom these rights are held – the state, or the group in question. Furthermore and critically, it is also uncertain how easily one can separate *cultural structure* from *cultural characteristics*. Is it not the case that *structure* is constructed with *characteristics*? And is *structure* not a *characteristic* itself? Even if the two can be separated, if particular cultural characteristics are not to be preserved and individual members are free to change their ideals and values whenever they see fit, it is arguable that cultural belonging is not in fact of central importance as Kymlicka claims.³⁵

2nd Approach
In contrast to the first approach which reconciles liberalism and the notion of group rights, a more conventional approach considers the recognition of group rights straight-forwardly as the recognition of rights that typically protect

---

33   Will Kymlicka, *Multicultural Citizenship* (Oxford University Press, 1995), p. 83.
34   *Ibid.*, pp. 82–84.
35   John Danley '*Liberalism, Aboriginal Rights and Cultural Minorities,*' Philosophy and Public Affairs 20(2) (1991), p. 168 ff.

group interests (sometimes at the expense of individual interests and well-being) and insists that such protection is legitimate, or at least justifiable, and necessary. This so-called *hard-multiculturalist* approach has been widely condemned, especially in relation to illiberal groups and their practices, which are the prime if not the only target. It thus makes sense to make illiberal groups the focus of attention in evaluating this second approach and anticipating its possible impact, during which process one will inevitably have to answer some fundamental questions of legal and political philosophy. A common *justification* of this hard-multiculturalist approach is based on the liberal principles of tolerance and neutrality; the most powerful *objection* to this approach, however, is also based on these same principles. Needless to say, like all significant legal and political concepts, interpretations of them are often open-ended and sometimes contradictory.

Before embarking on our discussion, it is necessary to first make a clear distinction between a *non-liberal group* and an *anti-liberal group*, which both seem to fall under the umbrella term *illiberal group* and are often used interchangeably. A non-liberal group is one that *does not place high value on* liberal ideas but does not necessarily denounce these values; whereas an *anti*-liberal group is one that *defines itself in opposition to* liberalism and core liberal norms. It thus seems that the difference between a non-liberal group and an anti-liberal group is to a certain extent a matter of degree (and also forms of resistance), which makes accurate labelling a hard task at times. What this tells us is that, just like the diversity of types of *group rights claims* examined in the first section, the diversity of types of *groups* is also so vast that it is impossible and irresponsible to develop a single attitude towards them *as a whole*. This is not to say that the umbrella term 'illiberal group' should be abandoned, but that we should be more cautious and more conscious when using it.

4 Group Interests, *Illiberal* Group Rights, the Principle of Toleration

Theorists disagree passionately about whether, how and to what extent illiberal group rights demands should be accommodated, and it is possible to divide them into three categories according to their respective views. In the first category are the hard anti-multiculturalists who aggressively oppose multiculturalist policies and are especially hostile to non-liberal cultures (e.g. Brian Barry). In the second category are those liberals who are sensitive to concerns of minority rights and demands voiced by illiberal groups, yet insist that minority groups especially illiberal groups still need to respect certain liberal values and recognise the importance of social unity (e.g. Will Kymlicka), and that toleration is only permissible to the extent that the existing order can be preserved (e.g. John Rawls). In the third category are the so-called *hard multiculturalists* who give the liberal principle of toleration paramount independent weight and argue for less social unity and maximum toleration (e.g. Chandran Kukathas).

While the precise content and nature of these groups' demands vary greatly, in general terms, they typically include demands to preserve cultural practices and community customs which severely restrict the freedom and opportunities of the members of the group in question – e.g. arranged marriages, limited freedom of movement, restricted access to education for women, and so on. In the vast majority of these cases, the practices and customs are opposed not because they harm the larger society, but because they harm the members of the minority group. These norms and practices are widely condemned to be morally unacceptable and legally unjustifiable largely but not only because they are so fundamentally different from the norms and practices which the liberal societies are familiar with, and accept.

In *Culture and Equality*, Brian Barry presents an aggressive uniform rejection of multiculturalism and group rights. He argues that multiculturalism is fundamentally flawed and dangerous because it promotes abuse of culture, inequality, and moral relativism. He is particularly against tolerating or granting group rights to illiberal groups, the public toleration of whom, he argues, creates a lot of private hells.[36] While his concerns are valid, his approach is completely blind to the diversity *within* theories of multiculturalism and group rights, blind to the fact that there is no such a thing as *the* multicultural theory or *the* notion of group rights as he falsely assumes, blind also to the fact that there have emerged various nuanced conceptions of group rights which are inspired and constrained by liberal principles. Thus, he has undermined his own case by failing to be sufficiently attuned to differences within multicultural theory. Perhaps this 'blindness' is symptomatic of his exclusionary form of liberalism, which inattentively represents *all* multicultural theorists as identical and misinformed. That said, Barry's views must not be carelessly brushed aside. He has issued a clearest warning against *excessive* protection of minority interests, traditions and cultures. His objection to group rights is also in line with the mainstream feminist view that, group rights supporters have largely ignored oppressions hidden in the private sphere, and given the troubling connection between gender and culture, minority group rights will exacerbate problems and oppressions experienced by women and other 'minorities within

---

36   Brian Barry, *Culture and Equality* (Polity Press, 2001), Chapter 4.

minorities.'[37] This observation alerts us to the urgent need of taking special care to tackle internal, more covert oppressions, and thereby sheds significant light on what a plausible notion of group rights must take into account. The issues concerning the rights of *'minorities within minorities'* will be examined in Chapter 5, but for the time being, it is enough to say that on Barry's account, liberalism does not permit formal recognition of minority group rights.

In contrast, in developing what some call *a liberal theory of multiculturalism*, Will Kymlicka interprets liberalism in a way as not just *permitting* but *requiring* formal recognition of *certain* minority group rights.[38] While remaining faithful to liberal values, Kymlicka emphasises the importance of cultural belonging and is anxious to ensure a voice and survival for cultural minorities within a larger political and cultural context. In other words, cultures, cultural structures and group interests should be protected since the *individuals* within the group will benefit from such protection. However, he makes a clear distinction between demands to preserve *'internal restrictions'* and demands for *'external protections,'* and argues that since the former cannot be justified within a liberal conception of minority rights, they should only be allowed in private voluntary associations and must not be accommodated in the public sphere.[39] That said, he expressly opposes coercive interference – 'there is an important difference between coercively imposing liberalism and offering various incentives for liberal reforms,'[40] both in cases of national minorities and foreign states.[41] Here it becomes clear that, despite his sensitivity to minority cultural demands, Kymlicka's approach is still one of *interventionism* – he believes in the existence of a superior, liberal, standpoint of morality, a universally accepted standard of human decency, and more importantly, he believes in the *liberation* of the illiberal – so long as the liberation process is nice and slow. Clearly his love for minority group interests and cultural structures is not unconditional.

There are several obvious problems with Kymlicka's approach. Firstly, he does not tell us what constitutes *'coercion.'* Surely coercion can be very nicely and slowly carried out, depending on one's definition of 'coercion' of course, say, by offering a carefully selected list of options in a decision-making process, by teaching children a restricted set of values and principles and presenting

---

37   See, for instance, Susan Moller Okin, *Is Multiculturalism Bad For Women?* (Princeton University Press, 1999).
38   See Will Kymlicka, *Multicultural Citizenship* (Oxford University Press, 1995).
39   *Ibid.*, Chapter 8.
40   *Ibid.*, p. 168.
41   *Ibid.*, pp. 166–170.

them in a highly particularistic way. Just what exactly distinguishes between *coercion* and *persuasion*? Does extremely persuasive persuasion constitute coercion? Where shall we draw the line? And who decides? And so on. Secondly, it is also unclear whether his distinction between *internal restrictions* and *external protections* can serve any useful purposes in real life. It is often difficult if at all possible to distinguish between the two, and indeed some rights demands can serve both purposes simultaneously, depending on the specific circumstances. Also, some demands which are intended and formally accommodated as demands for external protections might well have the side-effects of serving internal restrictions and oppression.

Thirdly, he also too readily assumes that a distinction can always be made between the private sphere and the public sphere. Such a simple, arbitrary distinction – along with other similar distinctions made by others, e.g. the distinction between the religious and the secular, between the comprehensive and the political – has distorted our understanding of the circumstances in which minorities live, of the demands voiced and thus the protections required. Again, from a feminist point of view, such a distinction ignores the private sphere in which a great deal of oppression is allowed to continue to take place, which gives rise, very rightly, to one of the most persistent objections to the granting of group rights. This is not to say that a practically workable and morally defensible account of group rights must not rely on this distinction – to the contrary, as will be demonstrated in Chapters 3, 4 and 5, such an account must keep this distinction firmly in mind, but the purpose of doing so is to develop under one concept two corresponding, separate, limbs of group rights to reflect the distinction, to protect rights in the public sphere as well as rights in the private sphere.

John Rawls takes a very similar stand as Kymlicka. While Rawls is sensitive to minority group demands and upholds liberty, equality and autonomy as fundamental values, he nevertheless emphasises the vital importance of establishing a common experience and building up a consensus in a pluralistic society.[42] In *A Theory of Justice*, he discusses whether or not justice allows or even requires the toleration of illiberal groups.[43] While he acknowledges that the differences between these groups and the mainstream society might be so profound that reconciliation by reason is impossible, he nevertheless argues that we should be able to agree on the *principle of equal liberty* if we adopt *the Original Position*, which requires people to choose political principles that shape their common life without knowing where they themselves or anyone

---

42   See John Rawls, *A Theory of Justice* (Harvard University Press, 1971).
43   *Ibid.*, pp. 216–221.

else will be placed in the resulting society, so that impartiality is guaranteed.[44] And that the freedom of these groups should only be restricted 'when the tolerant sincerely and with reason believe that their own security and that of the institutions of liberty are in danger. The tolerant should curb the intolerant only in this case.'[45] The key words are 'security' and 'liberty.'

Since Rawls and Kymlicka's theories overlap in several respects, many of the criticisms are applicable to both. Just like Kymlicka, Rawls's theory is seemingly very tolerant. It upholds toleration on the basis of the two principles of justice – the principle of liberty and the principle of equality – and considers *autonomy* as the fundamental value in society, the right to which applies to all minority groups including the illiberal ones. That said, he also maintains that breaches of liberty in the name of *public order* are legitimate, and that whether or not any minority cultures and practices should be tolerated must always be determined by their compatibility with the *liberal* conception of justice based on principles of liberty and equality.[46] In his own words, *'liberty is governed by the necessary conditions for liberty itself.'*[47] Whilst Kymlicka has failed to specify what constitutes *'coercive interference,'* Rawls has failed to spell out the implications of his reliance on a purely *liberal* conception of justice, which sees liberty, equality, and individual autonomy as *fundamental goods* in society. Obviously not all groups will agree with this conception, and it is not beyond the realm of imagination that a state, a cultural majority, or an organisation which adopts this purely liberal conception of justice will be to a certain extent hostile to those minority groups and cultures that do not share this conception – even though those minority groups do not necessarily pose any threat to the larger society.

Bearing this likelihood of hostility in mind, since Rawls also maintains that all members of society (which include members of minority groups) should possess knowledge of basic human rights, and that they should all be, 'in effect though not in intention,' educated to become 'fully cooperating members of society,'[48] his promise of tolerance, based on his conception of justice, seems rather empty. The difference between what he opposes and what he supports is not entirely clear, and on the whole, if my understanding of his arguments is accurate, his approach seems more invasive than Kymlicka's. However, it must

---

44 *Ibid.*, p. 220.
45 *Ibid.*
46 *Ibid.*, p. 215.
47 *Ibid.*
48 John Rawls, *'The Priority of Right and Ideas of the Good,'* Philosophy and Public Affairs (1988), p. 251, at p. 268.

be noted that in his later work *Political Liberalism*, Rawls advances his 'political liberal project' by making a clear distinction between *'political liberalism'* and *'comprehensive liberalism,'* and maintains that his theory of liberalism is not a *comprehensive* liberal theory; rather, it is a purely *political* conception that separates *political* and *moral* values with the specific aim of providing a *neutral* framework between rival comprehensive beliefs and doctrines.[49]

Rawls argues that peoples or groups with different *comprehensive* doctrines can co-exist peacefully in one single society only if they can develop an *'overlapping consensus,'* agreeing to share a neutral, value-free *political conception* in the *public realm*, and to forgo the search for the dominance of any one particular *comprehensive* doctrine.[50] Rawls is not claiming that a political society should have no ethical or moral foundation at all; rather, he is arguing that such a moral foundation can be and should be based on a variety of values, theories and justifications.

As promising as it sounds, Rawls has made three presuppositions. First, he assumes that all people are more or less reasonable beings who want to and indeed are in a position to help build up this 'overlapping consensus.' In so assuming, he seems to be 'in effect though not in intention' arguing for the dominance of one particular *comprehensive* doctrine over all others. Secondly, he also seems to assume that his restricted version of liberalism (based on the most basic human rights and liberties and a separation of the political and the comprehensive) is compatible with the values and ideals of *all* minority cultural groups. This is simply not the case. The reason that group rights and especially the possible illiberal group rights are so controversial is precisely that certain illiberal or 'traditional' practices or ways of life are deeply incompatible with the most basic human rights and liberties, and yet members of the groups insist on preserving them and refuse to compromise. From Rawls's views on children's education and his firm objection to unconditional respect for 'the dictates of conscience,' one can draw a safe conclusion that Rawls would find ways to *liberate* minority groups, to *educate* minority groups especially the illiberal ones into 'fully cooperating members of society,' to equip them with his conceptions of autonomy, justice, liberalism, and with good knowledge of basic constitutional and civil rights.[51] Once again, his principle of *toleration* expands into one of *intervention*, and it is not clear under what circumstances and in what fashion it is legitimate for it to so expand.

---

49   See John Rawls, *Political Liberalism* (Columbia University Press, 1996).
50   *Ibid.*
51   See John Rawls, *'The Priority of Right and Ideas of the Good,' Philosophy and Public Affairs* (1988), p. 251, p. 267 and p. 268.

The third, related, assumption Rawls makes in distinguishing between *political* and *comprehensive liberalism* is that liberalism can indeed be so simply divided (in a similar fashion to Kymlicka wrongly indicating that a clear distinction can always be made between *internal restrictions* and *external protections*, as discussed above). As Gaus and Kukathas rightly argue, it is impossible to so divide liberal doctrines as they evolve from and touch on ideas from a broad range of disciplines which themselves have continuously evolved and touch on ideas from a broad range of disciplines.[52] In reality, no minority cultural or religious groups are opposed by the mainstream society *merely* because they are culturally different and hold on to views and ways of life that are different from those of the majority. Rather, they are opposed because members of the majority fear the potential political consequences of these cultural views and ways of life. Cultural, social and religious views are not at all isolated from political views – far from it – the former form the *comprehensive* bases upon which *the latter* are built, and political decisions are often made against a comprehensive background which gives rise to meaning, expectations, and judgments. This reminds us of Kymlicka's argument, previously examined, that having a rich cultural structure is vital for individuals to be aware of the options available in life and to assess their cultural and political values intelligently.

What does all this mean to this project of developing a plausible account of minority rights? Despite the limitations, it is very clear that both Rawls and Kymlicka are sensitive to demands voiced by minority groups including illiberal groups. Both have aimed to develop a *liberal* theory of *multicultural* citizenship and have imagined a societal structure which is both liberating and constraining, with clearly drawn boundaries. However, while both theorists argue to varying extents that minority group interests should be protected, the claims they make on behalf of minority groups are very modest, and in their view, the liberal principle of toleration can benefit only a selected few – *those who remain within liberal boundaries*. This is hardly a solution in reality, as the most persistent and controversial group rights demands come precisely from those who remain firmly *outside* liberal boundaries. As already discussed in earlier sections, it is unwise to view minority groups (even the illiberal ones) as a single class, and it is equally unwise to condemn their demands (even the illiberal ones) as a single class without attentively considering where they are coming from and tentatively interpreting the messages without jumping to premature conclusions. Intervention when and where necessary must be informed, well-founded, and well-intentioned. An option between *integrating*

---

52   Gerald Gaus &. Chandran Kukathas (eds.), *The Handbook of Political Theory* (Sage Publications, 2004), p. 100.

(*or 'being liberated'*) and *being recognised and protected* is not (always) an option.

This points to two possible solutions: first, generously expand group rights and grant them potentially to all cultural groups including the most illiberal ones, even at the expense of social unity (the importance of which both Rawls and Kymlicka have emphasised and the lack of which is considered by both a pressing concern – to this point I will return later). Or second, develop a more fluid, proceduralistic, dialogical account of minority rights. Instead of looking at whether the group in question is liberal (enough) to be worthy of protection, a dialogical account will require us to take a step back from choosing which values and practices to affirm, and instead focus on whether or not certain procedural standards have been satisfied in the process of voicing, hearing, interpreting, evaluating, accommodating or rejecting demands. Far from being 'hands-off' like some of the other approaches, this approach places the greatest importance on communication and dialogue, and protects rights to certain *procedures and dialogues,* not *rights to certain ends.* Developing this second solution is the core of this project, and as will be demonstrated in the next chapter, a commitment to proceduralism and dialogue will result in a *fusion of group rights and individual rights.* But before moving on, we must first take a closer look at the first possible solution i.e. rapid expansion of group rights, as it sheds significant light on what needs to be done and thereby sets the stage for further analysis.

One of the leading defenders of expansion of group rights is Chandran Kukathas, who criticises the views of Rawls and Kymlicka as naively assuming a common standpoint of morality and human nature.[53] He argues that if we were to choose between greater social unity and greater toleration, we ought to choose the latter, and that even the most illiberal cultures should be tolerated and liberalism requires it. Although his approach offers a rival interpretation of the liberal principle of *toleration,* it itself is in fact not built upon it; rather, it builds upon the Kantian critique of pure reason.[54] In *The Critique of Pure Reason,* Kant says the following:

> Reason must in all its undertakings subject itself to criticism; should it limit freedom of criticism by any prohibitions, it must harm itself,

---

53 Chandran Kukathas, *The Liberal Archipelago* (Oxford University Press, 2003), p. 64.
54 See Immanuel Kant, *The Critique of Pure Reason,* translated by Norman Kemp Smith, (Palgrave Macmillan, 2nd edition, 2005); Chandran Kukathas's '*Cultural Toleration*' in Ian Shapiro &. Will Kymlicka (eds.), *Ethnicity and Group Rights* (New York University Press, 1997), Chapter 3, pp. 79 and 80.

drawing upon itself a damaging suspicion. Nothing is so important through its usefulness, nothing so sacred, that it may be exempted from this searching examination [...] *Reason depends on this freedom for its very existence. For reason has no dictatorial authority; its verdict is always simply the agreement of free citizens, of whom each one must be permitted to express, without let or hindrance, his objections or even his veto* (italics added).[55]

What Kant is saying is that a free public realm is the precondition for the existence of reason, and that *tolerance* is the precondition for the existence of this free realm. Kukathas argues exactly along these lines, that toleration is not only instrumental, '*it is the condition which gives judgments worth*.'[56] Thus, as long as we are not *convinced beyond doubt* of the correctness of our own values and practices or of the incorrectness of other people's values and practices which are contrary to our own, there are reasons to tolerate.[57] For Kukathas, the theories of anti-multiculturalists are unacceptable as they aggressively oppose tolerating illiberal cultures in the public realm and thereby, Kukathas would argue, disallow the latter the existence of their realm of reason and freedom. But the theories of those liberals who are sensitive to minority demands, such as Rawls and Kymlicka, are also seen as unacceptable: there are way too many strings attached and protection is too hard to come by – toleration has no independent value of its own and depends on numerous other factors for its realisation – no doubt only very little real protection can derive from it.[58]

Thus, whether Kukathas's theory is defensible depends on whether *toleration* ought to be granted independent weight. It seems that he has failed to distinguish between the normative value of toleration on the one hand, and the specific policies on the other, which are no doubt inspired by the normative value and distribute rights and benefits to particular persons or groups. While his theory largely focuses on the normative value of toleration, his major objections to what he considers to be 'intolerance' mainly concern the practical aspect. It is not always clear where exactly he draws the line. For instance, while he argues for maximum toleration for minority groups including and

---

55 Immanuel Kant, *The Critique of Pure Reason*, translated by Norman Kemp Smith, (Palgrave Macmillan, 2nd edition, 2005), p. 736.
56 Chandran Kukathas's '*Cultural Toleration*' in Ian Shapiro &. Will Kymlicka (eds.), *Ethnicity and Group Rights* (New York University Press, 1997), Chapter 3, p. 79.
57 Ibid.
58 Ibid.

perhaps especially illiberal groups, he also defends the members' *'right to exit'* when they no longer wish to adhere to the rules of the group. Thus it seems that his defence of group rights and tolerance of illiberal groups is based on the notion of 'voluntary association.'[59] Though he does not say whether this will mean that groups that do not allow their members to exit freely and easily must not be tolerated, or if members of the group can only exit with the help of the larger society, should such 'help,' or 'influence,' or 'intervention,' be allowed, and if so, under what circumstances and to what extent.

In other words, it is unclear which one of the two rights – the *group's right to autonomy* and *the individual's right to exit* – that Kukathas considers to be more important, or which one he deems to be weightier in justifying toleration of illiberal groups. While these two types of rights will be examined in detail in Chapters 4 and 5, it is worth pointing out in passing here that the vast majority of the minority groups we are concerned with in this project are *not* 'voluntary associations' as Kukathas wishes them to be – not only in the sense that group membership is not *chosen* (except certain religious and social groups), but also that exit is neither easy nor practical.[60] It thus seems that the foundation of Kukathas's approach is shaky. He has not only failed to show that toleration ought to be granted independent weight but has also left some of the most pressing questions unexplored and unanswered.

This leads to the second objection to Kukathas's approach. Implicit in his argument is the belief that a 'hands-off' approach is necessarily beneficial to group autonomy and a 'hands-on' approach is necessarily detrimental, which is a belief shared by many hard-multiculturalists. Is this so? In *Toleration and the Limits of Liberalism*, Susan Mendus discusses the condition and development of *individual* autonomy and their different requirements.[61] She argues that while the notion of *distance* is central to the *characterisation* of individual autonomy, the *development* of autonomy requires *proximity* to society, as autonomy does not form itself automatically from scratch; it must be learned, and sustained once learned, which requires a background of values and options against which knowledge can be gained, interpretations and decisions can be made, and self-construction, maintenance and continuous development can

---

59 See, for example, Chandran Kukathas, *The Liberal Archipelago* (Oxford University Press, 2003), Chapter 3 *'Freedom of Association and Liberty of Conscience,'* for his discussions on voluntary association. See also Chandran Kukathas, 'Are There Any Cultural Rights,' *Political Theory*, 20/1 (1992): pp. 105–139, at pp. 115–116.

60 See also Bhikhu Parekh, *Rethinking Multiculturalism: Cultural Diversity and Political Theory* (Palgrave MacMillan, 2006), pp. 161–162.

61 Susan Mendus, *Toleration and the Limits of Liberalism* (Macmillan, 1989), pp. 69–109.

take place.⁶² Although Mendus is concerned with *individual* autonomy, it seems that her argument applies also to *group* autonomy: while *distance from the larger society* is central to the *characterisation of* minority group autonomy, the *development* of group autonomy requires *proximity to the larger society*, since autonomy must be *learned and sustained*, which requires a background pool of values and options against which self-construction, interaction and continuous development can take place. Much also depends on the nature of the group in question. As will be shown in Chapter 6, not all groups are capable of meaningfully holding rights and becoming politically autonomous, and the right to autonomy must not be granted simply because it is wanted. But for the purpose of this section, it is sufficient to say that Kukathas is naive in assuming that a 'hands-on' approach is necessarily detrimental to group autonomy.

Mendus's discussion on the maintenance and development of autonomy deserves closer attention: we can subtract two ideas from it upon which my account of group rights might build: first, *the dialogical nature of the idea of autonomy, of identity*, and second, the importance of *proximity* to the larger society in the maintenance and development of autonomy, of identity. I shall consider each in turn.

5 The Dialogical Nature of Identity, of Minority Rights

This idea is not new. It was first advanced by Charles Taylor in *Multiculturalism: Examining the Politics of Recognition*, published in 1994. Partly due to Taylor's own lack of effort in thoroughly explaining the idea and specifying its practical implications, and partly due to the changing international contexts within which issues of cultural identity are situated and examined, this idea has not received wide-spread recognition and so far appears to have had little impact in the field of minority rights. This idea sheds important light on what a plausible dialogical concept of minority rights should look like, and if explained and applied properly, can help us break out of the downward spiral. In the book Taylor says the following:

> [A] crucial feature of human life is its fundamentally *dialogical* character [...] We define our identity always in dialogue with, sometimes in struggle against, the things our significant others want to see in us [...] [T]he making and sustaining of our identity [...] remains dialogical throughout our lives. Thus my discovering my own identity doesn't mean that I work it

---

62   *Ibid.*, p. 96.

out in isolation, but that I *negotiate it through dialogue, partly overt, partly internal, with others* (italics added).[63]

For this idea to form the basis of our account of minority rights, we must first examine it in conjunction with two issues already discussed in the first chapter: first, the indeterminacy of the meaning and scope of culture, and second, the difficulties in deciding which cultural values and practices to recognise and why.[64] Seeing identity as dialogical in nature has many advantages over the essentialist view of seeing identity, especially cultural identity, as something one passively inherits and maintains rather than actively develops and renews – which is still a mainstream view.

Firstly, it simply makes better sense. All cultures evolve, continue to evolve and interact with other cultures from which characteristics and values are 'borrowed' and integrated into the domestic culture. Cultural interaction and clashes are further facilitated and intensified through the process of globalisation and immigration, producing, among others, 'multicultural' members of society – people who have more than one cultural identity, practise more than one culture, speak more than one language, and possibly hold more than one nationality. Which cultural group do these people belong to? Which cultural values can we call purely and distinctly *theirs* and not *ours*? Which cultural values must we affirm and recognise and who decides? And so on.

Not seeing cultures and identities as fixed and settled therefore avoids the impossible task of having to choose which cultural values to recognise, which is a highly sensitive matter and has caused a great deal of confusion, controversy, even outrage and hatred. That said, one must not emphasis entirely on subtle change of focus and ignore the bedrock. Of course, it is arguable that no matter how 'multicultural' one appears, one still possesses one dominant cultural identity, or considers oneself to do so – for instance, a British born Chinese might consider herself more British than Chinese, or more Chinese than British. But this does not defeat our argument in favour of seeing identity as dialogical in nature. It in fact affirms that cultural boundaries are fluid, and that cultural identities can be 'born with' as well as 'taken on.'

Secondly, seeing identity as dialogical in nature allows us to challenge, from a different angle, the much criticised approach which sees all cultures as possessing *equal value* and therefore deserving *equal respect, equal recognition* and *equal protection* – an essentialist view which prevents us from understanding culture

---

63   Charles Taylor, *Multiculturalism: Examining the Politics of Recognition* (Princeton University Press, 1994), pp. 32–34.
64   See Chapter 1 of this book.

and cultural belonging progressively. Seeing identity as dialogical in nature assigns to members of cultural groups the very active role of expresser, communicator and negotiator; it is not some *fixed cultures* that are of equal value and deserve equal respect; it is not their preservation or certain *outcomes* that must be guaranteed; it is the dialogical processes that must be kept alive – dialogue between cultures, between academic disciplines, between different sectors of society, and, crucially, between minority group rights and their individual rights.

This leads us to the final and third major advantage of the view: it points to the possibility of a *dialogical* concept of minority rights. The next chapter, *A Dialogical Translation of the Concept of Minority Rights*, examines in detail what this means exactly. But for now we must turn to the second significant element in Mendus's discussion – the importance of *proximity* to the larger society in the development of autonomy, and, I might add, the maintenance of cultural identity.

6 'Proximity' and a Dialogical Concept of Minority Rights

It is necessary to examine Mendus's notion of proximity in conjunction with the two approaches we considered in Sections 3 and 4 – the first seeks to reconcile liberal principles and group rights by formulating group rights as rights protecting *individual* interests; the second considers group rights as typically protecting *collective* interests and sees no need to reconcile seemingly irreconcilable principles. Which of the two approaches should we adopt as the theoretical and moral justification of group rights? Do we have to choose? On the whole, it is undoubtedly more convenient to adopt the first approach, as once liberal values and the notion of group rights are reconciled, there is very little left to defend normatively. That said, the second approach, however controversial it sounds, is far from meritless, not least because it has alerted us to two different types of toleration – *passive* toleration (i.e. let it be for the sake of letting it be), and *active* toleration (i.e. a conscious decision inspired by knowledge and understanding). Neither approach can on its own justify the notion of group rights, but each sheds important light on a more plausible concept of group rights.

It might be worthwhile to look beyond the obvious differences between these two opposing approaches and instead look for inherent similarities and common standards: none of the theorists considered above, not even Brian Barry, has denied the importance of cultural belonging; but all of them, even Kukathas to some extent, have attempted to articulate a conception of group toleration and autonomy that is consistent with certain degrees and forms of external intervention. In other words, what divides opinions is not the importance of cultural belonging, but the appropriateness, degree, means, forms, and consequences of outside influence, assistance, and intervention.

Taking into account Mendus's views on the relation between autonomy and proximity, it seems that exactly how much toleration ought to be granted should at least partly depend on *how closely connected the group is, or should be, to the rest of the society*. Should intervention take place, the degree and form of which should correspond to the nature of the group and its degree of independence. If the group's *internal affairs* touch on matters which the state rightly regulates, there is no reason to grant maximum autonomy (if any at all will depend on the circumstances). On the other hand, if the group is largely self-dependant and isolated from the rest of the society culturally and institutionally (e.g. in the case of indigenous peoples), there seems to be no reason *not* to grant maximum toleration, no matter how illiberal the group is – *in the absence of compelling state interests* and *humanitarian concerns.*

Of course, the issue concerns not only the normative justifications but also the practicalities and particularities of outside intervention and assistance. We are in need of a theory of legitimate state interests to make the approach work. Chapters 4 and 5 will look at this in greater detail. Furthermore, it seems implausible that any group (with the exception of very remote indigenous groups) can ever completely go it alone without any form of interaction with the outside world. As long as there is interaction in the slightest degree, there is the possibility of outside influence and intervention. This is especially the case for groups (illiberal or not) without internal decision-making bodies and a clear set of governing rules and principles, who tend to have ambiguous values and fluid boundaries which are the source of internal and external disputes.

This has three implications. First, in order to benefit from a high degree of autonomy, a group should have sophisticated and competent internal governing bodies and mechanisms. Second, if the group in question lacks such mechanisms and/or a clear identity, there is good reason to treat its claims with caution, and further investigation is required. And last, the state ought to assist qualified groups in governing capacity-building which is a pre-condition for greater autonomy. Issues concerning construction and development of group agency will be examined in detail in Chapter 6.

What are the theoretical and political implications of employing a notion of *proximity* in the conceptualisation and attribution of group rights? This notion sends out a clear message that first, not all things of the slightest value can give rise to 'rights,' to 'group rights'; second, not all 'rights' are 'human rights' in the classical sense; third, 'group rights' are 'rights' but not 'human rights' in the classical sense. This message goes against the belief held by many of the theorists quoted in this book, who seek to interpret group rights as human rights, and therefore naturally argue for reform of the existing international human rights documents in order to bring about better protection to cultural minorities.[65] While I have clearly extracted elements from many of the arguments advanced by these theorists to form foundations of this dialogical account of group rights, I have failed to see the merit, or necessity, of equating 'recognising group rights' with 'expanding the list of human rights.'[66] In fact, I would argue that it is precisely this insistence on granting group rights the status of human rights that has unintentionally generated profound confusions and fears (among theorists as well as the general public), which have severely jeopardised the group rights project.

To say that 'group rights' are not 'human rights' is not to say that they are inferior to 'human rights' (or *individual* human rights); but it is primarily to deny them a *universal status*. While all individuals are entitled to particular human rights simply by being human, no cultural group is entitled to particular group rights simply by being a group. Thus denying a cultural group particular group rights (especially the strong ones such as rights to autonomy and self-determination) must not automatically be seen as *violating human rights*. On the other hand, to say that 'group rights' are not 'human rights' is not to claim that cultural groups are nothing more than private, free, organisations based on voluntary membership (which does seem to imply the legitimacy of various forms of internal disciplines – some of which amounts to oppression).

All this sheds important light on the account of minority rights I aim to develop in this book and on the possible means of implementation. It points to the need to bring in better drafted minority rights documents with mechanisms built in to deal with – first, the 'interaction' between group rights and individual human rights; second, the specification and interaction of short-term aims and long-term goals; and third, the maintenance of a balance between the pursuit of ethno-cultural justice on the one hand, and social unity and geo-political security on the other. The next three chapters will build on what has been discussed so far and flesh out this dialogical account of minority rights by showing that, first, this account is dialogical in nature; second, for this account to be plausible, it should necessarily be *a fusion of group rights and individual rights*, and consists of two separate limbs: *rights against the state* (examined in Chapter 4), and *rights against the group* (examined in Chapter 5); and third, this account is not as illiberal as it first appears.

---

65 See, for example, Neus Torbisco Casals, *Group Rights as Human Rights* (Springer, 2006).
66 Having said that, it should be noted that as will be shown in the concluding chapter, since *minority* rights are firmly embedded in the larger *human* rights system, reform of the former will inevitably mean reform of the latter. But *'reform'* does not mean *expanding the list of human rights*.

CHAPTER 3

A Dialogical Translation of the Concept of Minority Rights

1   Substantive, Procedural, Dialogical: What's In a Name?

It is necessary to first explain the title of this chapter – what exactly does it mean to *translate* the existing concept of minority rights? In the previous two chapters, attention was focused on the notion of group rights, which is widely interpreted as largely substantive in nature. A simplistic distinction is often made between substantive and procedural rights. Substantive rights often refer to the class of rights which are intended, formulated and interpreted as guaranteeing particular outcomes and substances; procedural rights, on the other hand, often refer to the class of rights which are intended, formulated and interpreted as guaranteeing certain procedures rather than promising certain ends. Therefore, simplistically speaking, 'the right to life,' 'the right to an adequate standard of living' are two examples of substantive rights, as they both guarantee an end – 'living' and 'adequate standard of living'; 'the right to a fair trial' and 'the right to be tried by jury,' by contrast, are procedural rights, as they do not promise any particular verdict but rather demand fairness during proceedings.

It is questionable though whether a distinction between the two types of rights can be so simplistically made. It may be argued that 'the right to a fair trial,' in some circumstances, is merely a derivative of, and remains an integral component of, 'the right to life.' Vice versa, 'the right to an adequate standard of living' can easily and arguably more adequately be interpreted as a right to certain procedural actions which will gradually and eventually bring about an adequate standard of living for the persons concerned. This leads one to question not only the distinction between substantive and procedural rights but more specifically also the very idea of *procedural rights*. This technical difficulty is the first of the several reasons which have led me to avoid using the term 'procedural' and instead advance a *dialogical* concept of minority rights.

The second reason has already been thoroughly explained in Chapter 2, which is that only a *dialogical* account can accurately reflect the *dialogical* nature of cultural identity.[1] The third and related reason is that, although *dialogue* is certainly a *process*, it is clearly distinguishable from, and more

---

1   See Chapter 2 of the book, Parts 5 and 6.

specific than, process, in the sense that *dialogue* is by definition a *two-way process* which presumes and requires *equality* between the parties engaging in dialogue. It is important to be precise as choice of terminology has practical policy implications. The fourth reason, as will be shown below, is that a dialogical account could help promote cross-cultural consensus by reducing distance between cultures, facilitating meaningful communication and thereby diminish inter-cultural hostility. Lastly, *'dialogical translation'* simply means the communication of essentially the *same* essence and meaning of minority rights in a *different, dialogical,* language. The *essence* and *meaning* of minority rights communicated here are their necessity, theoretical validity, and moral defensibility. Expressing these in a new dialogical language means, in theory, that only the *tools of expression* have changed; in reality, as will be illustrated in this chapter, it will necessarily result in a fusion of minority group rights (available *only* to minorities) and individual human rights (available to *all including* minorities).

But before moving on to demonstrate what, if any, has been lost in translation and what has newly emerged, it is necessary to first reveal the source of philosophical inspiration for the dialogical concept.

2   Legitimacy of Law and Dialogical Minority Rights

In *Between Facts and Norms*, Habermas examines the relationship between political theory and the philosophy of law, exposes the tension between the facticity of law and its normative claim to validity, and reconciles what he calls 'private autonomy' and 'public autonomy,' 'human rights' and 'sovereignty.' He makes the case for law as viewed through *'the deliberative paradigm,'* and argues that in modern complex societies, the coercive force of law *alone* does not grant law its legitimacy – *legitimacy* cannot simply be derived from *legality* – rather, legitimate law can only emerge from the consent of the governed, from 'the achievements of mutual understanding on the part of the communicatively acting subjects,' from 'the discursive opinion and will-formation of equally entitled citizens of a state.'[2] In other words, the meaningful exercise of private autonomy is granted through acts of public autonomy. Habermas thus sees law as the primary medium of social integration in modern complex societies which stabilises the separation between facticity and normative validity resulting from secularisation.[3]

---

2   Jürgen Habermas, *Between Facts and Norms: Contributions to a Discourse Theory of Law and Democracy*, translated by William Rehg, (Polity Press, 1996), Chapter 3.
3   *Ibid.*

His secular view of the law emphasises the role of *communication* and *mutual understanding* as the primary mechanism for governing and mediating spheres formerly governed by traditional religious and/or secular authorities. In his own words, 'informal public opinion-formation generates "influence"; influence is transformed into "communicative power" through the channels of *political elections*; and communicative power is again transformed into "administrative power" through *legislation*. This influence, carried forward by communicative power, gives law its *legitimacy*, and thereby provides the political power of the state its binding force (italics added).'[4] In other words, legitimate law-making takes place in an open procedure of public opinion and will formation.

Habermas considers the traditional authorities in society, religious as well as secular, as having been replaced by new, complex, more democratic, communicative modes of social interaction. One obvious problem with this view is that traditional forms of governance and social interaction, religious as well as secular, still exist. It can be argued that it is precisely because of the continuing presence of traditional authorities that Habermas's communicative modes of social interaction, which not only generate legitimate law-making but also enable cultural expression and knowledge-building, are so vital. In seeking to preserve traditional forms of life, one will inevitably be confronted with issues of modernity, diversity, reconciliation, and toleration. As we have seen before in Chapters 1 and 2, *preservation* in a modern plural society no longer means *sameness,* but *adaptation* and *change*, and it is through communicative dialogue and interaction that such 'preservation' takes place.

This is the source of inspiration for this dialogical concept of minority rights. At least four broad inter-related questions need to be addressed. Firstly, how can/should traditional authority be asserted in a modern cultural context? Secondly, how can the minority group in question find and maintain a balance between tradition on the one hand, and modernity, plurality and democracy on the other? Since this inevitably requires some form of 'internal transformation,' it leads us to, thirdly, enquire about the role of the state and the wider society in the group's internal transformation, and the crucial but often over-looked role of group members in the transformational processes of the group in which they belong. And fourthly, since law cannot be separated from society, with all the changes, actual and anticipated, taking place in the latter, how responsive should the former be in reflecting these changes? More specifically, what is the role of the law in the evolution of societal and cultural changes, understandings of these changes, and their consequences? It is through answering these four broad questions and applying Habermas's communicative

---

4 Jürgen Habermas, *Three Normative Models of Democracy*, Constellations, Volume 1, No. 1, (1994), p.8.

modes of social interaction that the dialogical account of minority rights comes into being.

As already seen in previous chapters, mainstream liberalism's conception of *law as individual rights* can be and has been criticised as establishing the rights of individuals as peremptory, pre-political and unrealistically disassociated from the good and the aims of community and society; and that although the newer development of liberalism expressly rejects many of the older assumptions regarding the notion of group rights, it itself is built on a number of assumptions. The mainstream liberal conception has played and continues to play a central role in the modern understanding of human rights theory and law, sometimes resulting in a disconnection between rights and responsibilities, fuelled by excessive individualism which enhances competitiveness and limits possibilities of dialogue and understanding.[5] This conception of human rights justifies individual *rights* against others, society, the state, but does not emphasise *obligations* to the public and other members of society. From this, some would argue, follows the decadence of social responsibility, mutual trust and respect, as well as cultural sensitivity.[6]

Indeed, Habermas, relying on something other than rational autonomy, contends that the mainstream liberal conception of human rights has to some extent misunderstood the nature of the argument for human rights. He argues that human rights are not pre-political (i.e. derived solely from philosophical argumentation and function independently of and above the political process); rather, they are very much *political* and *social* and must have a source of *legitimacy*.[7] He re-examines the relationship between law and politics with respect to human rights in two contexts: firstly, in the context of the relationship between private and public autonomy, and secondly, in the context of the conflict between human rights and popular sovereignty. He sees private and public autonomy as *co-original* and reinforcing each other. The former provides for the rights of the individual; the latter signifies popular sovereignty, or public will formation, or the consent of the governed. He also argues that we should understand human rights as the *rights citizens must accord one another* if they want to legitimately 'regulate their living together by means of positive

---

5 See, for example, Wiktor Osiatyński, *Human Rights and Their Limits* (Cambridge University Press, 2009), p.196.

6 See, for example, *ibid.*, Chapter 4; and Charles Taylor's *'Conditions of an Unforced Consensus on Human Rights,'* in Joanne R. Bauer &. Daniel A. Bell (eds.), *The East Asian Challenge for Human Rights* (Cambridge University Press, 1999), p.130.

7 Jürgen Habermas, *Between Facts and Norms: Contributions to a Discourse Theory of Law and Democracy,* translated by William Rehg, (Polity Press, 1996), pp.290–295.

law.'[8] In so arguing he decisively departs from the Kantian tradition and refrains from deriving rights from individual autonomy and liberty, but instead from the inter-subjective relations of citizens who would grant those rights to one another *through consent*.[9]

In other words, on this account, the sphere of law and law-making is *social, relational*, not *individual*. The legitimate basis of human rights claims is *social, relational*, not *individual*, and requires the establishment of unforced consensus. Having said that, one must not forget that there are very many different categories of rights claims, and especially that it is widely agreed that there exists a distinction between *legal* rights and *moral* rights – while the former may lead to legal consequences brought about by legal enforcement, the latter are protected only through appealing to ethical and moral standards and influencing public opinion.[10] It is arguable that Habermas's appeal to consensus, achieved through public communication and deliberative democracy, is more applicable in the case of moral rights and less, if at all, relevant in the case of legal rights. The distinction between legal and moral rights will be explored in greater detail in Chapter 5.

Placing Habermas's theory of law and rights, and especially his emphasis on the necessity of communication and consensus, in the specific context of minority rights, it is clear that his view is in line with Charles Taylor's claim that cultural identity is *dialogical* in essence.[11] The widespread determinist (and confrontational) approach to minority rights, favoured by both human rights practitioners and minority groups, has prevented a progressive understanding of culture and cultural belonging, and has thereby alarmingly deterred knowledge and sensitivity building, causing issues of minority rights to be caught between contradictory understandings, intentions, and policies. This has led many to call for the establishment of channels for meaningful intercultural and inter-religious dialogue. It is thus surprising that, few, if any, have called for meaningful *dialogue between minority rights law and minority cultures*. This seems like a misconceived accusation at first, considering the large number of international and regional minority rights documents all with the specific aim of recognising and accommodating cultural specificity and demands. But there are several reasons why this accusation is fair.

Firstly, accommodating demands is not the same as establishing channels of dialogue. In fact, passive accommodation often has adverse effects on the

---

8   *Ibid.*, p.126.
9   *Ibid.*, p.496.
10 Wiktor Osiatyński, *Human Rights and Their Limits* (Cambridge University Press, 2009), p.105.
11 See Chapter 2 of the book, Part 5.

perceived necessity of dialogue. Secondly, as already mentioned above, it is plainly wrong to equate *dialogue between cultures* with *dialogue between law and culture*. Although it is arguable that in order for *dialogue between law and culture* to emerge, constructive *dialogue between cultures* must be in place first. But the opposite might also be true, that without meaningful *dialogue between minority rights law and culture*, any effects of *dialogue between cultures*, however positive, will be limited.

Thirdly, as already shown in Chapter 1, rights provisions especially minority rights provisions in international legal documents are often vague. There are several reasons for this. The first is that they are necessarily products of compromise. One might even go as far as to say that, in order to generate enough support from a vast diversity of parties with a vast diversity of interests and values, they cannot afford to be too specific. The second reason relates to the special nature of minority rights, which fall into the broad category of 'cultural rights.' Cultural rights, along with social and economic rights, belong in the category of 3rd generation rights. There are significant differences between 3rd generation rights and the classical 1st and 2nd generations of civil and political rights. The former are expressed in extremely vague terms and are often seen as standards to be gradually implemented through state policies rather than laws giving rise to judicial enforcement, which is available to 1st and 2nd generations of civil and political rights. This distinction resembles the one between moral and legal rights, the former are 'protected' through appealing to universal moral standards, whereas the latter are non-negotiable and guaranteed and enforced by legal enforcement.

Fourthly, some might argue that the active participation of non-Western parties in the drafting of international rights documents is clear enough evidence of dialogue 'between law and culture,' 'between law-making and culture,' and thus the end product should be seen as reflecting a cross-cultural consensus generated through inclusion and communication. This is not so. The apparent consensus over these rights norms, especially the 3rd generation rights norms, is limited to content and does not extend to practical entailments or methods of enforcement.[12] Some have even argued that what makes the 3rd generation rights so distinct is precisely the lack of agreement on the immediate judicial enforcement of them.[13] Thus, the apparent, modest, consensus has obscured serious ideological and cultural differences and

---

12   See, for example, Wiktor Osiatyński, *Human Rights and Their Limits* (Cambridge University Press, 2009), p.146.
13   *Ibid.,* p.111.

equally valid local, non-legal, cultural, understandings of rights and human dignity.

It has also given the misleading impression that conflicts between interpretations of rights are conflicts between good and evil, between parties that respect and disrespect human dignity, overlooking the possibility of genuine interpretive disagreements generated by clash of values and other deep-rooted historical, political, cultural, social and even emotional and personal causes. Although standards and rules are laid down by international law, application of these rules is always, as it should be, left to national governments. Thus a top-down approach can never be sufficient in the absence of local support, as understandings and interpretations of international standards are always contextual and cultural, influenced and determined by a complex interplay of factors. Acknowledging this is not to deny the universality of human rights. It is to say that the realisation of at least parts of that rationale is unavoidably a troublesome task. This signifies a shift of emphasis, if not a change of direction, from the *moral substance of human rights* to *interpretative conflict resolution*, and it is mainly through conflict resolution that genuine dialogue between law and culture takes place, and that such a dialogue should gradually resolve interpretative conflicts.

Constructive and genuine dialogue between law and culture cannot be generated by mass production of vague legal norms, which will inevitably cause inflation of, and the consequent devaluation of, standards and norms – although establishing international standards is essential and necessary as it recognises, not least symbolically, the importance of what ought to be protected. Genuine dialogue emerges from honest and tentative re-examination of the relevant legal and cultural issues, and from confronting these issues head-on. I have already argued previously that it is essential to first clarify the basic, often taken-for-granted, concepts upon which law and policy are built, and then move from concepts to re-conceptualisation; and that a good concept of minority cultural rights must not be one that aims at protecting and sustaining *elements* of a minority culture at any given moment in time, but should instead aim at protecting and allowing sufficient *space* for *continuity* as well as *development* and *change*. To enable this shift of emphasis in law and policy, Part 3 below fleshes out the dialogical concept; Part 4 looks at its likely impact on the wider human rights system. It is worth repeating that the aim of developing this dialogical concept is *not* just to establish dialogue between cultures, which will be a sure and welcome side-effect; rather, it aims to establish dialogue between law and culture, to ensure as far as possible that law accurately reflects minority cultural needs.

3   A Dialogical Concept of Minority Rights

The previous chapters have defended the notion of group rights, which is largely ***substantive in nature***. A dialogical translation of minority rights does *not* call for the elimination, or even reduction, of substantive group rights *claims*, as classified in Levy's taxonomy, which I examined in Chapter 2 and to which I will return later in this chapter.[14] Rather, a dialogical concept re-conceptualises the general idea of minority rights by formally embracing group rights and – crucially – specifying how group rights and individual rights interact in minority rights protection. In other words, it is a concept based on the *relation* and *interaction* between minority rights that are collective in nature and those that are individualistic in nature, and resolving the disputes and conflicts that such interaction will inevitably generate.

This concept aims to accomplish four main tasks: first, to divide minority rights into two separate categories of *'rights against the state'* and *'rights against the group,'* and to justify such a division; second, to formulate and defend *rights to external dialogue, and rights to internal dialogue*; third, to add to existing collective rights claims a dialogic dimension; and fourth, to enable and justify the grouping together of the dialogical rights (to external and internal dialogue) and substantive group rights into one single coherent framework, through which notions of *dialogue and well-being* run. In other words, existing substantive group rights claims occupy a significant place in the new concept. But in order for them to be able to give rise to valid rights, instead of functioning on their own, I argue that they must be incorporated into this *dialogical framework* and be supplemented by other minority rights including the dialogical rights. I shall address each of these four aims in turn.

(1)   *Rights against the State and Rights against the Group*

A distinctive feature of this dialogical account of minority rights is that, while existing international human rights are always addressed to and claimed against the state *only*, this account has two limbs: minority rights against *the state*, and minority rights against *the group* itself. I shall deal with the rights against *the state* first. As clearly shown in the diagram, 'minority rights against the state' also have two sub-categories, A and B. In sub-category A are *rights held by the group as a collectivity* and contains all of Jacob Levy's eight types of group rights claims, which I already examined in Chapter 2.[15] The rights in

---

14   It is important to note that group rights *claims* do not automatically translate into group *rights*.

15   These rights claims are: total exemptions, autonomy and self-government, assistance rights, enforcement/recognition rights, external rules restricting non-members, internal

sub-category A can be further divided into three categories: *rights to self-determination, rights to state assistance,*[16] and *rights to external dialogue*. All three rights are collective in nature. Sub-category B, by contrast, contains *individual rights held by individual members* of the minority group, not by the group as an entity. Sub-category B rights also contain three branches: *the right to cultural belonging, the right to assistance and intervention,*[17] *and (also, an individualistic version of) the right to external dialogue*.

The second limb of this dialogical concept is *rights against the group*, which are held *only by individual members of the group* and consists of *the right to equal concern, the right to internal dialogue* and *the right of exit*. While the precise content, characteristics, functions and enforcement of these rights will be explained in detail in Chapters 4 and 5 – Chapter 4 deals with the first limb (rights against the state), and Chapter 5 looks at the second limb (rights against the group) – one key question must be addressed here and now: why is it necessary to have two separate limbs of minority rights, more specifically, why is it necessary to impose a duty of enforcement, which is usually held exclusively by the state, on the minority group in question and thereby splitting the duties between the state and the group?

There are three main reasons. The first is conceptual. As I have already argued previously, it is the intention of this book to reconceptualise minority rights. Once we acknowledge that minority rights, as with other types of human rights, can be enforced in different ways (legally, morally and politically), and *by different entities* and not just state, we have in effect broadened the concept of minority rights which should give rise to new interpretations, understandings, and solutions. Of course, a minority group can never 'enforce' rights in the same way the state can, due to the lack of resources, capacity, and legitimacy, which is why, as shown on the right hand side in the diagram, I have limited the 'rights against the group' to three narrowly framed rights only: *the*

---

rules governing group members, guaranteed representation demands, and symbolic demands.

16 It is arguable that rights to state assistance are not exactly rights *against* the state but rights *through* the state (see Wiktor Osiatyński, *Human Rights and Their Limits* (Cambridge University Press, 2009) p.110), or rights *with respect to* the state. As Osiatynski has argued (but in relation to *social* and *economic* rights), certain cultural rights claims (especially those to do with provision and redistribution of resources) are 'entitlement rights' claims which are in theory directed against the *society* at large but in reality (can only be) fulfilled by the *state* due to the society's lack of formal mechanisms to realise those rights. Whilst I recognise the distinction, in the moral sense, between rights *against* the state and rights *through* the state, I do not consider it to be of crucial importance to the analyses in this book.

17 See note above.

right to equal concern, the right to internal dialogue, and *the right of exit.* Common sense tells us, and Chapter 5 will reinforce it, that these three types of rights concern domestic matters of the group. Although it cannot be denied that they may touch on wider issues over which the state has, and should have, a certain degree of control – including but not limited to issues of equality and freedom of association – which renders state intervention and assistance legitimate and necessary, when needed. I have taken this into account, which is why, as shown in the diagram, there are *two separate 'rights to intervention and assistance,'* one held by the group as a collectivity against the state, and the other held by individual members of the minority group also against the state. As will be shown in Chapters 4 and 5, these two 'rights to intervention and assistance' are designed to interact with and counterbalance powers of the group; more specifically, the 'right to intervention and assistance' *held by group members against the state* aims to influence and affect decisions of the group's *internal decision-making bodies,* which, as will be demonstrated in Chapter 6, the state has a duty to help develop as part and parcel of the progressive realisation of the group's 'right to self-determination.'

This leads to the second reason for the distinction of duties between the state and the group, which stems from a renewed proceduralist and dialogic understanding of 'self-determination' and 'autonomy,' which will be the subject of Chapter 6. Contrary to conventional liberal interpretations of these two concepts, which wrongly derive from them a requirement of drawing arbitrary fixed boundaries between groups, the proceduralist and dialogic approach departs from putting up fences and moves towards establishing channels of communication, from a hands-off approach to a very much hands-on strategy focusing on *assisted capacity-building* as a necessary transitional measure.[18] Assigning duties of enforcement to minority groups has two main consequences. Firstly, it gives the groups a sense of responsibility as well as real control over their own domestic matters and especially the well-being of their members. This, of course, gives rise also to possibilities of internal abuse and oppression. Secondly, the special nature of the three rights for which the group is responsible (in particular, *'the right to internal dialogue,'* which requires the group to establish channels of dialogue between its members and its own decision-making bodies, and *'the right of exit,'* which guards/opens the borders between the group and the outside world, and the realisation of which requires cooperation between the group and the state[19]) means that effective communication, internal and external, cannot be avoided, and therefore the distance

---

18 See Chapter 6 for details.
19 See Chapter 5 for details.

between the minority group and the wider society is significantly reduced, minorities are thereby drawn closer into the wider world without having to compromise their cultural independence and sense of control. By 'independence,' I mean cultural autonomy exercised with good faith and a sense of responsibility towards not only the wider society but also, and especially, group members. This is, of course, all based on the assumption that effective internal decision-making bodies have been or can be established and maintained. And through catering for the rights and needs of their own members, minority groups can further develop their capacity to self-govern. All this will be explored in detail in Chapter 6.

This leads us to consider the exception to the rule: while some groups will be willing and able to develop capacity of self-government with the help of the state and to develop policies which respect and promote the members' rights and well-being, others will not be, and some, especially anti-liberal groups, will fiercely oppose any such move. This gives rise to the third reason for the distinction of duties of enforcement between the state and the group. In particular, it explains why it is necessary for individual members of the group to possess a *right to external dialogue* as well as a *right to internal dialogue*, and why *the former is claimed against the state*, whilst *the latter is claimed against the group*.[20] As will be explained in more detail in the next chapter when I turn to look at the precise characteristics of these rights, the individual's *right to external dialogue* has many functions. One of the most important is to ensure as far as possible that members of minority groups can engage in constructive dialogue with the outside world, *especially but not only when* meaningful *internal dialogue* is not guaranteed by the group. In other words, when the members' *right to internal dialogue* (against the *group*) is violated, it is through exercising the *right to external dialogue* (against the *state*) that they can voice their concerns and take further action.

(2)   *Rights to External and Internal Dialogue vs. Freedom of Expression*
It is stating the obvious to say that these two types of *rights to dialogue* are essential to this dialogical account of minority rights. Care must be taken to avoid inflating the rights system by inventing unnecessary new rights. Rights to dialogue are necessary only if no other existing right can serve the same purpose they aim to serve, which is, broadly speaking, to guarantee as far as possible not just that a particular voice is heard in public, but more specifically, that it is heard *in dialogue*. Traditional freedoms of expression and association, which are amongst the most basic human freedoms, all aim to promote

---

20   See diagram.

communication of opinions and beliefs to others. What can the rights to dialogue provide that these freedoms have not already? In other words, what distinct characteristics do these rights to dialogue possess which render them absolutely necessary? My answer is three-fold.

a   Freedoms vs. Rights

Firstly, *freedoms* are not the same as *rights*, in the sense that while the former indicate only a passive duty of the state not to interfere with the said freedoms, the latter imply an obligation to take positive action to bring about the realisation of the said rights. That said, one must avoid always judging the book by its cover: *political freedoms* of speech and association are *rights* as well as *freedoms*, as they clearly impose an obligation on the state to take steps to provide necessary measures to enable the realisation of those freedoms. However, no-one can seriously suggest that the *freedoms for cultural purposes*, or *cultural rights,* are rights in the same way political freedoms are. As already examined in Chapter 1, international documents do not provide for effective judicial enforcement of freedoms for cultural purposes. There are three broad types of reason for this. The first is *theoretical*, the second, which stems from the first, is *practical*, and the third, which arises out of the second, is *financial.*

On the *theoretical* level, it is difficult to award 3rd generation rights, minority cultural rights included, the same legal status and sense of urgency attached to 1st and 2nd generation civil and political rights. This is not to deny that the international community's effort in advancing 3rd generation rights has been genuine and consistent, and that we have come a long way in a relatively short period of time; but rather, despite all the struggles and improvements, 3rd generation rights are still seen as qualitatively different from, and catering for less important human needs, and therefore deserving less serious attention than, classical 1st and 2nd generations of human rights. In fact, their very status as *human rights* is still in dispute.

Associated with this lack of a proper status are *practical* problems of judicial enforcement. Minority rights are not enforced partly because they *cannot be* enforced and partly because it is believed that they *ought not to be* enforced. The reasons why they *cannot* be enforced have already been examined previously. One main reason that they *ought not to be* enforced is probably *financial.* An argument against 3rd generation rights is that they are more costly than civil and political rights. This claim is problematic at first sight as clearly *all* rights and freedoms cost money and resources. That said, the statement becomes more credible when phrased slightly differently. It has been argued that 3rd generation rights impose constraints upon civil and political rights and especially the freedom of market actors in the sense that, while civil and political rights serve self-interests (not least one's own civil rights and liberties), 3rd generation rights must be provided *by* others,[21] *for* others, e.g. through taxation and preferential policies, and in a sense require us to move in the opposite direction of pursuit of self-interests and instead put others and the common good first. Since the post-war political order and the international legal system have been founded on civil and political rights which allow and encourage pursuit of self-interests, the climate has not been one in which 3rd generation rights can comfortably grow. It is in this sense that the 3rd generation rights (minority rights included) are more costly than civil and political rights – they appear to benefit *others*, *The Other*, more than *ourselves*.

Two propositions arise. Firstly, despite a few exceptions, freedoms and rights are not the same. Calling something a right instead of a freedom more strongly indicates an obligation to take action, to realise, and to enforce the said rights. It is mainly for this reason that the 'rights to dialogue' here are framed as *rights* rather than *freedoms*. This leads one to, secondly, enquire whether the 'rights to dialogue' will be immediately enforceable. While leaving the more detailed construction of these rights to the next chapter, I will lay the foundations here by demonstrating that, firstly, they will be *as enforceable as some civil and political rights*, in the sense that a breach can be easily identified and that appropriate action can and should be immediately taken. Though, secondly, they *differ from civil and political rights* in that effects of implementation will be gradual and much less predictable, and that their enforcement need not be judicial. Thirdly, while civil and political rights are ends in themselves, 'rights to dialogue' are means to other ends *as well as* ends in themselves. This makes them *more*, rather than *less*, important.

'Rights to dialogue' *must* be implemented 'here and now' because they protect an essential interest, a vital process, through which we make sense of the world, of ourselves, and of each other. They cater for essential basic human needs: the need to relate, to belong, and to express, in an understanding and enabling environment. In the specific context of minority rights, they enable cultural expressions, reflect changes in and exchange of cultural understandings, through meaningful ongoing communication. As shown in the diagram, this dialogical concept of minority rights contains three separate but related 'rights to dialogue': the group's *collective* right to *external* dialogue, against *the state*; individual members' *individual* right to *external* dialogue, against *the state*; and individual members' *individual* right to *internal* dialogue, against

---

21 See, for example, Alex Kirkup &. Tony Evans, 'The Myth of Western Opposition to Economic, Social and Cultural Rights?: A Reply to Whelan and Donnelly,' in Human Rights Quarterly 31 (2009), pp.221–238.

the group. As will be shown in greater detail in Chapter 4, the first right is concerned with the minority group as a collectivity engaging in dialogue and communication with the outside world. And while the second protects the members' right to engage in dialogue with the outside world when necessary, the third is concerned with communication and discourse within the group itself. These rights can be implemented 'here and now' in quite the same way some civil and political rights are. Unlike the conventional substantive cultural rights, the rights to dialogue are rights to a specific process. By focusing on process instead of outcome, they strongly resemble certain classical civil and political rights, especially *participatory rights*, such as the right to vote and freedom of speech, which both require the state to take steps to enable *participation in a process* rather than to guarantee a particular outcome.

Neither do the rights to dialogue 'suffer from' the 'defect' of benefiting others more than ourselves, which, sadly but quite understandably, often produces scepticism and hostility in those who are not able to benefit. Although they are granted to minority groups and their members *only,* they differ significantly from other differential minority rights in that they aim to guarantee *participation in a dialogue*, which is *two-way process* which presumes and requires *equality* between whomever engaged in the process, members of minority or not. So in a sense, these rights, at least the two *rights to external dialogue,* are in a sense universally available to and benefit all, not just minorities. Thus, if these rights have more in common with participatory human rights than with other minority rights, why can/should they not be implemented 'here and now' like other participatory rights? It is for this reason that so formulating the rights to dialogue could alter the position of minority rights in the wider human rights system.

One possible objection is that, secondly, although these rights may *resemble* certain civil and political rights, they *are not* civil and political rights. While civil and political rights are implemented 'here and now' and enforced *judicially*, 'rights to dialogue' need not and should not be enforced judicially. One major reason for this is that the 'rights to dialogue' are more complex than other existing participatory rights. I have already argued in previous chapters that the so-called 'minority problem' is a multidimensional problem which requires a multidimensional solution. In order to develop, enable and implement the 'rights to dialogue,' cooperation of different fields is a must. This has two practical implications. The first is that from formulation to implementation it is going to take a long time, and full implementation is probably never going to happen. If there is one thing we must not expect, it will be immediate change. The second implication is that a necessarily multidisciplinary and multidimensional approach also renders judicial enforcement and legal remedies impossible. It will be detailed in Chapter 5 how these rights may be sufficiently protected politically and morally.

Thirdly, just because a right is not judicially enforced does not mean it is unimportant. Not all human rights are binding norms; and not all binding norms can or should be judicially implemented. While classical civil and political rights are widely seen as ends in themselves, the rights to dialogue as formulated here are important means to other ends as well as ends in themselves. In the minority rights context they are *means to other ends* in the sense that, firstly, by enabling and promoting dialogue, internal and external, they have in effect enabled and promoted dialogue not just between groups but also *between law and culture*; secondly, the *right to internal dialogue* specifically aims to give voice to members of the group, to acknowledge individual variations that the culture talk tends to obscure and conceal, thereby protecting rights of individual members which have previously been neglected in the name of their protection and group autonomy; thirdly, rights to dialogue are means to other ends also because of the likely spill-over effect of dialogue in law on the wider society. All of these *ends* are significant *ends* which have been largely ignored so far by the existing rights *means*. The rights to dialogue are *ends in themselves*, like all other human rights, in the sense that they ought to be pursued even if for no other reason besides the fact that they, like all other human rights, serve the realisation of essential human needs. In other words, they need not be, although they can be, justified, by more fundamental considerations.

b   Rights against the State vs. Distinction of Duties
There is a second significant difference between the classical *freedom of expression* on the one hand and the three *rights to dialogue* on the other which renders the latter absolutely necessary: while the former is claimed exclusively against the state, the latter consist of one collective right against the state, one individual right against the state, and one individual right against *the group*. The key reason for this distinction of duties has already been presented in the first part of Part 3, so I shall not repeat what has been said before, except to point out that the rights to dialogue are a lot softer, more delicate and more precise than freedom of expression. The distinction between the three types of rights to dialogue reflects the complex and intertwined relationship between the individual and his/her cultural group, between the individual and the wider society, and between that cultural group and the wider society. The distinction emphasises inter-connectedness instead of separateness: while the *individual right to internal dialogue* firmly places the individual within the group to which he/she belongs, the two *rights to external dialogue*

(one collective and the other individual) connects the individual, as well as the group, to the outside world. The broad *freedom of expression* cannot serve this crucial purpose. In fact, since *freedom of expression* is so often and so widely misunderstood as implying and warranting the *freedom to offend*, it can close channels of dialogue and sever much needed connections. This leads us to consider the third crucial difference between freedom of expression and the rights to dialogue.

c   'Rights to *Dialogue*,' not 'Rights to *be Heard*'

Freedom of expression guarantees that one's voice is *heard in public, not* necessarily that it is *heard in dialogue,* which is the primary aim of the rights to dialogue. Therefore the responsibility of defending the three *rights to dialogue* can be discharged while avoiding the problems of conventional freedom of expression. Freedom of expression as commonly understood is a universal fundamental human right. Rights activists often take an all-or-nothing view of this right in the sense that nothing less than full realisation of it is acceptable, even though no-one knows what 'full realisation' means. They are also often hostile towards any so-called cultural justifications of departure from *their understanding* of freedom of speech and label them cultural relativism. Lots of social harms can be and have been inflicted in the name of realisation and protection of freedom of expression – e.g. violent protests, profanity, which, in any reasonable person's view, are gross *abuse* of rather than *realisation* of freedom of expression.

However, this (very often well-intentioned) single-minded dedication is not always easy to refute and in a way demands respect. But its lack of consideration of genuine ideological and cultural disagreements and political and social alignment of the communities or states accused of having violated freedom of speech is a serious deficiency in the understanding of human rights and is itself a stubborn obstacle to the full realisation of human rights. Those who are critical of (strong or weak versions of) cultural relativism should stop to think if cultural relativism is present in their own thinking and reasoning. The answer is most likely yes. All understandings of human rights are to some extent cultural and contextual. It is highly arguable that the reason that human rights are better protected in the West than anywhere else in the world is precisely that human rights are born out of the Western culture, are a Western idea, and thus do not conflict with Western cultural norms. The rights that do to varying extent conflict with Western cultural norms have far from received growing support, illustrated by the various attempts to ban headscarves in schools, the spreading burka ban in Europe, and the minaret controversy in Switzerland. It must be noted that I do not seek to defend cultural relativism;

rather, I wish to issue a warning against lazy labelling and to suggest a reconsideration of conventional understandings of freedom of expression, which should entail a tentative rethinking of the multidimensional impact of culture on understandings of human rights. The most feasible way to achieve this is through the establishment of constructive dialogue about varying interpretations of human rights caused by varying cultural norms.

It is due to these three main differences between the conventional *freedoms of speech and association* and the *rights to dialogue* that the existence of the former does not render the latter unnecessary. The rights to dialogue are, of course, a manifestation of freedom of speech and cannot function properly unless freedom of speech is readily available. Similarly, the necessity of the *rights to dialogue* does not diminish the validity of existing *substantive* group rights claims. They will, however, add to them an additional dimension.

(3)   *Substantive Collective Minority Rights with a Dialogical Dimension*
I aim to address three questions here. Firstly, what does it mean to add to existing substantive collective cultural rights claims a dialogical dimension? Secondly, why is it necessary to do so? And thirdly, how can this be achieved? As shown in Chapter 2, what is considered to be most objectionable about collective rights is that they are formulated and widely understood as *rights of groups,* or even *rights of cultures,* which are held and exercised by the group as a collectivity. These collective rights are substantive in nature and insist on the imposition of perceived fixed notions of culture and rights, sometimes at the expense of the well-being and interests of individual members of the group. While acknowledging serious objections to the moral defensibility of some of these rights raised primarily by liberal and feminist theorists, the previous two chapters have nevertheless defended the validity and necessity of collective rights. But the objections have been taken into account in developing the dialogical concept.

As shown in the diagram and will be further examined in the next chapter, all existing collective cultural rights claims as categorised by Jacob Levy[22] continue to occupy a place in the new system and are now incorporated into the first limb: '*rights against the state.*' Adding a dialogical dimension to these substantive collective rights is primarily achieved by dividing this category of collective rights into three sub-categories: *rights to self-determination and autonomy, rights to assistance and intervention,* and the group's *collective rights to external dialogue.*[23] These three sub-categories of rights are both separate

---

22   See Part 1 of Chapter 2.
23   See diagram.

from and yet defined in terms of each other. They are separate because they cater for different needs and serve often oppositional purposes. They are defined in terms of each other because, firstly, their division highlights the fact that group rights cannot be defended or defeated as a whole, as they consist of a variety of claims – some promote greater independence whilst the others facilitate connection. Secondly, one sub-category cannot exist without the other two, as no group, a minority or a majority, can flourish in isolation (hence the first sub-category alone is insufficient), and no minority group should be required to trade their identity for state assistance and benefits (hence the second sub-category alone is inappropriate). To promote the co-existence of these sub-categories is to make acknowledgment of the authority of the group compatible not only with the group's right to development and its connectedness to the wider society, but also with the protection of the rights of individual members of the group.

'Adding a dialogical dimension' has another meaning. Effective dialogue and communication should lead to what Habermas calls *communicative rationality,* which should cause us to approach substantive collective rights claims less fanatically. We must acknowledge not only that it is often impossible to guarantee the desired outcomes, but also that we do not always know what 'desired outcomes' constitute, what it is that we, or those we aim to protect, desire. The most urgent task before us is thus to work out, through intellectual deliberation and exchange, reliable criteria of effective recognition and protection when we do not know what it is desired, or what it is reasonable and rational to desire. In other words, the potential for rationality is inherent in communication itself and is the necessary outcome of successful communication. And the group's *collective right to external dialogue* functions to keep the channels of communication open.

Before moving on to consider the likely impact of this dialogical concept of minority rights on the wider human rights system and on society, it is necessary to quickly summarise what has been said so far. As the diagram shows, this dialogical concept consists of a complex network of inter-connected rights. There is one other way of categorising these rights other than dividing them into *rights against the state* and *rights against the group.* Firstly, there are the strong cultural rights: the *collective* rights to self-determination and autonomy, and the members' *individual* right to cultural belonging. Secondly, there are the 'transitional rights' which are intended to create space for supererogation: the *collective* rights to appropriate intervention and assistance, the members' *individual* rights to appropriate intervention and assistance, the *group*'s right to *external* dialogue, the *individual* right to *external* dialogue, and the *individual* right to *internal* dialogue. Lastly, there is a 'last-resort right': the right of exit.

The co-existence of such a diversity of rights reflects the wide range of needs of cultural minorities; it also, in my view, reflects Habermas's distinction between ethics and morality. Although 'ethics' and 'morality' are often used interchangeably, and the former is widely understood to be the philosophical study of the latter, Habermas argues that in a modern pluralist society, normative issues should be separated from issues of the good life. Thus, deeply contextualist interpretations and claims should be allowed to stand as valid ethical claims. An ethical claim gives rise to normative issues and has implications for everybody in society only when it comes into conflict with another competing ethical claim, as it inevitably will in a modern pluralist society. The law's job, in Habermas's view, is to govern and stabilise such a society through the *deliberative paradigm*.[24] The strong cultural rights under this dialogical concept aim to allow the continuance of traditional, contextualist, ethical claims. The transitional rights, especially the rights to dialogue, create and protect the space in which competing ethical claims come into conflict and give rise to normative disagreements, and thereby facilitate and enhance communication and the deliberative paradigm. The right of exit is a necessary last resort in case of failed communication and deliberation. The most significant benefit of so categorising minority rights is that it has in effect prioritised them.

4 Minority Rights and their Prioritisation

All minority rights matter, but prioritisation of them (and any other rights) for pragmatic reasons should be a widely acknowledged necessity. There should also be little disagreement that the more important the human need, the more essential the interest, the greater priority the relevant right deserves. It is difficult, and wrong, to attempt to put all minority rights in order of significance and priority; but for all the reasons I have presented so far in this chapter, it should be reasonable to claim that the three transitional rights – *the group's collective right to external dialogue against the state, individual members' right to external dialogue against the state,* and *individual members' right to internal dialogue against the group* – should take top priority as leading indicators of a healthy minority rights scheme. In the absence of a consensus on the value and entailment of minority rights, the three rights to dialogue lay down procedural rules of behaviour, rules that should be and can be observed by opponents in a similar fashion as two sides of a debate being bound by the same set of rules and procedures. The efficiency of rights enforcement agents can be

---

24   See Jürgen Habermas, *Between Facts and Norms: Contributions to a Discourse Theory of Law and Democracy*, translated by William Rehg, (Polity Press, 1996), Chapter 7.

judged by the deliberative and communicative standards created by these rights to dialogue, i.e. by determining whether positive and efficient steps have been taken to enable dialogue and communication.[25]

As regards the substantive group rights claims and the right of exit, as Chapter 6 will show, in the absence of many minority groups' capacity of self-government, it is unrealistic and damaging to insist on immediate implementation of the stronger substantive group rights, especially the rights to self-determination and autonomy. They ought not to be the focus of attention at this early stage of development but might very well be the ultimate goal which can only be achieved through state-assisted capacity-building as a necessary transitional measure. The right of exit, being a 'last-resort right,' is by no means less significant. As will be demonstrated in Chapter 5, making exit real requires a sophisticated multidimensional solution, but efforts should always be directed towards enabling *options* while inside rather than printing exit tickets to get out.

5 Conclusion: Contextualising Dialogic Processes in Law and Society

The legitimacy of this dialogical account of minority rights derives not only from theories on the dialogical nature of cultural identity, legitimate law-making, and communicative rationality, but also from the fact that international minority rights law is not merely a collection of rules and standards, but also an institution responsible for introducing, interpreting, revising, and enforcing these rules and standards. The indispensability of a system of minority rights laws and policies that accurately reflect the cultural needs and concerns of minorities points to the need for re-conceptualisation of minority rights. I have in this chapter laid the foundations for a dialogical concept, which, I believe, will serve the purpose.

A relationship of interaction and interdependence not only exists between the minority rights scheme and the wider human rights system; such a relationship also exists between the entire rights system (minority rights included) and the wider society in which the rights system is necessarily situated, and in which the formation and development of public opinion and policy take place. Feminist scholars have made strong contributions to the case that we cannot possibly understand social policy without examining its cultural determinants. By the same token, we will not be able fairly and efficiently to legislate in the field of minority rights without first understanding culture, our own as well as others,' its profound influences in both normative and cognitive forms on, and how it *constitutes*, laws and policies through both background and foreground

---

25 For details see Chapters 4 and 5 of the book.

processes of interaction with other ideational dynamics.[26] In other words, 'understanding culture' means so much more than mechanically identifying beliefs and practices. It requires one to approach not only *culture* but also *discourse* and *interactions* as constitutive elements of opinion formation, law-making and policy development. Once we appreciate this true meaning of 'understanding culture,' we should also be able to grasp the essence of minority rights protection: it requires more than simply affirming the beliefs and practices we have previously mechanically identified. It must not only identify different processes of discourse and interaction but also strive to protect and further facilitate these processes. Since law cannot be separated from society, writing dialogue into legal concepts and law should lead to not only more realistic and more legitimate law-making, but also better understandings of, and a more democratic and more inclusive, society.

---

26   Ideational scholars have thoroughly examined these interactive processes. See, for example, Tasleem J. Padamsee *'Culture in Connection: Re-Contextualizing Ideational Processes in the Analysis of Policy Development'* in *Social Politics: International Studies in Gender, State, and Society*, Volume.16, No. 4, winter 2009, p.413–445, at p.418.

CHAPTER 4

Minority Rights against the State

As examined in the previous chapter, the dialogical concept of minority rights divides group rights into two broad categories: group rights against the *state*, and individual rights against the *minority group*, under both of which rights are further divided into sub-categories. This chapter examines in detail the first limb: group rights against the *state*. As shown in the diagram, such rights are held against the state by *both* the group in question as a collectivity and by the members of the group as individuals. In the case of the group, the rights in question take the form of the group's rights to autonomy and self-determination, the rights to state assistance and appropriate intervention, and very importantly – the right to *external* dialogue. In the case of the group members, such rights take the form of the member's right to cultural belonging, also a right to state assistance and intervention, and also a right to *external* dialogue which is individual in nature. I will demonstrate that under this dialogical account of minority rights, the group's collective rights and the members' individually held rights are not only compatible but also constitute two necessary internal components of the same concept, and that they can and must co-exist in order to bring about just and effective protection. Against the background of international and regional human rights instruments, especially the UN Declaration on the Rights of Indigenous Peoples, particular attention is paid to the notion of 'national interests,' its role in state intervention and especially in marking the boundaries of group autonomy and self-determination.

1   Minority Rights Held by the *Group* against the *State*

(1)   *Rights to Self-determination and Autonomy*

This category of group rights contains *all but one* of the traditional group rights claims as categorised by Jacob Levy, and is applicable to national minorities, indigenous peoples, and to a lesser extent, immigrant communities. As already examined in Chapter 2, Levy's non-exhaustive taxonomy of group rights, which is based on types of demands not types of groups, divides group rights claims into eight categories. In the first category are *total exemptions,* which aim at allowing cultural practices that contrast with those of the majority or even infringe upon the majority's legal rules and/or social norms – e.g. using illegal substances in traditional cultural ceremonies, and female genital mutilation.

In the second category are *self-government rights,* which cover a broad range of claims including partial or total control of cultural and public affairs, usually claimed by national minorities. In the third category are the so-called *assistance rights*, which, contrary to the purposes of the claims in the first two categories, demand assistance in overcoming the obstacles to engage in the majority's practices – e.g. preferential educational policies for members of certain cultural and linguistic minorities.

In the fourth category are the so-called 'hard multiculturalist' *enforcement rights, or recognition rights*, a common claim of which is for certain religious or cultural legal codes to be recognised as valid law, even if they conflict with aspects of state law – e.g. Sharia law. In the fifth category are certain *external rules* aimed at restricting the liberty of *non-members* so that the *minority* culture in question can be preserved. This approach is commonly referred to as '*cultural preservationism*.' In the sixth category are certain *internal rules* aimed at restricting the freedom of *members* of a minority group so as to, again, preserve the group's distinct characteristics and identity. In the seventh category are *guaranteed representation demands*, which aim at guaranteeing presence and participation of cultural minorities in central and/or regional decision-making bodies. And in the eighth category are the *symbolic demands*, which commonly aim at gaining permission to display minority cultural symbols in public places.

With the exception of indigenous peoples, minority rights are not framed as collective rights in international and regional instruments, though there are enough collective elements in them to suggest that these rights should not only be enjoyed by members of minority groups *individually* but also with the rest of the minority community *collectively*. Jacob's detailed categorisation of groups' rights demands is not reflected exactly in international documents. But it is worthwhile to explore the possibility of injecting this categorisation into international law through, I argue, incorporating them into the new dialogic framework, in the following way.

As seen in the diagram, all except the so-called *assistance rights* (Levy's Category 3), which now fall into the category of 'rights to state assistance and appropriate intervention,' will now fall under the heading 'collective rights to self-determination and autonomy.' A few questions need to be addressed. First, what is the main advantage of so dividing these rights claims? The advantage is that, as shown in the diagram, now there exist two distinct categories of collectively held rights against the state – one contains rights demands for greater autonomy and independence, warranted by cultural distinctiveness; the other invites appropriate intervention in appropriate circumstances. To be explicit, the seven rights claims that demand greater autonomy are: total exemptions, self-government, enforcement/recognition rights, external rules restricting the liberty of non-members, internal rules restricting the freedom of members, guaranteed representation, and symbolic recognition.

International minority rights law as it stands is one-sided, in that it places much greater emphasis on minorities' needs and rights to be distinct and separate (which not *all* minorities share) than on their needs and rights to connect with the larger society. Where it does permit state intervention and assistance, it is a particular kind of intervention and assistance – the kind that affirms and further strengthens their cultural distinctiveness – and such permission is always expressed in very mild terms without specifications. For instance, article 1(3) of the International Covenant on Economic, Social and Cultural Rights states that '[t]he States Parties to the present Covenant [...] shall promote the realization of the right of self-determination, and shall respect that right, in conformity with the provisions of the Charter of the United Nations.' Similarly, article 1 of the United Nation's 1992 Declaration on the Rights of Persons Belonging to National or Ethnic, Religious and Linguistic Minorities provides that 'states shall protect the existence and the national or ethnic, cultural, religious and linguistic identity of minorities within their respective territories, and shall encourage conditions for the promotion of that identity.' Clearly, state intervention and assistance are not explicitly expressed as such; rather, they are *implied* in open-ended phrases such as *'shall promote'* and *'shall encourage conditions.'*

It is worth repeating here that for the seven categories that now fall under the heading 'collective rights to self-determination and autonomy,' the central concern is cultural distinctness. They are seven broad categories of rights *demands*, not yet *rights*. Demands do not automatically translate into rights. Thus, the second question that ought to be addressed is whether international minority rights law does, is supposed to, and indeed can, cater for all of these collective rights demands and recognise them as 'rights.' Before I proceed, I would first like to point out that given the special nature of indigenous identity, the collective rights of self-determination and autonomy of *indigenous peoples* will be considered separately in Chapter 6.[1] I will not repeat the detailed examination of the relevant legal documents here which has already been done in the first chapter. Though it is necessary to note that, although these seven categories of demands have not given rise to mirroring categories of rights in international minority rights law, several international and regional documents have attempted to specify a bundle of minority rights, and the

---

1   Many indigenous peoples refuse to take on the title 'minorities,' arguing that their plight is distinguishable because of significantly differing historical circumstances.

interests and needs represented in the seven categories are mostly covered, to varying extents, albeit often loosely. Some sort of recognition and justification of protection can always be derived from international law. However, the lack of an internationally accepted, precise, enumeration of minority cultural rights means that national laws necessarily play a central role in the protection of minorities.[2]

There is a large number of literature on the more conventional types of group rights demands. What I want to focus on here are the two group rights demands on which laws and policies have been understandably silent: external rules restricting the freedom of non-members, and internal rules restricting the freedom of their own members. Of course, the absence of formal permission does not mean the practice is forbidden, not least because the seven categories are not mutually exclusive: for instance, *self-determination* and *recognition rights* (both of which are recognised by international law) inevitably overlap with some external rules and internal rules. The reasons for the silence of law and policy over some minority demands are fairly obvious. In some cases, the demand in question is considered to be unworthy of formal recognition. As previously stated, there cannot possibly be a right to all things of the slightest value. In other cases, the demand in question is considered to be worthy of formal protection, but it is unclear how or what form of recognition is to take place. But the most dominant reason is that many of these demands are contrary to the ideals of Western liberalism, individualism, and conceptions of human rights. A good example of this last objection is article 5 of UNESCO's 2001 Universal Declaration on Cultural Diversity, which states:

> Cultural rights are an integral part of human rights, which are universal, indivisible and interdependent. The flourishing of creative diversity requires the full implementation of cultural rights as defined in Article 27 of the Universal Declaration of Human Rights and in Articles 13 and 15 of the International Covenant on Economic, Social and Cultural Rights. All persons have therefore the right to express themselves and to create and disseminate their work in the language of their choice, and particularly in their mother tongue; all persons are entitled to quality education and training that fully respect their cultural identity; and all persons have the right to participate in the cultural life of their choice and conduct their own cultural practices; *subject to respect for human rights and fundamental freedoms* (italics added).

---

2 Francesco Francioni &. Martin Scheinin, *Cultural Human Rights* (Martinus Nijhoff Publishers, 2008), p.171.

(2)   *The Limits of Toleration and the Boundaries of Autonomy*
Indeed, 'respect for human rights and fundamental freedoms' is, and should be, a condition for exercising collective rights to self-determination and autonomy. But could there be anything wrong with drawing the line at breaches of rights and freedoms? It depends on which rights and which freedoms we are talking about. As seen in Chapter 2, while both Rawls and Kymlicka argue to varying extents that minority cultural values and practices should be protected, in their view the liberal principle of toleration should only be allowed to benefit a selected few – *those who remain firmly within liberal boundaries.* This is not always a solution in reality, as the most persistent and controversial collective rights demands come precisely from those who remain firmly *outside* liberal boundaries – e.g. the exclusionist Muslims who maintain strict gender segregation and practices that are harmful, in a modern Western eye at least, to women. The question thus becomes, specifically, whether these groups and practices should be accommodated and included in public reasoning. It is in this context that I shall examine the '*external rules limiting the liberty of non-members*' and the '*internal rules restricting the freedoms of members.*'

(1)   Group *Illiberalness* and Degrees of Toleration
A key word that often makes frequent appearances in discussions of minorities and cultural diversity is 'toleration,' which is different from acceptance, or respect – quite the opposite, for the concept is conceptually inseparable from non-acceptance, disagreement, and disapproval. As Michael Walzer rightly points out, a defence of toleration is not necessarily a defence of difference.[3] And as Susan Mendus observes, one usually only tolerates what one considers bad. In other words, the statement 'so-and-so ought to be tolerated' contains an inherent judgement as to the (lack of) intrinsic value of the tolerated.[4] Furthermore, like all principles, the principle of toleration has limits – there ought to be circumstances in which tolerance is wrong and intolerance is right. This means that the word 'toleration' is not right for all cases, and that it is necessary to distinguish between cases where the principle of toleration applies and those where it does not.

a   *External Rules Limiting the Liberty of Non-Members*
Under the dialogical account, demands for restricting external rules now fall into the broad category of 'collective rights to self-determination and

---

3   Michael Walzer, *On Toleration* (Yale University Press, 1997), preface, xii.
4   Susan Mendus, *Justifying Toleration: Conceptual and Historical Perspectives* (Cambridge University Press, 2009[1988]), p.3.

autonomy,' as they are often argued to be an extension of self-determination rights claims, and it seems that only those groups that have valid self-determination claims could legitimately set restricting external rules. The rationale behind such demands is reservationist in nature – namely, in order to preserve and protect a particular culture it is necessary to restrict the liberty of non-members whose free exercise of freedoms will have damaging effects on the minority culture in question. Thus two assumptions are implied. First, cultures need to be preserved. Second, (some elements of) cultures are fragile. Such principles can hardly fall within the liberal framework of the state, which is why whilst the demands are common their official recognition is rare.

The most striking and thoroughly debated example is undoubtedly Quebec's legal restrictions on the use of languages other than French. Serious dispute over Quebec's language policies started to grow in 1974, in which year *la Loi sur la langue officielle* (Official Language Act) was passed which made French the province's official language, and the language of contracts and corporations. *La Charte de la langue française* (Charter of the French Language) enacted by the National Assembly of Quebec in 1977 built upon the Official Language Act and declared French to be the only language allowed on commercial signs in the province. English education became restricted to children already in the English-speaking system and whose parents were temporarily posted to Quebec. With very few exceptions, the use of the English language was banned.

In 1993, the UN Human Rights Committee ruled that, by restricting 'the freedom to express oneself in a certain language' 'outside the spheres of public life,' Quebec's language restrictions on signs violated article 19 of the International Covenant on Civil and Political Rights.[5] This ruling led to the introduction of

---

5 Ballantyne, Davidson, McIntyre v. Canada, Communications Nos. 359/1989 and 385/1989, U.N. Doc. CCPR/C/47/D/359/1989 and 385/1989/Rev.1 (1993). The UN Human Rights Committee decided on the McIntyre case: 'While the restrictions on outdoor advertising are indeed provided by law, the issue to be addressed is whether they are necessary for the respect of the rights of others. The rights of others could only be the rights of the francophone minority within Canada under article 27. This is the right to use their own language, which is not jeopardised by the freedom of others to advertise in other than the French language. Nor does the Committee have reason to believe that public order would be jeopardised by commercial advertising outdoors in a language other than French. The Committee believes that it is not necessary, in order to protect the vulnerable position in Canada of the francophone group, to prohibit commercial advertising in English. This protection may be achieved in other ways that do not preclude the freedom of expression, in a language of their choice, of those engaged in such fields as trade. For example, the law could have required that advertising be in both French and English. A state may choose one or more official languages, but it may not exclude, outside the sphere of public life, the freedom to express

Bill 86[6] in 1993 and a series of court cases which would eventually allow English to appear on outdoor commercial signs *but only if* the French lettering is markedly predominant. A provincial court ruling in 1999 said that the province should not continue to impose restrictions on the use of languages other than French on commercial signs unless it could prove the fragility of the French language in Quebec. But this decision was overturned in 2000 by the Superior Court and the Quebec Court of Appeal, which cited the province's unique geographical and linguistic situation as a French-speaking province on a vast English-speaking continent.[7] The Supreme Court of Canada decided not to hear the case.

In March 2005, the Supreme Court ruled on a case filed by French-speaking parents who wanted the free choice to enrol their children in English-speaking schools. It ruled against the parents and upheld the legitimacy of language laws which prevented Quebec's Francophones from placing their children in English-speaking schools. However, the court did require that the government should make some changes in the legislation so as to comply with the Canadian Charter of Rights and Freedoms, and laid down new criteria which would make it easier for native Canadians and immigrants (who had already had some English education) to enrol in English-speaking schools in Quebec.[8]

Several observations can be made from the case of Quebec's language laws. Firstly, *external rules* are seldom *just* external rules. They are often also at the same time *internal rules* restricting the choices of members of the group. There are of course exclusively external rules, for instance, restricted mobility, property and voting rights for non-Indian Americans in Indian areas – the creation of which, Kymlicka has argued, is essential for the preservation of Indian culture.[9] Secondly and related, in the case of the Quebec language restrictions, the key issue is one concerning conflicts between freedoms and rights, especially between individual autonomy and group autonomy. Thus, thirdly, since in order for one side to win the other will have to lose, it seems that the ultimate

---

oneself in a certain language. The committee accordingly concludes that there has been a violation of article 19, paragraph 2.' Despite the disproportionate impact of the law on the English-speaking community, the Human Rights Committee found no violation of article 26, since French speakers also could not advertise in English. In other words, the focus was not on inherent linguistic rights but on anti-discrimination, to ensure that no linguistic group is discriminated against because of the law.

6 The Act to amend the Charter of the French Language.
7 R. c. Entreprises W.F.H. [2011] R.J.Q. 2557 (C.A.) ('The Lyon & the Walrus Case').
8 See John Geddes's article *'Tweaking the language laws,'* Maclean's, 5 April 2005, at: https://www.mcgill.ca/continuingstudies/files/continuingstudies/languagelaws5April05.pdf.
9 Will Kymlicka, *Liberalism, Community, and Culture* (Oxford University Press, 1989), p.136.

test for whether or not external rules are justifiable in any given circumstance should be *whether what is or may be lost is of considerable value to the cultural well-being and flourishing of group members, especially in comparison to what the other side would have lost had the case been decided differently.*

For instance, in the Quebec case, the test should be whether preservation of the primacy of the French language and culture is of considerable value to the cultural well-being and flourishing of the group, whether it is of greater value than having free choice and more options. As demonstrated by the increasing number of legal challenges to Quebec's language laws[10] (especially from parents who demand freer access to English schools), and the fact that the French language continues to dominate but the proportions of population who claim to be bilingual or multilingual have vastly increased in the past decades, and that the great advantages and opportunities that bilingualism and multilingualism will bring, it seems that what is lost – French exclusivity – is of no considerable value. This affirms the argument presented in previous chapters that cultural preservation in this globalised and multicultural age is no longer about sameness; rather, it is about adaptation, change, and continuous development. This is perhaps more relevant to restricting internal rules, which are even more difficult to formulate than restricting external rules.

b   *Internal Rules Restricting the Freedoms of Members*

Restricting internal rules are typically collective claims to restrict the range and availability of the options available to the group's membership on the grounds of their duty to the preservation and survival of the group's customs and traditions. Such claims have three underlying assumptions. First, group survival depends on the duty of the membership to conform to their prescribed roles and inherited cultural norms. Second, cultural boundaries are fixed and cultural particularities can only be expressed in one particular, fixed, and pre-determined, set of culturally sanctioned beliefs and practices. Third, it is acceptable for the group to impose internal restrictions on the membership to maintain its cultural structure and prevent changes to the collective character of the group. It cannot be denied that all cultural minority groups have some forms of internal rules, and while international norms prohibit the exercise of cultural and religious practices that contravene internationally proclaimed human rights and freedoms, rather few are considered absolutely intolerable.

---

10   For example, Quebec (Attorney General) v. Quebec Protestant School Boards (1984), Ford v. Quebec (Attorney General) (1988), Ballantyne, Davidson, McIntyre v. Canada (1993), the Bill 104 case (2009).

I aim to address two main issues. Firstly, I shall examine the different criteria for and the limits of toleration, and work out what restricting internal rules that the dialogical account of minority rights can accommodate. Secondly, under the dialogical account, the right to have internal rules is held collectively by the group against the state. I shall therefore consider what forms of state intervention is appropriate when and where necessary.

Theorists have proposed different criteria for toleration of restricting internal rules. For instance, the mainstream liberal claim is that, internally, members should be free to choose amongst a broad range of options, and in order for them to be able to do so a sufficiently wide range of alternatives ought to be tolerated by the group as a collectivity. Disagreement and dissent may or may not be successful, but the group's restriction on individual members' freedom to disagree and disobey cannot possibly be justified, and to use group autonomy to end individual autonomy is not only controversial but simply wrong. This recalls J.S. Mill's principle of self-contradiction in his essay *On Liberty*, where he argues that it is self-contradictory and therefore absurd, irrational, and wrong, to use freedom to end freedom.[11] In other words, freedom ought not to be granted where it may contravene the principle of freedom itself. Furthermore, Mill's harm principle could also be considered to have determined the boundaries of toleration of restricting internal rules. The principle states that the only justification for interfering is to prevent harm being caused to others. There should be no doubt that one can be harmed by being denied what is due to him – be it food, shelter, affection, or life choices. But harm is difficult not only to define but also to measure, not least because harm is often subjective i.e. what is considered harmful to one may not be considered as harmful or at all to another. There are also many different types of harm and many different degrees of harm. They are not all comparable or measurable.

Kymlicka also condemns 'internal restrictions' and argues that groups must not be allowed to restrict the basic civil liberties of members of the group in the name of the 'sacredness' of a particular cultural or religious practice, as the nature of cultural values and practices is only instrumental, not intrinsic.[12] Similarly, Dworkin also offers an argument, based on equal concern for individuals, for internal tolerance of those who disagree and dissent, guaranteed by rights. He argues that 'the value of [an individual's] own life depends on the

---

11 J.S. Mill, *On Liberty* (Penguin, 1974[1859]), Chapter III.
12 Will Kymlicka, *Politics in the Vernacular: Nationalism, Multiculturalism and Citizenship* (Oxford University Press, 2001), p.62.

success of his own community treating everyone with equal concern.'[13] In a similar vein but stronger terms, feminist theorists have alerted us to the lack of attention to the internal diversity of minority groups and the fact that some minority groups have used self-determination rights to oppress or discriminate against their own members, especially the female members.[14]

So what are the implications for the dialogical account of minority rights? How may it determine the boundaries of restricting internal rules? The dialogical spirit of this work requires that we examine these liberty-limiting rules *in the context of transition* and that we think more about the possibility of *internal reform* and less about external intervention and imposition of liberal values.[15] There are three main reasons for this. Firstly, the principle of self-determination and autonomy makes it difficult to justify external intervention in groups' internal affairs. And internal rules fall within the domain of internal affairs. Secondly, many internal rules and norms restricting the liberty of members are not formal rules let alone law. Neither are they always enforced coherently or coercively, if at all. Their 'enforcement' often takes the form of 'peer pressure' or pressure from the family or local community (e.g. forced marriage). This makes it difficult for the relevant state authorities to decide when and where to cut in. Thirdly, under this dialogical account of minority rights, there exist other rights (e.g. the group's collective right to external dialogue, individual members' right to external dialogue and to state assistance, members' right to internal dialogue, and their right of exit) that could help discover the right balance. It is often through protecting these other rights that the state can in effect limit and redress the practice of restricting internal rules. In other words, restricting internal rules may be, and sometimes may only be, counterbalanced indirectly.

As already examined in the previous chapter, the dialogical nature of these rights determines that their enforcement methods are a lot more tentative and fall far short of 'intervention.' The interaction of them could also lead the state to adopt preventive and corrective policies and measures and promote awareness of the liberty-restricting nature of these internal rules so that such rules

---

13 Ronald Dworkin, *'Liberal Community,' California Law Review*, 77(3) (1989): pp.479–504, at p.501.
14 See, for instance, Susan Moller Okin's essay *'Is Multiculturalism Bad For Women?,'* in which she argues that multicultural accommodation could worsen the situation of 'minorities within minorities,' especially women, as self-government powers are attributed to groups which neglect women's autonomy and their right to equality and systematise their oppression.
15 But it must be acknowledged that internal reform is often the result of interaction with the outside world.

may (or may not) be abandoned gradually and eventually. Direct and forceful intervention should only take place in the most serious and most urgent cases. I shall refrain from attempting to provide an exhaustive list of allowable internal rules. In each case, we shall determine whether the rule or practice in question is consistent with the limits and principles of toleration established above, and then decide whether or not to directly intervene.

(2)   *National Interests* as Limits of Toleration and Autonomy

It is not just the restricting internal rules whose limits need determining. It is also the category of 'collective rights to self-determination and autonomy' as a whole (see diagram). Another way of determining the limits of group autonomy is through tracing the influence of cultural identity on national interests and security. Commentators in the field can be loosely sorted into three categories. In the first category are those who see a connection between cultural identity and national interests and yet do not go beyond the simple assertion that cultural identity, in one way or another, plays an important role in state interests and foreign policy, and offer only vague and imprecise definitions and analyses. In the second category are those who are sceptical of the notion of cultural identity and its influence on state interests, and argue that state policies can be much better understood in terms of *interest* only, and that national interests alone, not the concept of *identity,* explain why states adopt certain policies and not others. In the third category are those who see *cultural identity* as playing a direct and vital role in how states define and pursue their interests and goals. Some have even gone as far as to say that national interest and security *depend on* national identity.[16]

The most relevant issue that concerns both minority self-determination and national interests is perhaps *separatism,* real or perceived. As already examined in previous chapters, there has been long-standing debate over whether group autonomy or self-determination is merely a principle and not a proper right. And whilst both the UN and regional organisations have spoken variously and continuously of minority self-determination,[17] understandably all have been cautious on this matter, and there remains a consensus that there is no general right to secession and that the exercise of internal self-determination must not damage the sovereignty and territorial integrity of the state.[18] Since

---

16 Paul A. Kowert's *'National Identity: Inside and Out,'* in Glenn Chafetz, Michael Spirtaz &. Benjamin Frankel (eds.), *The Origins of National Interests* (Frank Cass Publishers, 1999), p.1.
17 See Chapter 1 of the book.
18 Even the UN Declaration on the Rights of Indigenous Peoples 2007, which spells out strong and expansive rights including the right to self-determination and the right to

the international community is and will continue to be state-dominated, it is unlikely that any forms of minority rights to secession or independence will be formally recognised in the foreseeable future.

However, with the spread of democratic movements around the globe (successful or not), it is very possible that some variations on the idea – e.g. freedom from political and cultural oppression – will have greater influence on international minority rights law. But such 'freedom' does not need to take a territorial form. Indeed, studies have shown that strict territorial autonomy and secession often make ethnic relations worse, because they tend to oversimplify problems and legalise and glorify confrontations.[19] The dialogical spirit of this work determines that any minority claims to territory-based self-determination and autonomy must be treated with great caution, and that any extension of the existing principle of self-determination must be strongly and persistently resisted, as they address only the symptoms and not the cause. Instead, as will be shown below, states ought to focus on facilitating the groups' exercise of their *collective right to external dialogue*, which can help, through interaction with other minority rights and human rights, find the right balance between autonomy and connectedness. Self-determination should be a constant work in progress, not an immediate entitlement.

Thus, to conclude this section, generally speaking, the category of 'collective rights to self-determination and autonomy' under this dialogical concept of minority rights should consist of the following non-exhaustive list of rights and entitlements.

- Total exemptions;
- Non-territorial self-government rights (with the exception of indigenous peoples);
- State enforcement and recognition of customary laws;
- External rules restricting the liberty of non-members;
- Internal rules restricting the liberty of members;
- Right to establish the group's own internal decision-making bodies;
- Guaranteed representation in the state system;
- Symbolic recognition;
- Right/freedom to maintain relations with cultural kin cross national borders;

---

freely determine their political status, stops short of providing for the possibility of secession and independence.

19 Donald Horowitz, *'Self-Determination,'* in Ian Shapiro & Will Kymlicka (eds.), *Ethnicity and Group Rights* (New York University Press, 1997), p.433.

- Language rights;
- Rights to practise the group's own culture and/or religion;
- (For major religious groups) Right to establish faith schools.

(3) *Rights to State Assistance and Appropriate Intervention*

I now move to the second sub-category of collectively held rights against the state (see diagram) – the rights to state assistance and intervention. It is not easy to make a sharp distinction between rights to collective self-determination and rights to state assistance and intervention, for the realisation of the former necessarily requires the latter, but the latter often conflicts with and hinders the former. In the present context, the collective rights to state assistance refer *specifically* to minority groups' entitlements to state policies which assist with *strengthening their cultural autonomy and independence*. There is a strong 'promotion' element, which should give the relevant authorities competence to extend its promotion of minority cultures to a wide range of policy areas at various levels. Thus, minority groups can expect that such efforts will be attempted in various fields.

- Minority groups should have sufficient access to economic and social means provided by the state to practise their own culture and religion, should such needs arise.
- Minority groups should have sufficient access to economic and social means of dissemination of their culture and religion – e.g. media, public exhibitions, and other projects that celebrate minority traditions.
- The state has the duty to assist minority groups in establishing their own internal decision-making bodies, via which the group can meaningfully exercise the right to self-determination and participate in state decision-making.[20]
- The state has the duty to assist qualified religious groups to establish schools of their own faith and other social and cultural institutions.
- Minority groups have the right to economic and social help from the state in preserving aspects of their own culture and religion, e.g. sacred sites, language, art, and local knowledge, and in practising their own lifestyles.
- These minority rights also apply to indigenous peoples, who, in addition to these rights, also enjoy certain special rights aiming to protect both the tangible and intangible aspects of their unique indigenous identity – e.g. rights

---

20   Detailed examination in Chapter 6.

concerning the use of their land and natural resources, oral tradition, local knowledge, and human remains.[21]
- The state should, at the request of minority communities, offer legal or other forms of assistance in specific cases to help the communities in question resolve disputes and problems.

It needs to be underlined that the group's *collective right to state assistance* here aims to serve the sole purpose of *maintaining the cultural structure and integrity of minority groups*. As will be shown in Part 2 of this chapter, under this dialogical account there exists another *individually held right to state assistance and intervention* – a right held by individual members of the group and which has the main purpose of *aiding integration* into the wider society when and where such needs manifest. There are three major reasons why this distinction is necessary. Firstly, the design of this dialogical concept is meant to precisely divide rights demands according to actual needs, with the *collective* branch serving the chief purpose of maintaining minority cultural structure and strengthening autonomy. Secondly and related, it makes less sense to speak of integration of *groups* into society than to speak of integration of *individuals*. Thus, as will be shown in Part 2 below, the latter purpose is better served by *individually held* rights to state assistance. Lastly, for reasons identified in the previous chapters, and further demonstrated throughout this book, when it comes to protection of minority groups and their relation with the state and the rest of the population, the most urgent need is not to *integrate*, but to *communicate*.

(4)   *The Collective Right to External Dialogue*

Along with the two individually held rights to dialogue, the group's right to *external* dialogue against the state, collectively held by the group, is the most significant addition to minority rights under this dialogical account.[22] It has already been demonstrated in Chapter 3 that freedom of expression has significant limitations and cannot serve the purpose of, and sometimes hinders, inter-cultural dialogue, which serves the human need to relate, to belong and to culturally express oneself. It is an essential interest and a vital process through which we make sense of the world and of each other, and must be and can be protected as a right. Although this human need is universal irrespective

---

21 Detailed examination in Chapter 6.
22 Individual members of the group have the right to *external dialogue, against the state,* and the right to *internal dialogue, against the group*. The first right will be examined in Part 2 of this chapter, and the second will be examined in the next chapter.

of cultural backgrounds, cultural minorities ought to be singled out for special consideration due to their weaker bargaining position in society which often muffles their voices. The cultural distinctness of some minority cultures also renders their expression hard to apprehend for the rest of the society, which calls for additional assistance.

Unlike the more conventional collective rights, the right to external dialogue is a right to a specific dialogical process. It is a participatory right that requires the state to take positive steps to enable constructive dialogue between the minority group in question and the society at large, not to guarantee any particular outcome. It is a means to other ends as well as an end in itself. With these general principles in mind, we may formulate the right to external dialogue and the corresponding state duties along the following lines:

- Minority groups, as collectivities, have the right to initiate and to participate in constructive dialogue with the state and the rest of the society, with the specific purpose of establishing and maintaining channels of communication and enabling greater mutual understanding and respect.
- Minority groups are entitled to organise and to participate in inter-cultural and social events, such as lectures, exhibitions and television programmes, either through social and cultural institutions of their own or of the state, with the specific purpose of promoting cultural knowledge and understanding.
- To promote such knowledge and understanding, the state should, through the media, education and other institutions, provide the general public with opportunities to be educated about cultural diversity and minority cultures.
- Events and programmes that aim to generate and strengthen intercultural and inter-religious dialogue in all aspects of the public domain should be encouraged and made accessible to the general public.
- The state and public agencies should take all necessary steps to ensure as far as possible that minority groups are aware of the existence of this right and of the procedures involved. It is essential that the state (as well as the minorities) demonstrates willingness and good faith.

Four inter-related questions arise and must be addressed in detail. The first is: what does it mean exactly for groups collectively to hold this right as opposed to individual members holding it? I have already explained the difference between the group's *collectively held rights to state assistance and intervention* and the individual members' *individually held rights to state assistance and intervention* – namely, while the former aim to strengthen minority cultural structure and enable meaningful cultural autonomy, the latter serve the purpose of enabling (if not facilitating) integration into the wider society. The two rights to external dialogue against the state (the group's collective right on the one hand and individual members' individual right on the other) are different also in the same way – namely, the *group's collective right to external dialogue* serves the main purpose of enabling and communicating cultural expressions, of representing and presenting the group's values and collective identity to the outside world; the *individual members' individual right to external dialogue*, as will be demonstrated below, is intended to help the individuals express concerns and individual needs to the state and the wider society, especially but not only in case of internal conflict and oppression. In other words, the *collective right to external dialogue* and the *individual right to external dialogue* are pulling in opposite directions and serve oppositional purposes, with the specific aim of providing options and enabling choice. As will be shown in greater detail in Chapter 6, collectively held minority rights will be exercised on behalf of the membership by the group's internal decision-making bodies – which, of course, are made up of individuals.

The second question that must be addressed is whether minorities have a right to refuse dialogue. The short answer is 'yes.'[23] But, I will argue, minorities are highly unlikely to refuse communication and dialogue if good faith and willingness to engage in dialogue are demonstrated by the authorities and the rest of the population, and that if the principle of fairness of the dialogical processes is upheld. There are three claims to support this optimistic proposition.

Firstly, research has shown that people's willingness to comply with state policies and laws is shaped to a large extent by the degree of procedural fairness demonstrated by the authorities during the process of law and policy-making. When laws and policies are fairly and transparently made, they tend to gain widespread support even among those to whom the policies are not entirely acceptable.[24] Tom Tyler has identified two main factors that can determine voluntary acceptance and compliance: morality and legitimacy.[25] In other words, people are more likely to comply with a rule or a process if they think it is morally right, and if they think the authorities initiating that rule or process is legitimate and ought to be obeyed.[26] It should be significantly easier for the minorities to agree to engage in external dialogue than for them to

---

23   Also, to acknowledge minorities' right to external dialogue is not to determine how the rest of the population should respond to it.
24   Tom R. Tyler (ed.), *Procedural Justice*, Volume I (Ashgate, 2005), Chapter 16.
25   *Ibid.*, pp.391–392.
26   *Ibid.*

accept substantive state policies and laws. Not only do the minorities participate in the making and exercise of the rules ('the rules' being invitation/ requirement to engage in dialogue), but also that through participation they can evaluate for themselves whether the process is fair and just. Thus the 'legitimacy' criteria can be easily satisfied. And since the main goal of external dialogue is to enable collective cultural expression, mutual understanding and respect, the 'morality' criteria can also be easily satisfied.

The second claim to support the proposition is related to Rawls's notion of 'overlapping consensus,' which has already been examined in Chapter 2. The key question is whether, despite our cross-cultural differences, there can be a consensus about dialogue as a possible solution. Not everyone will choose to express themselves culturally through dialogue; nor will everyone agree on the criteria that define a fair dialogical process. As already established earlier, the focus of attention is now on *conflict resolution* – conflict between cultures, between interests, between interpretations and opinions, and between rights. The desired result of conflict resolution is of course *peace*. As Melissa Williams rightly points out:

> When peace is the motive, we look for those forms of living-together that are mutually acceptable, and are willing to accept the proposition that compromise has an appropriate place in our decision-making. The search for mutually acceptable arrangements does not presuppose that one or the other group's practices will prevail. Perhaps the solution that will be acceptable to both sides will be a moderated form of one group's practice; perhaps it will be a combination of both groups' practices; or perhaps the solution will be found in an entirely new practice. In the quest for peaceful accommodation none of this is prejudged.[27]

In other words, despite all differences, if peace-seeking and peace-keeping can form our 'overlapping consensus,' more constructive and creative forms of deliberative engagement between minorities and the majority are likely to emerge, which will have long lasting impacts and further increase willingness to engage in dialogue. Of course there will always be those who will refuse dialogue and disturb peace, which will leave the state with no choice but to restrict their activities and actions. But as a general issue, it seems that in many situations neither the state nor the minorities have expressed enough openness

---

27 Melissa S. Williams, *'Tolerable Liberalism,'* in Avigail Eisenberg &. Jeff Spinner-Halev (eds.), *Minorities within Minorities: Equality, Rights and Diversity* (Cambridge University Press, 2005), p.37.

to the other, enough curiosity, enough willingness to listen to and learn from each other. The collective right to external dialogue is intended to make this happen. And since most minority groups are by nature inwardly focused, they will require additional assistance – in the form of a right to external dialogue against the state – to really bring out their voice.

Yet, neither 'dialogue' nor 'peace' is a guaranteed solution let alone an immediate solution to problems. This is the third issue about the right to external dialogue that must be addressed – its limitations. Firstly, it can be extremely frustrating to kick start and maintain dialogue. It is frustrating to have to sort through a great multiplicity of views and opinions, which is likely to cause uncertainty and anxiety. Secondly, as David Bohm points out, what is widely considered to be 'dialogue' tends to focus on negotiation, which is in fact only the preliminary stage of the dialogical process, and not a sign of a meaningful close relationship.[28] There is no guarantee that the parties will ever move from this early stage onto genuine dialogue about the deeper issues. But then without the preliminary negotiations nothing more will ever happen. I shall make a few suggestions in the concluding chapter as to how to keep things going. Thirdly, on the part of the minorities, the meaningful exercise of the right depends on minority groups having reasonably representative and competent internal decision-making bodies, which are precisely what most of them lack. This will be examined in detail in Chapter 6.

The fourth and arguably the most important question that needs to be addressed is whether the collective right to external dialogue is 'all-inclusive.' There are two inter-connected but separate aspects to this question: Firstly, *what* should *not* be the subject matter of dialogue, if any? In other words, is there a limit to *what* can be discussed? Secondly, *who* is *not* entitled to the rights to dialogue, if any? In other words, is there a limit to *who* may be allowed to take part? The same questions apply to the two individually held rights to dialogue, which I shall examine in respective sections below. Once again, these questions concern the boundaries of toleration and hence the scope of inclusion. As established previously, without 'good cause,' the mere fact that certain views and practices are irrational, illiberal, or even ill-conceived is not reason enough for the state not to tolerate. In other words, the principle of toleration should hold generally except in circumstances where trumping considerations exist to render intolerance and exclusion permissible and justifiable.

Furthermore, as indicated at the beginning of the paragraph above, it is important to clearly distinguish between 'views' and 'holders of views,' and to specify what we mean by exclusion – in particular, exclusion *from what*. In the

---

28   David Bohm, *On Dialogue* (Routledge, 1996), p.21.

context of the collective right to external dialogue, exclusion means exclusion from the dialogical processes, from exercising the collective right to dialogue against the state. Thus, three inter-related questions need to be answered. As regards the 'views': firstly, can dialogue legitimately exclude certain views? If so, secondly, what are the criteria for exclusion/inclusion? And thirdly, what is the point of dialogue if not all views are included, publicly considered and debated? As regards the 'holders of the views,' the same questions apply: firstly, can dialogue legitimately exclude certain people? If so, secondly, what are the criteria for exclusion/inclusion? And thirdly, what is the point of dialogue if not all people are allowed to take part in the dialogical processes?

To successfully answer these questions requires us to look back to Rawls's notion of 'overlapping consensus' which was examined in Chapter 2. Rawls argues that peoples or groups with different *comprehensive* doctrines will be able to co-exist peacefully in one single society if they can develop an 'overlapping consensus,' agreeing to share a neutral, value-free *political conception* in the *public realm*, and to forgo the search for the domination of any one single particular *comprehensive* doctrine over all others.[29] This must not be taken to mean that a political society should have no ethical or moral foundation at all, but that such a foundation can be and should be based on a variety of norms, values, theories and justifications. In Rawls's own words, having an 'overlapping consensus' means in reality that '[a]s reasonable and rational, and knowing that they affirm a diversity of reasonable religious and philosophical doctrines, they should be ready to explain the basis of their actions to one another in terms each could reasonably expect that others might endorse as consistent with their freedom and equality.'[30] Furthermore, Rawls holds that reasonableness requires that 'on fundamental political matters, reasons given explicitly in terms of comprehensive doctrines are never to be introduced into public reason.'[31]

Chapter 2 raised, among others, the issue of incompatibility between Rawls's restricted version of liberalism and the values and practices of illiberal groups. While I shall not repeat the arguments here, particular attention will inevitably focus once again on illiberal groups in the following paragraphs. It is clear that Rawls talks about 'overlapping consensus' as a means to avoid conflict and achieve peace – not through meaningful interaction with or constructive understanding of each other – but through precisely the opposite, through

---

29   See Chapter 2 of this book; John Rawls, *Political Liberalism* (Columbia University Press, 1996).
30   *Ibid.*, p.218.
31   *Ibid.*, p.247.

skirting around the most fundamentally conflicting issues and letting it be, through *avoidance*. In so arguing, Rawls appears to be in favour of a *hands-off, substantive*, approach to the accommodation of seemingly unbridgeable differences. The context here, by contrast, is not about substantive principles of passively living with The Other, but about hands-on interaction through dialogue. It does concern Rawls's 'overlapping consensus,' but of a different kind – one that determines the inclusiveness of dialogue, one that is achieved through extensive interaction. The question is thus *not* whether illiberal values and practices should be tolerated *in general*, but rather whether they should be included and considered throughout *the dialogical processes*.

Can Dialogue Legitimately Exclude Certain Views or People?

Rawls is of the view that his notion of overlapping consensus refers only to *reasonable* doctrines endorsed by reasonable people – namely people who see society as a fair system of cooperation between free and equal participants, and who accept what Rawls calls the 'burdens of judgment' and reasonable pluralism.[32] These 'burdens of judgment' are factors which explain why persons in a diverse society are likely to hold different, often incompatible, conceptions of the good. These burdens include: 'difficulties in assessing evidence and difficulties in weighing it, indeterminacy of concepts and conflicts of interpretation, experiential and normative divergences, the diversity of values and variations in selecting and ordering them.'[33] Rawls sees these 'burdens of judgment' as the free use of human reason and an irreducible feature of liberal, diverse, democratic societies. And recognising the consequences of these burdens of judgment, Rawls holds, should lead us to relinquish the expectation to achieve a political community based on a comprehensive agreement amongst all values, beliefs, and convictions.

The key notions, therefore, seem to be 'conflict avoidance' and 'reasonable disagreement.' It is in this way that Rawls's overlapping consensus is a consensus only amongst reasonable people, in order to ensure that justice is not held hostage to the views and practices of the unjust and the unreasonable. Three key questions arise, which I shall address in turn. Firstly, what are the positive and indeed negative consequences of such a cautious conflict-avoidance approach? Secondly, is it ever right to pre-determine what can be included in dialogue before dialogue has actually taken place? And thirdly, will the inclusion in the dialogical processes of the usually excluded issues and persons

---

32   *Ibid.*, pp.54–60.
33   See Thomas McCarthy, *'Kantian Constructivism and Reconstructivism: Rawls and Habermas in Dialogue,'* in *Ethics* 105 (October 1994), pp.44–63, at p.58.

necessarily be divisive and detrimental to dialogue itself and the protection of minority rights?

This conflict-avoidance approach does have some advantages (albeit, I argue, mostly short-term and skin-deep). It is not hard to imagine that by not bringing up certain subjects of contention, some doctrinal conflicts can indeed be avoided. This of course is based on the assumption that doctrinal conflicts are irresolvable. At first sight, this conservative approach of concealment seems to be the safest method of conflict avoidance as there appears to be no risks involved, as no views, feelings or opinions are revealed or exchanged on that particular matter. Less exposure means less confrontation, less conflict. But just because certain views are not publicly expressed does not mean they are not continued to be held. Neither does it mean conflicts caused by these doctrinal differences are extinguished. Rather, they are merely muted in public and suppressed into the private sphere, within which those views continue to grow and differences continue to widen as misunderstanding, and lack of understanding, remain. It is in this way that divisive conflicts can be heightened by the limitations placed on what can or cannot be debated in public or in the political sphere.

Furthermore, Rawls himself is fully aware of the problems of his political liberalism and acknowledges that, if truly divisive issues are excluded from the public sphere (as he advocates), we will encounter great difficulties in measuring societal and political change.[34] We will have problems explaining, for example, how the abolition of slavery could have come about at that particular time in history. This realisation has led Rawls to put forward a more inclusive, what he considers to be a more 'correct'[35] version of public reason, which '[allows] citizens, in certain situations, to present what they regard as the basis of political values rooted in their comprehensive doctrine, provided they do this in ways that strengthen the ideal of public reason itself.'[36] I shall consider this more inclusive version of public reason in greater detail below. Apart from societal and political change, the exclusive conflict-avoidance approach will also have problems measuring change within the comprehensive views (which are far from static but constantly evolving) and therefore have difficulties measuring ideological trend and predict future directions, both of which are vital for effective conflict avoidance and management.

A further problem is that this very exclusive account of public reason makes it rather difficult for us to justify liberalism especially to those who do not

---

34 John Rawls, *Political Liberalism* (Columbia University Press, 1996), p.157 ff.
35 *Ibid.*, p.248.
36 *Ibid.*, p.247.

already share liberal values. I shall deal with this issue in greater detail later in this chapter when I move to answer the question 'what is the point of dialogue if not all are included?'. For the time being, it must be said that the dialogical spirit of this work determines that whether or not this conservative conflict-avoidance method is defensible and workable depends on whether it is used as a *permanent* method of disposing a matter or as a *temporary* means of buying time i.e. putting off a public, potentially heated and damaging, confrontation until later when enabling opportunities present themselves. Common reading of Rawls's political liberalism seems to favour the former – i.e. the motivation behind Rawls's assertion that 'reasons given explicitly in terms of comprehensive doctrines are never to be introduced into public reason'[37] seems to be *permanent* elimination of issues of comprehensive doctrinal differences from the public sphere. This leads me to consider the second question presented above – is it ever right to pre-determine what can or cannot be included in dialogue before dialogue has actually taken place?

The short answer is 'no.' It is important to note that the dialogical approach introduced in this book, like Rawls's political liberalism, also favours an approach that does not aim to generate agreement on all issues, but it proceeds rather differently than Rawls in getting limited agreements on issues of common concern. The dialogical approach may very well involve, just like Rawls's political liberalism, avoiding certain issues over which people fundamentally disagree. But unlike Rawls's approach which places the emphasis on deciding *in advance* what can or cannot be part of public debate and dialogue, the dialogical approach is about establishing and firmly adhering to theoretical and practical principles that govern dialogue and public reason. Conflict avoidance is indeed one of the key principles under this approach, but it is employed as a temporary method to buy time and enable continuous dialogue rather than a permanent means of disposal of certain views. Under this more inclusive account, what matters is not *whether* matters of doctrinal differences can be publicly expressed, but rather *how* they are publically expressed.

There are many reasons behind this approach. Firstly, it recognises the need to develop essential skills to exchange views and opinions with people who do not already share ours, and to hear, consider and take into account of theirs in an increasingly inter-connected and inter-dependent society. Secondly and importantly, it recognises the fact that issues of fundamental doctrinal differences come in many forms and can be expressed in many different ways. What needs compromising is not necessarily those doctrinally

---

37   *Ibid.*

conflicting views themselves but rather the means of expressing and realising them, and especially how those views are employed politically. This is not to say that *all* doctrinally conflicting issues should be included and considered in public reason, not least because *some* comprehensive views are harmful and dangerous either to society at large or particular groups of people (e.g. racism, gender segregation). But the correct way of dealing with these views and issues is not to suppress them into the private sphere where they may continue to grow strong in silence, but to let them be confronted and worked out in the processes of democratic politics, in public reason, in dialogue. Indeed, some would argue that public reason and democratic politics may be endangered by such views and practices. But they may also be enabled and enhanced by them. The key point is that there is simply no guarantee either way. What kind of a place these views and practices will occupy in public reason and democratic politics can and should only be worked out in the very context and practice of public reason and democratic politics itself – theoretically, pragmatically, and contextually – being subject to the conditions and rules of dialogue. This practice always carries the risk of intensifying conflict and chaos, which no democratic theory or dialogical process could ever eliminate, let alone the elimination of the very practice of democracy and dialogue itself.

This leads to the third and related reason behind this more inclusive approach, namely that a less restricted account of public reason will not *necessarily* be divisive and detrimental to dialogue and minority rights protection. Public expression of doctrinal differences could indeed lead to conflict and division, but many aspects of conflict and division can be managed, not least because the cause of division is as much the *reaction* to those differences as the *expression* of them, especially how these differences are socially and politically employed. Once again the focus of attention is on the *processes,* on *interaction.* I wish to tackle this issue in three stages.

1st Stage

Firstly, it is very important to realise that a divisive issue is distinguishable from a mere difference of opinion, as the latter (which is common and inevitable in any context) can easily be misinterpreted, exaggerated and therefore perceived as the former, intentionally or unintentionally, in processes of democratic politics and dialogue. A divisive issue is a source of tension and conflict in any social or political context among different people and interest parties. There is a wide range of divisive issues, covering all spheres of life, especially politics, economics, culture, education and social policies, etc. Understandably what is divisive very much depends on the context within which those issues are situated. But what all divisive issues have in common is that they all relate to matters of considerable importance to the well-being and advancement of certain groups or persons, be they political, social, cultural, or material well-being and advancement. Such issues are often phrased in highly emotional terms, based on historical claims, and related to entitlements to certain human, minority or group rights – conflicting interpretations and understandings of which tend to hugely complicate the matter. In reality, however, the line between a divisive issue and a mere difference of opinion cannot easily be drawn. It is often a matter of degree and the boundaries are fluid.

2nd Stage
Once we acknowledge this important but subtle distinction between a divisive issue and a mere difference of opinion, we should be able to say with greater certainty that the inclusion in the dialogical processes of seemingly doctrinally conflicting issues will not necessarily be divisive or detrimental to dialogue itself and the protection of minority rights. To the contrary, it is necessary and beneficial to dialogue and unity if managed properly. Not all doctrinally conflicting issues are conflicting to the same degree or in the same form. If we can keep the sometimes subtle distinction between divisive issues and differences of opinion in mind during processes of democratic politics and dialogue, some doctrinal conflicts to a lesser degree *may* begin to appear more as differences of opinion than doctrinally divisive issues. And since we tend to much more readily tolerate, accept, and thus co-exist with 'differences of opinion' than with 'divisive issues,' we might be able to better handle these less conflicting issues. This must not be misunderstood as saying *all* 'divisive issues' can be reduced to mere 'differences of opinion' – rather, it is a warning against equating 'doctrinal conflicts' with 'absolute truth claims,' and especially against treating *all* doctrinal conflicts as the same.

Rawls would exclude the public expression of 'absolute truth claims,' or 'fundamental convictions' (save those of political liberalism, whose claim to truth yields to the claim to 'reasonableness,' which Rawls seems to equate with 'reasonable disagreement' in the context of public reason and democratic politics). He rightly claims that the practice and expression of absolute truth claims and fundamental convictions, which tend to give rise to the strongest doctrinal conflicts, tend towards self-righteousness, are ones that one is neither able nor willing to rationally justify, which is precisely what makes them 'fundamental' and 'absolute,' and therefore unfitting in democratic politics which functions on the basis of reasoning, justification, and most importantly, compromise. Similarly, Hannah Arendt is also against the inclusion of fundamental convictions in public reason, arguing that the nature of such convictions means that they tend to preclude all debate and reasoning.[38] Thus whilst Rawls fears conflict, Arendt fears silence, though the causes of their seemingly oppositional concerns are both the absolutist nature of fundamental convictions. Yet, even for these absolutist claims, which cannot easily be reduced to mere differences of opinion, their inclusion in public reason may not be harmful but may even be beneficial to dialogue, the practice of democratic politics and the protection of minority rights. It will be particularly beneficial to those marginalised minority groups who tend to favour an emotive, rhetorical, less logical and less analytical mode of public discourse.[39] By allowing them to rely on what they consider to be the whole truth, public discourse becomes less demanding and more inclusive.

3rd Stage

But *whether* or not their inclusion may be beneficial depends on *how* they are included. It is essential to recognise that inclusion requires effort and cooperation from both sides. Instead of seeing inclusion as the sole responsibility of the democratic system and dialogical processes, minorities, those who make absolute truth claims and hold absolutist values, must make a conscious effort in order to have themselves and their views included. In this respect, I shall consider two questions in detail: firstly, on the part of the claim holders, is it ever possible to hold on to absolute claims while mastering the art of political compromise? Secondly, what changes, if any, must take place on the part of democratic and dialogical processes in order to accommodate absolute truth claims?

As regards the first question, if we are indeed to include all issues including absolute truth claims in the processes of dialogue, it is essential that all parties observe a basic requirement of reasonableness and are constantly aware of the danger of absolutism. It is important to note that this is not necessarily a requirement to realise the danger of the absolute *convictions* themselves (though they are indeed dangerous in most people's opinion), but rather a requirement to recognise the danger of *expressing* these convictions in an absolutist manner in political and dialogical processes. Though it is highly questionable whether it is ever possible to express absolutist convictions in a non-absolutist manner, this requirement is feasible in the present context. Holders of absolute convictions should be reminded during dialogical

---

38   Hannah Arendt, *Truth and Politics*, The New Yorker, February 25 1967, p.49, at: http://www.newyorker.com/magazine/1967/02/25/truth-and-politics.

39   See, for example, Iris Marion Young, *Inclusion and Democracy* (Oxford University Press, 2000), Chapter 2.

processes that, although observing this basic requirement of reasonableness should lead all parties to demonstrate some degree of willingness to compromise, it does *not* require them to give up their absolute convictions (though it may happen); rather, it requires them to be willing to fine-tune how they express and pursue the realisation of their convictions. In other words, the requirement is a procedural one, not a substantive one. Should they consider it to be in their best interest to participate in dialogue and so wish to be included, they should be willing to adopt a reasonably, or even only minimally, reflexive and accommodating attitude, demonstrating 'dialogical reasonableness' and 'dialogical correctness.' It is their choice.

Holders of absolute convictions could also be reminded that, by adopting such an attitude, they in fact have a better chance of spreading their convictions. Hence, it is by separating the *absolute convictions* from their *means of expression and realisation* that it *may* become possible for those who hold absolute truth claims to learn to make political compromises and yet continue to hold on to those claims. It is very important to note that anyone's sense of political and dialogical correctness can only be generated in the very process of making political and cultural claims. Thus it is not certain *views* that should be excluded from the very beginning *before* dialogue has actually taken place, but rather those *persons* who refuse to compromise *during* dialogue and *while* public expression is taking place. This is in fact consistent with Rawls's less known, more inclusive, view of public reason, namely that comprehensive doctrines should be admissible provided that they are presented in ways that strengthen the ideal of public reason itself.'[40]

As regards the second question, it is difficult to specify an exclusive list of political and democratic conditions that may enable the accommodation of absolute truth claims. But given the potential of intensifying conflict and further division, the focus should clearly be on dialogue enablement and management. Two related questions ought to be considered: What should happen during these dialogical processes to avoid further division, if possible? What are the signs of good dialogue management?

The 'dialogical processes' that we are concerned with here can consist of several forms, some are more political, coercive, organised and systemic, others less so and more to do with common sense and 'everyday sensitivity' so to speak. Relatedly, the precise means of dialogue may also vary, e.g. face to face or over the internet. While the aim of this book has been to develop and defend a dialogical concept and theory of minority rights, it is essential to realise that concepts and theories can get in the way of practice. This is not at all to deny

---

40 See John Rawls, *Political Liberalism* (Columbia University Press, 1996), pp.247–248.

that good practice must have its basis in sound concepts and theories, or that it is helpful to articulate norms and standards about how we should go about dialoguing; rather, it is to acknowledge that since all concepts and theories are to some extent detached from the practical context, it is important that when laying down rules of dialogue, we make extra efforts to ensure as far as possible that the dialogical concept and theory of dialogue do not get in the way of dialogue itself.

What this means in practice is that: firstly, dialogical processes should consist of *dialogue about dialogue*, which has the specific purpose of consciously and continuously engaging all relevant parties in conversations about how best to keep dialogue going when dialogue is already taking place, and addressing the deficit of dialogue before it leads to the development of misunderstanding and conflict. In other words, the most important task of *dialogue about dialogue* is, through observing past and on-going dialogical processes, evaluating, correcting and renewing principles and rules of dialogue. This requires conscious engagement rather than mere sharing for the sake of sharing without any thought.

What, then, secondly, are the principles and rules of dialogue? Intercultural dialogue of the type that we are concerned with should be governed by fundamental moral principles and practical rules that are built on the foundation of the ethics of reciprocity or mutuality. It is impossible to provide a definite list of rules that are applicable in all situations, but as mentioned earlier, all parties must demonstrate a certain level of communicative reasonableness and dialogical correctness. This principle of reciprocal restraint regularises cooperation, however minimal, and dampens rivalry, however fierce, aiming to consciously create and maintain a space of dialogical stillness in which views may be expressed fully and honestly with minimal expressions of blame or demands, and in which reflection and dissolution may be formed. This, arguably, is idealistic expectation, especially considering it is the expression of absolute truth claims that we are concerned with. While recognising that this goal is likely to remain hard to reach, it is nevertheless reasonable to say that the more closely the parties involved in a dialogical process are able to adhere to this principle of reciprocal restraint, the nearer the process will be to being effective and ideal, though in reality all dialogical processes must suffer imperfections, setbacks, and irremovable obstacles. Yet, it is also reasonable to expect that as long as the desire to express and to engage in dialogue is strong enough, moving towards this distant goal, however slowly and reluctantly, is possible.

A related second principle is that, when it comes to the precise means or activities of dialogue, especially if we are to include absolute truth claims in dialogical processes, we ought to promote face-to-face interaction, *real* moments of meeting, and rely less on distant, say, internet, engagement. The rationale is as follows: by enabling and encouraging fast expression and instant response, internet interaction gives the wrong impression that dialogue takes only words and does not require careful digestion or thoughtful evaluation of information. A serious side-effect is the lack of attention and sensitivity, both of which should come from common sense and are critical for meaningful dialogue. This is not to say that internet communication should be abandoned entirely (nor is it ever possible); neither is it to claim that there is no hope for effective internet communication when it comes to bringing together people and groups of conflicting views. Rather, it is to recognise that the goals of dialogue cannot be achieved instantly or thoughtlessly.

It should be noted that while only face-to-face interaction and online engagement have been mentioned here, there is neither limit nor consensus on the sorts of activities dialogue can consist of, or cannot consist of. While one can speak of dialogue as one particular kind of conversation realised through some particular means, it is also possible to define it in more general terms as encompassing a broad range of conversations, activities, and means, all with the specific purpose of bringing about better relations and enhanced understanding. This diversity of possible activities and means of dialogue is an important point for both theorists and practitioners to bear in mind if we are to avoid embarking on dialogue in a culturally insensitive and thoughtless manner. In particular, it is essential for all to realise that what we see as an obvious and preferred means of dialogue may not be familiar or appealing to people of a different cultural background, with whom we seek to engage. And it is only through dialogue that we can discover what their preferred means might be.

This leads to the third related principle that should govern dialogical processes, namely that to prevent thoughtless and culturally insensitive dialogue, conditions and rules ought to be in place. First and foremost, one must speak honestly and defends only what one sincerely believes to be the truth. Neutrality is neither required nor desirable, and emotion is natural and conveys important messages. Secondly, it is important to avoid ambiguous and contradictory expressions and stick to the common meaning, the 'common language' that everyone speaks and understands. Yet, thirdly, dialogue must not be rigid – room for doubt and error is both necessary and beneficial and must not only be allowed but should also be maintained. Fourthly, all parties involved ought to demonstrate sensitivity towards diversity and openly endorse an obligation to listen and consider. It should be noted that, fifthly, although dialogue presumes and requires equality among all involved, it is not an equality of power as such, which is neither necessary nor possible. Rather, it is an equality of opportunity to take part in dialogue, based on demonstration of willingness to participate.

What this means is that, sixthly, anyone willing and competent to take part in dialogue should be allowed to, in theory. In practice though, while willingness might be easy to establish, difficulty will arise as to how competence may be judged. While there is competence in a general sense, there are also matter-specific and context-specific kinds of competence, associated with specific means of dialogue, skills and capacities. Seventhly, when dialogue is on-going, it is essential to keep separation of concerns in mind and not to mix issues together. Those taking part in dialogue tend to be more clear-headed when they can be specific and present in the concrete reality. One demonstration of being specific is that, eighthly, the best as well as worst outcomes of dialogue need to be anticipated, stated and discussed during the dialogical processes, with the specific purpose of helping those involved realise the best as well as the worst-case scenario. Once the limits are drawn, it becomes easier to anticipate how to achieve good and avoid bad, what good might be achieved and what bad might occur. Lastly, it is essential for those involved in dialogue to have a sense of the common good in mind, though selflessness is not at all a requirement.

By way of concluding this part, the arguments made so far must not be misinterpreted as saying that the dialogical concept demands *all-inclusiveness*. It does not. It demands *maximum* inclusiveness. As previously pointed out, some views and persons ought to be excluded as they are harmful to public reason and dialogue itself. This is a familiar territory for political theorists, especially liberal theorists, who have done a lot of work on the so-called 'intolerable.'[41] The mainstream liberal view is that unreasonable doctrines and practices which contradict the fundamental values of a liberal democratic society ought to be excluded by public reason. This does not mean that adherents to those doctrines and practices are not entitled to basic rights and benefits, only that they ought not to be part of the public discourse that determines what those rights and benefits should be.[42] This liberal conception of toleration is too narrow for the dialogical concept, the spirit of which requires us to be aware that people who are generally reasonable may sometimes make unreasonable or

---

41   See, for instance, D.D. Raphael, *'The intolerable,'* in Susan Mendus (ed.), *Justifying Toleration: Conceptual and Historical Perspectives* (Cambridge University Press, 2009[1988]), p.137.

42   They will inevitably be part of the internal constituency that determines rights and benefits within the group to which they belong. I shall examine this in detail in later chapters.

harmful requests, and vice versa. The goals of dialogue are to enhance understanding, establish trust, gain recognition and further communication. It is those who cannot adhere to the dialogical rules that aim at these goals, and during dialogical processes hinder the advancement of these purposes and goals, should be excluded from dialogue. Their exclusion does not weaken the point of dialogue. It enhances it.

2 Minority Rights Held by *Members* of the Group against the *State*

This is the less controversial branch of minority rights under the dialogical account, and I shall spend less time on it. I aim to answer four main questions in the remaining sections though not necessarily in the following order. Firstly, what are these individually held minority rights? Secondly, what purposes does this branch of rights serve which cannot be served by the *collective* rights? Thirdly, to what extent, if at all, can the minority rights regime entrench these individually held minority rights as well as the collectively held ones – in other words – can the two types of minority rights co-exist within the same legal discourse and form complementary components of a solution? And fourthly, since the co-existence of individual and collective minority rights is unlikely to be peaceful, how might the inevitable conflicts be managed and resolved?

(1) *Individually Held* Rights to Cultural Belonging

As shown in the diagram, this branch of individually held minority rights consists of three sub-categories: rights to cultural belonging, rights to state assistance and appropriate intervention, and a right to external dialogue. The existence of this branch of individually held rights is rendered necessary primarily by the observation that 'cultural freedom' is multi-layered, in that a group's *collective freedom* to practise its culture is not the same as its members' *individual freedom* to practise their culture, although they are interdependent and overlap in many respects. As shown in previous sections, one troubling fact which defenders of collective rights cannot argue away is that the group's 'collective cultural freedom' is sometimes exercised at the expense of group members' certain freedoms. In other words, it is sometimes the case that the freer the collectivity is culturally speaking, the less free the individual members are culturally speaking, which is evidence that cultural needs are enormous and diverse and cannot be sufficiently satisfied collectively. The multi-layered dialogical concept of minority rights addresses this issue. Broadly speaking, the *existing* minority rights regime provides for the following rights to cultural belonging:

- Members of minority groups have the right to freely participate in their cultural life and assert their cultural identity, and to express themselves culturally without interference from the state. These include but are not limited to the right to use their own language, the right to an interpreter in court proceedings, (in the case of religious minorities) the right to be educated in schools of their own faith, and the right to take part in their own cultural and religious activities.
- The state must take positive steps to protect such free participation in minority cultural life from interference from others, be they state authorities, individuals, other groups, or corporations.
- Members of cultural minority groups have the right to non-discrimination and equal treatment when it comes to their cultural identity and practices. In other words, members of minority groups should be able to identify themselves as such without facing inequality in a range of areas related to public and private life, and that the state must not, in its policy and action, favour members of particular groups over others.

These are the best known broad categories of rights to cultural belonging of members of minority groups held by them *as individuals*. But clearly, collective and individual cultural rights are intertwined and not always easily separable. For instance, the *individual* right to *be educated* in schools of one's own faith depends on the group's *collective* right to *establish* faith schools. And the rights to practise one's own cultural and religion and to speak one's own language are held and exercised both collectively and individually. But this is not what I will focus on here. Evidently, the law in the area of minority cultural rights is unquestionably one-sided. This phenomenon, in my view, has been brought about by a determinist understanding of culture, cultural belonging and cultural autonomy, which has already been looked at in detail in Chapter 2. Since no right exists in a vacuum, in order to realistically understand the implications and impact of having certain rights, it is necessary to interpret them in conjunction with their co-existing rights which might enhance or conflict with them.

Freedoms of expression and association are fundamental human rights which apply to all irrespective of cultural backgrounds. But freedoms to express and to associate only make sense if there are corresponding freedoms *not* to express and *not* to associate. Consider this in conjunction with the above listed minority rights, we will reach the conclusion that members of cultural minority groups should not only have the right to participate in cultural practices of the group, they should also have the right *not* to participate; they should not only have the right to attend schools of their own faith but also the right to choose *not* to; they should not only have the right to use their own language but also the right *not* to. The individualistic notions of freedom and autonomy upon which the human rights system is built mean that the choice element is embedded, but not explicitly expressed. In the case of minority rights, I argue, the cultural freedoms *not* to participate ought to be emphasised and expressly stated in relevant documents. Thus, to achieve this, *in addition to* the existing individually held minority rights, the dialogical account contains also the following rights *against the state*: rights to state assistance and appropriate intervention, and the individually held right to external dialogue.

(2)   *Rights to State Assistance and Appropriate Intervention*

As detailed previously in the section on collectively held rights to state assistance, it is not always possible to make a sharp distinction between rights to collective self-determination and to state assistance, for the implementation of the former necessarily requires the latter.[43] By the same token, the individual rights to cultural belonging and the individual rights to state assistance and appropriate intervention are also interdependent. For instance, where it might be threatened, the right to freely practise one's own culture and religion cannot be realised unless the state takes steps to ensure it.

I have already argued earlier that the group as a collectivity and members of the group as individuals require different kinds of state assistance and intervention. Whilst the collective right to state assistance aims at strengthening collective cultural autonomy and independence, the individual members' right to state assistance emphasises on helping them integrate into the wider society when and where necessary. In other words, while the *collective right to state assistance* (together with the collective rights to self-determination and the individual rights to cultural belonging) affirms and strengthens cultural identity, and maintains the minority cultural structure and atmosphere, the *individual right to state assistance* (together with the rights to dialogue, the right to internal equality, and the right of exit) provides options, channels and opportunities of connecting to the outside world, and thereby counterbalances the constraining effects of the collectively held rights.

With these in mind, provisions of individual rights to state assistance under this dialogical account should be worded along these lines:

---

43   See Part 1 sub-section (3) of this Chapter.

- If they so wish, members of minority groups are free to choose *not to participate* in cultural practices of the group to which they belong, and the state should ensure as far as possible that no negative consequences may ensue as a result of such a choice. The cultural autonomy of the individual must be recognised and protected.[44]
- When and where such needs arise, the state should adopt positive measures to ensure, as far as possible, the *integration* of members of minority groups into the larger society, through, for instance, preferential educational policies. Affirmative action, however, must not amount to *forced* assimilation.
- Members of minority groups have the individually held right to *external dialogue* with the state.[45] The state must take necessary steps to guarantee opportunities and to establish and maintain channels of communication.
- In the event that all lines of communication and dialogue (external as well as internal) have failed and the individual is forced to exercise the right of exit,[46] the state should act promptly and efficiently to provide necessary transformative accommodation to enable transition.[47]

(3) *Individual Right to External Dialogue*

As already argued above, the two rights to external dialogue against the state (the group's collective right on the one hand and individual members' individual right on the other) serve different purposes. Whilst the former aims to enable and to communicate cultural expressions, to represent and present the group' values and collective identity to the outside world, the latter is intended mainly to help individual members express concerns and their individual needs to the state and the wider society, especially but not only in case of internal conflict and oppression. Their first point of contact can be social services or any public agency. This right may be formulated along the following lines:

- Members of minority groups, as individuals, have the right to initiate and to participate in constructive dialogue with the state and the rest of the society, with the specific purpose of getting their voices heard, expressing their

---

44   As will be shown in Chapter 5, apart from these rights held against the state, individual members also have the right to equal concern, the right to internal dialogue, and the right of exit, all three of which are held against the group and can be activated in cases of internal coercion and cultural dissent.
45   See sub-section (3) below for more details.
46   Detailed examination in Chapter 5.
47   This task can only be accomplished if the state shares duties and burdens with the minority group in question. This will also be examined in detail in Chapter 5.

individual needs, voicing concerns and demands regarding their cultural autonomy and well-being, and especially articulating their concerns about internal cultural pressures or practices.
- The state and public agencies have the duty to take all necessary steps to enable minority members' exercise of their right to external dialogue, and provide necessary support services, identify and remove obstacles that discourage or prevent minority members from exercising the right.
- The state and public agencies must take all necessary steps to ensure as far as possible that members of minority groups are aware of the existence of this right and of the procedures involved. They must not operate on the assumption that minority members are fully aware of their rights and options.
- When and where necessary, the state and public agencies should take all necessary steps to provide guarantees of privacy and anonymity, which are of crucial importance in cases of internal coercion.
- It is the duty of the state and the relevant public agencies to ensure that the minority member who is exercising the right stays informed regarding the professional assistance he/she is entitled to, the procedure, and progress of the case.
- Cultural sensitivity must be demonstrated at all times on the part of the state and the public agencies during the entire process. It must not be taken as an opportunity to denounce, to convert, or to impose values of one's own.[48]
- In cases where children and people with disabilities are involved, the state and relevant public agencies must ensure, during the entire process, the provision of special professional support, dedicated facilities, and a safe environment.
- Upon completion of the process, it is the duty of the state and the relevant public agencies to carefully review all relevant facts of the case, and pay special attention to the minority member's personal circumstances, if any, before deciding on further action.

3 Conclusion

It has been the main task of this chapter to reconceptualise the existing concept of minority rights by – firstly, formally endorsing and internalising the

---

[48] This will require the state and public agencies to provide training and continuous professional support on minority rights, cultural diversity, and cross-cultural communication to members of staff.

notion of group rights to reflect the collective aspect of cultural identity which cannot be adequately protected by individual rights; secondly, making a clearer distinction between collective rights and individual rights while acknowledging that they tend to overlap and are often interdependent; and thirdly, formally endorsing, defending, and distinguishing between two separate but related rights to external dialogue, i.e. the group's collectively held right to external dialogue, and the members' individually held right to external dialogue, and by doing so directing attention to the fact that the minorities' need to relate is just as strong as their need to be distinct. The existing minority rights law, as I have detailed, is one-sided in that it predominantly emphasises the latter and has largely failed to consider the former.

This is indeed the key advantage of (this branch of) the dialogical concept of minority rights – that it more accurately and more tentatively reflects the needs and demands of minority groups and their members, which are not only enormous but also diverse. I have also demonstrated in places how different minority rights interact and conflict with each other. I shall examine this issue in greater detail at the end of Chapter 5 once I have fleshed out the other branch of minority rights under this dialogical account, i.e. 'rights against the minority group,' held by individual members of the group.

CHAPTER 5

Rights against the Minority Group

In the previous chapter, I examined the minority rights held against the state under the dialogical account. I argued against a determinist understanding of culture and cultural belonging, and especially against a conventional hands-off approach to substantive collective rights claims which, in my view, is falsely viewed by many as the most effective if not the only means of protecting group identity and autonomy. I have argued that autonomy and independence in the context of minority rights *must not* mean establishing and maintaining arbitrary boundaries, especially if the group in question lacks the necessary self-governing capacities.

In this chapter, I turn to examine the second limb of minority rights under this dialogical account: individually held rights against *the minority group*, which consist of three separate but related rights: the right to equal concern, the right to internal dialogue, and the right of exit. These rights are held only by the members of the minority group as individuals and not by the group as a collectivity. Discussions on legitimate state intervention will continue here, focusing largely on the position and treatment of the so-called 'minorities within minorities.' The aim is adequately to address the troubling connections between internal oppression and group autonomy, between restrictions on human freedom and cultural belonging, between gender inequality and cultural preservation. Attention will inevitably focus on the treatment of illiberal groups, which can be further divided into two sub-categories: *non*-liberal groups, and *anti*-liberal groups. Particular attention is paid to the so-called *'right to stay'* suggested by some political theorists, and why, I argue, it must be re-formulated as *'the right to internal dialogue,'* and how.

1 Why is this Limb of Minority Rights Necessary?

As already argued in Chapter 3, this sub-category of rights is an essential component of the dialogical notion of minority rights for a variety of reasons, which I will not re-state here.[1] I also looked at freedom to associate in the context of minority rights and relabelled it 'the right to cultural belonging.' Freedom to associate only makes sense if there is a corresponding freedom not

---

1 See Chapter 3, Part 3.

to associate. Freedom not to associate could have various meanings and degrees. It could mean liberty to leave the group once and for all; it could also mean liberty to depart from the mainstream teachings and beliefs of the group while retaining group membership. The former is often formulated as 'the right of exit,'[2] and the latter simply 'the right to remain.' This binary formulation is problematic – it does not capture what lies in between. Three inter-related points have been strongly emphasised in previous chapters. The first is that cultural belonging is essential in shaping a person's identity and thus must be valued and protected. The second is that, despite the importance of cultural belonging, cultural boundaries are to varying degrees fluid and the nature of culture to varying degrees ever-changing, thus a determinist understanding of culture and cultural belonging is simply wrong. The third point is that it is unwise to view culture as something one can readily pick up or disregard.

There is a diversity of interpretations of different types of human rights, but on balance, rights, minority rights, especially minority cultural rights have often been formulated and interpreted as emphasising, even exaggerating, differences and ignoring similarities, and thereby creating, maintaining and accentuating distance between nations, between cultural communities, between some members of the group and the rest. We ought to find a balance, a middle course, between cultural belonging and individuals' rights and freedom. This middle course must be one that affirms cultural community and the sense of cultural belonging, but *a particular form* of cultural community and *a particular sense* of cultural belonging. Recent development in the field has witnessed a version of multiculturalism that focuses on the individual's 'exit right' as a form of protection against internal oppression and undue pressures. As shown in Chapter 2, while hard multiculturalists want all cultural communities to be left alone to live and develop as far as possible, they do nevertheless emphasise that individual members must be free to leave the group if they so wish.

However, many political theorists have criticised exit rights as offering insufficient and unrealistic protection. Anne Phillips, for instance, has provided us with a comprehensive analysis of the 'right of exit,' and gives several sets of reasons why, while it sounds good in theory, it might not work in reality.[3] Firstly, the conditions that make the right of exit realisable are often absent, which renders it a paper guarantee, an empty promise.[4] To make exit a realistic option, many requirements need to be satisfied: the person in question must

---

2   See, for example, Anne Phillips, *Multiculturalism Without Culture* (Princeton University Press, 2007), Chapter 5.
3   *Ibid.*
4   *Ibid.*, p. 138.

be properly equipped to lead a life outside of the group, financially and psychologically; he/she must be able to overcome the fear of losing his/her cultural identity and being cut off from family and friends.[5] It is thus hardly surprising that, for many, the option of exit is not really an option, as, in Jacob Levy's words, 'everything about a culture is an exit barrier. To have a culture whose exit is entirely costless [is] to have no culture at all.'[6] Unless all other means have been exhausted, it is unlikely that people will voluntarily *choose* to exit.

This is the second set of difficulties associated with exit: not everyone wants to leave, largely but not merely due to the likely unbearable financial and emotional costs, but also that many would wish to challenge the mainstream teachings of the group *from within* without having to risk their group membership being taken away. It thus seems that although 'the right of exit' plays an important role in theories on multiculturalism and minority rights, it alone is insufficient. A disproportionately heavy reliance on exit right can once again be attributed to an essentialist and non-interventionist understanding of multiculturalism and minority rights,[7] against which I have argued throughout the book. The dialogical spirit of this work demands a decisive departure from the determinist approach, which means, conceptually, rephrasing the empty and substantive 'right to remain' as the *'right to equal concern'* and the *'right to internal dialogue,'* and institutionally, reflecting this conceptual shift in governmental and organisational set-up and design.

2   The Right to Equal Concern

Equal concern (or 'qual respect', 'qual consideration') is a very abstract concept and can mean many different things to many different people. In *A Theory of Justice*, John Rawls accepts a distinction between two conceptions of equality:

> Some writers have distinguished between equality as it is invoked in connection with the distribution of certain goods [...] and equality as it applies to the respect which is owed to persons irrespective of their social

---

5   Ibid.
6   Jacob Levy, *The Multiculturalism of Fear* (Oxford University Press, 2000), p. 112; Anne Phillips, *Multiculturalism Without Culture* (Princeton University Press, 2007), p. 138; see also Leslie Green's consideration of the exit argument in *'Internal Minorities and Their Rights,'* in Will Kymlicka (ed.), *The Rights of Minority Cultures* (Oxford University Press, 1995), pp. 264–266.
7   As is the case with strong autonomy and self-determination rights, as presented in previous chapters.

position. Equality of the first kind is defined by the second principle of justice [...] But equality of the second kind is fundamental. It is defined by the first principle of justice and by such natural duties as that of mutual respect; it is owed to human beings as moral persons.[8]

The right to equal concern and respect, which derives from the general principle of equality, can be said to be the fundamental concept of Rawls's theory of justice, and his 'original position' aims to enforce it in the design of political institutions and arrangements. Dworkin, in *Taking Rights Seriously*, makes a similar distinction between two rights to equality – the right to *equal treatment*, which he describes as 'the right to an equal distribution of some opportunity or resource or burden,' and the right to *treatment as an equal*, which is 'the right to be treated with the same respect and concern as anyone else.'[9] Like Rawls, Dworkin also sees the second right as fundamental and the first derivative and therefore restrictive.[10] A potential difficulty in applying Rawls's and Dworkin's theory in the context of minority groups is that the fundamental assumption of their theory seems to be the assumption of liberalism – in other words, the protection of the right to equal concern and respect requires a liberal constitution. But most minority groups are not liberal institutions, and I have already discussed in previous chapters the danger and impracticality of attempting to liberalise non-liberal minority groups. I shall further demonstrate in the section below that a certain degree of paternalism and an emphasis on tradition rather than autonomy may well be compatible with the requirements of human well-being, which should be our main concern.

So what exactly does the right to equal concern entail *in the context of minority members' claims against their group?* It clearly does *not* entail *identical* treatment in general: it does not entail an absolutely equal, the same, distribution of opportunities, material resources, goods, or indeed duties and responsibilities. But it does entail equal treatment as regards maintaining at least *minimal* reasonable standards of living and at least *basic* standards of welfare. It also entails that in the group's internal decision-making processes one's needs and interests be treated as sympathetically and as fully as the needs and interests of any other member of the group. It also entails that individual members of the group have a right to equal concern in the design, administration and reform of the group's internal decision-making mechanisms. Very importantly, a right to equal concern is also owed to individuals irrespective of

---

8   John Rawls, *A Theory of Justice* (Harvard University Press, 1971), p. 511.
9   Ronald Dworkin, *Taking Rights Seriously* (Harvard University Press, 1977), p. 227.
10 *Ibid.*

their social position and background to guarantee access to and meaningful participation in processes of *internal dialogue* with the group. It is true that, in Dworkin's words,

> the right to treatment as an equal must be taken to be fundamental [...], and that the more restrictive right to equal treatment holds only in those special circumstances in which, for some special reason, it follows from the more fundamental right.[11]

3   Well-being, Happiness, and the Right to Internal Dialogue

What is 'well-being' and how is it relevant here? There are two main approaches to individual well-being. One is the *objective* well-being approach, which emphasises socially determined requirements for a good life; the other is the *subjective* well-being approach, which emphasises an individual's own assessment of their level and degree of well-being. While these two perspectives are often considered to be oppositional, in reality they are inseparable and often combined. In psychology, philosophy and sociology, well-being is a convenient umbrella term sheltering both *objective* well-being and *subjective* well-being, and the dividing line between the two types is not always clear. Well-being, generally speaking, is most commonly described in philosophy as 'what is non-instrumentally or ultimately good for a person,'[12] and is 'bound up with ideas about what constitutes human happiness and the sort of life it is good to lead,'[13] at least some aspects of which, e.g. the psychological aspect, are highly *subjective*.[14] Quality of life, on the other hand, might simply be defined as the *degree* of well-being felt by individuals or by groups of individuals, which, unlike standard of living, cannot easily be measured and which are again, at least some aspects of which are highly *subjective.*

Although it is beyond the scope of this chapter to consider in great detail theories of well-being, it is essential to examine some of the findings, conclusions and complexities as they shed important light on the dialogical notion of

---

11   Ibid., p. 273.
12   See 'well-being' in Stanford Encyclopaedia of Philosophy: http://plato.stanford.edu/entries/well-being/.
13   See 'well-being' in Ted Honderich (ed.), *Oxford Companion to Philosophy* (Oxford University Press, 2005).
14   See E. Diener, E. Suh & S. Oishi, '*Recent findings on subjective well-being,*' *Indian Journal of Clinical Psychology*, 24 (1997), pp. 25–41.

minority rights and especially on the right to internal dialogue. I shall demonstrate that, while the multipurpose right to internal dialogue attends to both *objective well-being* and *subjective well-being* of individuals, it more clearly advances the latter.

(1)   *Objective Well-being and the Right to Internal Dialogue*

'Objective well-being' could be seen as just another name for universal 'basic human needs' which ought to be satisfied in order for one to lead a dignified life. The relationship between *human needs* and *human rights* is difficult to define. The two are certainly intimately and correlatively linked. Human rights are widely considered to serve human needs, and the more important the need, the more fundamental the right. But this popular needs-based approach to human rights assumes that all people have valid human needs that ought to be protected by rights. There are three major problems. First, clearly not all needs give rise to rights, and yet it is not always clear which ones do and which ones do not. Second, there is a wide range of instruments other than human rights to fulfil these human needs. Third, it is often hard to distinguish between what one *needs* and what one *wants*, and it is often the case that the more one *has*, the more one *wants*, and the more one (feels that he/she) *needs*. While there is no doubt that human rights serve human needs, it does not mean that all human needs can be realised by claiming human rights.

This leads us to think more carefully about the function of the *right to internal dialogue*: which human needs or which aspects of objective well-being should it aim to serve? Since what we are concerned with is the well-being of individuals in minority groups, we ought to identify not only the fundamental human needs which are ontologically universal and invariant in nature, but also and especially those that are most relevant, most likely not to be satisfied, within a minority cultural environment.

Objective universal human needs seem fairly straightforward. All human beings, irrespective of cultural background, have certain physiological needs: breathing, food, water, sleep, shelter, clothing, a decent standard of living, etc. We also all have various security needs: personal security, financial security, a stable and supportive family, a safe living and working environment, etc. We also all have certain social needs: the need to relate and to belong, friendship, romantic love, close relationship with family, the need for attention, and for respect. Some would argue, respect for these needs is respect for human dignity; hence, they would argue, the rights that serve these needs are rights that serve human dignity. Linking human rights to human dignity so straightforwardly is unwise and especially unhelpful for the task before us. Culture frequently underpins notions of human dignity which are different from the concept of human rights. While all cultures have underlying, indigenous, concepts of human dignity, only the Western culture, traditionally, developed the concept of human rights. Thus, while it may be appropriate to consider human rights as implying human dignity, it will be culturally insensitive, even cruel in some circumstances, to claim that human dignity implies human rights.

In an ideal world, should any of the basic human needs be inadequately served, the right to internal dialogue will be activated to grant the individual in question an independent voice to express concerns and thus the opportunity to right wrongs. However, we do not live in an ideal world. It will be wholly unrealistic to expect the right to internal dialogue to be able to bring real, immediate, relief, which is what is often needed when people's objective well-being is at stake. Rather, the right to internal dialogue serves as a *transformative device* which helps bring certain problems into the spotlight and to the attention of appropriate bodies and mechanisms. But solution and relief are going to have to come from elsewhere. This is the first function of the multipurpose right to internal dialogue. In contrast, the impact of the right is much more direct and immediate in cases concerning *subjective well-being* of minority group members.

(2)   *Subjective Well-being and the Right to Internal Dialogue*

The subjective aspect of human well-being is a great deal more complex. Jeremy Bentham argues that mankind is constantly under the governance of two sovereign masters – pleasure and pain, and that well-being is the greatest balance of pleasure over pain.[15] According to this hedonistic view, well-being, which can be described as what is good *for* one, is naturally linked to what *seems* good *to* one, and since pleasure seems good and enjoyable *to* most, therefore pleasure is good *for* most; by the same token, pain is bad for most.[16] According to this simplistic account of Hedonism, the more pleasure one has in one's life, the better life will be, and the more pain one encounters, the worse life will be; and that the value of pleasure and pain can be measured by, first, their *duration*, and second, their *intensity*.[17]

The most obvious objection to this account is that it places all types of pleasures and all degrees of pleasantness on a par, and fails to acknowledge that, in the absence of a single common strand of pleasantness running through all the

---

15   Jeremy Bentham, *An Introduction to the Principles of Morals and Legislation* (Oxford University Press, (1996 [1789])).
16   See 'well-being' in Stanford Encyclopaedia of Philosophy: http://plato.stanford.edu/entries/well-being/.
17   Jeremy Bentham, *An Introduction to the Principles of Morals and Legislation* (Oxford University Press, (1996 [1789])).

different experiences and sensations human beings enjoy, what is pleasurable for one might not be so pleasurable for another, if at all, and what is painful for one might not be so painful for another, if at all.[18] Also, some types of pleasantness are incommensurable. For instance, it might be hard to choose between a long but uneventful life and a short but wildly successful one. Again it is very much a matter of personal preference.

One way to get around this objection is to claim that *any* view of pleasure and pleasantness is valid, and equally, *any* view of pain and unpleasantness is valid – in other words, *well-being is purely subjective*. There are three objections. Firstly, obviously well-being is *not exclusively* subjective – it clearly has an objective, universal, aspect – e.g. the basic human needs examined above. Secondly, it fails to acknowledge that, just like human rights, pleasures conflict with each other, also, they sometimes come hand in hand with pain, and vice versa – e.g. giving birth and raising children. Thirdly, as already mentioned above, Bentham's concept of well-being is too simplistic to be of any real analytical use, as it does not sufficiently distinguish between different types and degrees of pleasure.

Indeed, categorising pleasures is by no means easy if at all possible. John Stuart Mill famously argues that some pleasures are by nature more noble and more valuable than others and give more pleasure than an equal quantity of lower pleasures, thereby adds a qualitative element to Bentham's two quantitative elements of duration and intensity, and divides pleasures into 'higher' and 'lower' ones according to their 'quality.'[19] A straightforward example will be that, according to Mill, reading Shakespeare is a higher pleasure than watching porn and gives more pleasure than porn. Thus, by 'quality,' Mill means 'nobleness,' 'goodness,' 'decency.' The problem is that not everyone agrees on the weightiness of nobleness and decency in determining pleasure and well-being, and not everyone agrees on what is decent and what is not. If 'higher pleasures' are more valuable than 'lower pleasures' because certain aspect of their nature makes them more noble and morally better, then that aspect of their nature has absolutely nothing to do with the pleasure itself. Mill employs a property that is external to pleasure to determine the worthiness of pleasure – a property intimately linked to a particular conception of the good, the better. In other words, his conception of well-being has a conception of the good built into it, and for him, nobleness and pleasure are correlatively linked.

This presents a huge problem as regards minority rights and in particular the individual members' right to internal dialogue. The danger of imposing

---

18   See also Ronald Dworkin, *Sovereign Virtue: The Theory and Practice of Equality* (Harvard University Press, Cambridge, Massachusetts), pp. 42–44.
19   John Stuart Mill, *Utilitarianism* (Oxford University Press, 1998 [1863]), Chapter 2.

mainstream values on minority groups has already been considered in previous chapters. The same arguments apply here regarding the group's treatment of its own members. It is inevitable that a minority cultural group should have its own mainstream philosophy, a philosophy that is considered to be most noble, most decent, most correct, from which cultural practices derive and to which all members of the group are required to adhere. It is extremely difficult for people to think or act outside the political and cultural frameworks within which they are acculturated and educated, which is why dissidents are rare in any group. Neither are they popular with the rest of the group (not just the elites but also fellow members), as anyone who departs from what is collectively held to be most decent and most noble is likely to be considered *bad, indecent*, which warrants condemnation and suppression. In other words, sometimes intolerance and oppression are born out of a natural human need, personal and collective, to be in the company of people who are *alike* us, and who *like* us.

However, the representation of culture as a *political* rather than a purely cultural construct in contemporary feminist literature should lead us to resist the temptation of asserting cultural identity to be fixed and permanent, which should in turn alert us to the need to allow and hear contesting interpretations of collective norms and practices instead of blindly accepting one canonical reading. It is important to note that the right to internal dialogue is intended to benefit not just dissidents. Its availability may at best offer encouragement to those who have not previously had the courage to differ, and at worst open the floodgates. The latter, in my view, will be an undesirable outcome and is not the aim of the right to internal dialogue. The aim of this right is to allow expression of concerns, dissatisfaction, and grievances, and to enable them to tell their stories and state their claims, thereby enable internal transformation *indirectly*, where and when necessary, not to directly cause or encourage it.

The very fact that the sense of well-being is often subjective and culturally determined tells us that the mere fact that *I* think someone's situation is intolerable is no sufficient reason for condemnation and intervention; vice versa, just because someone else thinks my situation is intolerable is no paramount reason for me to rebel. This is particularly relevant as regards non-liberal and anti-liberal groups. There are of course groups that fall into the category of 'the intolerable.' While those theorists are right in seeing human beings as rational revisers who are capable of choosing their ends,[20] as Kukathas argues, the importance and desirability of choice and autonomy in human rationality must not be over-stated.[21] There are often practical constraints which render

---

20 E.g. John Stuart Mill, John Rawls, Ronald Dworkin, Will Kymlicka.
21 Chandran Kukathas, *The Liberal Archipelago* (Oxford University Press, 2003), p. 56.

one ill-equipped to pursue one's chosen good, and the reality is often that the chosen good is not better than the imposed good. This is not at all to claim that an imposed way of life is necessarily good; nor is it to say that internal oppression is defensible and ought to be tolerated. It is to say that there are circumstances where, quoting Kukathas, 'the unexamined life may well be worth living.'[22] It is worth repeating that, what the outside world can and should do is to enable revision and internal transformation should they be necessary, not to cause or encourage it. Transformation and change should come from the inside.

With these principles in mind, we can formulate the right to internal dialogue along the following lines:

- Minority groups must not use their self-determination rights to oppress or discriminate against their own internal minorities.
- Minority groups must be willing to allow internal disagreement and to hear a variety of interpretations of norms and practices which are deemed canonical and previously uncontested. This, however, does not have to lead to immediate recognition or accommodation.
- Minority groups should give sufficient room to the possibility that members of the group may not always act 'reasonably' or according to the group's collective standards.
- Minority groups should be willing to engage in debates and discussions, be they formal or informal, with the membership over issues of concern.
- Minority groups should be willing to give reasons for favoured norms and practices and thereby subject disputed norms or practices to internal scrutiny.[23]
- Internal decision-making bodies of minority groups have the duty to make group members fully aware of the existence, purpose, and function of their right to internal dialogue with the group, as well as the procedures involved.
- Minority groups must guarantee as far as possible that all those who wish to take part in processes of internal dialogue can, and should provide necessary assistance according to the specific needs of the members.
- Minority groups must guarantee as far as possible that their members do not suffer discrimination or any other form of ill treatment as a result of exercising their right to internal dialogue.

---

22   Ibid., p. 59.
23   See Anne Phillips, *Multiculturalism Without Culture* (Princeton University Press, 2007), p. 161; and also Bhikhu Parekh, *Rethinking Multiculturalism: Cultural Diversity and Political Theory* (Palgrave Press, 2000).

- Minority groups should pay special attention to the needs and concerns of young people, women, the elderly, and other under-represented internal minorities.

One important conclusion we can draw from the discussion so far is that, in order for the concept of well-being to be of the slightest analytical value to this project, we must break it up and be specific and critical about its meaning and implications. There is little use in talking about it in the abstract. There can be no doubt that objective well-being and subjective well-being both matter, but they demand different forms of protection. And it seems that subjective well-being will only become a matter of concern when one's basic human needs (i.e. objective well-being) have been properly attended to. In other words, objective well-being is the foundation of all, but not necessarily more important. Since people's life situations vary, it is inevitable that for some, objective well-being is more important, whilst for others, subjective well-being matters more. This may change when one's life circumstances change.

Since the advancement of the well-being of members of minority groups is the ultimate goal of the right to internal dialogue, the fact that different types of well-being matter to different people must be reflected in the function of that right. Among other things, it tells us not only what kind of protection is needed, but also how much and what form of intervention, if any, is appropriate. Advancing subjective well-being is understandably more difficult than attending to objective well-being, as the only way of achieving objective protection of something subjective is through safeguarding freedom and autonomy. But freedom and autonomy in the traditional liberal sense are precisely what many cultural minority groups are reluctant to embrace, and no-one is in a position to impose these values and beliefs on them. Autonomy is not universally valued since not everyone wants or needs it to the same degree as others. Sometimes one should simply acknowledge that different people want different things in life, and that people's well-being, objective and subjective, is largely and ultimately up to them. As will be demonstrated in the sections below, the duty (of the group and the state) to protect and promote the well-being of members of minority groups falls short of a duty to ensure the flourishing of their lives.

4   Theory in Practice: Cases

The individual right to *internal* dialogue aims to enable two types of dialogue: dialogue among group members themselves, and dialogue between group members and group elites/internal decision-making bodies. Thus, by 'internal dialogue,' I mean both 'personal encounter' as well as 'formal constructive engagement,' although the latter carries more weight than the former. As already made clear at the very beginning, cultural minority groups are the concern of this book – membership of which tends to be by birth rather than by choice, identity-conferring rather than identity-neutral. Since the right to internal dialogue is most relevant to illiberal groups, but since groups demonstrate different degrees of illiberalness, it is necessary to differentiate between the more liberal groups and the less liberal groups (the latter can be further divided into *non*-liberal groups and *anti*-liberal groups), between general group matters and matters that are issue-specific, and between matters that are identity-conferring and identity-neutral.[24]

Having these distinctions in mind, I here move to apply the theory to three groups of so-called 'minorities within minorities': firstly, cultural dissidents, secondly, minority children, the elderly, and the mentally incapacitated, and lastly, minority women. All 'minorities within minorities' to whom the right to internal dialogue is most relevant can be sorted into either one of these three groups, which inevitably overlap.

Group 1: Cultural Dissidents' Right to Internal Dialogue

A cultural dissident, broadly defined, is a member of a cultural group who challenges the group's established doctrines and policies.[25] I use the term in a broad sense so as to include *religious* dissidents. *Political* dissidents are not considered here as the book is exclusively on the rights of cultural minorities, although the arguments may equally apply to them. For cultural dissidents, *subjective well-being* is more of a concern than objective well-being. This is not to say that their basic human needs must all have been properly catered for, but that their most urgent concern is to be able to express their own interpretations of established cultural norms, which often have practical consequences. The right to internal dialogue of cultural dissidents serves two main purposes. The first is to simply let live by letting talk in the face of disagreement and conflict, and the second is to establish the truth.

In *'Cultural Dissent,'* an article published in the Stanford Law Review in 2001, Madhavi Sunder discusses the case of *Boys Scouts of America v. Dale* (2001) in

---

24 Daniel M. Weinstock's *'Beyond exit rights: Reframing the debate,'* in Avigail Eisenberg &. Jeff Spinner-Halev (eds.), *Minorities within Minorities: Equality, Rights and Diversity* (Cambridge University Press, 2005), pp. 234 and 235.

25 For some examples, see the first paragraph in Madhavi Sunder, *'Cultural Dissent,' Stanford Law Review*, Vol. 54 No. 3, December 2001, pp. 495–567.

her exploration of cultural belonging and dissent.[26] James Dale's membership in the Cub Scouts, of which he had been a member since the age of eight, was revoked when the local council of the Boy Scouts discovered that he was gay. He sued the association for discrimination on the grounds of sexual orientation. The US Supreme Court held that the group had the right to determine its own membership rules, and since the association's mandate was to oppose homosexuality, the revocation of Dale's membership was justified. As Sunder argues, the Supreme Court had refused to accord enough significance to the evidence that had been presented demonstrating a wide range of views on homosexuality within the Boy Scouts. In the face of considerable internal disagreement, the Court nevertheless chose to adopt an essentialist view on cultural autonomy and thereby denied dissident members like James Dale their right to association.

This is a difficult case, as cases of this nature usually are. There should be no doubt that cultural groups and organisations ought to have the right to determine their own membership rules; but at the same time it seems grossly unjust to take away someone's membership because of something over which he has no control. In this particular case, as regards further actions, Dale's best option is of course *exit*. But should he wish, he can exercise the right to internal dialogue which will require institutions, where internal differences exist, to be true to these disagreements and conflicts, acknowledge their presence, and provide institutional channels for the expression of these alternative views. Thus, instead of revoking Dale's membership, the local council of the Boy Scouts ought to accept the need carefully to balance Dale's interests with those of the Boy Scouts, Dale's associational freedom and right to belong with the group's right to cultural autonomy. This can be achieved through hearings and panel meetings, in which Dale ought to be invited to take part to present his case.

This must not be understood as a requirement on the part of the group not to ever banish dissidents. Rather, it is a requirement that the group ought to acknowledge what is already true, that disagreement and conflict are a very normal part of life, of group life, and that engaging dissidents in the face of conflicts of moral principles and rights is a necessity. Such dialogic processes may well sustain and even strengthen the group's beliefs rather than undermine them. Both sides should know that dialogue is not an attempt to convert. It is an opportunity to present.

---

26 *Ibid*. It is important to note that the Boy Scouts of America is an organisation, not exactly a 'culture' in a strict sense. But the arguments apply equally and are especially relevant to minority cultural dissidents whose group opposes homosexuality.

Obviously the groups that readily accept these arrangements are not the problem. The problem rests with the deeply anti-liberal, isolationist, groups, with whom we face more than one structural dilemma. Firstly, internal dialogue is particularly necessary and urgent in these groups as exit is either impossible or extremely costly. But the isolationist nature of these groups render them most unlikely to grant more voice to their members, least of all to dissidents. It is thus understandable why in dealing with these groups most advocate either rough-and-ready intervention – e.g. the spreading burqa ban in Europe, or the right of exit – hoping that exit will eventually contribute to voice.

Another structural dilemma associated with the more isolationist groups is that the cases involving them are much more controversial and have a much greater impact on not only the well-being of the group members but also on the moral conscience of the larger society. These cases often concern deep religious and cultural beliefs, competing interpretations of *the truth* and its entitlements. A good example is the Wahhabi movement of Islam, which aims to purify Islam by rejecting foreign innovations and progressive interpretations, insists on stringent gender segregation and uses regulation and open discrimination to keep women at home. Many (probably 'most') Muslims see the intolerant Wahhabi interpretation as threatening and wrong. It is thus very important for people of the Muslim faith to continue discussions and dialogues among themselves about whether Wahhabism, or any other branch of Islam, is the most authentic representation of their faith.

In the previous chapter I looked at cultural groups' collective right to external dialogue, which works hand in hand with the members' individual right to internal dialogue – communication with the outside world will inevitably inspire internal transformation. Despite this, and perhaps because of this, it is essential to note that, when we are dealing with isolationist cultural groups, we should, for the time being, place greater emphasis on the group's right to external dialogue than on their members' right to internal dialogue. There are several reasons. Firstly, as mentioned above, isolationist elites tend to fiercely oppose ideas of equality and democracy. Thus, over-emphasising their members' right to internal dialogue is likely to generate anger and defensive reactions in the short term, which are going to hinder chances of internal transformation in the long run. Secondly, evidence shows that closer connection with the outside world – which can be best facilitated by exercising the collective right to external dialogue – has caused minorities within minorities to push for changes and reforms within even the most isolationist groups and countries, e.g. Iran, Afghanistan, and Saudi Arabia.[27]

---

27 See Isobel Coleman, *Paradise Beneath Her Feet: How Women are Transforming the Middle East* (Random House, 2010), for examples of case studies across the greater Middle East.

A crucial and interesting fact which is often ignored by the outside world is that, while pushing for change from within, 'minorities within minorities' often have to skirt around the most urgent issues and start with a 'safer,' less controversial, set of matters, i.e. matters that the governing elite feels comfortable discussing. This is a necessary, culturally acceptable and sustainable way forward. Change in one area gradually opens up opportunities to change in another. Changes spread. Furthermore, it is also important to stay within the rules in order to challenge the rules. For instance, given the deeply entrenched religious set-up in Saudi Arabia, minorities (especially women) pushing for reform must take great care to couch their efforts within Islamic discourse. This is another reason why I argued earlier that change must and can come from within – equipped with knowledge of their own culture, members of minority cultures know what works and what does not and why. Since isolationist groups often use puritanical interpretations of their religion and culture to justify maltreatment of 'minorities within minorities,' by pushing the limits, 'minorities within minorities' have set themselves on the path to rebut such interpretations and search for a different meaning of their culture and faith.

Some may argue though that, if internal transformation is already happening within isolationist groups without the right to internal dialogue, why is the right still necessary? At least in the short run, the right to internal dialogue will mainly serve as a distant reminder to 'minorities within minorities' in isolationist groups that there may be reason and room for change. In the same way the presence of human rights and women's rights has inspired many women in these groups to push for tolerance and better treatment. Have international human rights and women's rights *directly* bettered women's lives in these isolationist groups? Probably not. Women in these groups enjoy far fewer legal rights than women elsewhere. But had there not been awareness that these rights are widely available *elsewhere*, women in these groups would probably not have gained the courage or acquired a sense of direction. It is hoped that the right to internal dialogue can serve this same purpose for the time being.

Group 2: Minority Children, the Mentally Incapacitated and the Elderly

I group these three categories of people together for a common feature they share: compromised (under-developed or diminished) moral and mental capacity. I recognise that each category has its own distinctive characteristics. They can also overlap (e.g. a mentally incapacitated minor, a mentally incapacitated old person). Unlike cultural dissidents, *objective well-being* is a more urgent concern than subjective well-being for these three categories of 'minorities within minorities.'

(1)   Minority Children

Severe criticisms of collective cultural rights are voiced most frequently concerning the rights of minority minors. There is no universally accepted definition of children's rights, and they can be and have been defined in numerous ways covering a wide spectrum of civil, political, cultural, social and economic rights. These include both rights enjoyed by adults as well as rights specifically for children, and include both general rights – e.g., rights to a decent standard of living, rights to health care and education – and the more particular rights – e.g. the right to an end to military use of children.[28] These rights are provided in a broad range of conventions and rights instruments, with the Universal Declaration of Human Rights being a basis for all international standards for children's rights, and the United Nation's 1989 Convention on the Rights of the Child being the first legally binding international instrument to incorporate a wide range of civil, political, cultural, social and economic rights of children.[29] However, despite evidently strong international commitment, issues concerning children's rights remain controversial and ambiguous, especially but not only in the context of minority cultural rights. The discussion here is not on children's rights as a general category, but on specifically the *right to internal dialogue* of cultural minority minors.

The right to internal dialogue is particularly difficult to defend when the potential beneficiaries are minors, as, more than anything, such a right aims to grant an independent voice, which minors do not, and should not, as many would argue, have.[30] Despite the apparent popularity of the term 'children's right,' it is highly arguable that children do not have all of the rights that the international instruments, children's organisations and academic writers say they have. While there can be no doubt that they have basic human rights, it is unclear whether, and if so to what extent, they have, for instance, *freedom of choice, autonomy,* and intimately related to both – the *right to internal dialogue*. This objection can be understood on both theoretical and practical levels, but it is mainly of a practical cast. On the theoretical level, it is often argued that minors, especially the very young ones, lack the moral capacity necessary to hold and exercise rights. On the practical level, it can be argued that in order for children to properly prosper physically and psychologically, they ought to

---

28   See Amnesty International 'Children's Rights' section, 'A Safe Childhood is a Human Right': www.amnestyinternational.org/our-work/issues/children-s-rights.

29   Available at: http://www.ohchr.org/en/professionalinterest/pages/crc.aspx.

30   For a discussion on the conflict between paternalism and autonomy in the context of children's rights, see Claire Breen, *Age Discrimination and Children's Rights: Ensuring Equality and Acknowledging Difference* (Martinus Nijhoff Publishers, 2006), Chapter 1.

be protected from the adult world, in particular from making decisions and shouldering responsibilities which ought to be made and shouldered by adults.

Given the unique role played by parents in a child's life, this argument brings to light the troubling relationship between *children's autonomy* and *parenting*, which is a conflict of rights in essence, as *parenting*, according to article 9 of the 1989 UN Convention on the Rights of the Child, is an essential *children's* right. The idea of children having rights could make people feel uneasy because it goes against the conventional view that matters concerning children are really matters concerning their parents, their guardians, the family home. While the society at large has a whole set of responsibilities concerning a child's well-being, for instance the provision of public education and health care, there can be no doubt that the central relationship that a child has is the one with his/her parents or guardians, and despite current patterns of social harm and damage done to children, the prevailing approach remains largely one of non-interventionism.[31]

All this makes defending a child's right to internal dialogue a particularly daunting task. Issues are further complicated if the child is a member of a cultural minority group, in which case the parents' and the group's responsibilities for the care of the child often shield the child from public view and their treatment from public scrutiny. However, it is essentially for this reason that the right to internal dialogue is potentially vital for minority minors, as they are undoubtedly the most vulnerable members in any group, for whom exit is out of the question. This right aims to, firstly, give a child an independent voice and a fair hearing *in appropriate circumstances*, and, secondly, to *affirm* rather than *sever* family and cultural ties, through *fostering* and *aiding* internal communication. A crucial task, therefore, is to identify these *appropriate, exceptional, circumstances*.

An exceptional circumstance will be where it is blatantly obvious that the child in question has been made subservient to his/her parents' interests for the benefit of the parents and to the disbenefit of the child. In other words, for a cultural minority minor to be able to exercise the right to internal dialogue, two criteria must be satisfied: first, the mistreatment must be obvious, and second, the child is subservient to the interests of the parents and/or the group. I shall consider the two criteria in turn before demonstrating what it means to hold and exercise this right once qualified.

Regarding the first criterion, one might argue that in obvious cases of child mistreatment, social services and the law will step in, thus the right to internal

---

31   See, for example, Laura Beth Nielson, *Theoretical and Empirical Studies of Rights* (Ashgate, 2007), Chapter 7.

dialogue is wholly unnecessary, and it seems too mild to be effective anyway. This is not so. The children we are talking about here are members of minority groups, to whom social services do not always have adequate access, and where and when they do have access, failure to act is often justified by a conventional understanding and demonstration of cultural sensitivity which takes the form of non-intervention. The problem with this first criterion is that most cases of child mistreatment are not 'blatantly obvious,' not only because they often take place in the private home, but also that children are often reluctant, as well as lack the capacities and skills, to talk about such issues, often fearing what might happen to their parents and consequently what might happen to themselves.

Too little intervention is dangerous, so is too much. There is no universal agreement over what constitutes child mistreatment – e.g. corporal punishment is considered in many cultures as a justified form of discipline, not child abuse. And in the specific context of minority cultural rights, it is highly arguable whether, for instance, forcing a child to attend a religious school against his/her wishes constitutes mistreatment and abuse, or whether it is simply a normal exercise of parental power. Furthermore, social services often lack cross-cultural competency. This is not only a matter of language barriers but also that the risk assessment instruments they employ tend to be racially and culturally biased resulting from a lack of cross-cultural interaction. For example, avoiding direct eye contact is considered respectful in many foreign cultures, but in Western countries, it is often seen as a sign of deceptiveness in adults, and in children – a sign of abuse. Misunderstandings will inevitably lead to inappropriate treatment, confusion and resentment.

Furthermore, the concern here is not just *any* child mistreatment, but specifically mistreatment in the cultural sphere. A classic example of a case which satisfies this first criterion is *R v. Adesanya*, where a Nigerian mother resident in Britain was prosecuted for ceremonially scarring the cheeks of her sons, who were nine and fourteen years of age respectively.[32] She was convicted but given an absolute discharge. The scarification was a normal part of Nigerian custom, and neither the local Nigerian community nor the mother herself was aware that the practice was contrary to English law. Furthermore, both children were said to be willing participants in the ceremony. In my view, this seems to be a fairly straight-forward example of a scenario where the (physical) harm done to the children was obvious[33] – even though they were said to have consented to the scaring – the first criterion has been satisfied.

---

32 Unreported, noted in [1975] 24 ICLQ 136.
33 Although it can also be argued that whilst the *pain* caused was obvious, the *harm* was arguable.

This case is clearly distinguishable from the Muslim headscarf cases, where it is often claimed that young Muslim girls are coerced by their parents into wearing a hijab – something they might not have otherwise chosen to do. The problem is, children have underdeveloped capacities, and it is the duty of their parents to protect them and act in their best interest (which, of course, is value-laden and culturally specific), which often means making decisions on their behalf. Children do not and should not have a say over much in their lives, and it is unclear why being told to wear a hijab should be seen as any less acceptable than being told not to associate with a friend who is seen by the parents as a bad influence. Obviously the parents' right to make such educational and social decisions for the child is not unlimited. Parents cannot make decisions that will harm their children's basic well-being and interests, or leave them unprepared to fully function in society. But in the absence of significant harm directly resulting from wearing the hijab,[34] seeing personal autonomy and freedom of choice as the highest good in such cases regarding children is inappropriate. As established at the beginning of this section, *objective* well-being matters much more than *subjective* well-being to children.

The second criterion which must be satisfied in order for a child to exercise the right to internal dialogue is that it must be shown that the he/she is subservient to the parents' or the group's interests *to their disadvantage*. An example will be a forced marriage against the child's wishes, and from which, for instance, the parents gain a large dowry. But even the case of forced marriages is not clear-cut. Where there is no overriding evidence of coercion, or of gain on the parents' part and loss on the child's, which is sometimes the case, the situation is much more complicated. In *Alhaji Mohammed v. Knott*, a girl of thirteen and a man of twenty six entered an Islamic marriage in Nigeria before moving to the UK shortly afterwards.[35] The first instance court held that the marriage was 'repugnant to any decent-minded English man or woman' and issued a care order, which was subsequently revoked on appeal by the Divisional Court, which held the marriage to be valid and 'entirely natural' *for a Nigerian girl, 'as they develop sooner.'*[36]

Understandably, this case and later similar cases generated a great deal of controversy in the UK and subsequently caused the changes in the Immigration Rules 1986, which barred spouses under the age of 16 from entering the UK. The age of admission was eventually raised to 18. However, one can confidently say

---

34 This is not to deny that there are cases where being forced to wear the hijab has caused direct and significant harm, in particular emotional and psychological harm.
35 [1969] 1 QB 1.
36 *Ibid.*

that, should a similar case arise again before an English court, the marriage would still be held valid. In the present case, it is unclear whether the child bride in question has been used as a means to other ends for the benefits of her parents, her husband or her community. Although she has not reached the legal age of consent, it can be argued that a mature thirteen-year old may well be capable of evaluating the pros and cons of marrying a grown man. It thus seems that the validity of the marriage should hinge on whether, given the particular circumstances of the case, the girl could be deemed to have willingly and meaningfully consented.

It is clear that, as always, some cases are easy, others are hard. The right to internal dialogue should not be expected to serve the same purpose in all cases, although the ultimate goal should always be to advance children's *objective* well-being, over autonomy. In a hard case, such as *Alhaji Mohammed v. Knott*, the right to internal dialogue can be of assistance in helping establish the crucial facts especially whether the child in question has been subject to serious harm and repression. It was a hard case because, despite the fact that the bride in question was underage, there was no clear evidence that she was married against her wishes. Neither was there evidence that her husband was in any way harmful to her; or that her parents or her husband used her as a means to other ends. This should not be interpreted as a defence of underage marriage generally, but it is possible that the marriage had provided her with a safe home, financial support and companionship. But we must also recognise that entering into a long-term sexual relationship at a young age is probably going to lead to serious lifelong physical, and possibly psychological, consequences. It would also mean that she would have to shoulder the duties and responsibilities of a wife at a young age, which was likely to include, for example, bearing and raising children, and looking after her husband. By contrast, in an easier case, such as *R v. Adesanya*, the right to internal dialogue can serve a more proactive purpose by granting the child in question an independent voice to present their own opinions and, if necessary, to challenge the established doctrine and practice. Both are borderline cases in their own way.

(2)   The Mentally Incapacitated in Minority Groups

With respect to internal dialogue, the situation of minority minors is very similar to that of the mentally incapacitated in minority groups. All the arguments and conclusions above are equally applicable to them. However, there exists a key difference between the two groups: while the former are often subjects of excessive protection (sometimes with oppressive effects), the latter are almost always victims of discrimination and systemic exclusion. We must not forget that mentally incapacitated people are likely to be facing other stresses which may be far more problematic than those associated with disability. It is likely that it is not the impairment that presents the biggest challenge, but poverty and discrimination. In other words, advancement of the overall *objective* well-being of the mentally incapacitated in minority groups should be the goal of the right to internal dialogue.

It is not immediately apparent why human rights and disability rights alone are not sufficient for the protection of mentally incapacitated minorities. But upon closer inspection, we will see that the situation of the mentally incapacitated members of minority groups is not dissimilar to that of cultural dissidents in isolationist groups, in that they are completely powerless in the face of larger forces – in the case of cultural dissidents such larger forces are orthodox forces, and in the case of the mentally incapacitated these larger forces are simply the everyday cultural surroundings to which they do not have adequate, meaningful, access due to their impairment.[37] In other words, the element of choice is likely to be completely lacking in their cultural life. And life may be doubly challenging should they be members of an isolationist group. But the obvious difference between cultural dissidents and the mentally incapacitated is that, given adequate opportunities, the former have the capacity to enable change from within, whereas the latter do not.

Given that they are undoubtedly amongst the most vulnerable of all the 'minorities within minorities,' all things considered, and largely for humanitarian reasons, I would suggest that the responsibility for the well-being of the mentally incapacitated in minority groups should rest with the *state* rather than the group. This would mean that the state should have a much greater say regarding the group's treatment of its mentally incapacitated members than any other categories of 'minorities within minorities,' if at all. Their right to internal dialogue should be exercised with the specific aim of periodically communicating their life situations to the outside world – the state, social services and relevant NGOs – and then reporting the latter's opinion and advice back to the cultural community within which they will continue to reside. Since they are likely to lack the capacity to present their own case, representation as well as investigatory mechanisms will always be necessary. Thus, the right to internal dialogue of the mentally incapacitated aims to facilitate a form of joint governance to ensure proper protection of the most vulnerable of all.

(3)   The Elderly in Minority Groups

Treatments of the elderly vary greatly among ethnic and cultural groups. It is very common in many minority groups that the elderly are also the elites, to

---

37   Mentally incapacitated people in the majority culture also face the same challenges.

whom the right to internal dialogue is clearly not relevant. However, minority elders can also be found at the other extreme. Studies have shown that multiple forms of elder abuse among minorities exist: neglect, physical abuse, psychological abuse, domestic abuse, and even sexual abuse.[38] Elder abuse is difficult to detect for several reasons. First, again, it takes place in the private domain, to which the public does not have easy access. This has resulted in lack of research in this crucial area of minority social life. Second, old people are most unlikely to report abuse or seek help due to their old age, limited mobility, financial vulnerability, and a sense of shame. And it is often the case that there are simply no available social services, or they are unaware of the services, or do not believe that they can solve their problems. They cannot be blamed for this, as their expectations of public services are shaped by their life histories, and it is unlikely that they had grown up in an environment in which a competent social service network functioned, thus in old age, they are much less likely than those who have grown up in such an environment to request assistance from these services.

Furthermore, cultural values and beliefs also greatly influence how an old person copes with maltreatment and determine whether or not he/she is going to seek help. Clearly, the advancement of *objective* well-being is a greater concern for old people in minority groups than *subjective* well-being, which matters most to dissidents. Since the situation of and the problems faced by minority old people are not dissimilar to that of minority minors, I propose that the right to internal dialogue with respect to them should be exercised in the same fashion as with respect to minors. I shall not repeat the discussion here.

Group 3: Minority Women's Right to Internal Dialogue
It must be noted at the outset that the focus here is not on women's rights as a general category; rather, it is on women as members of cultural minority groups holding and exercising the specific *right to internal dialogue*. The case of minority women is the most complex out of all 'minorities within minorities.' The picture presented is one of huge contrasts. On the one hand, significant gender disparities continue to exist in all cultural groups. In some, the treatment of women is at the forefront of a long deadly battle between the extremists and the reformists with progressive views. But on the other hand, women, even in the most isolationist groups and countries, are very much the driving force behind social, political and legal reforms. And their efforts often constitute an

---

38 See, for instance, the website of the National Committee for the Prevention of Elder Abuse of the United States: http://www.preventelderabuse.org/.

essential part of the community's, and the nation's, broader reform movement.[39] However, despite progress, multi-dimensional structural difficulties facing women in many cultural minority groups persist. Once again, the issue at hand is often concerned with seemingly irresolvable conflicts of rights – for example, conflicts between religious freedom and gender equality, between cultural belonging and gender equality, between group self-determination and the individuals' right of exit, and so on.[40]

Common contemporary controversies in this area include but are not limited to cases concerning, for instance, forced marriage, veiling, and genital mutilation. Forced marriage is a relatively easy case. Despite a blanket ban in Europe and an overall decline in the number of forced marriages around the world, the chances of young women being forced into a marriage against their will are still high in those minority communities that traditionally practise it.[41] As regards veiling, a great deal has been written about it due to the spreading burqa ban in Europe. I do not wish to repeat the arguments here but will present a detailed examination in the concluding chapter when I look into conflicts of rights. It is possible to consider cases of veiling and forced marriage together in developing general guidelines on internal dialogue for minority women, as they share common characteristics.

First, both are concerned with adult women, who can generally be presumed to know their own minds,[42] capable of expressing and conveying their emotions, feelings, and opinions. Second, both are concerned with controversial cultural practices which have given rise to competing views and interpretations. In the case of forced marriages, whilst most condemn the practice, some do argue that parental supervision and approval is a determinant factor

---

39 Some examples of women driven reforms, e.g. in Saudi Arabia, have already been mentioned in my earlier discussion of isolationist groups. For more case studies, see Isobel Coleman, *Paradise Beneath Her Feet: How Women are Transforming the Middle East* (Random House, 2010).

40 As will be shown in the concluding chapter, it is in fact not always helpful to approach these claims as competing rights claims, not least because it generates a simplistic misunderstanding of gender being distinct from culture. See also Anne Phillips's *'Dilemmas of gender and culture'* in Avigail Eisenberg &. Jeff Spinner-Halev (eds.), *Minorities within Minorities: Equality, Rights and Diversity* (Cambridge University Press, 2005); and Martha Nussbaum, *Women and Human Development: The Capabilities Approach* (Cambridge University Press, 2000), Chapter 3.

41 See Anne Phillips, *Multiculturalism Without Culture* (Princeton University Press, 2007), p. 119.

42 There is, however, the issue of 'false consciousness.' But it is beyond the scope of this chapter to examine it in detail.

in the stability of family life. As regards the practice of veiling, whilst many condemn it as a symbol of women's subordination, others see it as a sign of modesty and submission to God, an expression of a woman's moral agency. The rule of thumb is that we must not look at these cases as a whole class; rather, when determining whether the right to internal dialogue is applicable in a given case, it is necessary to first identify whether *force* is involved. If elements of force are lacking – as they sometimes are in cases of veiling, contrary to common belief – then the right to internal dialogue does not need to be called upon. But if force has been used, further investigation is required, and the internal governing bodies of the group have a duty to enable the exercise of the women's right to internal dialogue as fleshed out in Part 3 above.

But how much force is enough force? The 2007 Forced Marriage (Civil Protection) Act of the UK defines 'force' as 'coerce by threats or other psychological means (and related expressions are to be read accordingly).'[43] And for the purposes of the Act, 'a person ("A")' can be considered to have been 'forced into a marriage if another person ("B") forces A to enter into a marriage (whether with B or another person) without A's free and full consent.'[44] 'In deciding whether to exercise its powers under this section and, if so, in what manner, the court must have regard to all the circumstances including the need to secure the health, safety and well-being of the person to be protected.'[45] And 'in ascertaining that person's well-being,' the court must have regard 'to the person's wishes and feelings (so far as they are reasonably ascertainable) as the court considers appropriate in the light of the person's age and understanding.'[46]

Clearly, whether or not unacceptable force has been used is very much context-dependent and should be determined on a case-by-case basis. This point can be better illustrated using the example of genital mutilation, a practice with deep religious and cultural roots and significance in a number of African, Middle Eastern, South American and Southeast Asian countries, and intimately connected to those cultures' interpretation of gender and sexuality. Whilst it is easy (and right) to condemn female genital mutilation as a general practice regardless of its religious or cultural significance because it undoubtedly causes permanent harm to females, it is nevertheless essential to distinguish between genital mutilation of *young girls*, of *non-consenting adult women*, and of *consenting adult women*.[47]

---

43 The Forced Marriage (Civil Protection) Act 2007, Section 63A(6).
44 *Ibid.*, Section 63A(4).
45 *Ibid.*, Section 63A(2).
46 *Ibid.*, Section 63A(3).
47 It should be noted that the UK's Female Genital Mutilation Act 2003 only protects *girls*.

Genital mutilation of young girls is an easy case to decide. As discussed earlier in the section on minority children, the *objective* well-being of children is more important than their *subjective* well-being. In the case of genital mutilation of young girls, the *objective* well-being in question is the young girls' physical, mental and sexual health. Unless it can be shown in a given case that a surgical operation conducted by an approved person is necessary for the girl's physical and mental health,[48] since the practice undoubtedly causes permanent and irreversible harm, its cultural significance seems irrelevant. By the same token, genital mutilation of *non-consenting adults* also cannot be justified. In both scenarios, there are likely to be elements of force, lack of consent (e.g. due to young age), which render the nature of the procedure involuntary.

By contrast, genital mutilation of *consenting adult women* is a much harder, and often overlooked, case. As Carens points out, in cases where women, for whatever reason, voluntarily undergo genital mutilation and thus no force is involved, the question becomes whether the state, or anyone, has the power to restrict their *conscious life choices*, and whether genital mutilation should be treated differently from the other forms of bodily mutilation which are permitted.[49] In such cases, it is one thing to condemn and entirely another to prohibit.[50] While widespread public accommodation of the procedure will be too much and is unlikely to happen, a blanket ban seems too invasive, especially considering there are many different types of genital mutilation – some are much less harmful than others.[51] Thus, it does seem that in cases where genital mutilation is *voluntary*, the woman's right to internal dialogue is largely irrelevant, except in circumstances where the minority group in question condemns the practice and should therefore be willing to give reasons.[52]

5 The Right of Exit

Although the overwhelming emphasis of this approach is on dialogue, it is nevertheless necessary to prepare for when internal accommodation and dialogue fail. The right of exit is a last-resort right, and, as Phillips observes, 'one of the few uncontested rights in these debates,'[53] which constitutes an option open to

---

48   Female Genital Mutilation Act 2003, Section 1(2), (3), (4) and (5).
49   Joseph H. Carens, *Culture, Citizenship, and Community* (Oxford University Press, 2000), pp. 147 and 148.
50   *Ibid*. The same argument applies to the issue of the burqa.
51   *Ibid.*, p. 150.
52   See Part 3, sub-section (2) of this chapter.
53   Anne Phillips, *Multiculturalism Without Culture* (Princeton University Press, 2007), p. 136.

a member of a minority group to leave the group, usually due to unbearable internal oppression, and join the wider society instead. It is also widely agreed that this right *alone* does not adequately protect against internal cultural and social pressure, for the threat of exclusion and isolation is often enough to cause someone to abandon the thought of exit.[54] The dialogical nature of this concept of minority rights determines that even this last-resort right should be procedure and future oriented and play a much more proactive role than simply providing an open door as traditionally assumed. With this principle in mind, the right can be formulated to contain the following key elements:

- Minority groups have the duty to ensure that their members are fully aware of the availability, purpose and characteristics of the right of exit, as well as the relevant procedures involved in order to activate and exercise the right.
- The right of exit should become available not only at the point of exit; rather, it is available at three stages: before, during and after the manifestation of internal oppression.
- The right of exit can be called upon to protect vulnerable members from further oppression during the process of exit.
- It is part and parcel of the exit right for the group and the state to jointly provide necessary assistance and resources without which exit cannot take place. This may include temporary accommodation, financial assistance, and emotional support, and so on.
- If the exercise of the right of exit concerns vulnerable parties such as women and minors, the group and state institutions must pay particular attention to their general well-being, with the specific aim of minimising the physical, psychological, emotional, financial, and other associative costs of exit.

It is important to note that whilst this is a right held by minority members against the group, the duty to protect is jointly exercised by the group's internal decision-making bodies and the state. Since the very nature and purpose of the right is to enable movement from one group to another,[55] which requires transformative decision-making and accommodation, it is thus essential that both sides work together, as singular accommodation is clearly not a plausible solution.[56]

---

54 *Ibid.*, p. 137.
55 Culturally, physically, or both.
56 Having said that, it must be noted that in some contexts and circumstances, it may not be clear precisely what belonging, staying or leaving all mean, let alone how they can be adequately accommodated.

CHAPTER 6

Group Agency and the Capacity to Self-govern
From Dependency, through Assisted Capacity-Building, to Meaningful Autonomy

The focus of this chapter is on one persistent argument against the recognition of strong group rights – i.e. groups' lack of moral agency and requisite capacity to hold and exercise rights. This is a particularly important issue for the dialogical concept of minority rights, as on this account minority groups must now play a much more active role than they were previously required to, not only to exercise collectively held rights, but also to enhance and enforce the branch of minority rights held against the group by its membership, as well as to participate in and contribute to state decision-making in the form of dialogue.

The aims are three-fold. The first is to challenge the assumption that autonomy is a precondition for holding and exercising rights, and to challenge also the assumption that group autonomy and *moral* agency are the preconditions for a group's exercise of group rights (as formulated in Chapters 2, 3 and 4). The second aim is to examine nevertheless the *practical necessity* of groups having internal decision-making bodies in order to hold and exercise group rights, the reasons for and means and purposes of the creation of these internal bodies, their maintenance and functioning, and whether the state owes a *duty* to certain groups to establish them. The last and most important aim is to argue, against the background of the UN Declaration on the Rights of Indigenous Peoples 2007, that the current approach to indigenous self-determination and autonomy is well-intentioned but unrealistic. If self-determination is to remain as the ultimate goal, we must not neglect the future-influencing duty of the international community and ought to start focusing our efforts on upgrading the self-governing capacities of indigenous communities.

1   Moral Agency, Capacity, and Group Rights

I have examined, in the first two chapters, the main concerns that often motivate talk of collective rights, and whether it will be feasible for liberals to endorse the notion. Since rights signal degrees of urgency among moral considerations, and theories of rights seem to elevate their subject matter above other aspects of morality, defenders of collective rights would naturally want to capture this urgency for the sort of moral concerns that they consider as giving rise to collective rights. Thus, they would wish to show that, in addition to universal peremptory individual concerns, there are also peremptory collective concerns. I have embraced and thoroughly examined this claim, and argued that, instead of upholding individual rights as the only valid rights, we ought to re-conceptualise the notion of collective rights, inject it into the minority rights system, find and maintain a balance between the rights of individuals and the rights of groups, not least because individual interests and collective concerns are not always separable, and the protection of the latter often, but not always, contributes to the promotion of the former. Thus, it is through widening the concept of 'rights' that I have sought to widen the appeal of the notion of collective minority rights. And it is through dividing the broad category of 'minority rights' into various sub-categories of collectively held rights and individually held rights, and introducing three separate but related rights to internal and external dialogue, that I have sought to widen the concept of 'minority rights.'[1]

I now wish to turn to the *capacity conditions* of groups holding and exercising rights, by first making a clear distinction between the capacity to *hold* rights and the capacity to *exercise* rights, and to proceed in three steps. First, I wish to challenge the assumption that autonomy is a precondition for *holding* rights; second, to challenge by extension the assumption that *group* autonomy and *group moral* agency are the preconditions for a group's *holding* of collective rights; and last, to show nevertheless the *practical necessity* of groups having some form and degree of capacity of agency – e.g. in the form of internal decision-making bodies – in order to *exercise* collective rights.

It is commonly argued that autonomy and moral capacity are logical preconditions of having rights, which of course is more in line with the 'will' or 'choice' theory of rights than with the 'interest' theory. In its simplest form, the 'will theory' of rights holds that the purpose of rights is to grant the rights-holder the freedom to control the duties that others legitimately owe to him/her, ultimately it is to protect and foster individual autonomy of the rights-holder. By contrast, the 'interest theory' of rights claims that rights exist in order to serve relevant interests of the rights-holder, and thus are instrumental in achieving human well-being.

The view that minority groups lack capacities for moral agency and reciprocity and therefore cannot be rights holders is widely held, conventional, but not entirely persuasive. Neil MacCormick has offered influential arguments *against* the will theory, and argues that if it is correct – that a right is a power of waiver over the enforcement of a duty, and the right-holder is a person who is capable of demanding performance or choosing to waive the duty – then a young child

---

1 See diagram.

does not have any rights as he/she obviously does not possess such moral capacity and power.[2] But since young children obviously do have rights, the will theory of rights is false.[3] In other words, what determines that young children have rights is something other than 'capacity for moral agency and reciprocity.' The justification of their rights derives from the mere fact that they are human and also from the rights' contribution to the rights holders' well-being.

The same argument can be made to defend collectively held self-determination rights. I would not repeat here the arguments made in the first two chapters in defence of the necessity and moral defensibility of the notion of collective rights, except that human dignity, interests and well-being cannot and must not be expressed in narrowly individualistic terms, and that individual rights are not a cure-all solution to all the problems – some aspects of *individual* human well-being and dignity must be pursued and protected *collectively*, through the exercise of collective rights.

Furthermore, it is naive to assume that just because collectivities such as minority groups are not adult persons, they must lack the *capacity* for moral agency that adult persons have. Institutional bodies and decision-making processes possess such capacities of moral agency.[4] This view is in agreement with H.L.A. Hart's defence of the will theory of rights, which says that, for instance, in the case of children, we ought to make a distinction between *moral* and *legal* rights. While it might not be correct to ascribe *moral* rights to young children, it is appropriate to ascribe *legal* rights to them, except that it is the child's parents or guardians instead of the child himself/herself who make decisions and exercise *the child's rights* on behalf of the child.[5] Another way to put it is to say that, while children *have* rights despite lacking in capacities of moral agency (which they do not need in order to *possess* rights), they *need* those capacities to effectively *exercise* those rights, and until they have acquired those capacities, their rights will be exercised by accredited representatives on their behalf.

Similar arguments apply to self-determination rights. As already shown in Chapter 2, although a minority group should not be viewed as possessing a moral status similar to that of a human being, it will be wrong to think that rights are ways of recognising and respecting *only* a pre-existing moral status.

---

2   Nigel Simmonds, *Central Issues in Jurisprudence: Justice, Law and Rights* (Sweet &. Maxwell, 2nd edition, 2002), p. 311.
3   *Ibid.*
4   Bhikhu Parekh, *Rethinking Multiculturalism: Cultural Diversity and Political Theory*, (Palgrave Press, 2nd edition, 2006), pp. 213–214.
5   Nigel Simmonds, *Central Issues in Jurisprudence: Justice, Law and Rights* (Sweet &. Maxwell, 2nd edition, 2002), p. 312.

They are also ways of *conferring* moral status when and where we think it desirable and appropriate. Hence the question is not whether or not minority groups have moral status, but whether they *should* have it and can be the bearers of rights. This question has been answered affirmatively in Chapter 2. However, moral status *per se* does not render the group in question capable of *exercising* rights. There is a practical necessity for them to possess certain core capacities in order to do so. And it is through building up and strengthening their internal institutional decision-making bodies and processes that this can be achieved.

2   The Practical Necessity of Internal Decision-Making Bodies

In order for a group to acquire the core capacities necessary to perform tasks and meaningfully exercise rights, it must formulate an institutional decision-making structure that defines leadership positions, assigns powers and responsibilities, and specifies how powers are to be exercised and responsibilities fulfilled. Leaders of the group, through this decision-making structure, can propose and approve collective goals of the group and determine strategies required to realise them. The internal decision-making body also evaluates actions, reviews and renews strategies and plans, and regulates relations between group members and with the outside world. When a group is able to do all or at least most of these things, it can be said to possess moral agency and the capacity for deliberation, and thus in a position to *exercise* rights.

In order to later determine which particular capacities are required, it is necessary to first consider what and whose *incapacities* there are. There are three separate but interconnected incapacities in question: first, the incapacity of international and regional laws to develop the self-governing capacities of minority groups; second, the state's incapacity to cater for the self-governing needs and interests of minority groups and indigenous communities; and last, the minorities' own incapacity to efficiently govern themselves. My focus is on the third but it is necessary also to briefly cover the first two, as there is an unbroken causal link between the three. I shall start with international law.

3   Upgrading Self-governing Capacities

(1)   *Self-determination and Self-governance in International Law*

A good example is the UN Declaration on the Rights of Indigenous Peoples 2007. As already outlined in Chapter 1, the instrument contains a series of *collective rights*, including but not limited to the right to self-determination and self-governance (Articles 3 and 4); the right to maintain and strengthen distinct political, legal, economic, social and cultural institutions and to participate fully, *if they so choose*, in the political, economic, social and cultural life of the State (Article 5); the right to practise and revitalise their cultural traditions and customs (Article 11); the right to manifest, practise, develop, and teach their spiritual and religious traditions, customs and ceremonies (Article 12); the right to revitalise, use, develop and transmit to future generations their histories, languages, oral traditions, philosophies, writing systems and literatures, and to designate and retain their own names for communities, places and persons (Article 13(1)); the right to establish their own media in their own languages (Article 16(1)); the right to participate in decision-making in matters which would affect their rights, through representatives chosen by themselves in accordance with their own procedures, as well as to maintain and develop their own indigenous decision-making institutions (Article 18); the right to determine their own identity or membership in accordance with their customs and traditions (Article 33(1)); the right to determine the responsibilities of individuals to their communities (Article 35); and the right to maintain and develop contacts, relations and cooperation with their own members as well as other peoples across borders (Article 36(1)).

The chief inadequacy of this document (as well as international minority rights law in general) is that it manifests a single-minded determination to realise immediately an absolute right to substantive self-determination, self-governance and autonomy. It seems that it neither recognises that in order to exercise these rights certain core collective capacities are absolutely required, nor acknowledges the fact that most if not all of these communities are to varying extents unequipped and unprepared for meaningful self-governance. Furthermore, since nowadays even the most isolated groups have to face interaction with the outside world and therefore change and transformation, by predominantly emphasising their radical *otherness* and the rights owed to them on the grounds of their radical *otherness*, international minority rights law needs to consider – if the circumstances of these groups change as a result of interaction with other cultures and traditions, which will inevitably diminish their *otherness* and undermine the *cultural distinctiveness* that has given rise to these self-government rights in the first place, are these groups to lose these rights?

Having said that, it is impossible for international minority rights law to do anything more than lay down the most basic principles and guidelines regarding capacity-building for self-governing minorities. But perhaps it is time for it to shift the focus to providing opportunities for adequate learning, developing and enhancing capacities of self-government with international and state assistance, and to encourage domestic measures of accommodation. The attractive doctrine of substantive self-determination seems very tempting, but the temptation must be resisted at this early stage. No amount of self-determination can give cultural expression to groups that are incapable of realising it.

(2) *Interpretations of the Right to Self-determination: Three Approaches*
Although self-determination is not principally a problem for international law but for states, the flaws in international law have caused consequences in laws and policies of states. Here I move to consider the second incapacity mentioned above – that of the state to cater for the self-governing needs and interests of minority groups and indigenous communities – through examining three different approaches which states around the globe have adopted.

(1)   Paternalism and Welfare Dependency
In an article published in 2009, Sarah Maddison criticises the then Australian government for its wide range of coercive measures in the name of combating serious social and economic problems such as widespread violence, substance abuse, welfare dependency and child sexual abuse in indigenous communities in the Northern Territory.[6] Examples of the measures were alcohol restrictions, market-based rents and tenancy arrangements, restricting welfare payments based on behaviour (e.g. school attendance), pornography ban, and compulsory health checks for all children.[7] These measures received mixed responses from the relevant communities. Having long acknowledged child abuse as a widespread serious problem, many indigenous people were thankful that the government was finally taking steps to tackle it. But a large number of these measures especially the enforcement methods employed, e.g. greater control and surveillance, generated not only widespread criticism and fear but also increasing suspicion concerning the government's true intention.[8]

This reveals one common extreme attitude to indigenous self-determination, namely that indigenous communities have problems that the state must help solve, and restrictions and tight control are the solution. This paternalistic approach, which is assimilationist in essence, has been said to be able to solve the problem of *welfare dependency*,[9] which is central to all critiques of the

---

6   Sarah Maddison, *'Australia: Indigenous Autonomy Matters'* in *Development* (2009) 52(4), pp. 483–489.
7   *Ibid.*, p. 484.
8   *Ibid.*, pp. 484 and 485.
9   *Ibid.*, p. 486.

welfare state.[10] It is argued that unconditional welfare destroys recipients' incentive to improve and develop as they become increasingly accustomed to living on the benevolence of the state.

It needs pointing out though that these paternalistic measures were a mixed bag of policies, some had positive impacts whereas others produced disastrous results. Maddison failed to reach any meaningful constructive conclusions, and in failing to provide any evidence to prove her case, her repeated statements 'more, not less, autonomy is the answer to dependency' were devoid of substance. There are at least three key issues that deserve greater attention. Firstly, the relevant policies were in fact not as shocking as the author suggested, considering that meaningful indigenous self-determination and self-governance had never been tried in Australia.[11] And taking into account the undeniably troubling issues such as child sexual abuse, widespread violence, suicide and community decline, it can be argued that these indigenous communities were simply not in a position to self-govern due to the lack of necessary capacities – a situation which the state had done little if anything to help improve.

Secondly, the government rightly identified 'institutionalised welfare dependency' as a problem, but did not seem to realise that this passivity problem was created partly by earlier top-down interventions and sustained by continuing interventions of the same nature. Simply righting wrongs does not create capacities and skills, but rather places the indigenous communities forever at the receiving end. Capacities will come only with education and adequate learning, open communication and policy experimentation which would allow indigenous communities a certain degree of freedom to try things out and make mistakes while developing their own solutions. The government diminished the effectiveness of its policies by failing to constructively engage with the indigenous peoples it intended to help and support.

---

10 Cf. see Chapter 3 in Iris Marion Young, *Justice and the Politics of Difference* (Princeton University Press, 1990), for a general defence of the welfare state as necessary and humane, but also a warning that it depoliticises the public and restricts social conflict and discussion largely to distributive issues, leaving out important background institutional issues such as policy formation. Of particular relevance to the dialogical concept developed in this book is Young's argument that only when oppressed groups are able to publically express their concerns and interests on an equal basis with other groups can domination be really avoided.

11 Avril Bell, *Relating Indigenous and Settler Identities: Beyond Domination* (Palgrave Macmillan, 2014), p. 151; Sarah Maddison, 'Australia: Indigenous Autonomy Matters' in *Development* (2009) 52(4), p. 483.

Thirdly, while the author is right in quoting that 'if treated like children, [indigenous communities] will always behave like children,'[12] and that 'it is time [for them] to be given responsibility in the right way,'[13] she seems to suggest that to give responsibility 'in the right way' is to grant immediate greater autonomy including real political and economic powers. It is irresponsible to suggest a leap from dependency straight to self-determination without going through the necessary stage of *assisted capacity-building*, or to think that autonomy is somehow a cure-all solution that can make all difficulties magically disappear. This unrealistic 'solution' is potentially chaotic and may collapse into two further approaches: one is *modernisation*, and the other *abandonment*.

(2)   Modernisation

Many have painted depressing pictures of how the arrival of modernity will damage and eventually extinguish indigenous societies and traditional practices of ethnic minority groups, as, according to them, modernity is brutal and refuses to tolerate the ignorant and the pre-modern. Indeed, the need to modernise is frequently cited as a justification for state intervention in ethnic groups' especially indigenous communities' internal affairs. Underlying the justification is of course the hierarchical belief that modernity is a higher level of societal and cultural development. Whilst there is no doubt that in parts of the world state-sponsored modernisation projects have thrown indigenous societies and other minority groups into cultural confusion and social turmoil with devastating consequences, there are also cases where the groups have coped with the arrival of modernisation and managed to maintain traditional characteristics at the same time.

In fact, with the exception of a tiny number of un-contacted groups, indigenous communities and similar groups have long been influenced by modernity. Such influence is expressed most profoundly in their tireless efforts to globalise their struggle and to develop international legal standards on indigenous rights. The results of their efforts are, among others, the UN Working Group on Indigenous Populations, the UN Permanent Forum on Indigenous Issues, and of course the UN Convention on the Rights of Indigenous Peoples 2007. Clearly, in order to ensure the survival of their pre-modern and traditional characteristics, indigenous peoples have had to engage with modernity (as the institution and function of law is most relevant and most significant

---

12   Sarah Maddison, 'Australia: Indigenous Autonomy Matters' in *Development* (2009) 52(4), pp. 483–489, at p. 487.
13   *Ibid*.

in conditions of modernity), and by doing so they have contributed to international law-making and re-making and remoulded international perceptions of the relationship between indigenousness and modernity.

Yet, there can be no doubt that during this process some aspects of their identity have been re-negotiated, compromised, even lost, for as long as there is interaction, there will be influence and change. A distinction must be made between voluntary encounter with and adoption of modernity on the one hand, and state-sponsored modernisation projects on the other. The key problem with many state-sponsored projects is that they are too future-oriented, whilst many, though not *all*, minority and indigenous communities weigh the future in favour of the past. These projects also seem to function on the assumption that the transition process from pre-modernity to modernity will one day be completed. This may never be the case considering how indigenous peoples have learned to use modernity to protect and retain their distinctive traditional characteristics, thus their indigenous identity is now bound up with, and expressed through, modernity, not replaced by it.

It can thus be argued that indigenous and similar attempts to achieve self-determination and self-governance do not flow from a need to secure absolute adherence to 'the old ways'; rather, their claims are concerned with preventing *unjustified* outside influences to force them to abandon 'the old ways.' Change is permitted, but it must come from the inside. Accordingly, it becomes arguable that state-sponsored modernisation projects may become more justifiable if they could slow down and shift the focus from transition to indigenous self-governing capacity-building (which may well lead to transition). In particular, attention must be on developing capacities which will help indigenous communities build up a harmonious relationship between tradition and modernity and achieve a healthy fusion of traditional and modern cultural characteristics. Sub-section 3 below will examine precisely what capacities are needed and how to develop them.

(3)   Indifference and Abandonment

In great contrast to the first and second approaches is that of abandonment.[14] It must be noted that complete abandonment is rare, as in countries with indigenous inhabitants it is often the case that the governments exercise much more direct control over the lives of indigenous peoples than it does over the rest of the population, not least because indigenous groups often occupy areas of land that are rich in natural resources (e.g. the Kgeikani Kweni in Botswana) or have great geo-political significance (e.g. the Tibetans in China). It seems

---

14   Though the three very different approaches have led to similar consequences in reality.

that abandonment, or perhaps more accurately *indifference*, often takes place *after* state-sponsored projects of assimilation have taken place and failed in some way, and typically takes the forms of poor standards of living (especially in government-built settlement villages), lack of access to decent health care, and lack of professional advice and support in exercising their land rights.

In *A Way of Life That Does Not Exist*, Samson brings to light the tragedies of the Canadian authorities relocating the Innu people to purposely built villages which are overcrowded and lack running water and basic sanitation, where they are cut off from their own hunting world and yet remain unconnected to the outside world.[15] Studies like Sanson's as well as reports of NGOs such as Survival International and Minority Rights International have warned that severe undernourishment has made many indigenous communities particularly vulnerable to diseases such as malaria, measles and tuberculosis.[16]

It is clear from these three approaches that there is in fact little disagreement over the key ingredients of the notions of indigenous self-determination and self-governance, namely: freedom to decide one's own fate coupled with some degree of state support. What *is* in dispute though is how much freedom and how much state support. Self-determination should not be about letting indigenous peoples run programmes designed by someone else. Neither should it be about the state irresponsibly transferring decision-making powers immediately, once and for all, to unprepared and unequipped indigenous communities to let them sort themselves out. Self-determination should be a long-term process, during which the state consistently provides programmes, resources and opportunities to gradually, step by step, develop self-governing capacities of indigenous communities, and nurtures a strong and stable policy environment that encourages and supports indigenous solutions. Substantive self-determination is the ultimate goal – not the first step.

(3) *From Dependency, through Assisted Capacity-Building, to Autonomy*
As already shown, critics of paternalistic approaches to self-determination are of the view that *greater, rather than less, autonomy* is the gateway to improvement

---

15   See Colin Samson, *A Way of Life That Does Not Exist: Canada and the Extinguishment of the Innu* (Verso Books, 2003).

16   For example, a 2007 study of the Javari Valley in the Brazilian Amazon warned that rates of malaria and hepatitis were spiralling out of control, with an estimated 90% of indigenous peoples in the area suffering from malaria in 2006 and 85% carrying hepatitis A and 25% carrying hepatitis C. See 'Malaria and hepatitis threaten Javari Valley tribes,' Survival International, 27 April 2007: www.survivalinternational.org; Minority Rights Group International: Brazil: Brazil Overview: www.minorityrights.org.

of indigenous lives and meaningful self-determination, but are often somewhat ambiguous about what this means. Maddison, for instance, seems fully aware of the danger of the unrealistic assumption that indigenous communities will be able to assume immediate self-determination after having materially depended on the state for so long.[17] She sees the danger of creating a 'social void' and clashes between traditional ways of life and newly introduced internal community governing structures (e.g. community councils with elected representatives).[18] That said, she continues to argue that indigenous peoples ought to be given meaningful political and economic power, and especially greater control over decisions that affect their daily lives.[19] She argues so without providing any specifics.

While I agree with Maddison's critique of the top-down coercive indigenous measures, I do not share the view that greater autonomy, in the sense of increased control over community internal affairs, could be an *immediate solution* for all indigenous communities. There are no immediate solutions. At the centre of my objection is the observation that many indigenous communities do not have the capacity to effectively self-govern, which has historical and geographical causes – e.g. historical injustices, geographical and social isolation, welfare dependency, and so on – which have led to, among other problems, educational deficiencies. They also often perceive themselves as victims, powerless, and neglected. I would therefore argue that in order effectively to move from material and rights dependency to meaningful autonomy, we ought to speak less of autonomy at this early stage, and shift the focus, in law and policy, to *assisted capacity-building*, i.e. assisting indigenous communities in developing and upgrading self-governing competence and core capacities. I shall now examine, in the context of the dialogical concept of minority rights, what these core capacities are.

(a)   Which Capacities?
It must be noted at the outset that what is presented here is only a general guideline, which will not be a perfect fit for *all* indigenous groups which manifest a great variety of needs and demands. In order to work out what capacities need developing one must first determine what challenges there are. Indigenous peoples today face many challenges apart from mere preservation of their own customs and cultures, which was once upon a time their primary,

---

17   Sarah Maddison, 'Australia: Indigenous Autonomy Matters' in *Development* (2009) 52(4), pp. 483–489, p. 486.
18   *Ibid.*
19   *Ibid.*, pp. 486 and 487.

if not the only, concern. Nowadays indigenous peoples face rapid change in all aspects of life, and it has become less and less likely if at all possible for anyone to remain totally cut-off from the mainstream society. The traditional idea that indigenous peoples prefer not to be participants in the larger society and that self-determination rights should function to put up fences between them and the rest is looking increasingly like a product of history rather than well-thought out argument based on actual experience. Rapid, massive, changes currently underway open up new possibilities for social and cultural evolution within indigenous communities as well as present open-ended prospects for the better (and also for the worse). Thus, the first core capacity that self-governing indigenous groups ought to develop is the capacity to cope with and take advantage of unprecedented change swiftly and effectively. Failure to do so will not only incur short-term costs but also inflict long-term harm which will diminish chances of meaningful self-determination.

Secondly, in the face of rapid change, the preservation of collective indigenous cultural identity is in danger. While Chapter 2 has argued that it is not the precise characteristics of certain cultures at any given time in history that ought to be protected – rather, the dialogic account of minority rights aims to, broadly speaking, protect an open space within which change, as well as continuity, can take place. This must not be taken to say that steps must not be taken to ensure cultural continuity. Thus, the second core capacity to enable meaningful self-determination in the long run is the capacity to maintain aspects of alternative ways of life, traditions and norms that are considered valuable and essential to the indigenous identity, in the conditions of modernity. What should be avoided at all costs is the old culture being abandoned and the new culture being perceived as alien and inconsistent with group identity. The result will inevitably be that group members are left with very few cultural resources, having been deprived of their own culture and yet unable to properly adopt another.[20]

A third, related, core self-governing capacity that must be developed is the ability to identify the group's own interests and (cultural, social, economic) needs, evaluate opportunities, and develop shared purposes and goals. It is an ability to evaluate the group's well-being and future prospects. But this, at least in the short run, is more of a task for the state and independent professional bodies than for the groups themselves, since as demonstrated by the three approaches to self-determination examined above, the disadvantaged status, the cultural and economic marginalisation, and the self-governing capacities deficiency of indigenous peoples are entirely the direct result of the actions

---

20   This also applies to many other types of minority groups.

and non-actions of the state and non-indigenous societies. In order to develop the said capacity, indigenous communities need resources and opportunities which only the state and independent bodies are in a position to provide; but in order for these resources and opportunities to properly serve the interests and needs of indigenous communities, the ideas, institutions and processes which systematically marginalise these communities must be dismantled first. The key word is *co-operation*.

But no co-operation can take place in the absence of a continuing relationship of trust. This is the fourth core capacity – the capacity to build up and maintain such relations with the state and independent bodies such as NGOs. Arguably this is not a capacity as such but a practical need. Understandably, good relations with NGOs will be significantly easier to establish than those with the state, considering the long history of inequality and broken promises in the relationship between indigenous communities and the state. An important aspect of group-state co-operation is participation by indigenous peoples (and other self-governing minorities) in state decision-making which impacts upon their cultural heritage and daily lives. This is reflected in recent UN and UNESCO instruments which aim to enable such participation,[21] and also in the shaping of the UN Millennium Development Goals which have tentatively incorporated indigenous concerns and have confirmed that there is an urgent need for indigenous peoples to convey their own definitions and understandings of discrimination, poverty and development, and that there should be full participation of indigenous peoples in the realisation of the Goals.[22]

Given that the Goals' overall target date is 2015 and that the UN has admitted to not having managed to fully address the Goals' principles and practices in relation to welfare of indigenous peoples,[23] it is likely that the Post-2015 Development Agenda is going to pay particular attention to indigenous issues such as equality, sustainability and to ensure their effective participation in law and policy making. Thus, the capacity to engage and participate in state

---

21 For instance, article 8(j) of the Convention on Biological Diversity; article 11(b) of the Convention for the Safeguarding of the Intangible Cultural Heritage; the Revised Operational Guidelines for the Implementation of the World Heritage Convention.

22 See 'Indigenous Peoples and the Millennium Development Goals' on the website of the UN Permanent Forum on Indigenous Issues: www.un.org/esa/socdev/unpfii/en/mdgs.html.

23 'Indigenous Peoples and the Post-2015 Development Agenda,' United Nations Permanent Forum on Indigenous Issues: http://undesadspd.org/IndigenousPeoples/Post2015Agenda.aspx.

and international decision-making and goal-setting is the fifth core self-governing capacity.

(b) Beyond Claim and Provision: Governance and Participation through Dialogue

The sixth and seventh related, vital, core capacities that indigenous groups ought to develop should they aim for meaningful self-determination and autonomy in the long run are, respectively, the capacity to develop and maintain a dialogic relationship between the group's internal decision-making bodies and its members, and the capacity to hold and engage in external dialogue with the outside world. Needless to say, these two capacities are particularly relevant to the promotion of the dialogical notion of minority rights that this book has aimed to develop.

In Chapter 3 I examined the necessity of a division of duties between the state and the minority group. I argued that a necessary separation between the state's duties and the group's duties stemmed from a renewed proceduralist and dialogic understanding of the notions of 'self-determination' and 'autonomy.' This dialogic approach allows and requires us to depart from the conventional liberal interpretations of the two concepts, which wrongly derive from them a requirement of drawing arbitrary fixed boundaries between groups, and move towards establishing channels of communication, from a hands-off approach to a very much hands-on *assisted capacity-building, as a necessary transitional measure.*

In the specific context of indigenous self-determination, assigning duties to the group has two significances. The first is that it gives the groups a sense of responsibility and real control over their own domestic matters and especially the well-being of their members, while at the same time, secondly, the special nature of the three rights for which the group is responsible – *'the right to equal concern,' 'the right to internal dialogue'* (which requires the group to establish channels of dialogue between its members and its own decision-making bodies) and *'the right of exit'* (which guards/opens the borders between the group and the outside world, and the realisation of which requires cooperation between the group and the state) – means that effective communication, internal and external, cannot possibly be avoided. Therefore the distance between the minority group and the wider society is significantly reduced, and minorities are drawn closer into the wider world without having to compromise their sense of independence and autonomy, as they remain in control.

But what does it mean and require in order for self-governing groups to develop capacities of internal and external dialogue? I shall attempt to answer this question in a broader, more general, context, by considering a non-exhaustive list of tasks facing *both* the self-governing minorities and the states.

(c)   Main Tasks and Obstacles

(1) *Internal Decision-Making Bodies*: Self-government will only be possible if internal decision-making bodies with at least basic structures and minimal functioning capacities have already been established. Relevant details should be specified in autonomy agreements with the state. It must be stressed that there is no general abstract model that can be a perfect fit for all self-governing groups; neither is there a universally valid operational conception of the best types of self-governing bodies. This is because the desirability of different structures and methods of self-governance very much depends on the particular histories, specific values and beliefs, and the current situation of the group in question. However, it is possible to lay down a few ground rules, which are, of course, open to interpretation and further development.

Firstly, when developing internal decision-making bodies, it is important to keep in mind the seven core capacities identified above, as they correspond to the main challenges facing self-governing groups in the 21st Century. Thus being committed to them should improve their chances of survival and prospects for long-lasting self-governance. Secondly, since, with the exception of very few uncontacted groups, interaction between self-governing communities with the outside world is inevitable, change is inevitable. Internal decision-making bodies should therefore pay special attention to the group's pace and direction of change, and aim to make sense of, and control, them. Thirdly, so far claims of self-determination are made almost solely on the basis of cultural distinctiveness and historical injustice. One is concerned with culture and identity, and the other with domination and oppression of culture and identity. Whilst cultural distinctiveness is undeniable, and the use of law as an instrument to achieve reconciliation is widely acknowledged, when designing and strengthening internal decision-making mechanisms, it might be sensible to focus on the group's weaknesses instead of strengths.[24]

It would be a good start to be able to identify the principal weaknesses of the group as a whole and of the group's internal governing mechanisms in particular, analyse the consequences that these weaknesses have caused, if any, and then develop counter-measures. One likely 'weakness' of such self-governing bodies is, fourthly, the domination of local elites. This is almost inevitable in indigenous communities. While it will be wrong to expect indigenous self-governing bodies completely to cohere with the formal and democratic governance

---

24   I consider distinctive culture and identity to be *strengths*.

systems of the developed world, on the dialogical account of minority rights, self-governing institutions should serve as a means to resist not only *external* discrimination and oppression, but also and especially *internal* exploitation and exclusion. As already thoroughly argued throughout the book, this is partly achieved through external and internal dialogue.

Thus, fifthly, when designing and operating the internal decision-making mechanisms, the greatest emphasis must be placed on dialogue. Both the decision-making bodies and the membership of the group must be able to see the importance of dialogue, and be willing to work with it. It is difficult to lay down precise rules for dialogue, though common sense tells us that it requires, among other things, giving enough space for people to convey their opinions, to be listened to, and to have these opinions taken into account when the internal mechanisms are making decisions.

(2) *Deliberation and Well-being*: In order for internal decision-making bodies of the groups to see the importance of and be willing to engage in dialogue, they have to *learn*, not necessarily *accept*, the values and requirements of deliberation and its relationship with human well-being. They should *be aware of* this reflective way of thinking and reasoning, this rational process of receiving and evaluating a wide range of alternatives, and eventually choosing the most suitable one(s) for the group. To fit deliberation values and processes into systems that are historically *not* deliberative is a difficult if not impossible task, which is why at the very early stage we can only expect these groups to *be open* to the deliberative values and processes, to be *willing to consider* them.

These internal governing bodies will also need a strong sense of responsibility towards not only the wider society but also and especially their own membership. Opinions will undoubtedly differ as to what is good, better, and the best for the well-being of the members. But disagreements can be best solved by argument and negotiation. Deliberation in the form of dialogue should generate more negotiations and debates and will thereby produce more careful and repeated considerations as to what well-being means and requires.

(3) *Education and Enlightenment*: Knowledge should be a rather obvious requirement for self-governance, though surprisingly it is ignored in much of the modern thinking on claims of self-government and autonomy. Achieving deliberation, well-being and self-government depends on having knowledge of the relevant issues and the ability to function. And it is largely through learning that people acquire these skills. In the specific context of self-governing minorities, it is important for their internal decision-making bodies to be trained in all the fundamental aspects of the self-government ideals and processes, including but not limited to the historical development of the idea of self-governance, knowledge of traditional and newly emerged models and trends, skills

associated with administration, accounting, policy research and analysis, and management.

It is also essential for such bodies to know what has worked and what has not worked both locally and globally. It must be noted that education is not just an issue for the self-governing communities. It is also and perhaps especially important for the state and the non-indigenous population to acquire in-depth knowledge of the lived experiences of indigenous communities. There are strong indications that people today are ill-equipped to understand the rationale and practice of self-determination. This, coupled with the states' general unwillingness to accommodate self-government demands, makes meaningful dialogue and improvement of the lives of self-governing peoples extremely difficult.

(4) *Conflict Resolution*: Another difficult task that is facing both the self-governing peoples and the state is that of conflict resolution. There are three overlapping senses of conflict in concern here: the first is conflict between tradition and modernity, the second is conflict between different rights, and the third is conflict when people disagree, when dialogue breaks down. The inevitable clash of traditional *values* and the modern, alien, ones, have already been covered previously, and I shall not repeat what has been said before. But self-governing communities should also be prepared for clashes between traditional community and organisational *structures* and newly emerged models and governing methods. While change seems inevitable, stability *during* and *after* change is not guaranteed.

The second sense of conflict (between rights) has also been touched on previously and will be further explored in the concluding chapter. The need to sort out competing rights claims is an unavoidable challenge in modern societies. Kymlicka, in *Multicultural Citizenship*, argues that the strong self-government rights of self-governing peoples sometimes raise serious moral dilemmas for the state and others. As, while self-governing rights do not justify potential violation of individual rights, given the assertion of rights to autonomy and self-governance, should conflicts between these rights and members' individual rights take place, 'there is relatively little scope for legitimate coercive interference,' and relations between these groups and the state 'should be determined by peaceful negotiation, not force.'[25]

In my view, in the context of self-governing indigenous communities, the problem of rights conflicts is in a way simplified, due to the fact that internally these groups are much less diverse in terms of culture and mentality, which will mean less opportunities of dispute and conflict. It is perhaps not

---

25   Will Kymlicka, *Multicultural Citizenship* (Oxford University Press, 1995), pp. 167 and 168.

unreasonable to expect that in such communities – fragile, with a history of colonisation and oppression, and continue to suffer discrimination and exploitation – if they are convinced that they absolutely must choose between the more liberal rights (e.g. the right to equal concern and the right to internal dialogue) and the rights that aim to affirm communal values and practices (e.g. the group's right to self-determination), many will choose the latter at the expense of the former.

We should perhaps pay less attention to *what* they choose than *why* they choose it. It is to do with social psychology and expectations – you do not abandon your own safety net and embrace the values of those who have historically rejected and continue to reject you. I shall explain in the concluding chapter that there are more nuanced approaches than framing the relevant issues in terms of *'conflict of rights'* (which only seems to generate more conflicts, more confrontations, and more dilemmas). For the purposes of this section, it is sufficient to say that while at present conflict of rights is not the most serious challenge facing indigenous communities, it might become more of an issue as interaction with the outside world increases. And they should be prepared for it.

The third sense of conflict that both self-governing communities and the state ought to be prepared for is conflict during and after dialogue has taken place. This is essentially an issue of dialogue management, which I will examine in detail in the concluding chapter. There are of course other challenges and tasks facing self-governing communities and the state which I do not have time and space to explore in this book. What should be clear though is that self-governing capacity-building is not just about upgrading capacities of self-governing communities; it is about upgrading capacities of *all* concerned. And although the emphasis is on dialogue, dialogue does not stand alone. Its proper place is dependent on many other measures and activities of many different players. Apart from international law and the states, another key player in the field is non-governmental organisations.

(d)   The Role of NGOs

Non-governmental organisations have played and will continue to play a vital but supporting role in the process of indigenous capacity-building, mainly through providing the state with regional and international experiences about how best to bring about real improvements in state policies relating to indigenous peoples' cultural, social, collective and individual well-being.[26] As shown

---

26   Apart from deploying their activities within domestic frameworks, NGOs also seek to influence international decision-making.

earlier in this chapter, governments and bureaucracies are not the best agents of positive change when it comes to improving the health and well-being of the indigenous populations. As impartial and well-meaning third parties, NGOs, both local and overseas ones active in the country, are in a much better position to kick-start processes of capacity-building in those communities. Governments should not only support their work but should also actively seek advice from them. In this way, NGOs can potentially play a very significant role in establishing channels of dialogue between the state and its indigenous communities, and between indigenous communities' decision-making bodies and their members, thereby promoting and realising the rights to external and internal dialogue.

Having said that, although the name 'non-governmental organisations' implies independence from governments and political parties, in reality the vast majority of NGOs rely heavily on governments for funding as well as co-operation.[27] This is potentially controversial, as the whole point should be to respond to people in need with acts of solidarity and assistance irrespective of the government's opinion, and with or without its support.[28] But there exists also an opposite, arguably more serious, problem: NGOs sometimes present a very negative image of themselves as zealous and overly aggressive watchdogs who are ready to cause trouble and do battle with the states at the slightest sign of perceived mistreatment of minorities and others in need.[29]

While it is not uncommon for NGOs to have a different conception of justice and human rights than the governments, they often seem to fail to realise that, in most if not all cases, the surest way to bring about better protection of minorities is through building a solid and continuing working relationship between the NGOs and the state institutions. This will require both sides to clearly define and agree on the necessity of partnership and co-operation, and respective responsibilities; identify shared purposes and interests as well as disagreements; establish and maintain channels of dialogue and communication; constantly search for new and effective instruments of action; and most importantly, share experiences, successes and failures, and learn from each other. In reality, starting such a relationship will be extremely time and

---

27 Christian Tomuschat, *Human Rights: Between Idealism and Realism* (Oxford University Press, 2003), p. 239.
28 In parts of the world, NGOs are also widely seen as of Western inspiration. This coupled with the fact that they are funded by (Western) governments is a main reason why their presence and watchdog function are despised in some non-Western countries.
29 In relation to indigenous peoples, a good example is Survival International, a human rights organisation that campaigns for indigenous rights.

resources consuming, and once such a relationship is formed, it is necessary for it to last long enough in order to make a change, which will further cost time and resources. But common sense tells us that confrontation does not bring about easy agreement and whole-hearted commitment. Perhaps it is time for some NGOs to tone down and soften up.

(e)   Fallacy of Rights Sequentialism?

To recap, this chapter has argued that the short term aim of self-governance should be to enable self-governing minorities to develop core capabilities to self-govern, not to grant them straightaway whatever they ask for or whatever we consider ourselves to be morally and humanitarianly obligated to grant at a particular stage of their historical development. That said, it cannot be overstated that this approach with an emphasis on capacity-building can easily distract our attention from our original intention and ultimate goal, which is sequentially to lay down foundations for meaningful self-determination and autonomy for these communities. Albeit realistic, such *'rights sequentialism,'* if one may so call it, has a dark side. No doubt aspects of it are useful and necessary correctives to the excesses associated with the indigenous rights cause, by recognising that rights promotion takes time, and that neither in the short run nor the long run it is to be a universal cure-call solution to all difficulties facing self-governing peoples. But there is a list of potential problems associated with rights sequentialism regarding the promotion of the rights of self-determination and autonomy.

Firstly, since capacity-building is going to take time, and that it is likely to take a significantly longer period of time and greater effort with some communities than others, there is the danger that over time, intervention (however well-meaning) may become the norm, and governments may gradually and habitually develop inherent contradictions to the idea of genuine self-determination in the long run. Secondly, rights sequentialism requires and presumes good faith. States are presumed to genuinely and consistently want to bring about indigenous self-determination. Unfortunately, this is often not the case.

Thirdly, since clearly the interest theory of rights is a better approach than the will theory for thinking about indigenous self-determination[30] (and rights generally), not only because it focuses the attention on the underlying interests involved and the moral and theoretical arguments required to justify those interests and them giving rise to rights, but also that since interests change over time and according to changing circumstances, we should not only expect our understanding of self-determination rights to be similarly alterable but

---

30   See, for instance, Peter Jones (ed.), *Group Rights* (Ashgate, 2009), p. 482.

also the policies and laws that protect those rights. This could potentially greatly complicate things not least by, among others, providing the state with excuses for indefinitely putting off core elements of self-determination. One can thus confidently predict that rights sequentialism in relation to indigenous self-determination will be favoured not only by realists, traditional developmentalists, but also power holders.

Fourthly, there are too many factors that are not always within our control, the future is thus unpredictable. Even consistent push towards meaningful self-determination could end up somewhere surprising or bring about little systemic change. However, one should be able to claim that when several or all of those factors lean decisively in a positive direction, there is a better chance of succeeding. Nevertheless, it will probably be more realistic to speak in terms of *likelihood* rather than *certainty*.

4   Conclusion

I have dedicated a chapter to self-governance, because it challenges the state system in a fundamental way and will remain a challenge for many countries around the globe. It is the hardest right to defend within the dialogical framework that this book has aimed to develop. It also sits uncomfortably in the international human rights regime, as it does not easily blend in within the generic rights system due to its collective nature; neither does it fit easily into the minority rights framework, not only because indigenous peoples reject their categorisation as 'minorities,' arguing that the difficulties they are facing have very different historical roots; but also that even if indigenous self-determination could be considered a minority right, as I have done in this chapter,[31] it certainly seems to have a very different purpose than the other minority rights – it functions to convert a governed minority group into a self-governing majority in a land which they have historically occupied.

The reasons for indigenous self-determination demands are various; as are the reasons for recognising them. But they tend to flow from a sense that an indigenous community constitutes a political and cultural entity of its own, and their aspirations to collectively decide their own fate are legitimate. This chapter has aimed to show that self-determination should not be an absolute and immediately available right, associated with a high degree of political

---

31 Despite their distinct circumstances, indigenous peoples can be considered 'minorities' for the purposes of this book because they are numerically so, can be defined in terms of a cultural identity, are discriminated against and dominated.

independence; rather, it should be *a process* which consists of three key stages: dependency, assisted capacity-building, and autonomy. The realisation of self-determination has significant implications for its interrelation with other minority rights under the dialogical account, especially the three dialogical rights. It is to be realised through a complex network of political, social and cultural measures within a larger state which ensures meaningful participation of groups with distinct identities. However, there should be no granting of extensive autonomy unless steps have been taken to first develop core capacities of the group in question in order for them to be in a position to efficiently govern themselves. While promotion of self-governing rights constitutes a nation's internal affairs, it has been shown that a wide range of institutions and organisations can and should all potentially play a role in the process of indigenous capacity-building.

CHAPTER 7

The Rights Culture vs. A Dialogical Rights Culture
The Conclusion

> Dialogue is really aimed at going into the whole thought process and changing the way the thought process occurs collectively. We haven't really paid much attention to thought as a process. We have engaged in thoughts, but we have only paid attention to the content [...] Participatory thought is a different way of perceiving and thinking [...] Literal thought aims at being a reflection of reality as it is – it claims just to tell you the way things are [...] as long as we stick only to this literal thought, there is no room in it for participation [...] participation is absolutely necessary if anything is to be done collectively.[1]

In this book I have sought to develop a dialogical notion of minority rights, the legitimacy of which derives not only from theories on the dialogical nature of cultural identity, legitimate law-making, and communicative rationality, but also from the fact that international minority rights law is not only a collection of rules and standards, but an institution responsible for introducing, interpreting, reviewing and revising these rules and standards. The indispensability of a system of minority laws and policies that accurately reflect the cultural needs and concerns of minorities points to, in my view, the need for re-conceptualisation of minority rights and a shift of focus from substantive norms to procedural justice and informal as well as structured dialogical practices, with the specific aim of orienting the rights discourse towards problem understanding, consensual action, and conflict resolution.

The idea of dialogue as a social device is hardly new. It is widely employed in all fields to build better relationships between peoples, cultures, religions and states; to increase awareness and understanding of multiple perspectives; to broaden one's horizon and enable self-betterment; and to reach solutions. While cross-cultural and multi-faith dialogues are very important and necessary, especially in the field of minority protection, as I have aimed to show in this book, in order for fundamental and long-lasting changes to take place, dialogue needs to be written into law, into the very concept of minority rights. The solution I have proposed is the dialogical notion of minority rights. In this concluding chapter I aim to complete four main tasks. The first is to provide a

---

1 David Bohm, *On Dialogue* (Routledge, 1996), Chapter 7.

complete picture of the issues and challenges confronting the minority rights project. The second is to summarise the main arguments presented in the book and to provide a definitive statement of the dialogical notion. The third is to examine the pros and cons of 'dialogue' as a means through which minority rights can be protected. And the last is to forestall some possible misunderstandings that might have arisen from my analysis and especially my talk of 'dialogue.'

1   Minority Rights in the Human Rights System: Pros and Cons

As examined in the opening chapter, for a rather long period of time, minority rights have not been on the top of the list of international rights concerns. Despite a revival of interest, it is still widely, and erroneously, believed that they are less significant than the traditional civil and political rights. Upon closer inspection, however, it becomes clear that very few of the apparent opponents to minority cultural rights deny the importance of culture, cultural diversity, and cultural belonging. Neither do they turn a blind eye to the destructive trends facing the world's cultural minorities, in particular indigenous peoples. They do, however, question the value of some cultures in comparison to others, and more importantly the appropriateness of expressing cultural identity in the language of rights. In other words, while they accept that cultural identity ought to be protected, they do disagree as to the scope and methods of protection.

I have argued in this book that minority cultural rights ought to exist and function within the broader framework of human rights. This does not mean hammering more entitlements into the existing regime; but rather, it requires the establishment of, within the sphere of international law, a cultural territory with more clearly drawn boundaries – which can partly be achieved by the provision of essential definitions which have been lacking so far. The vagueness of the various existing minority rights has been a major obstacle to attributing clear responsibilities to the state and thereby ensuring implementation. But within these boundaries, greater sensitivity and creativity are needed when drawing up and implementing rules in order to reflect the vast complexity of the concept and content of 'culture.' A key implication of this – having divided the general concept of minority rights into *collectively* and *individually* held rights – is that the notion of *collective rights* must now be formally endorsed, a direct effect of which is an apparently broader concept of 'minority rights.'

While this may raise questions as to whether minority cultural rights should/ can remain within the existing human rights framework, there are both normative and practical reasons why they should, can, and must. Firstly, we should respect, protect and fulfil minority cultural rights as key human rights for their profound significance for human dignity. Secondly, minority cultural issues have always been and continue to be linked to large-scale conflicts (societal, political, military), therefore the proper handling of which offers hope of peace and might go a long way towards resolving long-standing disputes. Furthermore, the international human rights regime is the only universal vocabulary that can make the ethical, moral and political relevance of the relevant issues most vividly felt.

Thirdly, minority rights are already enshrined in many of the most profound and broadly ratified international human rights instruments, such as the International Covenant on Civil and Political Rights and the UN Declaration on the Rights of Persons Belonging to National or Ethnic, Religious and Linguistic Minorities. By voluntarily signing up to them, states are obligated and under international pressure to honour their commitment to these minority rights, which are a formal and integral part of international human rights law, and to take necessary steps to protect and promote them. This would not be the case if minority rights were to be situated outside the human rights framework. This also means that, fourthly, human rights mechanisms of international and regional organisations can legitimately set and renew standards for implementation of these minority rights and monitor the performance of the states.

Fifthly, minority cultural rights being part of the human rights system also means that non-governmental organisations and other parts of civil society can cooperate with the international human rights bodies in the monitoring and promotion of these rights. The international human rights regime, being a source of inspiration and motivation for all in the field of minority rights protection, provides not only a concrete legal and policy framework of protection but also institutional machinery of monitoring, assistance and cooperation. Having said that, while there is no question that the international human rights regime in general and the minority rights system in particular have done a great deal of good, as detailed in this book, despite continuous developments in the field, the status of minority rights is far from as prominent as it should be. Sadly, it is being within the human rights regime that has in part caused the problem. There are six related arguments to support this claim.

Firstly, the rights language is narrow, assertive, confrontational, and absolutist enough to encourage conflict and foreclose possible development of meaningful dialogic processes during which calm discussions, exchange and discoveries take place and where necessary compromises are considered and evaluated. As a fashionable and dominant language of speaking about human dignity, welfare and social justice, proud speakers of the rights language often refuse to acknowledge the existence of other equally valid emancipatory languages and policies that are not expressed in the rights vocabularies but may well be, and have been, serving exactly the same end, sometimes with better results. By announcing or implying that the rights language is the *only* acceptable vocabulary to express concerns about human welfare, one is in effect refusing to acknowledge the magnificent contributions made by well-meaning people in non-Western and non-democratic cultures, where the stress has historically and culturally been placed on the fulfilment of responsibilities rather than realisation of rights.[2] This has and will continue to generate resentment, hatred, and consequently unwillingness to comply with *international* rights standards (often perceived as *Western* standards). It will also impair our imaginative capacities of discovering and developing alternative, equally workable if not more so, means of advancement of human welfare.

Furthermore, the black-and-white rights language has also been used as a political weapon, to name and shame, to condemn, to attack. Without providing either the specifics or means of discovering the specifics upon which informed judgement can be made, it can serve as a hard shield of willingness to attentively examine reality, especially other peoples' reality. In other words, by (sometimes selectively) re-framing a social or political harm as a 'human rights violation,' attention is drawn, division is created, sometimes at the expense of better human rights protection. Being part and parcel of the international human rights regime and expressed in the human rights language, whatever resentment consequently generated against human rights in general will also inevitably affect minority rights in particular.

A second, perhaps unintended, consequence of the obsession with expression in the language of human rights is that, whatever that is *not* expressed in that language dose not attract as much political attention or societal emotion, and often generates much less commitment, for they are regarded as less urgent, less serious and less sufficient, even though they may give rise to equally valid claims, but simply framed and expressed differently.[3] Less attention means less effort; less effort means less resources; less resources means less results. Among other reasons given in this book, this explains why, despite a

---

2 For cross-cultural and non-Western perspectives, see, for example, Patrick Hayden, *The Philosophy of Human Rights* (Paragon House, 2001), Part 1, Section 4; Abdullahi Ahmed An-Na'im (ed.), *Human Rights in Cross-Cultural Perspectives: A Quest for Consensus* (University of Pennsylvania Press, 1992).

3 David Kennedy, *The Dark Sides of Virtue: Reassessing International Humanitarianism* (Princeton University Press, 2005), p. 9.

vast wealth of international legal sources and consistent efforts, minority cultural rights remain inadequately developed, and their status as true human rights remains doubtful. Relevant provisions contained in the existing legal instruments do not give rise to genuine legal rights with corresponding, precise, enforceable, obligations. Rather, they create expectations and fuel desires:

> [They] become a phatasmatic supplement that arouses but never satiates the subject's desire. Rights always agitate for more rights; they create new areas of claim and entitlement but these must always prove insufficient. We keep inventing new rights in an endless attempt to fill the lack but this only defers desire.[4]

There are greater, more stubborn, obstacles. As demonstrated in the earlier chapters, the third, most widely debated, 'problem' with human rights in relation to minority protection is its (perceived) close connection with Western liberal values and (excessive) individualism. Many have firmly objected to the claim that the human rights movement is the product of the post-Enlightenment, secular, liberal movement in the West, the product of a specific culture and a specific historical moment in time.[5] They argue that human rights values are really universal, with cross-cultural validity though often expressed differently. Some present as proof that non-Western countries have not only signed up to international rights instruments but have always taken part in the consultation processes. In other words, their voices had been heard and their concerns taken into account and reflected in the resulting documents, then the end product must have represented a high degree of global consensus. This claim is not wrong though only reveals the partial truth.

In examining theories of commitment to international obligations, Simmons looks at different reasons why countries sign up to and ratify international human rights instruments, and divides them into three categories: sincere ratifiers, false negatives, and strategic ratifiers.[6] She finds that, not surprisingly, while European democracies are by far the most likely to sincerely

---

4 C. Douzinas (2001), 'Human rights, humanism, and desire,' in *Angelaki*, 6(3): pp. 183–206, at p. 197; Saladin Meckled-García & Başak Çali, *The Legalization of Human Rights* (Routledge, 2006), pp. 192–193.
5 See, for example, Joseph Runzo, Nancy M. Martin &. Arvind Sharma (eds.), *Human Rights and Responsibilities in the World Religions* (Oneworld Publications, 2003); Abdullahi Ahmed An-Na'im (ed.), *Human Rights in Cross-Cultural Perspectives* (University of Pennsylvania Press, 1992).
6 Beth Simmons, *Mobilizing for Human Rights: International Law in Domestic Politics* (Cambridge University Press, 2009), Chapter 3.

commit to international instruments,[7] non-Western countries, especially non-democratic countries, whose cultural and social values fit uncomfortably with the norms reflected in the international instruments and whose domestic political and legal institutions resist the acceptance of the international human rights regime, have been systematically most reluctant.[8] The result is that they either do not sign up, or they appear supportive in principle but remain uncommitted and fail to ratify (the *'false negatives'*), or they ratify for purely strategic reasons (the *'strategic ratifiers'*) – to gain good press, to improve image, for political, diplomatic or economic gains. In such cases, the apparent 'commitments' are meaningless trade-offs which bring about only instrumental adjustments of external behaviour and no internal change.[9]

Political variations and cultural differences are undeniable. Neither is the fact that international human rights instruments seek to promote idealistic and unduly abstract ideals as to what human interests and aspects of human well-being ought to be protected without offering any detailed instructions as to how or why. This is the fourth problem. The international rights regime is there to set vague standards and to make announcements. But it is one thing to announce protection and quite another to make protection reality. An inevitable consequence of this one-size-fit-all practice is that it generalises too much and downplays genuine variations and particularities of human and cultural experiences, the recognition of which is vital to the spread of the universal value of human rights.

This book has shown that the mainstream notion of minority rights as it stands has inherited this problem. As with other human rights in general, minority cultural rights as they are have been too narrowly and unstably constructed, consisting of general goods and evils, abstract rights and wrongs, failing to reflect the rich diversity of minority interests and concerns and thereby rendering realistic protection impossible. It is convenient and fashionable to blame it all on the lack of political will, but the root of all evil, I have argued, are unstable generalising conceptual tools. As this book has aimed to show, it is both necessary and possible to re-conceptualise minority rights by making it less substantive and more procedural, focusing on building dialogical procedures and particularities into the concept itself, in order to generate better knowledge and greater understanding. Minority rights protection must not be an overwhelmingly one-way street; its realisation requires participation and contribution from both sides. And it is through

---

7   *Ibid.*, p. 61.
8   *Ibid.*
9   *Ibid.*

these two-way dialogues that alternatives can be presented and considered, and solutions may be reached.

Part and parcel of conceptual generalisation is an inevitable fifth problem, that the human rights language/regime constructs problems as well as solutions dangerously narrowly,[10] which is why given particular political climate and social context, human rights can not only do good but can also be used to commit evil, intentional or unintentional.[11] The case in point is the French burqa ban. Both sides were playing the human rights card – whilst those who were pro-ban emphasised freedom from oppression, those who were anti-ban emphasised freedom of religion and belief. In this way, an enormously complex case was reduced to a simple, black and white, issue of conflict of rights.[12] The impression given was that we would have no choice but to choose between two sets of incommensurable values and practices, between good and bad, between justice and evil. Such simplistic mindset caused many to become selectively deaf to the comments of many burqa-wearing women, who insisted that they wore the garment out of free choice.[13]

In my view, the whole debate went down the wrong path, which was partly if not largely due to the inherent deficiency of the rights language. The pressing question was not whether the burqa was an Islamic requirement, or whether some women had been forced to wear it, or whether those who wore it voluntarily were so oppressed that they did not know how to be free and thus ought to be liberated. Participants and observers of the debate did not seem to realise that individual (and indeed governmental) motivations and intentions were often way too complex for us to accurately interpret. This is not at all to deny there were serious problems, serious problems concealed by the burqa. But what we should have been concerned with was whether a simplistic ban could effectively solve those problems. If so, what would be the price to pay? Would it be too high a price? Would it not be possible to deal with the issue in more nuanced ways? Had we exhausted all other means (e.g. social services)? And so on.

It is unlikely that such a ban will solve underlying problems. Far from it. Since the law does not function in isolation, a legal ban can only be properly

---

10   See Wiktor Osiatyński, *Human Rights and Their Limits* (Cambridge University Press, 2009); David Kennedy, *The Dark Sides of Virtue: Reassessing International Humanitarianism* (Princeton University Press, 2005), pp. 10 and 11.
11   See Michael Freeman, *Human Rights* (Polity, 2002), p. 117; Will Kymlicka, *Multicultural Citizenship* (Oxford University Press, 1995), pp. 4–5.
12   More details on conflicts of rights in Section 2 below.
13   This is a good example of the kind of scenarios where the rights to dialogue are necessary.

understood once placed in the wider social and political context. It is not beyond the realm of imagination that an attack on the burqa can easily evolve into an attack on Muslims as a group, on minorities as a whole. Soon there might be more 'controversial' minority cultural practices that would need to be banned. The scariest thing about this ban was the fact that it was carried out in the name of minority protection. This stopped people from inquiring – 'if the practice constitutes rights violation, it can't be good!' There was no longer any need to pay attention to subtle details, and all things became black and white, good or bad, right or wrong. This naive and idealistic take on rights matters has created a false sense of righteousness, entitlement, over-entitlement, which has resulted in means of expressing concerns that are arrogant and offensive, therefore damaging and counter-productive.

The reality is that how successfully rights are protected depends on a complex interplay of different factors, social, economic, cultural, historical, and moral. As Kennedy rightly observes, one of the areas which human rights sometimes turn a blind eye to is distribution of wealth and resources; instead it tends to single-mindedly foreground liberal freedom and democratic participation.[14] Noting the obsession with the rights language and a subsequent unwillingness to explore alternative solutions, Kennedy went as far as to say that 'a practice of rights claims against the state may actively weaken the capacity of people to challenge economic arrangements,' within which remedies to many social wrongs, which are often expressed in the rights language, lie.[15] In other words, the current approach to rights protection treat only the symptoms and neglect the deep-rooted causes, for instance, social inequality and poverty, which cannot always be easily or accurately expressed in the language of rights, and as a result are often either unaddressed or under-addressed.

The combined effect of all these problems is that, lastly, the human rights regime as it is (within which the minority rights system is uncomfortably situated) promises much more than it can ever deliver.[16] While the invaluable contribution of rights defenders must be recognised and applauded, their action sometimes gives the misleading impression that we can be presumed always to know right from wrong and how to right wrongs using the rights tools. This is

---

14 David Kennedy, *The Dark Sides of Virtue: Reassessing International Humanitarianism* (Princeton University Press, 2005), p. 11.
15 *Ibid.*
16 See Wiktor Osiatyński, *Human Rights and Their Limits* (Cambridge University Press, 2009), pp. 40–60; Christian Tomuschat, *Human Rights: Between Idealism and Realism* (Oxford University Press, 2003), Chapter 14; Michael Freeman, *Human Rights* (Polity, 2002), Chapter 6; Will Kymlicka, *Multicultural Citizenship* (Oxford University Press, 1995), p. 4.

simply not the case. Successful rights protection requires knowledge more than it does passion, skills more than it does beliefs, yet knowledge and skills are precisely what is often lacking.

Very few have seen the need to study the *negative* impacts of rights discourse and interventions, how incomplete or false knowledge can lead to irresponsible and counter-productive interventions, or to critically examine how well-intentioned, enthusiastic, well-meaning and righteous rights defenders can go wrong and end up, often unknowingly, entrenching the very ideals and practices they fight to denounce.[17] And when things do go wrong, their belief in the divinity of human rights leads them readily to place the blame elsewhere.[18] In other words, their firm belief that neither rights nor rights defenders can ever do any wrong gives them no incentive to critically re-assess their own beliefs or take responsibility for actions that, however well-intentioned, may have led to negative consequences.[19] Unfortunately, the problem is exacerbated by the often simplistic rights reporting in the media, caused by the lack of legal expertise at many newspapers, symptomatic of what some see as the 'general decline of the legal correspondent.'[20] Since the general public tends to rely solely on locally and readily available resources, they run the risk of being permanently misinformed.

It must be noted that this is not a general critique of human rights or their defenders, but rather a realistic presentation of their limits and short-comings. The dialogical notion of minority rights has aimed to address these limits and short-comings by slowing things down and softening things up, in the hope of gradually removing the 'language barrier' between cultures and countries, which has long been generating misplaced hatred and unnecessary conflict. The dialogical notion functions on the belief that what matters is not only *what* is being said, but more importantly *how* it is being said. Taking rights seriously should not only mean tirelessly striving for their realisation but also taking their limits and short-comings seriously, starting with a tentative and honest re-assessment of our *own* beliefs, commitments and means of expression.[21]

---

17 David Kennedy, *The Dark Sides of Virtue: Reassessing International Humanitarianism* (Princeton University Press, 2005), p. 35.
18 *Ibid.*, p. 30.
19 *Ibid.*
20 See, for instance, 'Inaccurate human rights reporting will not help either side of the debate,' by Adam Wagner, The Guardian, 17 January 2011; 'Legal opinions – Joshua Rozenberg reflects on 25 years covering the law,' by Alex Aldridge, Legal Week, 24 March 2011.
21 See, for example, Steven C. Greer, 'Being "Realistic" about Human Rights,' *Northern Ireland Legal Quarterly*, 60(2) (2009), pp. 145–159; Stephen Kinzer, 'End human rights imperialism now,' The Guardian, 31 December 2010.

2 Minority Rights and Dialogue: Limits, Challenges, Possibilities

As shown in the opening chapter, the minority rights project has been on a rocky path. And as demonstrated in Part 1 of this chapter, being part and parcel of the human rights system means that minority rights carry with them all the downsides (and upsides) of human rights, both theoretical and practical. Traditional engagement with and objection to them are inspired by the belief that the recognition of some minority cultural rights (especially the strong collective ones) is an unjustified extension of human rights and will overburden the very concept and the system. This view maintains that, there cannot possibly be a right to every single thing that is worthy of some sort of protection; neither should the state be expected to protect someone's identity simply because it is distinctive; and many of the things that minority rights proponents claim to be worthy of protection are not in fact so. This is a legitimate and well-intentioned concern. If there is a right to every good thing, the distinctive power and appeal of human rights will be severely depleted. Yet, it is equally arguable that it is never possible to fix an absolute limit on rights claims and aspirations.

Furthermore, the observation of the critics should primarily be viewed as a good sign – it is an inevitable outcome of the overall success of the human rights framework. Successes help further expand the framework, its appeal becomes greater and wider, thereby inviting more and more attempts to push in new directions. These, however, are abstract arguments, and one must not stop at abstract arguments. No-one can predict with absolute certainty as to the future of particular notions of rights, such as the dialogical one developed in this book. Their success or failure can only be determined in practice. And in order for this to happen, the rights, including and especially the ones that are collective in nature, must be considered proper *rights* to begin with. In other words, treating minority cultural rights as proper legal rights, both in theory and in practice, is the first essential step. Thus the question we should be focusing on now is not whether or not minority rights are proper rights, but rather what their boundaries are: what exactly do they protect, where does the protection begin and where does it end? This book has attempted to arrive at a possible answer, but the argument will continue and develop in new directions. Now I shall go through the key findings and conclusions of this book, with the specific aim of forestalling some possible misunderstandings that might have arisen from my analysis.

Firstly, an emphasis on dialogue is intended to generate opportunities for exploration of alternative assumptions of meaning, thinking and understanding, through which fuller knowledge, clearer reasoning, and greater understanding may emerge. It is not at all a call for absolute cultural or moral relativism in the protection of minority rights. Quite the opposite – its ultimate goal is to bring about the endorsement of minority rights across existing normative divides. It is necessary to be aware of the subtle but crucial distinctions between two claims: the first is that rights interpretations are contextual and their protection has cultural foundations; and the second is that rights interpretations are purely subjective and perspectival, with no absolute or universal standards. The second claim signifies absolute cultural and moral relativism. The first claim is the one this work adopts.

One can indeed go as far as to say that *all* conceptions of human rights are contextual. As shown in previous chapters, it is highly arguable that the reason that human rights are in general better protected in the Western world is precisely because the notion was born out of the Western context, the Western culture, and therefore does not clash with Western values and norms. Until very recently, Western conceptions of rights and human dignity dominated the human rights system. They still do, but to a lesser extent, and in the face of continuing challenges, most notably from the Chinese and the Muslim world, the international rights regime has been forced into increasing and repeated contacts with doubts over the cross-cultural legitimacy of human rights universalism. While it is necessary to acknowledge that every conception has a context, one must guard against going too far, not least because to speak about contextual understanding is potentially to generate more contextual *misunderstanding*, which can be problematic. In 'Are There Any Cultural Rights?' Kukathas argues:

> If to do justice is to give each person his or her due, the answer [...] depends on what we think a person is due. The problem is that different cultural communities have different conceptions of what individuals are due or entitled to, and in many cases, these conceptions will not value those freedoms and equalities which figure prominently in liberal conceptions of justice.[22]

This is unproblematic *per se*. But Kukathas claims that, even though there are behaviours and actions in these groups which will constitute injustices according to liberal standards, the liberal ideal of tolerance requires that we allow these conceptions of justice be put into effect. Clearly, as Barry observes, what

---

22 Chandran Kukathas, 'Are There Any Cultural Rights?', *Political Theory*, 20/1 (1992): pp. 105–139, at p. 132.

Kukathas calls 'tolerance' is in fact a form of moral and cultural relativism.[23] A good reason why we ought to reject Kukathas's claim is that membership of these communities are often *unchosen*, and unchosen inequalities and harm caused by internal restrictions must be compensated for, in some way.[24] The question is – in what way?

The dialogical notion of minority rights addresses this question, though it is an incomplete answer to it. The three rights to dialogue – the group's collective right to *external* dialogue, the members' individually held right to *external* dialogue, and the members' individually held right to *internal* dialogue – are particularly relevant.[25] Whilst the first right aims to enable collective cultural expression, to represent and present the group' values and conceptions of justice to the outside world, the second right is intended to enable individual members to convey their own interpretations, express concerns and their individual needs to the state and the wider society, especially but not only in case of internal conflict and oppression. And, as shown in Chapter 5, it is through exercising the individual right to internal dialogue that individual members of the group can voice their concerns, dissatisfaction, and grievances to the internal decision-making bodies of the group.

Furthermore, as stated at the outset of the book, this dialogical approach is far from hands-off, although it does recognise that intervention and assistance should take place within limits. But since it is much more nuanced and tentative than direct state intervention and condemnation, even though liberal ideals of human rights and participatory democracy are embedded, it can realistically be expected to be embraced by even illiberal minority groups. All relevant parties should take full advantage of these dialogical processes of inquiry to establish appropriate interpretative, behavioural and communicative standards, trusting in conversation and dialogue as clarifying, liberating, and connecting. It is in this way that cross-cultural consensus on minority rights *may* be established.

Yet, secondly, it is important to realise that the result of dialogue is not *necessarily* consensus, even under the most favourable circumstances. Neither does the operation of the dialogical notion of minority rights, especially of the three rights to dialogue, presumes the absolute necessity of agreement or

---

23   See also Brian Barry, *Culture and Equality* (Polity Press, 2001), pp. 131–132.
24   See Susan Mendus, *Toleration and the Limits of Liberalism* (Macmillan, 1989), p. 135; Dworkin also makes two distinctions between what one chooses and what one suffers, and between what one wants and what one needs, and argues that 'suffered needs' must be accommodated.
25   See diagram.

consensus. Rather, it requires norms similar to what Allan Gibbard calls 'norms of accommodation' – i.e. values and procedural norms to which parties engaged in dialogue commit in order to communicate and interact with each other.[26] The end result may be consensus, may be further divergence, and may also be something in between – we may have moved closer to each other, just not close enough.[27]

Since consensus is not guaranteed, then, thirdly, enough attention must be paid to conflict resolution. In Chapter 6 I briefly discussed the issue in the specific context of self-governing peoples. In this concluding chapter it is necessary to provide an analysis of a more general nature. Due to the complexity, variety and conflicting nature of human interests (which human rights and minority rights represent, reflect, and protect), conflicts of rights are inevitable.[28] Waldron argues that conflicts between rights are best understood as conflicts between the duties that the rights give rise to and by which they are protected.[29] Unlike rights, duties are much more flexible and are therefore negotiable. On his account, conflicts of rights can be resolved by either choosing duties that are compatible with each other, or by compromising amongst duties. In this way we can avoid having to choose one right over another, which is often an impossible task. Waldron further argues that, in those circumstances where there are no compatible duties, we should turn to examine the purposes of the rights in conflict and then determine which duties best serve those purposes.[30] The result would be step-by-step, manageable, alterations and change.

In reality, however, the assumption that all rights conflicts can be resolved this way (or in any other way) is highly implausible, not only because the purposes of rights are not always beyond doubt, let alone the duties that best serve them; but also that the areas in which rights conflicts take place tend to be the very areas of human life in which the most important and fundamental interests and values are implicated. Compromises are not often possible. However, it is important to note that Waldron's search for externally conflicting but internally related considerations is a highly sensitive and contextual approach

---

26   Allan Gibbard, *Wise Choices, Apt Feelings: A Theory of Normative Judgement* (Oxford University Press, 1990), p. 241; see also discussions on John Rawls's 'overlapping consensus' in Chapter 2.
27   But needless to say, the more agreement we can generate concerning interpretations and implementation of rights and policies the better, as it helps ensure consensus-based social stability and unity.
28   See Jeremy Waldron, *'Rights in Conflict,' Ethics*, Vol. 99, No. 3, April 1989, pp. 503–519.
29   *Ibid.*
30   *Ibid.*

to conflict resolution. It shares the same spirit with the dialogical account of minority rights, in that both are nuanced and proceduralistic, and emphasise *how* we reach our decisions rather than *what* decisions we reach. The three rights to dialogue on the dialogical account are also particularly useful for establishing purposes of rights and discovering internally related considerations and duties, thereby helping to achieve compromises. Although, given the variety and complexity of rights claims, any attempt to develop a general theory of rights conflicts is likely to fail,[31] it is worthwhile to conclude the discussion with a few general points as to how best to approach and cope with these conflicts, and especially how the dialogical notion of minority rights may be of assistance in developing constructive strategies.

First, it is necessary to rethink the very expression of 'conflict of rights.' It seems that fixating on 'conflict of rights' diverts our attention from the fundamental problem at hand: competing cultural values and interests. As McDonald points out, by focusing the attention more precisely on the values and interests which ground the rights in conflict, and thereby leaving behind the 'excesses of "rights-talk" or "the rhetoric of rights", we may be able to engage in more contextual and culturally sensitive talks which may in turn give rise to resolution of conflicts.[32] This is not to say that a direct examination of the relevant interests and values will produce an easy solution to rights conflicts. Rather, as McDonald argues, until the values and interests behind the rights on each side are more carefully considered, we are not in a position to pose, let alone answer, meaningful questions that accurately reflect the problem at hand.[33] Thinking in terms of 'conflict of rights' also forces us to think too narrowly and to aim to solve a simplistic either-or dilemma of choosing one right over another, leaving a complex network of background values and interest unexamined, in which the cause of and potential solution to the conflicts lie.

However, investigation into underlying differences is not enough. Conflict resolution requires also, secondly, intellectual coherence and that we actually believe in the possibility of meaningful co-existence of seemingly competing values, cultures, and peoples. Bohm repeatedly stresses that the greatest

---

31   See Leslie Green's *'Internal Minorities and Their Rights'* in Will Kymlicka (ed.), *The Rights of Minority Cultures* (Oxford University Press, 1995), Chapter 11.

32   Leighton McDonald, *'Can Collective and Individual Rights Coexist?', Melbourne University Law Review*, Volume 22 (1998), pp. 310–336, at p. 334; see also Avigail Eisenberg, 'The Politics of Individual and Group Difference in Canadian Jurisprudence,' *Canadian Journal of Political Science*, Volume 27 No.1, March (1994), pp. 3–21.

33   Leighton McDonald, *'Can Collective and Individual Rights Coexist?' Melbourne University Law Review*, Volume 22 (1998), pp. 310–336, at p. 335; see also discussions on the rights language in the first section of this chapter.

challenge in dialogue is simply let it be – i.e. allowing multiple interpretations and points of view to be – as our natural instinct to agree with those who hold similar views and to disagree with those who differ is too powerful.[34] In other words, we tend to firmly hold on to our own personal meanings, however they came to be in the first place. Once these personal meanings become fixed, they become incoherent, and the degree of incoherence increases when we impose past meanings on present situations.[35] And when this incoherence occurs on a large scale, collectively, fixed personal meanings join forces and evolve into fixed collective meanings, and serve to divide and to maintain division.[36]

In order for meaningful dialogue to take place and for rights conflicts to be addressed and solved, collective coherent thinking and acting are absolutely required. But, as Senge says, '[...] collective coherent ways of thinking and acting only emerge when there is truly a flow of meaning, which starts with allowing many views, an approach that defensiveness precludes. [...] coherence is a way of living rather than a fixed state [...].'[37] In other words, before we can be in a position to resolve rights conflicts, we must engage ourselves in the enlightening process of first noticing, acknowledging and then tackling our own natural defensiveness, and learn how not to let strong impulses override reason. The dialogical notion aims to protect the space within which all this can take place.

Even more difficult to come about than coherence is an unwavering belief in the possibility of meaningful co-existence of different values, cultures, and peoples, which is well illustrated in the endless debate about the relation between group rights and individual rights. This leads to the fourth key conclusion of this book – that collective rights and individual rights *can* co-exist. It is difficult, and questionable in some circumstances, to sort rights into these two distinct categories, especially if we hold on to conventional conceptions, not least because the vast majority of collective rights are exercised by individuals;[38] but also because of the complexity of human well-being, which justifies and grounds rights and is often composed of a great network of interconnected interests with both collective and individual dimensions.[39] Thus, as McDonald points out, it is perhaps more accurate to say that a right has both collective

---

34   David Bohm, *On Dialogue* (Routledge, 1996).
35   *Ibid.*, *Preface*, by Peter M. Senge.
36   *Ibid.*
37   *Ibid.*, xi.
38   Will Kymlicka, *Multicultural Citizenship* (Oxford University Press, 1995), p. 45.
39   Leighton McDonald, 'Can Collective and Individual Rights Coexist?', *Melbourne University Law Review*, Volume 22 (1998), pp. 310–336, p. 320.

and individual aspects.⁴⁰ By doing so the inter-connectedness of the two seemingly competing rights categories is exposed. I do not wish to repeat here the arguments made earlier in this book, except to once again stress that traditional determinist conceptions of group rights and individual rights have caused a great deal of unnecessary and exaggerated fear by failing to recognise their interconnectedness and instead positioning them at opposite ends; and that there is no justification or evidence for the assertion that the mere *recognition* and *inclusion* of group rights into the rights system will necessarily systematically undermine individual rights.

This is not to deny that there are indeed 'gaps' between group rights and individual rights. There are also numerous cases of genuine conflicts between group rights and individual rights. I have aimed to show in this book that the rights to dialogue under the dialogical account help fill these gaps and help us cope with, if not resolve, the conflicts. It seems that if we want a solution we have to really believe in it first. As McDonald puts it, one way of constructively approaching conflicts between group rights and individual rights is to:

> [accept] the assumption of coexistence, rather than asserting pervasive irreconcilability, [and this] may lead to a transformation of our starting question, so we ask not whether coexistence is possible, but a more interesting and urgent question for multicultural societies: how can coexistence be achieved?⁴¹

The answer that I have proposed is the dialogical account of minority rights. However, both as a concept and a practical approach, it has great limits and faces enormous challenges. From here on I shall carry on presenting the key findings and conclusions of this book but with a specific focus on the limits of, and the challenges facing, the notion and practice of *dialogue*.

The challenges confronting the dialogical approach are best understood within a wider cultural and social context. Since dialogue is multi-dimensional and multi-layered, so are the challenges it presents and faces. Ever since the invention of democracy, the dialogic has been an important positive term in modern democracies and a wide range of disciplines. Indeed there is an integral link between the term 'dialogue' and the theory and practice of democracy, and it is stating the obvious to say that the more democratic a society, the greater demand there is for dialogue. Important it may be, the term is neither well understood nor consistently practised. Globalisation has further

---

40   *Ibid.*
41   *Ibid.*, p. 335.

complicated matters by generating and intensifying cultural clashes and religious tensions, and thereby rendering the notion and practice of dialogue inseparable not only from 'democracy' but also and especially from 'pluralism' and 'diversity'.[42] In the specific context of minority rights protection and minority-state relations, with the call for inter-cultural dialogue comes a recognition of the necessity of cultural and religious dissent, and the expression of minority views. It is a matter of engaging contradictions, establishing common interests, and taking action to end unjust sufferings. However, apart from the technical difficulties of enabling dialogue by employing the legal and political means examined in this work, dialogue presents us with an additional number of challenges, some are on-going, others are likely side-effects of the dialogical notion. I shall consider each in turn.

Firstly, this dialogical approach is likely to produce, as an unintentional but inevitable by-product, unhelpful relational and contextual conclusions that are distracting and do not deserve overwhelming attention. It may generate a great deal of open-ended questions, claims, and irrelevant data, which we are obligated to consider if we commit to the dialogical approach – an obligation overtly required by law and our sense of justice but covertly determined by a guilty conscience. The problem is that there are no easy methods of determining what is relevant and what is not; neither is there any guarantee that the dialogues will actually get somewhere. In other words, if mismanaged, the dialogical processes will not only be time-consuming, but also confusing, frustrating, and potentially a waste of time. As Walzer rightly observes, while all ordinary people can be presumed to have some capacity to *reason*, only extremely few can constructively *reason together*.[43] But it seems that there is no other way out except to *learn* through *doing*, to build up participatory and dialogical capacities and skills through actually taking part in the processes. Also, it may be possible as well as worthwhile to see the irrelevant and distracting data generated in the dialogical processes in a positive light. David Bohm sees distraction as an integral part of the process, that 'studying the distractions is part of the process of learning; it is crucial to see [valid data and claims] in the presence of distractions, as well as in a quiet place.'[44]

---

42 For discussions on democratic accommodation of cultural diversity, see, for instance, Chandran Kukathas, *The Liberal Archipelago* (Oxford University Press, 2003), Chapters 5 and 6; Bhikhu Parekh, *Rethinking Multiculturalism: Cultural Diversity and Political Theory* (Palgrave MacMillan, 2nd edition, 2006), Chapter 7; Joseph H. Carens, *Culture, Citizenship, and Community* (Oxford University Press, 2000); and Iris MarionYoung, *Inclusion and Democracy* (Oxford University Press, 2000).
43 Michael Walzer, *On Toleration* (Yale University Press, 1997), p. 145.
44 David Bohm, *On Dialogue* (Routledge, 1996), p. 108.

Secondly, the dialogical approach is not supposed to be costless. In fact it might be rather costly. But costs and benefits will not look the same to everyone. Neither are costs and benefits always immediately apparent or provable. The problem is, as with any system, the dialogical approach needs to be in place long enough to make a change. But cost-benefit issues are likely to cause impatience and diminished confidence in the workability and future prospects of the approach.

Thirdly, the so-called 'minority problem,' even in its most contemporary form, is not a recent phenomenon. Earlier in this chapter I emphasised on the important but often ignored issue of knowledge-building, which is vital to legal and social action and reform not only in the field of minority rights. However, in order to gain knowledge, people tend to rely solely on locally, presently and readily available resources (newspapers, television, social media). It is too often overlooked that a reflection on past actions, successes, failures and consequences can be a vital source of information and new understanding. And since the past is always present and continues into the future, it is important that defenders of, and those taking part in, the dialogical processes pay particular attention to how past experiences inform our future choices. It should be an open and honest dialogue not only with others but also and especially with ourselves.

The fourth challenge facing our efforts to develop and improve dialogue is to do with human emotions, which are persistent features in the cultural field and play a vital role in determining the future of dialogue. In particular, the emotion of *fear* needs to be singled out. Dialogue is a great paradox – it is meant to ease fears (be they rational or irrational), but in order to establish itself let alone achieve its goal, it must first overcome fear. There are many reasons why those who do not belong to minority groups might fear cultural and religious minorities. Firstly, minorities are often associated with the unknown, foreign, secrecy, cultures and peoples that come from the outside into our familiar world. Secondly, minorities are associated with not only difference but even more so with dissent. As Appadurai's says, minority is only the symptom, difference of a fundamental nature is the underlying problem.[45] Thirdly, minorities are commonly associated with unfair disadvantages and special treatments, which are often seen as threatening the common good and general interest.[46] Fourthly, some minorities, e.g. the Muslims, are feared and suffer prejudice not only for what they (are perceived to) represent culturally in general, but also

---

45 Arjun Appadurai, *Fear of Small Numbers: An Essay on the Geography of Anger* (Duke University Press, 2006), p. 11.
46 *Ibid.*, p. 62.

and especially because some have acquired the habit of simplistically associating them with mass crimes and terror since the September 11 attacks.

Thus, it seems that understandably, communicating with minorities could be an uncomfortable if not fearful experience in some cases, especially where the gulf is the biggest and dialogue is most urgently needed. We can say with confidence that much of the fear of minorities is irrational and caused by essentialist understanding of cultures and peoples. But we must also admit that even unreal, irrational, fears do not come from nowhere. They are usually rooted in genuine differences. The problem, however, is that the pattern has been to exclusively focus on and exaggerate those differences, with the 'help' of highly selective media reporting, which tends to leave the general public, who understandably have little knowledge of minority cultures let alone of human rights law, with a skewed picture.

However, it is unclear whether the public is simply misled or the prejudicing is more conscious. It may be fair to say that sometimes we are unwilling to let go of prejudices and partial understandings and fears just so as to ease our own fear, our own sense of insecurity and pain. In the face of vast differences in ideology and practice, what we often try to do, naturally, is to somehow eliminate those differences in order to create a much needed sense of certainty – a false sense of certainty, but a sense of certainty nonetheless. The problem is, in a world of increasingly blurred boundaries, this has become an increasingly distant if not impossible goal, which is bound to further generate and intensify fear, which will in turn lead to more prejudices and fear.

The dialogical approach aims to reverse this trend. Since the public tend not to look far but instead rely on readily available resources, the mass media can and should play a deciding role in easing fears and enabling dialogue – by consciously tipping the balance – e.g. by consciously directing more energy and resources towards presenting minority cultural goods instead of minority cultural bads, and towards shared interests instead of unbridgeable differences. This is not at all to turn a blind eye to differences or to the abuses and wrongs committed by the 'bad guys;' rather, it is to include also the lives and actions of the 'good guys' – who are certainly the majority – to make the picture complete. However, it is unclear whether the Western free media will be willing to, or capable of, working collectively towards a common good, especially considering that it may not be considered a common good. To achieve this requires greater specialist knowledge of minority rights, cultural diversity and cross-cultural dialogue in the media, which the dialogical approach to minority rights aims to help bring about.

But, fifthly, fear does not function alone. In examining why meaningful communication is so difficult to come by, Bohm draws our attention not only to emotions of *fear*, which push one away from critical questions and confrontations, but also to the sensations of *pleasure*, which, in his own words, '[attract ones'] thoughts and cause them to be occupied with other questions. So one is able to keep away from whatever it is that he thinks may disturb him.'[47] The result, Bohm tells us, is that one 'can be subtly defending his own ideas, when he supposes that he is really listening to what other people have to say.'[48] Clearly, in this context, *pleasure* and *fear* are two sides of the same coin. This is another major and potentially irremovable barrier to effective dialogue as it is so deeply embedded in human nature.

Sixthly, it is important to also note that since minority rights issues cannot be separated from politics, there will always be structural and political factors which may prevent dialogue from taking place. What this means is that although an emphasis on dialogue makes minority rights more approachable and more workable, and should thereby generate greater public interest and institutional efforts, which will no doubt contribute to minority rights attaining greater status; we must also be fully prepared to be creative when it comes to means of execution and implementation – they should be sufficiently diverse to cope with foreseeable and unforeseeable difficulties, and not just by formal, legal, means. In other words, making things legal and proper does not mean conversations about them should become rigid. Quite the contrary. People who are concerned with minority rights issues should be encouraged to rethink their concerns, and means of expression, and to think of the relevant issues as issues concerning their own '*duty*' to take an active interest in someone else's culture, rather than that someone else's '*right*' to cultural expression. In other words, we can grant others more rights by taking on more responsibilities ourselves. And sometimes less rights talk is more rights talk.

3 Conclusion: The Rights Culture vs. A Dialogical Rights Culture

Evidently, the challenges facing the dialogic approach to minority rights are varied and profound. The continuous development of the minority rights framework in a relatively short period of time has had a confirmable impact and has continued to inspire a global network of intellectuals and policy-makers who are increasingly intimately familiar with the importance and essence of the cultural aspect of minority protection. Yet, this commendable success hides a deeper failure. Attempts to significantly advance minority

---

47 David Bohm, *On Dialogue* (Routledge, 1996), p. 5.
48 *Ibid.*

rights have remained largely theoretical throughout the world. And where successes have been witnessed, in the presence of renewed and continuous demands of cultural minorities, the law, social policy as well as the general public have often proven to be ill-equipped. The remedy I have put forward – a dialogical concept of minority rights – is not intended to be a cure-all solution, if a solution at all. But it has significant advantages over the existing conceptions, and I believe it to be a step in the right direction. However, it is important for minority rights defenders to acknowledge that minority rights can only ever play a small part in minority protection. Only interdisciplinary, intercultural and intersectional analyses can continuously inform and develop our critical consciousness, which is crucial if we are to successfully manage this field of great complexity and controversy. A good minority rights defender should expect to be conversant with numerous other fields, and it is hoped that as the dialogical spirit spreads, those in other fields will also feel the need to become conversant with us.

Diagram

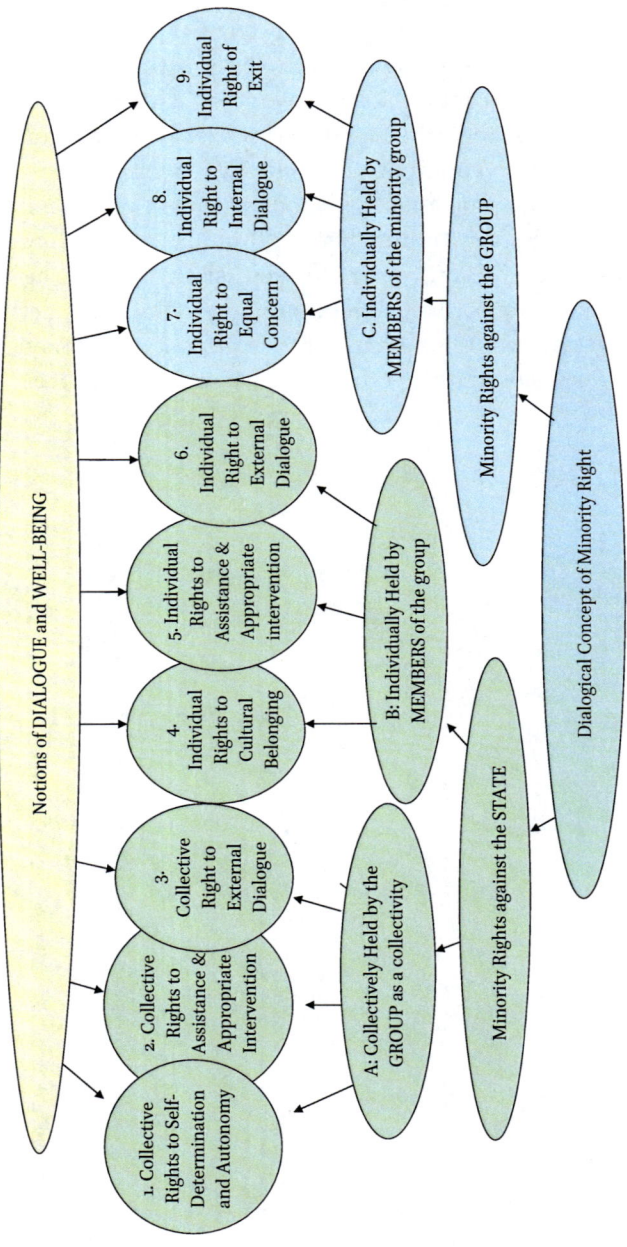

Bibliography

Books & Chapters

Ahmed, Tawhida (2011), *The Impact of EU Law on Minority Rights* (Hart Publishing, Oxford).

Andersen, Erik Andre & Lindsnaes, Birgit (eds.) (2007), *Towards New Global Strategies: Public Goods and Human Rights* (Martinus Nijhoff Publishers, Leiden).

Angle, Stephen C. (2002), *Human Rights & Chinese Thought* (Cambridge University Press, Cambridge).

An-Na'im, Abdullahi Ahmed & F. Deng (eds.) (1990), *Human Rights in Africa: Cross-Cultural Perspectives* (Brookings Institution, Washington, D.C.).

An-Na'im, Abdullahi Ahmed (ed.) (1992), *Human Rights in Cross-Cultural Perspectives* (University of Pennsylvania Press, Philadelphia).

Appadurai, Arjun (2006), *Fear of Small Numbers: An Essay on the Geography of Anger* (Duke University Press, Durham and London).

Arendt, Hannah (1998), *The Human Condition*, 2nd edition (The University of Chicago Press, Chicago).

Arendt, Hannah (2004), *The Origins of Totalitarianism* (Schocken Books, New York).

Arnold, Roberta & Quenivet, Noelle (2008), *International Humanitarian Law and Human Rights Law* (Martinus Nijhoff Publishers, Leiden).

Baehr, Peter R. (1994), *The Role of Human Rights in Foreign Policy*, 2nd edition (MacMillan Press Ltd, Basingstoke).

Banting, Keith & Kymlicka, Will (2006), *Multiculturalism and the Welfare State* (OUP, Oxford).

Barry, Brian (2001), *Culture and Equality* (Polity Press, Cambridge).

Bauer, Joanne R. & Daniel A. Bell (eds.) (1999), *The East Asian Challenge for Human Rights* (Cambridge University Press, Cambridge/New York).

Baumann, Gerd (1999), *The Multicultural Riddle: Rethinking National, Ethnic, and Religious Identities* (Routledge, New York).

Baumeister, Andrea (2000), *Liberalism and the 'Politics of Difference'* (Edinburgh University Press Ltd, Edinburgh).

Baylis, John & Smith, Steve (2005), *The Globalization of World Politics*, 3rd edition (Oxford University Press, Oxford).

Baynes, Richardson and Williams (2009), *Moral Universalism and Pluralism* (New York University Press, New York).

Bell, Avril (2014), *Relating Indigenous and Settler Identities: Beyond Domination* (Basingstoke: Palgrave Macmillan).

Bell, Christine (2003), *Peace Agreements and Human Rights* (Oxford University Press, Oxford).

Bell, Vikki (2007), *Culture and Performance: The Challenge of Ethics, Politics and Feminist Theory* (Berg, Oxford).

Bentham, Jeremy (1996 [1798]), *An Introduction to the Principles of Morals and Legislation* (Oxford University Press, New York).

Berridge, G.R. (1991), *Return to the UN: UN Diplomacy in Regional Conflicts* (MacMillan, Basingstoke).

Blattberg, Charles (2010), *Patriotic Elaborations: Essays in Practical Philosophy* (McGill-Queen's University Press, Montreal).

Bloed, Arie (1993), 'Monitoring the CSCE Human Dimension: In Search of its Effectiveness' in Arie Bloed et al (eds.), *Monitoring Human Rights in Europe – Comparing International Procedures and Mechanisms* (Martinus Nijhoff, Dordrecht).

Boeckx, Cedric (2006), *Linguistic Minimalism: Origins, Concepts, Methods, and Aims* (Oxford University Press, Oxford).

Bohm, David (1996), *On Dialogue* (Routledge, Oxford).

Bourdieu, Pierre (1991), *Language and Symbolic Power* (Polity, Cambridge).

Bradley, Harriet (1996), *Fractured Identities: Changing Patterns of Inequality* (Polity Press, Cambridge).

Breen, Claire (2006), *Age Discrimination and Children's Rights: Ensuring Equality and Acknowledging Difference* (Martinus Nijhoff Publishers, Leiden).

Brigham, John (1996), *The Constitution of Interests: Beyond the Politics of Rights* (New York University Press, New York).

Brubaker, Rogers (2004), *Ethnicity without Groups* (Harvard University Press, Cambridge, Massachusetts).

Buchanan, Allen (2003), *Justice, Legitimacy and Self-Determination* (Oxford University Press, Oxford).

Buchanan, Allen & Moore, Margaret (eds.) (2003), *States, Nations and Borders: The Ethics of Making Boundaries* (Cambridge University Press, Cambridge).

Calhoun, Craig (ed.) (1992), *Habermas and the Public Sphere* (The MIT Press, Cambridge).

Campbell, Tom (2006), *Rights: A Critical Introduction* (Routledge, Oxford).

Cape York Institute (2007), *From Hand Out to Hand Up: Cape York Welfare Reform Project, Design Recommendations* (Cape York Institute fro Policy and Leadership, Cairns).

Capps, Patrick (2009), *Human Dignity and the Foundations of International Law* (Hart Publishing, Oxford).

Carens, Joseph H. (2000), *Culture, Citizenship, and Community* (Oxford University Press, Oxford).

Carter, Ian (1999), *A Measure of Freedom* (Oxford University Press, Oxford).

Casesse, Antonio (1995), *Self-determination of Peoples: A Legal Reappraisal* (Cambridge University Press, Cambridge).
Castellino, Joshua & Domínguez Redondo, Elvira (2006), *Minority Rights in Asia* (Oxford University Press, Oxford).
Castellino, Joshua & Cavanaugh, Kathleen A. (2013), *Minority Rights in the Middle East* (Oxford University Press, Oxford).
Chafetz, Glenn, Spirtaz, Michael & Frankel, Benjamin (eds.) (1999), *The Origins of National Interests* (Frank Cass Publishers, London).
Christiano, Thomas (ed.) (2003), *Philosophy and Democracy* (Oxford University Press, New York).
Clark, Ian (2007), *International Legitimacy and World Society* (Oxford University Press, Oxford).
Claude, Inis (1955), *National Minorities: An International Problem* (Harvard University Press, Cambridge, Mass.).
Clayton, R. & Tomlinson, H. (2003), *The Law of Human Rights* (Oxford University Press, Oxford).
Coates, Ken (1988), *Think Globally, Act Locally* (Spokesman, Nottingham).
Cohen, G.A. (1995) *Self-ownership, Freedom and Equality* (Cambridge University Press, Cambridge).
Coleman, Isobel (2010), *Paradise Beneath Her Feet: How Women are Transforming the Middle East* (Random House, New York).
Cowan, Dembour & Wilson (eds.) (2001), *Culture and Rights* (Cambridge University Press, Cambridge).
Cram, Ian (2006), *Contested Words: Legal Restrictions on Freedom of Speech in Liberal Democracies* (Ashgate, Aldershot).
Crawford, James (ed.) (1992), *Language Loyalties* (University of Chicago Press, Chicago).
Dalacoura, Katerina (2003), *Islam, Liberalism and Human Rights* (I.B. Tauris & Co Ltd, London).
Dean, Hartley (ed.) (2004), *The Ethics of Welfare* (The Policy Press, Bristol).
De Bary, Wm. Theodore & Tu Wei-Ming (1998), *Confucianism and Human Rights* (Columbia University Press, New York).
De Feyter, Koen & Pavlakos, George (2008), *The Tension between Group Rights and Human Rights* (Hart Publishing, Oxford).
De-Shalit, A. & Bell, D.A. (eds.) (2003), *Forms of Justice: Critical Perspectives on David Millers Political Philosophy* (Rowman and Littlefield, Lanham, MD).
Donnelly, Jack (1985), *The Concept of Human Rights* (St Martin's Press, New York).
Donnelly, Jack (2003), *Universal Human Rights: In Theory and Practice,* 2nd ed. (Cornell University Press, Ithaca).
Donskis, Leonidas (2009), *Troubled Identity and the Modern World* (Palgrave, New York).

Dowding, Goodin & Pateman (2004), *Justice and Democracy* (Cambridge University Press, Cambridge).
Dror, Yehezkel (1994), *The Capacity to Govern* (Frank Cass Publishers, London).
Drzewicki, Krzysztof (2010), 'The OSCE Lund Recommendations in the Practice of the High Commissioner on National Minorities', in Weller & Nobbs (eds.) (2010), *Political Participation of Minorities: A Commentary on International Standards and Practice* (Oxford University Press, Oxford).
Dworkin, Ronald (1977), *Taking Rights Seriously* (Harvard University Press, Cambridge, Massachusetts).
Dworkin, Ronald (1998), *Law's Empire* (Hart Publishing, Oxford).
Dworkin, Ronald (2002), *Sovereign Virtue: The Theory and Practice of Equality* (Harvard University Press, Cambridge, Massachusetts).
Eisenberg, Avigail & Spinner-Halev, Jeff (eds.) (2005), *Minorities within Minorities: Equality, Rights and Diversity* (Cambridge University Press, Cambridge).
Elster, Jon (1983), *Sour Grapes: Studies in the Subversion of Rationality* (Cambridge University Press, Cambridge).
Evans, Malcolm (1997), *Religious Liberty and International Law in Europe* (Cambridge University Press, Cambridge).
Feldman, David (2002), *Civil Liberties and Human Rights in England and Wales*, 2nd edition (Oxford University Press, Oxford).
Fenton, S., & May, S. (eds.) (2002), *Ethno-National Identities* (Palgrave Macmillan, Basingstoke).
Feyter, Koen de & Pavlakos, George (eds.) (2008), *The Tension between Group Rights and Human Rights* (Hart Publishing, Oxford).
Flathman, Richard E. (1992), *Wilful Liberalism: Voluntarism and Individuality in Political Theory and Practice* (Cornell University Press, New York).
Ford, Richard T. (2005), *Racial Culture: A Critique* (Princeton University Press, Princeton).
Forsythe, David P. (2006), *Human Rights in International Relations*, 2nd edition, (Cambridge University Press, Cambridge).
Francioni, Francesco & Scheinin, Martin (eds.) (2008), *Cultural Human Rights* (Martinus Nijhoff Publishers, Leiden).
Fraser, Nancy (1997), *Justice Interruptus: Critical Reflections on the "Postsocialist" Condition* (Routledge, New York).
Freeman, Michael (2002), *Human Rights* (Polity Press, Cambridge).
Frey, R.G. (ed.) (1985), *Utility and Rights* (Basil Blackwell, Oxford).
Frey, R.G. & Morris, C.W. (eds.) (1993), *Value, Welfare and Morality* (Cambridge University Press, Cambridge).
Fromm, Erich (2001), *The Fear of Freedom* (Routledge Classics, Oxford).
Galbreath, David & Gebhard, Carmen (2010), *Cooperation or Conflict? Problematizing Organizational Overlap in Europe* (Ashgate, Surrey).

Galbreath, David & McEvoy, Joanne (2012), *The European Minority Rights Regime: Towards a Theory of Regime Effectiveness* (Palgrave Macmillan, Basingstoke).
Garcia, O., Skutnabb-Kangas., T. & Torres-Guzman, M. (eds.) (2006), *Imagining Multilingual Schools: Languages in Education and Globalization* (Multilingual Matters Ltd, Clevedon).
Gareau, Frederick H. (2002), *The United Nations and Other International Institutions* (Burnham Inc., Publishers, Chicago).
Gaus, Gerald & Kukathas, Chandran (eds.) (2004), *The Handbook of Political Theory* (Sage Publications, London).
Ghanea, Nazila; Stephens, Alan & Walden, Raphael (eds.) (2007), *Does God Believe in Human Rights?* (Martinus Nijhoff Publishers, Leiden).
Gibbard, Allan, *Wise Choices, Apt Feelings: A Theory of Normative Judgement* (Oxford University Press, Oxford).
Goodhart, Michael (ed.) (2009), *Human Rights: Politics & Practice* (Oxford University Press, Oxford).
Gow, David, D. (2008), *Countering Development: Indigenous Modernity and the Moral Imagination* (Duke University Press, Durham and London).
Gray, Christine (2008), *International Law and the Use of Force* (Oxford University Press).
Greer, Steven C. (2006), *The European Convention on Human Rights: Achievements, Problems and Prospects* (Cambridge University Press, Cambridge).
Habermas, Jürgen (1989), *The Structural Transformation of the Public Sphere,* trans. by Thomas Burger (Polity Press, Cambridge).
Habermas, Jürgen (1993), *Justification and Application* (Polity, Cambridge).
Habermas, Jürgen (1996), *Between Facts and Norms: Contributions to a Discourse Theory of Law and Democracy,* translated by William Rehg (Polity Press, Cambridge).
Habermas, Jürgen (2006), *The Divided West* (Polity Press, Cambridge).
Hale, Charles, R. (ed.) (2008), *Engaging Contradictions: Theory, Politics, and Methods of Activist Scholarship* (University of California Press, Berkeley).
Hastings, Adrian (1997), *The Construction of Nationhood: Ethnicity, Religion and Nationalism* (Cambridge University Press, Cambridge).
Hayden, Patrick (2001), *The Philosophy of Human Rights* (Paragon House, St. Paul).
Heeger, R. *et al.* (eds.) (1998), *Ethical Theory and Moral Practice,* Volume 1, No. 2, (Kluwer Academic Publishers, Netherlands).
Henrard, Kristin & Dunbar, Robert (eds.) (2008), *Synergies in Minority Protection: European and International Law Perspectives* (Cambridge University Press, Cambridge).
Hirschman, Albert O. (1970), *Exit, Voice, and Loyalty* (Harvard University Press, Cambridge, Massachusetts).
Hofmann, Rainer (2008), 'Implementation of the FCNM: Substantive Challenges' in Verstichel, Alen, De Witte & Lemmens (eds.) (2008), *The Framework Convention for the Protection of National Minorities: A Useful Pan-European Instrument?* (Intersentia, Antwerp).

Honderich, Ted (ed.) (2005), *Oxford Companion to Philosophy* (Oxford University Press, Oxford).

Honig, Bonnie & Mapel, David R. (2002), *Scepticism, Individuality and Freedom* (University of Minnesota, Minnesota).

Joachim, Jutta, Reinalda, and Verbeek (eds.) (2007), *International Organizations and Implementation: Enforcers, Managers, Authorities?* (Routledge, London and New York).

Jones, Peter (ed.) (2009), *Group Rights* (Ashgate, Surrey).

Kalantzis, Cope & Slade (1989), *Minority Languages and Dominant Culture: Issues of Education, Assessment and Social Equality* (Falmer Press, London).

Kant, Immanuel (1991), *The Moral Law: Groundwork of the Metaphysic of Morals*, trans. by H.J. Paton (Routledge, New York).

Kant, Immanuel (2005), *The Critique of Pure Reason*, translated by Norman Kemp Smith, 2nd edition (Palgrave Macmillan, London).

Kaufman, A. (2006), *Capabilities Equality* (Routledge, Oxford).

Keller, Helen & Sweet, Alec Stone (2008), *A Europe of Rights: The Impact of the ECHR on National Legal Systems* (Oxford University Press, Oxford).

Kelley, Judith (2004), *Ethnic Politics in Europe: The Power of Norms and Incentives* (Princeton University Press, Princeton).

Kelly, John Maurice (1992), *A Short History of Western Legal Theory* (Clarendon Press, Oxford).

Kelly, Paul (ed.) (2002), *Multiculturalism Reconsidered* (Polity, Cambridge).

Kelly, Paul (2005), *Liberalism* (Polity, Cambridge).

Kent, Ann (1999), *China, United Nations and Human Rights: The Limits of Compliance* (University of Pennsylvania Press, Philadelphia).

Kennedy, David (2005), *The Dark Sides of Virtue: Reassessing International Humanitarianism* (Princeton University Press, Princeton).

Kennedy, David (2006), *Of War and Law* (Princeton University Press, Princeton).

Kivisto, Peter (2005), *Incorporating Diversity: Rethinking Assimilation in a Multicultural Age* (Paradigm Publishers, Boulder).

Kontra, Phillipson, Skutnabb-Kangas & Varady (1999), *Language: a Right and a Resource* (Central European University Press, Budapest).

Koskenniemi, Martti (2006), *From Apology to Utopia: the Structure of International Legal Argument* (Cambridge University Press, Cambridge).

Kramer, Hilton & Kimball, Roger (eds.) (1999), *The Betrayal of Liberalism: How the Disciples of Freedom and Equality Helped Foster the Illiberal Politics of Coercion and Control* (Ivan R. Dee, Chicago).

Kramer, Matthew; Simmonds, Nigel & Steiner, Hillel (1998), *A Debate Over Rights: Philosophical Enquiries* (Oxford University Press, Oxford).

Krasner, Stephen (1999), *Sovereignty: Organized Hypocrisy* (Princeton University Press, Princeton).

Kukathas, Chandran (2003), *The Liberal Archipelago* (Oxford University Press, Oxford).
Kymlicka, Will (1989), *Liberalism, Community, and Culture* (Oxford University Press, Oxford).
Kymlicka, Will (1995), *Multicultural Citizenship* (Oxford University Press, Oxford).
Kymlicka, Will (ed.) (1995), *The Rights of Minority Cultures* (Oxford University Press, Oxford).
Kymlicka, Will (2001), *Politics in the Vernacular: Nationalism, Multiculturalism and Citizenship*, (Oxford University Press, Oxford).
Kymlicka, Will & Magda Opalski (2001), *Can Liberal Pluralism Be Exported?* (Oxford University Press, Oxford).
Kymlicka, Will (2002), *Contemporary Political Philosophy: An Introduction,* 2nd edition, (Oxford University Press, Oxford).
Kymlicka, Will & Patten, Alan (eds.) (2003), *Language Rights and Political Theory* (Oxford University Press, Oxford).
Kymlicka, Will & He, Baogang (eds.) (2005), *Multiculturalism in Asia* (Oxford University Press, New York).
Kymlicka, Will (2007), *Multicultural Odysseys: Navigating the New International Politics of Diversity* (Oxford University Press, Oxford).
Kymlicka, Will (2008), 'The Internationalization of Minority Rights', in Sujit Choudhry (ed.) *Constitutional Design for Divided Societies: Integration or Accommodation?* (Oxford University Press, Oxford).
Kymlicka, Will & Bashir, Bashir (eds.) (2010), *The Politics of Reconciliation in Multicultural Societies* (Oxford University Press, Oxford).
Laden, Anthony Simon & Owen, David (2007), *Multiculturalism and Political Theory* (Cambridge University Press, Cambridge).
Levy, Jacob (2000), *The Multiculturalism of Fear* (Oxford University Press, Oxford).
Lewin, Kurt (1948), *Resolving Social Conflicts: Selected Papers on Group Dynamics* (Harper & Brothers, 1st edition).
Locke, John (1988), *Two Treaties of Government,* ed. Peter Laslett (Cambridge University Press, Cambridge).
MacCormick, Neil (2007), *Institutions of Law: An Essay in Legal Theory* (Oxford University Press, Oxford).
MacGilvray, Eric (2004), *Reconstructing Public Reason* (Harvard University Press, Cambridge, Massachusetts).
Marshall, Jill (2009), *Personal Freedom through Human Rights Law?* (Martinus Nijhoff Publishers, Leiden).
May, Steven (2001), *Language and Minority Rights: Ethnicity, Nationalism and the Politics of Language* (Pearson Education Ltd, Essex).
May, Steven, Modood, Tariq & Squires, Judith (eds.) (2004), *Ethnicity, Nationalism and Minority Rights* (Cambridge University Press, Cambridge).

May, Steven, & Modood, Tariq (eds.) (2005), *Ethnicities,* Volume 5 (Sage Publications, London).

McDonough, Kevin & Feinberg, Walter (2003), *Citizenship and Education in Liberal-Democratic Societies* (Oxford University Press, Oxford).

McIlwain, Charles Howard (1940), *Constitutionalism Ancient and Modern* (Cornell University Press, Ithaca).

Meckled-García, Saladin & Çali, Başak (2006), *The Legalization of Human Rights* (Routledge, Oxford).

Mendus, Susan (1989), *Toleration and the Limits of Liberalism* (Macmillan, London).

Mendus, Susan (2009 [1988]), *Justifying Toleration: Conceptual and Historical Perspectives* (Cambridge University Press, Cambridge).

Mill, John Stuart (1974), *On Liberty* (Penguin, Harmondsworth).

Mill, John Stuart (1991), *Considerations on Representative Government* (original 1861), in *On Liberty and Other Essays* (Oxford University Press, Oxford).

Mill, John Stuart (1998 [1863]), *Utilitarianism* (*Oxford University Press, Oxford*).

Modood, Tariq (2005), *Multicultural Politics: Racism, Ethnicity, and Muslims in Britain* (Edinburgh University Press, Edinburgh).

Moïsi, Dominique (2009), *The Geopolitics of Emotion: How Cultures of Fear, Humiliation and Hope are Reshaping the World* (The Bodley Head, London).

Moravcsik, Andrew (1995), *The Choice for Europe* (UCL Press, London).

Murray, Rachel (2004), *Human Rights in Africa* (Cambridge University Press, Cambridge).

Nagel, Thomas (1991), *Equality and Partiality* (Oxford University Press, New York).

Nash, Kate (2009), *The Cultural Politics of Human Rights: Comparing the US and UK* (Cambridge University Press, Cambridge).

Nielsen, Laura Beth (2007), *Theoretical and Empirical Studies of Rights* (Ashgate Publishing Ltd, Aldershot).

Nowak, Manfred (1993), *U.N. Covenant on Civil and Political Rights: CPPR Commentary* (Kehl am Rhein: N P Engel Pub).

Nussbaum, Martha (2000), *Women and Human Development: The Capabilities Approach* (Cambridge University Press, Cambridge).

Okin, Susan Moller (1999), *Is Multiculturalism Bad For Women?* (Princeton University Press, Princeton).

Osiatyński, Wiktor (2009), *Human Rights and Their Limits* (Cambridge University Press, Cambridge).

Ostrom, Elinor (2005), *Understanding Institutional Diversity* (Princeton University Press, Princeton).

Otsuka, Michael (2003), *Libertarianism without Inequality* (Oxford University Press, Oxford).

Own, Nicholas (ed.) (2003), *Human Rights, Human Wrongs* (Oxford University Press, Oxford).

Packer, John & Myntti, Kristian (eds.) (1993), *The Protection of Ethnic and Linguistic Minorities in Europe* (Turku: Institute for Human Rights, Åbo Akademi University).

Parekh, Bhikhu (2000), *The Future of Multi-Ethnic Britain* (Profile Books, London).

Parekh, Bhikhu (2006), *Rethinking Multiculturalism: Cultural Diversity and Political Theory*, 2nd edition, (Palgrave Press, London).

Peerenboom, Randall (ed.) (2004), *Asian Discourses of Rule of Law: Theories and Implementation of Rule of Law in Twelve Asian Countries, France and the US* RoutledgeCurzon, London).

Pentassuglia, Gaetano (2009), *Minority Groups and Judicial Discourse in International Law: A Comparative Perspective* (Martinus Nijhoff Publishers, Leiden).

Phillips, Anne (1999), *Which Equalities Matter?* (Polity Press, Cambridge).

Phillips, Anne (2007), *Multiculturalism Without Culture* (Princeton University Press, Princeton).

Pojman, Louis & Westmoreland, Robert (1997), *Equality: Selected Readings* (Oxford University Press, New York).

Pridham, Geoffrey (2005), *Designing Democracy* (Palgrave Macmillan, New York).

Psychogiopoulou, Evangelia (2008), *The Integration of Cultural Considerations in EU Law and Policies* (Martinus Nijhoff Publishers, Leiden).

Quong, Jonathan (2010), *Liberalism without Perfection* (Oxford University Press, Oxford).

Rajagopal, Balakrishnan (2003), *International Law from Below: Development, Social Movements and Third World Resistance* (Cambridge University Press, Cambridge).

Rawls, John (1971), *A Theory of Justice* (Harvard University Press, Cambridge, Massachusetts).

Rawls, John (1996), *Political Liberalism* (Columbia University Press, New York).

Rawls, John (1999), *The Law of Peoples* (Harvard University Press, Cambridge, Massachusetts).

Raz, Joseph (1986), *The Morality of Freedom* (Oxford University Press, Oxford).

Raz, Joseph (1994), *Ethics in the Public Domain* (Clarendon Press, Oxford).

Rechel, Bernd (2009), *The Long Way Back to Europe: Minority Protection in Bulgaria* (Ibidem Verlag, Stuttgart).

Rechel, Bernd (2009), *Minority Rights in Central and Eastern Europe* (Routledge, London).

Richardson, Henry & Melissa Williams (2009), *Moral Universalism and Pluralism* (New York University Press, New York).

Rosen, Michael & Wolff, Jonathan (1999), *Political Thought* (Oxford University Press, Oxford).

Rousseau, Jean-Jacques (2004), *Discourse on the Origin of Inequality* (Dover Publications).

Runzo, Joseph, Sharma, Nancy M. & Martin, Arvind (2003), *Human Rights and Responsibilities in the World Religions* (Oneworld Publications, Oxford).

Russell, Bertrand (1949), *Authority and the Individual* (Routledge, London).

Sachedina, Abudulaziz (2009), *Islam and the Challenge of Human Rights* (Oxford University Press, New York).

Samson, Colin (2003), *A Way of Life That Does Not Exist: Canada and the Extinguishment of the Innu* (Verso Books, London).

Sandel, Michael (1998), *Liberalism and the Limits of Justice*, 2nd edition (Cambridge University Press, New York).

Sartre, Jean-Paul (1960), *Anti-Semite and Jew* (New York: Grove Press).

Selbourne, David (1994), *The Principle of Duty: An Essay on the Foundations of the Civic Order* (Sinclair-Stevenson, London).

Sen, Amartya (2001), *Development as Freedom* (Oxford University Press, Oxford).

Sen Amartya (2009), *The Idea of Justice* (Penguin Books, London).

Shachar, Ayelet (2001), *Multicultural Jurisdictions: Cultural Differences and Women's Rights* (Cambridge University Press, Cambridge).

Shapiro, Ian & Kymlicka, Will (eds.) (1997), *Ethnicity and Group Rights* (New York University Press, New York).

Shivji, I.G. (1989), *The Concept of Human Rights in Africa* (CODESRIA Book Series, London).

Siim, Berte & Squires, Judith (eds.) (2008), *Contesting Citizenship* (Routledge, London).

Simmonds, Nigel (2002), *Central Issues in Jurisprudence: Justice, Law and Rights*, 2nd edition (Sweet & Maxwell, London).

Simmonds, Nigel (2007), *Law as a Moral Idea* (Oxford University Press, Oxford).

Simmons, Alan John (1979), *Moral Principles and Political Obligations* (Princeton University Press, Princeton).

Simmons, Beth (2009), *Mobilizing for Human Rights: International Law in Domestic Politics* (Cambridge University Press, New York).

Skirbekk, Gunnar & Gilje, Nils (2001), *A History of Western Thought: From Ancient Greece to the Twentieth Century* (Routledge, London).

Skutnabb-Kangas, T. & Phillipson, R. (eds.) (1995), *Linguistic Human Rights: Overcoming Linguistic Discrimination* (Mouton de Gruyter, Berlin).

Skutnabb-Kangas, T. (2000), *Linguistic Genocide in Education or Worldwide Diversity and Human Rights* (LEA Publishers, London).

Sottiaux, Stefan (2008), *Terrorism and the Limitation of Rights* (Hart Publishing, Oxford).

Spinner-Halev, Jeff (2000), *Surviving Diversity: Religion and Democratic Citizenship* (John Hopkins University Press, Baltimore).

Sriram, Chandra Lekha (2004), *Confronting Past Human Rights Violations* (Frank Cass, Oxford).
Steiner, Hillel (1994), *An Essay on Rights* (Blackwell Publishers, Oxford).
Sunstein, Cass (2001), *Designing Democracy: What Constitutions Do* (Oxford University Press, New York).
Svensson, Marina (2002), *Debating Human Rights in China: A Conceptual and Political History* (Rowman & Littlefield Publishers, Maryland).
Tan, Gerald (2000), *Asian Development: An Introduction to Economic, Social and Political Change in Asia* (Times Academic Press, Singapore).
Tan, Sor-Hoon (2004), *Confucian Democracy* (State University of New York Press, New York).
Taylor, Charles (1991), 'Shared and Divergent Values', in Watts and Brown (eds.), *Options for a New Canada* (University of Toronto Press, Toronto).
Taylor, Charles (1994), *Multiculturalism: Examining the Politics of Recognition* (Princeton University Press, 1994).
Taylor, Ward, Henderson, Davis and Wallis (eds.) (2005), *The Power of Knowledge: The Resonance of Tradition* (Aboriginal Studies Press, Canberra).
Thio, Li-Ann (2005), *Managing Babel: The International Legal Protection of Minorities in the Twentieth Century* (Martinus Nijhoff Publishers, Leiden).
Tomuschat, Christian (2003), *Human Rights: Between Idealism and Realism* (Oxford University Press, Oxford).
Torbisco Casals, Neus (2006), *Group Rights as Human Rights* (Springer, Dordrecht).
Tyler, Tom R. (ed.) (2005), *Procedural Justice,* Volumes I and II (Ashgate Publishing Limited, Aldershot).
Tylor, Edward (1871), *Primitive Culture* (John Murray, London).
UNDP (2000), *Overcoming Poverty* (UN Development Program, New York).
Unger, Peter (1996), *Living High & Letting Die: Our Illusion of Innocence* (Oxford University Press, New York).
Van Cott, Donna Lee (1994), *Indigenous Peoples and Democracy in Latin America* (St Martin's Press, New York).
Van Cott, Donna Lee (2000), *The Friendly Liquidation of the Past: The Politics of Diversity in Latin America* (University of Pittsburgh Press, Pittsburgh).
Van Ness, Peter (1999), *Debating Human Rights* (Routledge, London).
Verstichel, Annelies (2010), 'Understanding Minority Participation and Representation and the Issue of Citizenship', in Weller & Nobbs (eds.) (2010), *Political Participation of Minorities: A Commentary on International Standards and Practice* (Oxford University Press, Oxford).
Walzer, Michael (1997), *On Toleration* (Yale University Press, New Haven).
Walzer, Michael (2006), *Just and Unjust Wars,* 4th edition. (Basic Books, New York).
Weatherley, Robert (1999), *The Discourse of Human Rights in China: Historical and Ideological Perspectives* (Palgrave, Basingstoke and New York).

Weil, Simone (2001), *Oppression and Liberty* (Routledge, London).

Weller, M. (ed.) (2005), *The Rights of Minorities in Europe: A Commentary on European Framework Convention for the Protection of National Minorities* (Oxford: Oxford Univeristy Press).

Weller & Nobbs (eds.) (2010), *Political Participation of Minorities: A Commentary on International Standards and Practice* (Oxford University Press, Oxford).

Wellman, C. (1997), *An Approach to Rights: Studies in the Philosophy of Law and Morals* (Kluwer Academic Publishers, Dordrecht).

Wheatley, Steven (2005), *Democracy, Minorities and International Law* (Cambridge University Press, Cambridge).

Wilkinson, Richard (1996), *Unhealthy Societies: The Afflictions of Inequality* (Routledge, Oxford).

Wilson, Catherine (ed.) (1999), *Civilization and Oppression,* Canadian Journal of Philosophy Supplementary Volume 25 (1999), (University of Calgary Press, Calgary).

Wilson, Richard (ed.) (1997), *Human Rights, Culture and Context: Anthropological Perspectives* (Pluto Press, London).

Winston, Kenneth (ed.) (1981), *The Principles of Social Order: Selected Essays of Lon L. Fuller* (Duke University Press, Durham, N.C.).

Wissenburg, Marcel (2009), *Political Pluralism and the State: Beyond Sovereignty* (Routledge, London).

Wolf, Martin (2004), *Why Globalization Works* (Yale University Press, New Haven).

Wolterstorff, Nicholas (2008), *Justice: Rights and Wrongs* (Princeton University Press, New Jersey).

Wright, Sue & Kelly-Holmes, Helen (eds.) (1998), *Managing Language Diversity* (Multilingual Matters Limited, Clevedon).

Young, Iris Marion (1990), *Justice and the Politics of Difference* (Princeton University Press, Princeton).

Young, Iris Marion (2000), *Inclusion and Democracy* (Oxford University Press, Oxford).

Young, Oran R. & Marc A. Levy (1999) 'The Effectiveness in International Regimes' in Young, Oran R. (ed.) *The Effectiveness of International Environmental Regimes: Causal Connections and Behavioural Mechanisms* (MIT Press, Cambridge, Mass. and London).

Articles

Arendt, Hannah (1967) 'Truth and Politics', The New Yorker, February 25 1967, p. 49, at: http://www.newyorker.com/magazine/1967/02/25/truth-and-politics.

Anaya, James S. (1993), 'A Contemporary Definition of the International Norm of Self-determination', *Transnational Law and Contemporary Problems* 3:131–164.

Bell, Daniel A. (1996), *'The East Asian Challenge to Human Rights: Reflections on an East West Dialogue'*, Human Rights Quarterly, 1996, Vol. 18, 641.

Blake, Michael I. (2000), *'Rights for People, Not for Cultures'*, Civilization, August/September, 50.

Brown-Blake, C. (2006), *'Fair Trial, Language and the Right to Interpretation'*, International Journal on Minority and Group Rights, Volume 13, No. 4, 391.

Buchanan, Allen (1993), *'The Role of Collective Rights in the Theory of Indigenous Peoples' Rights'*, Transnational Law & Contemporary Problems 3(1): 89–108.

Cariolou, Leto (2007) *'Recent Case Law of the European Court of Human Rights Concerning the Protection of Minorities'* in European Yearbook of Minority Issues, Volume 7, 2007/2008, 513.

Carothers, Thomas (2006), *'The Backlash against Democracy Promotion'*, Foreign Affairs, March/April 2006, 55.

Carothers, Thomas (2009), *'Democracy Assistance: Political vs. Developmental?'* Journal of Democracy, Volume 20, Number 1, January 2009.

Coomans, Fons (2003), *'The Ogoni case before the African Commission on Human and Peoples' Rights'*, 52 International and Comparative Law Quarterly, 749.

Cullity, Garrett (1995), *'Moral Free Riding'*, Philosophy and Public Affairs, Volume 24, 3.

Danley, John (1991), *'Liberalism, Aboriginal Rights and Cultural Minorities'*, Philosophy and Public Affairs 20(2) (1991), 168.

De Graaf, Vincent & Verstichel, Annelies (2006), *'Recommendations on Policing in Multi-Ethnic Societies'*, in: Institute for Peace Research and Security Policy at the University of Hamburg/IFSH (ed.), OSCE Yearbook 2006, Baden-Baden 2007, 317–330.

Diener, E., Suh, E. & Oishi, S. (1997), *'Recent findings on subjective well-being'*, Indian Journal of Clinical Psychology, 24, (1997), 25–41.

Dion, Stephane (2002), *'The Canadian Charter of Rights and Freedoms: The Balance between Individual and Collective Rights'*, Canadian Studies Lecture, Woodrow Wilson School, Princeton University, New Jersey, 1 April 2002.

Donnelly, Jack (1986), *'International Human Rights: A Regime Analysis, International Organization'*, 40:3, 559–642.

Douzinas, C. (2001), *'Human rights, humanism, and desire'*, Angelaki, 6(3): 183–206.

Durbach, Renshaw & Byrnes (2009), *"'A Tongue but no Teeth?' The Emergence of a Regional Human Rights Mechanism in the Asia Pacific Region"*, Sydney Law Review, Volume 31:211.

Dworkin, Ronald (1989), *'Liberal Community'*, California Law Review, 77(3): 479–504.

Eide, A. (1999), *'The Oslo Recommendations Regarding the Linguistic Rights of National Minorities: An Overview'*, 6(3) International Journal on Minority and Group Rights, 319–328.

Evans, G. (2001), 'Conflict Prevention with Regard to Inter-ethnic Issues, Including the Role of Third Parties: Experiences and Challenges from the Asian-Pacific Region', 8 International Journal on Minority and Group Rights, 38.

Eisenberg, Avigail (1994), 'The Politics of Individual and Group Difference in Canadian Jurisprudence', Canadian Journal of Political Science, Volume 27 No. 1, March 1994, 3–21.

Favell, A. (1998), 'Applied Political Philosophy at the Rubicon: Will Kymlicka's Multicultural Citizenship', Ethical Theory and Moral Practice, Volume. 1 (1998), 225–278.

Gilbert, Geoff (1996), 'The Council of Europe and Minority Rights' in Human Rights Quarterly, Volume 18, Number 1, February 1996, 160.

Greer, Steven C. (2009), 'Being 'Realistic' about Human Rights', Northern Ireland Legal Quarterly, 60(2), 145–159.

Griffin, James (2001), 'Discrepancies between the best philosophical account of human rights and the international law of human rights' in Proceedings of the Aristotelian Society, 101, 1–28.

Habermas, Jürgen (1994), 'Three Normative Models of Democracy', Constellations, Volume 1, No. 1, 1994.

Hafner-Burton, Emilie M. & Kiyoteru Tsutsui (2005), 'Human Rights in a Globalising World: The Paradox of Empty Promises', American Journal of Sociology, 110:5, 1373–1411.

Hafner-Burton, Emilie M. (2009), 'The Power Politics of Regime Complexity: Human Rights Trade Conditionality in Europe', Perspectives on Politics, 7:1, 33–37.

Heintze, Hans-Joachim (2013), 'The Significance of the Thematic Recommendations of the OSCE High Commissioner on National Minorities', in: IFSH (ed.), OSCE Yearbook 2012, Baden-Baden 2013, 249–265.

Henrard, Kristin (2005), '"Participation", "Representation" and "Autonomy" in the Lund Recommendations and Their Reflections in the Supervision of the FCNM and Several Human Rights Conventions', International Journal on Minority and Group Rights, 12:2–3, 133–168.

Herr, Ranjoo (2004), 'A Third World Feminist Defense of Multiculturalism', Social Theory and Practice, 30: 73–103.

Hessler, Kristen (2005), 'Resolving Interpretive Conflicts in International Human Rights Law', Journal of Political Philosophy, Volume 13, Number 1, 2005, 29–52.

Hooker, Juliet (2005), 'Indigenous Inclusion/Black Exclusion: Race, Ethnicity and Multicultural Citizenship in Contemporary Latin America', Journal of Latin American Studies, 37/2: 285–310.

Hughes, James & Sasse, Gwendolyn (2003), 'Monitoring the Monitors: EU Enlargement Conditionality and Minority Protections in the CEECs', Journal on Ethno-politics and Minority Rights in Europe, 1:1, 1–37.

Jackson-Preece (1997), 'Minority Rights in Europe: From Westphalia to Helsinki', Review of International Studies, 23:1, 75–93.

Kirkup, Alex & Evans, Tony (2009), *'The Myth of Western Opposition to Economic, Social and Cultural Rights? A Reply to Whelan and Donnelly'*, Human Rights Quarterly 31 (2009), 221–238.

Kukathas, Chandran (1992), *'Are There Any Cultural Rights?'* Political Theory, 20/1: 105–139.

Lennox, Corinne (2006), *'The Changing International Protection Regimes for Minorities and Indigenous Peoples'* (presented to Annual Conference of International Studies association, San Diego, March 2006).

Maddison, Sarah (2009), *'Australia: Indigenous Autonomy Matters'*, Development (2009) 52(4), 483–489.

McCarthy, Thomas (1994), *'Kantian Constructivism and Reconstructivism: Rawls and Habermas in Dialogue'*, Ethics 105 (October 1994), 44–63.

McDonald, Leighton (1998), *'Can Collective and Individual Rights Coexist?'*, Melbourne University Law Review, Volume 22 (1998), 310–336.

Modood, Tariq (1998), *'Anti-Essentialism, Multiculturalism, and the 'Recognition' of Religious Groups'*, The Journal of Political Philosophy 6 (4) (1998): 378.

Moravcsik, Andrew (2000), *'The Origins of Human Rights Regimes: Democratic Delegation in Post-war Europe'*, International Organization, 52:2, 729–752.

Nisan, Mordechai (1996), *'The Minority Plight'*, The Middle East Quarterly, September 1996, Volume III: Number 3.

Nowak, Manfred (1980), *'The Effectiveness of the International Covenant on Civil and Political Rights – Stocktaking after the first Eleven Sessions of the UN Human Rights Committee'*, 1 Human Rights Law Journal 136 (1980).

Okin, Susan Moller (2002), *'Mistresses of their Own Destiny: Group Rights, Gender, and Realistic Rights of Exit'*, Ethics 112(2): 205–230.

Packer, J. and Siemienski, G. (1996–7), *'Integration through education: the origin and devleopment of the Hague Recommendations'*, 4(2) International Journal on Minroity and Group Rights, 187–198.

Padamsee, Tasleem J. (2009), *'Culture in Connection: Re-Contextualizing Ideational Processes in the Analysis of Policy Development'*, Social Politics: International Studies in Gender, State, and Society, Volume.16, No. 4, winter 2009, 413–445.

Peerenboom, Randall (2005), *'Assessing Human Rights in China: Why the Double Standard?'*, 38(1) CILJ (2005), 71–164.

Phillips, Anne (2004), *'Defending Equality of Outcome'*, Journal of Political Philosophy 12(1): 1–19.

Phillips, Anne (2006), *"'Really' Equal: Opportunities and Autonomy"*, Journal of Political Philosophy 14(1): 18–32.

Rabinowitz, D. (2001), *'The Palestinian Citizens of Israel, the Concept of Trapped Minority and the Discourse of Transnationalism in Anthropology'*, 24(1) Ethnic and Racial Studies, 64–85.

Rawls, John (1988), 'The Priority of Right and Ideas of the Good', Philosophy and Public Affairs, 251.

Rechel, Bernd (2008), 'What has limited the EU's impact on minority rights in Accession Countries?', East European Politics and Societies, 22:1, 171–191.

Schmidtke, O. (2002), 'Naive Universalism: The Neglected Questions in Brain Barry's Culture and Equality', Ethnicities, 2/2. 268.

Smith, R.K.M. (2000), 'Preserving Linguistic Heritage: A Study of Scots Gaelic', International Journal on Minority and Group Rights, Volume 7, 173.

Squires, Judith (2002), 'Difference or Compromise?', Government and Opposition, Volume 37, 2002, 281.

Sunder, Madhavi (2001), 'Cultural Dissent', Stanford Law Review, Vol. 54 No. 3, December 2001, 495–567.

Tharoor, Shashi (1999/2000), 'Are Human Rights Universal?', World Policy Journal XVI(4).

Tilley, Virginia (2002), 'New Help or New Hegemony? The Transnational Indigenous Peoples' Movement and "Being Indian" in El Salvador', Journal of Latin American Studies, 34: 525–554.

Waldron, Jeremy, 'Rights in Conflict', Ethics, Vol. 99, No. 3, April 1989, 503–519.

Wheeler, Ron (1999), 'The United Nations Commission on Human Rights, 1982–1997: A Study of "Targeted" Resolutions', 32(1) Canadian Journal of Political Science (1999), 75–101.

Whelan, Daniel J. & Donnelly, Jack (2009), 'Yes, A Myth: A Reply to Kirkup and Evans', Human Rights Quarterly 31 (2009), 239–255.

Wright, Jane (1996), 'The OSCE and the Protection of Minority Rights', Human Rights Quarterly, Volume 18, Number 1, February 1996, 190.

Yee, Sienho (2004), 'The Role of Law in the Formation of Regional Perspectives in Human Rights and Regional Systems for the Protection of Human Rights: The European and Asian Models as Illustrations', 8 Singapore Yearbook of International Law (2004), 157–164.

Index

Page references marked in **bold** indicate a more in-depth treatment of the subject.

abandonment (state approach to self-determination rights)   95–196
absolute truth claims, in external dialogue   49–151
ACHPR (African Charter on Human and Peoples' Rights)   47, 48–49
ACJ (Advisory Council of Jurists, APF)   60
ACWC (ASEAN Commission on the Promotion and Protection of the Rights of Women and Children)   58
adaptation   21–22, 107
Advisory Council of Jurists (ACJ, APF)   60
aesthetic value, as basis for group rights   88
affirmative action   76, 158
   in Malaysia   53
   in North America   45–46
Afghanistan, minority rights regime in   63
Africa, minority rights regime in   47–49, 65
African Charter on Human and Peoples' Rights (ACHPR)   47, 48–49
African Union   47
AHRD (ASEAN Human Rights Declaration)   54–57
   Article 6 (human rights and corresponding duties)   55
   Article 7 (universal human rights)   55–56
   Article 8 (limitations)   56
   Article 26 (social and cultural rights UDHR)   55
   Article 32 (cultural participation)   55
   Article 33 (state obligations)   55
   criticism on   55–57
   prevalence of national laws in   56–57
   on sexual orientation   60
AICHR (ASEAN Intergovernmental Commission on Human Rights)   54
Ainu people (Japan)   51
Alhaji Mohammed v. Knott (1969, 1 QB 1)   79, 180
American Convention on Human Rights   42–43
   Article 1 (obligation to respect rights)   42
   Article 8 (fair trial)   43
   Article 11 (privacy)   43
   Article 12 (conscience and religion)   42
   Article 13, additional protocol (education)   43
   Article 13 (thought and expression)   42–43
   Article 14, additional protocol (benefits of culture)   43
   Article 14 (reply)   43
   Article 16 (association)   43
American Declaration of Independence (1776)   45
American Declaration on the Rights and Duties of Man   43
   Article 2 (equality before law)   42
   Article 3 (religion and worship)   42
   Article 4 (investigation, opinion, expression and dissemination)   42–43
   Article 5 (protection of honor, personal reputation, and private and family life)   43
   Article 12 (education)   43
   Article 13 (benefits of culture)   43
   Article 18 (fair trial)   42
   Article 22 (association)   43
Americas, minority rights regime in   41–47
anti-liberal groups   90, 161, 172, 174
   see also illiberal groups
anti-multiculturalists   90, 98
APF (Asia Pacific Forum of National Human Rights Institutions)   59–61
Appadurai, Arjun   226
Arab Charter on Human Rights (2004)   20, 62–63
Arab Committee of Human Rights   62–63
Arab nationalism   62
Arab Spring, impact on minority rights   64–65
Arendt, Hannah   149–150
Are There Any Cultural Rights? (Chandran Kukathas)   219
ARF (ASEAN Regional Forum)   58–59
ASEAN, minority rights regime of   54–62
ASEAN Charter (2008)   54

ASEAN Commission on the Promotion and Protection of the Rights of Women and Children (ACWC)   58
ASEAN Declaration on Cultural Heritage   57
ASEAN Human Rights Declaration *see* AHRD
ASEAN Intergovernmental Commission on Human Rights (AICHR)   54
ASEAN Regional Forum (ARF)   58–59
Asia, minority rights regime in   49–62, 65
'Asian Values' debate   49, 55
Asia-Pacific, minority rights regime in   53
Asia Pacific Forum of National Human Rights Institutions (APF)   59–61
assimilation   5, 21–22
assistance, right to   76, 113, 114, 121–122, 127, 138–139
   collectively right to   122, 139, 140
   individual right to   122, 139, 140, 157–158
   right to collective self-determination v.   138
assisted capacity building   194, 196–207
   capacities required for self-government   197–201
association, right to   161–162, 173
Auckland Declaration (PIF, 2004)   59
Australia, self-governance in   192–193
autonomy   93
   assisted capacity building as means to achieve   196–207
   boundaries of   130–138
   cultural   115, 138, 140, 156, 157, 158, 159, 173
   importance of distance/proximity   100, 102, 103
   limits of, national interests   136–138
   as precondition for holding and exercising rights   187, 188
   preconditions for   103
   see also children's autonomy; group autonomy; individual autonomy; self-determination; self-governance
autonomy, right to   20, 26, 80, 99, 121–122, 137–138
   as group right against the State   99, 126–130
   indigenous peoples   16, 187

Bangladesh, minority rights regime in   51
Barry, Brian   91–92, 102, 219–220
Bentham, Jeremy   167, 168

Between Facts and Norms (Jürgen Habermas)   106
Biketawa Declaration (PIF, 2000)   59
bilateral treaties, criticism on   2
Bloed, Arie   29
Bohm, David   143, 222–223, 225, 227–228
Bolzano/Bozen Recommendations on National Minorities in Inter-State Relations (2008)   30
Boran, Idil   87
Boy Scouts of America v. Dale (530 U.S. 640, 2000)   172–173
Burakumin people (Japan)   51
burqa ban (France)   215–216

Canada
   indigenous peoples in   46, 196
   language rights in   131–133
   multicultural policy in   45–46
Canadian Charter of Rights and Freedoms   46
Canadian Constitution   46
capacity building *see* assisted capacity building
capacity conditions for holding and exercising rights   188
   for self-government   197–201
Carens, Joseph H.   185
Casals, Torbisco   85
Castellino, Joshua   50–51
categorization of group rights   75–79, 121, 126
   diagram   230*ill.*
The Charter of the French Language (National Assembly of Quebec, 1977)   131–132
Charter of Fundamental Rights (CFR, EU)   36–38
   Article 21 (non-discrimination)   37
   Article 22 (cultural, religious and linguistic diversity)   37
   Article 51 (scope)   38
   legal status   37, 38–39
Charter of Paris for a New Europe (1990)   28
child marriages   179–180
child mistreatment and abuse   178
   in Australia   192
   forced marriages   179–180
   genital mutilation   185
children, objective well-being of   175, 179, 180, 185

INDEX   249

children's autonomy   176, 177
children's rights   189
    definition   176
    individual right to internal dialogue
        176–180
    moral v. legal rights   189
China, minority rights regime in   51–52
Chittagong Hill Tribes (Bangladesh)   51
'choice theory' of rights   188
Christians, in Middle East   62, 64
citizenship, in ICCPR   9–10
civilisation, concept/definition   72
civil rights, cultural rights v.   110, 210
Civil Rights Acts (US, 1964)   45
classification of group rights   75–79, 121, 126
coercion   92, 94
    persuasion v.   92–93
Cold War   3
collective rights   37, 121
    collective cultural rights   121, 155–156
    definition   67–68
    endorsement of   211
    individual v.   188, 223–224
    objections to   121
    rights against the state   112–113, 121
    right to assistance and intervention   122, 138–139, 140
    right to external dialogue   118, 120, 121–122, 123, **139–155**, 220, 222
    right to self-determination   122, 138
    term   1
    see also group-differentiated minority rights; group rights; minority (cultural) rights
Commissioner for Education, Culture, Multilingualism and Youth (EC)   35
Commissioner for Justice, Fundamental Rights and Citizenship (EC)   35
Committee on Constitutional Affairs (EU)   40
Committee on the Elimination of Racial Discrimination (Japan)   51
communicative rationality (Habermas)   122
communitarianism, correlation between group rights and   84
competing rights   183n40, 203–204, 215–216, **221–223**, 224
complex rights   68–69

comprehensive liberalism, political liberalism v.   95–96
conceptions of human rights   212, 219–220
concepts of minority rights   66, 70, 71
conflict prevention, management and resolution   30, 142, 145–146, 147
    conflicts between competing rights   183n40, 203–204, 215–216, **221–223**, 224
    conflicts between tradition and modernity   203
    conflicts during and after dialogue   204
    dialogue to solve   222–223
    distinction between minority rights and   27, 28–29
    'overlapping consensus' theory (Rawls)   144–145
Constitutive Act (African Union)   47
Convention on the Rights of the Child (UN, 1989)   9n27, 176
    Article 9 (parenting)   177
Copenhagen Document (1990)   27–28
    Article 35 (effective participation in public affairs)   28
costs of dialogical approach   226
Council of Europe   4, 21–26, 34–35
The Critique of Pure Reason (Immanuel Kant)   97–98
cross-border contacts, right to self-determination and   17–18
cross-cultural consensus   220–221
cultural autonomy   115, 138, 140, 156, 157, 158, 159, 173
cultural belonging   102–103, 162
    connection between individual autonomy and   88–89
    individual v. collective rights   122, 155–157
    restrictions on human freedom and   161
    right to   113, 156, 161
    see also cultural identity
cultural differences   83
cultural displacement   22
cultural dissidents   181
    right to internal dialogue   172–175
cultural diversity, as public good   87–88
cultural groups
    definition   79
    indigenous communities v.   80
    sovereign states v.   79–80

cultural identity   101
    definition   73
    dialogical nature of   100–102, 109
    influence on national interests   136
    see also cultural belonging
cultural interaction and dialogue   101, 103, 109
cultural minorities   71
cultural preservationism   77, 107, 127, 133
    gender inequality and   161
cultural relativism   120, 219, 220
cultural rights   10–11, 69, 87, 116
    civil and political rights v.   110, 116, 210
    cost of   116–117
    law   156
    legal enforceability of   116–117
    restricting freedom of group members   91, 155
    right to participate and not to participate in cultural practices   156–157
cultural values   101
culture
    concept/definition   71–73
    dialogue between law and   109–111, 209
Culture and Equality (Brian Barry)   91–92

Dale, James   172–173
decision making *see* internal decision making bodies
Declaration on Minority Rights (UN, 1992)   3–4, 5, 13–14, 211
    Article 1   128
    definitions in   14
Declaration on the Rights of Indigenous Peoples (UN, 2007)   15–21, 46, 79, 126, 187
    Article 18 (right to be represented in decision-making)   19
    Article 27 (recognition of indigenous' peoples laws and traditions)   20
    Article 35 (right to determine responsibilities)   20
    Article 36(1) (cross-border contacts)   17–18
    Article 44 (equal rights for male and females)   19
    Article 46(1) (territorial integrity and political unity)   16–17
    autonomy and self-determination in   16
    defects   16–20

    definitions in   18–19
    group rights in   15–16
    internal diversity and oppression in   19–20
    legal enforceability of   16
    risk of manipulation   19–20
    self-determination and self-governance in   190–191
deliberation values, internal decision-making bodies and   202
democracy, link between dialogue and   224–225
dialogical approach, costs of   226
dialogical approach to minority rights   97, **100–102**, 147, 209, 217, 219, 224
    challenges   224–228
    costs of   226
    diagram   230*ill.*
    distraction in the process   225
    impact on human rights system and society   122
    importance of knowledge building   226
    legitimacy of law and   106–112
    restricting internal rules and   135
    role of human emotions in   227–228
dialogue   209
    challenges to develop   224–228
    dialogue about dialogue   152
    dialogue management   204
    face-to-face interaction v. internet communication   152–153
    link between democracy and   224–225
    link with diversity   225
    link with pluralism   225
    principles and rules of   152, 153
    result of   220–221
    willingness and competence to take part in   154
dialogue, rights to   220, 224
    civil and political rights v.   117
    complexity of   118, 118–119
    diagram   230*ill.*
    legal enforceability of   117, 119
    necessity of   115–116
    rights to be heard v.   120–121
    see also external dialogue, right to; internal dialogue, right to
disability rights   181
disabled people   175, 180–181

INDEX 251

discrimination
  based on sexual orientation   173
  of mentally incapacitated people
    180–181
  of Palestinians   63
  of social minorities   71
distance, characterizing autonomy   100
diversity, link with dialogue   223
divisive/doctrinally conflicting issues
  definition   148–149
  inclusion in external dialogue   148–152
Domínguez Redondo, Elvira   50–51
Dunbar, Robert   30
duties
  division of duties between states and
    minority groups   200
  rights v.   119–120, 221
  see also state obligations
Dworkin, Ronald   135, 164, 165

Eastern Asia, minority rights regime in   50
EBLUL (European Bureau of Lesser Used
  Languages)   34
ECHR (European Convention on Human
  Rights)   38–41
  Article 14 (prohibition of discrimination)
    21–22
  Article 52 (inquiries by Secretary General)
    39
  EU accession to   40–41
ECJ (European Court of Justice)   39
  jurisdiction of   40
  relation with ECtHR   39–41
economic crisis   5
ECtHR (European Court of Human Rights),
  relation with ECJ   39–41
education, as requirement for
  self-governance   202–203
Egypt, minority rights regime in   63, 64–65
Egyptian Bill of Rights (2011)   64–65
Elbaradei, Mohamed   64
elder abuse   182
elderly people
  objective well-being   175, 182
  social services and   182
enforcement of rights   76–77, 124, 127
  by minority groups   113, 114
  by the state   115
equal concern, right to   113, 114, **163–165**, 200

equality, conceptions of   163–164
equality principle   94
equal liberty principle   93
equal treatment   21, 93, 101–102, 156
ethics, morality v.   123
ethnic violence   3, 5, 83
Europe, minority rights regime in   4, **21–41**,
  65, 83, 213–214
European Bureau for Lesser Used Languages
  (EBLUL)   34
European Charter of Regional and Minority
  Languages (1992)   22–23
European Commission   34–35
  cultural agenda   35–36
European Convention on Human Rights
  see ECHR
European Court of Human Rights see ECtHR
European Court of Justice see ECJ
European Parliament, resolutions   33–34
European Union   4, 31–41
  accession to ECHR   40–41
  cultural diversity   32–33, 36
  see also Europe
exit, right to   99, 113, 114, 122, 123, 124,
    162–163, 173, 185–186, 200
expression, freedom of see freedom of
  expression
external dialogue, willingness by minorities
  to engage in   141–143, 200
external dialogue, right to   113, 115, 137
  accommodation of absolute truth
    claims   149–151
  all-inclusiveness of   143, 154
  collective right to   118, 120, 121–122, 123,
    139–155, 220, 222
  dialogical processes   151–154
  exclusion of   143–155
    conflict avoidance approach
      145–146, 147
    public reason   147
  freedom of expression v.   115–121
  inclusion of doctrinally conflicting
    issues   148–152
  individual right to   118, 120, 122, 123, 141,
    158–159, 220, 222
  limitations of   143
  reasonableness/reasonable
    disagreement   145, 149, 150
  refusal of external dialogue   141

external protections, internal restrictions v. 92, 93, 96
external rules (category of group rights) 77, 127, 129
    limiting liberty of non-members 130–133

Far East, minority rights regime in 50, 51
far-right politics 5
FCNM (Framework Convention for the Protection of National Minorities) 5, 23–26
    acceptance of 24
    Article 14.2 (*education in minority languages*) 25–26
    Article 15 (effective participation) 26
    definitions in 24–25
    legal enforceability of 24
fear of minorities, challenging dialogue 226–228
Finland, minority regime in 26
forced assimilation 21–22, 158
Forced Marriage (Civil Protection) Act (UK, 2007) 184
forced marriages 179–180, 183–184
Framework Convention for the Protection of National Minorities *see* FCNM
France
    burqa ban 215–216
    minority regime in 26
freedom of expression 42, 131n5, 156, 169
    limitations to 139–140
    right to external and internal dialogue v. 115–121
    see also absolute truth claims
freedoms, rights v. 116–119
freedom to associate 161–162, 173
fundamental convictions 149

Gaus, Gerald 96
gender inequality 161, 174, 182
generic rights, accommodation with group rights 15, 81–84
genital mutilation 184–185
Germany, bilateral treaty with Poland 2
Gibbard, Alan 221
globalisation 224–225
Graaf, Vincent de 30
group autonomy 100
    individual autonomy v. 132
    internal oppression and 161

limitations of 136
as precondition for holding and exercising group rights 187, 188
group-differentiated minority rights 68
    historical development of 5–6
    promotion of 3–4
    retreat from 81
    substitution by generic human rights 2, 4–5
    term 1
    see also collective rights; group rights; minority (cultural) rights
group rights
    accommodation with generic rights 15, 81–84
    accommodation of individual rights with 81–84, 86–87, 102, 104, 106, **223–224**
    aesthetic value as basis for 88
    against the State,
        rights to assistance and appropriate intervention 138–139
        rights to external dialogue 139–155
        rights to self-determination and autonomy 126–130
    classification/categorization of 75–79, 121
    correlation between communitarianism and 84
    in Declaration on the Rights of Indigenous Peoples 15–16
    expansion of 97–99, 100
    hard-multiculturalist approach to 89–90, 91, 127, 162
    historical evolution of 1–7
    human rights v. 103–104
    liberal approach to 84–89, 91–93, 94, 102, 146, 147, 164
    political theorists v. lawyers 81–82
    rejection of 91
    requirements for necessity of 81
    as rights to public goods 87–88
    term/definition 1, 67–68
    theoretical validity and moral defensibility of 84–90
    see also collective rights; group-differentiated minority rights; minority (cultural) rights
group, rights against the *see* rights against the (minority) group

group rights proper   75
group-specific rights   68, 75
group-state co-operation   199
group-statistical rights ('funny rights')   75
guaranteed representation demands (category of group rights)   77

Habermas, Jürgen   106–109, 122, 123
Hague Recommendations Regarding the Education of Rights of National Minorities (1996)   29
Hanoi Plan of Action (1998)   54
'harm principle' (J.S. Mill)   134
Hart, H.L.A.   68, 189
HCNM (High Commissioner on National Minorities)   28–29, 61
headscarves   179
Helsinki Final Act (1975)   27
Henrard, Kirstin   30
High Commissioner on National Minorities (HCNM)   28–29, 61
human dignity, human rights and   166–167
human emotions, challenging dialogue   226–228
human freedom, cultural belonging and restrictions on   161
human needs
   human rights v.   166
   see also well-being
human rights
   conceptions of   49, 87, 88, 91, **108**, **219–220**, 223, 224
   group rights v.   103–104
   human dignity and   166–167
   human needs v.   166
   legitimate basis of   109, 213
   minority rights in system of   210–217, 218
   popular sovereignty v.   106, 108
   relation between law and politics with respect to   108
   third-generation   110, 116–117
   universalism and individualism in   2n4, 6
Human Rights Committee (UN)   9
   General Comment No. 23 (8 April 1994)   11–12
   McIntyre v. Canada   131n5
human rights language/discourse   211–213, 215, 217

IACHR (Inter-American Commission on Human Rights)   43–44
ICCPR (International Covenant of Civil and Political Rights)   3, 8, 51, 211
   Article 1 (self-determination)   12–13
   Article 19 (freedom of expression)   131
   Article 27 (Minority Clause)   9–12, 26, 50, 53, 62, 69
      citizenship in   9–10
      definitions in   10, 14
      individual human rights in   9, 10
      problems with clause   10–11
      state obligations in   10, 11
      universal, general rights in   10, 12
ICERD (International Convention on the Elimination of All Forms of Racial Discrimination)   8, 50
ICESCR (International Covenant on Economic, Social and Cultural Rights)   12–13
   Article 1(3)   128
   Article 1 (self-determination)   12–13
identity, dialogical nature of   100–102
illiberal groups   96, 144, 169
   liberalisation of   164
   non-liberal v. anti-liberal groups   90, 161, 172
   rights of   85
   toleration of   98, 130–136
independence, right to   137
India, minority rights regime in   50
indifference (state approach to self-determination rights)   195–196
indigenous peoples
   in Asia   51, 52
   assisted capacity-building for self-governance   196–207, 206
   in Australia   192–193
   in Canada   46, 196
   challenges faced by   197–198
   change in attitude towards   3
   cooperation with state and NGOs   199–200
   cultural groups v.   80
   definition   80
   duties of   200
   internal diversity and oppression   19–20
   in Latin America   46–47
   national minorities as   18–19

indigenous peoples (cont.)
   rights of self-determination and
      autonomy   128, 187, 196, 197
   welfare dependency   192, 197
   see also Declaration on the Rights of
      Indigenous Peoples
Indigenous Peoples' Act (Philippines, 1997)   52
Indigenous and Tribal Peoples Convention
   (ILO, 1989)   3, 16
individual autonomy   99–100
   group autonomy v.   132
   relation with cultural belonging   88–89
individualism in human rights   2n4, 6
individual rights   68, 81
   accommodation with group rights
      81–84, 86–87, 102, 104, 106, **223–224**
   collective v.   188, 223–224
   correlation between liberalism and   84
   in ICCPR   9, 10
   rights against the group   113
   rights against the state   113
   right to assistance and intervention   122, 139, 140, 157–158
   right to external dialogue   118, 120, 122, 123, 141, **158–159**, 220, 222
   right to internal dialogue   117–118, 119, 122, 123, **165–168**, 220, 222
   in TEU   37
   to cultural belonging   122
Innu people (Canada)   196
institutional capacity-building   60
integration   139
   law as medium of social   106
Inter-American Commission on Human
   Rights (IACHR)   43–44
Inter-American Court of Human Rights   44
inter-cultural dialogue   35–36, 109–110, 139–140
'interest theory' of rights   188, 206
Intergroup for Traditional Minorities,
   National Communities and Languages
   (European Parliament)   34
internal decision-making bodies
   ground rules for developing   201–202
   importance of deliberation values and
      processes   202
   importance of internal and external
      dialogue   202
   as precondition to hold and exercise
      group rights   187, 188, 190

relationship with members   200
see also self-governing capacities
internal dialogue, right to   113, 114, 115, 200
   freedom of expression v.   115–121
   individual right to   117–118, 119, 122, 123, **165–185**, 220, 222
   anti-liberal/isolationist groups   174
   cases   171–185
   children   176–180
   cultural dissidents   172–175
   elderly people   181–182
   mentally incapacitated
      people   180–181
   types of dialogue   171–172
   women   182–185
   objective-well being and   166–167
   subjective well-being and   167–171
internal diversity (within diversity
   groups)   135
internal oppression   19, 20
   group autonomy and   161
   see also internal rules
internal restrictions, external protections v.
   92, 93, 96
internal rules (category of group rights)   77, 127, 129
   enforcement of   135
   restricting freedom of members   130, 132, 133–136
internal self-determination, right of   16
International Convention on the
   Elimination of All Forms of Racial
   Discrimination   8, 50
International Covenant of Civil and Political
   Rights see ICCPR
International Covenant on Economic, Social
   and Cultural Rights see ICESCR
international documents, effectiveness and
   applicability of   66
international human rights instruments
   ratification by states   213–214
   shortcomings   214
international human rights regime
   dominance of Western conception in
      49, 66, 219
   minority cultural rights as part
      of   210–211
international law, incapacity to develop
   self-governing capacities of minority
   groups   190

INDEX

international minority rights law   7, 128–129
international minority rights regime   65–66
international rights standards, Western   212
interpretation of rights, conflicts between   111
inter-religious dialogue   109
intervention   220
    in case of restricting internal rules   135–136
intervention, right to   113, 114, 121–122, 138–139
    collective right   122, 138–139, 140
    individual right   122, 139, 140
    right to collective self-determination v.   138
Iran, minority rights regime in   63
isolationist groups
    right to internal dialogue   174
    women in   175
Israel, minority rights regime in   63

Jackson-Preece, Jennifer   8
Japan, minority rights regime in   51
Jews, in Middle East   62
Jordan, minority rights regime in   63

Kant, Immanuel   97–98, 109
Kennedy, David   216
knowledge-building, challenging dialogue   226
Kukathas, Chandran   100, 102, 169–170
    on conception of human rights   219–220
    on expansion of group rights   97–99, 100
Kymlicka, Will   3, 16
    on categorization of group-specific rights   68, 75–76
    on conflicts between competing rights   203
    on culture/cultural values   72, 130, 132
    on debates about minority rights   5, 26, 85
    on internal rules/restrictions   134
    liberal conception of group rights   88–89, 94
    liberal theory of multiculturalism   92–93, 96

language rights   10, 22–23
    education in minority languages   25–26
    Quebec   131–133

Laos, minority rights regime in   53
Latin America, minority rights regime in   46–47
law
    dialogue between culture and   109–111, 209
    as medium of social integration   106
    relation between political theory and   106–109
law-making
    public opinion and will formation influencing   107
    sphere of   109
lawyers, approach to group rights   81–82
League of Nations   2, 8
legal rights
    children   189
    moral rights v.   109, 110, 189
legitimacy of law, public opinion and will formation influencing   106
Lennox, Corinne   19
Levy, Jacob   76–78, 112, 121, 126, 163
liberal groups, illiberal v.   172
liberalism
    approach to group rights   84–89, 91–93, 94, 102, 146, 147, 164
    comprehensive   95–96
    individual rights and   84, 108
liberty-limiting rules *see* internal rules
liberty principle   94
Libya, minority rights regime in   63
Lisbon Treaty (Reform Treaty, 2009)   32, 36, 37, 41
Lund Recommendations on the Effective Participation of National Minorities in Public Life (1999)   29

Maastricht Treaty (Treaty on European Union, 1993)   32, 36
    Article 2 (founding values)   36–37, 38
    qualification of minorities in   37
MacCormick, Neil   68–69, 188
McDonald, Leighton   222, 223–224
McIntyre v. Canada (UN Human Rights Committee, 385/1989/Rev.1, 1993)   131n5
Maddison, Sarah   192–194, 197
majorities, minorities v.   70, 96
Malaysia, minority rights regime in   53
mass media, role in enabling dialogue   227
Mendus, Susan   99–100, 102, 103, 130

mentally incapacitated people   175, 180–181
Middle East, minority rights regime in
    62–65
migrant workers   9, 10
Millennium Development Goals (UN)   199
Mill, John Stuart   134, 168
Mindanao islands (Philippines)   53
minorities
    in African context   47
    change in attitude towards   3
    definition issue   66, 70–71
    fear of   226–228
    as individual human beings   2
    majorities v.   70
    see also national minorities
minorities within minorities   91–92, 172
    children   176–180
    cultural dissidents   172–175
    elderly people   181–182
    mentally incapacitated people   180–181
    women   182–185
minority (cultural) rights
    concept   66, 70, 71
    cross-cultural consensus   220–221
    prioritisation of   123–124
    in system of human rights   2–3, 210–217, 218
    term/definition   1, 67, 68
    treatment as proper legal rights   218
    see also collective rights; group-differentiated rights; group rights; individual rights
minority groups
    enforcement of rights   113, 114
    internal decision-making bodies   187, 188, 190, 200, 201–202
    see also rights against the (minority) group
Minority Rights International   196
minority rights protection
    in Africa   47–49
    in Americas   41–47
    in Asia   49–62
    in Europe   21–41
    factors of success   216–217
    in Middle East   62–65
    shortcomings   214–215
modernisation (state approach to self-determination rights)   194–195
Modood, Tariq   73

Montevideo Convention on the Rights and Duties of States (1933), *Article 1* (qualifications of a state)   79
moral agency, as precondition for holding and exercise of group rights   187–190
moral capacity, as precondition of holding and exercising rights   188
morality, ethics v.   123
moral relativism   219, 220
moral rights
    children   189
    legal rights v.   109, 110, 189
Multicultural Citizenship (Will Kymlicka)   75–76, 203
multicultural constitutionalism   46
multiculturalism   5, 71
    in Europe   65
    liberal theory   92
    rejection of   91
    retreat from   65, 81
Multiculturalism Act (Canada, 1988)   45–46
Multiculturalism (Charles Taylor)   100–101
multicultural policy (Canada)   45–46
Muslim sects   62

national interests   126
    influence of cultural identity on   136
    as limits of toleration and autonomy   136–138
    self-determination and   136–137
national minorities   23–26
    definition   21, 24–25
    in European minority rights regime   37, 38
    as indigenous peoples   18–19
negative rights   68
Nepal, minority rights regime in   51
NGOs
    cooperation with indigenous peoples   199–200, 204–206
    working relation with states   205–206
Nisan, Mordechai   64
non-discrimination, right to   11, 48, 57, 156
non-liberal groups   90, 161, 172
    see also illiberal groups
non-Western countries, ratification of international human rights systems   214
norms and values   76, 126

North America, minority rights regime in 45–46
North Korea, minority rights regime in 51

OAS Charter 41
OAS (Organization of American States) 41–44
objective well-being
  minority children, mentally incapacitated, elderly 175, 179, 180
  right to internal dialogue and 166–167
Official Language Act (Canada) 131
Okinawa people (Japan) 51
On Liberty (J.S. Mill) 134
Organisation for Security and Cooperation in Europe *see* OSCE
Organization of American States (OAS) 41–44
OSCE (Organisation for Security and Cooperation in Europe) 4, 27–31
  cross-regional exchange with ASEAN 61
Oslo Recommendations on the Effective Participation of National Minorities in Public Life (1999) 29
'overlapping consensus' theory (Rawls) 142, 144–147

Pacific Islands Forum (PIF) 59
Pacific Plan 59
Packer, John 66
pain, as indicator for well-being 167
Pakistan, minority rights regime in 50
Palestinians 63
parenting, relation between children's autonomy and 177
Paris Principles 61
participatory rights 118
  cultural participation 156–157
  right to external dialogue 140
paternalism (state approach to self-determination rights) 192–194, 196–197
peace-seeking and peace-keeping 142–143
  'overlapping consensus' theory (Rawls) 142, 144–147
Pentassuglia, Gaetano 3
persuasion, coercion v. 92–93
Philippines, minority rights regime in 52
Phillips, Anne 162, 185
PIF (Pacific Islands Forum) 59

pleasure/pleasantness
  challenging dialogue 228
  higher v. lower pleasures 168
  as indicator for well-being 167–168
pluralism, link with dialogue 223
Pogge, Thomas 75
Poland, bilateral treaty with Germany 2
political factors, challenging dialogue 228
political freedoms 116
political liberalism, comprehensive liberalism v. 95–96
Political Liberalism (John Rawls) 95
political rights, cultural rights v. 110, 210
political theory
  approach to group rights 81–82
  relation between law and 106–109
political unity 16–17
poly-ethnic rights 76
popular sovereignty 106, 108
positive discrimination *see* affirmative action
positive rights 68
poverty, mentally incapacitated people 181
preservationism *see* cultural preservationism
prioritisation of minority rights 123–124
private autonomy, relation with public autonomy 106, 108
private sphere rights 92
  public v. 93
procedural rights 105
Proposed Declaration on the Rights of Indigenous Peoples (Inter-American Commission on Human Rights, 1997) 4
protection of rights *see* minority rights protection
proximity
  consequences for group rights 103
  importance for autonomy 100, 102, 103
public autonomy, relation with private autonomy 106, 108
public goods, definition/concept 87
public goods, rights to, group rights as 87–88
public morality 56
public opinion, influencing law-making 107
public reason 146, 148, 151
public sphere rights, private v. 93
public will formation 108

quality of life, definition 165
Quebec, language rights in 131–133

Rabinowitz, D. 63n195
Rawls, John 130
  on absolute truth claims and public reason 146, 149–150, 151
  on equality 163–164
  liberal theory of multicultural citizenship 93–97
  'overlapping consensus' theory 142, 144–147
Raz, Joseph 72, 85–86
reasonableness/reasonable disagreement, in external dialogue 145, 149, 150
recognition rights 76–77, 127, 129
Recommendations on Policing in Multi-Ethnic Societies (Rotterdam Charter, 2006) 30
regional documents, effectiveness and applicability of 66
regional minority rights systems 65–66
Resolution on Racism, Xenophobia and Anti-Semitism and on Further Steps to Combat Racial Discrimination (European Parliament) 34
responsibilities, rights v. 212
right-holders 68
rights
  conflicts between competing 203–204, 215–216
  duties v. 119–120, 221
  freedoms v. 116–119
  holding rights v. exercising rights 187, 188
  responsibilities v. 212
rights against the (minority) group 112–115, 161–163
  right of exit 185–186
  right to equal concern 163–165
  right to internal dialogue 165–185
rights against the State 112–115
  collective cultural rights as 121
  collective v. individual rights 112–113
  distinction of duties v. 119–120
  held by members of minority group,
    rights to cultural belonging 155–157
    rights to state assistance and appropriate intervention 157–158
    right to external dialogue 158–159
  held by minority group,
    collective right to external dialogue 139–155
  limits of toleration and boundaries of autonomy 130–138
  rights to self-determination and autonomy 126–130
  rights to state assistance and appropriate intervention 138–139
  subcategories 121–122
rights claims, limitations on 218
rights sequentialism 206–207
right to assistance 76, 113, 114, 121–122, 127
right to association 161–162, 173
right to autonomy *see* autonomy, right to
right to cultural belonging *see* cultural belonging
right to dialogue *see* dialogue, rights to
right to equal concern 113, 114, **163–165**, 200
right to exit 99, 113, 114, 122, 123, 124, **162–163**, 173, **185–186**, 200
right to independence 137
right to internal self-determination 16
right to intervention *see* intervention, right to
right to non-discrimination 11, 48, 57, 156
right to public goods 87–88
right to secession 136–137
right to self-determination *see* self-determination, right to
right to state assistance 113, 138–139
Rotterdam Charter (2006) 30
R v. Adesanya (unreported) 178, 180

Saudi Arabia 175
  minority rights regime in 63
scarification 178
secession, right to 136–137
Second World War 2
security 94
  minority rights and 27, 28–29
self-determination 206
  external rules and 130–131
  in international law 190–192
  national interests and 136–137
  see also autonomy; self-governance
self-determination, right to 80, 86, 113, 121, 129
  approaches of states,
    indifference and abandonment 195–196
    modernisation 194–195
    paternalism and welfare dependency 192–194, 196–197

INDEX 259

collective right 114, 122, 137–138, 189
cross-border contacts and 17–18
as group right against the State 126–129
in ICESCR and ICCPR 12–13
indigenous groups 128, 187
internal self-determination 16
interrelation with other minority rights 208
reasons for demanding right 207–208
rights to state assistance and intervention v. 138
self-governance
    in Australia 192–193
    in international law 190–192
    main tasks and obstacles 201–204
        conflict resolution 203–204
        deliberation and well-being 202
        education and enlightenment 202–203
        internal decision-making bodies 201–202
    see also autonomy; internal decision-making bodies; self-determination
self-governing capacities
    assisted capacity-building to achieve 196–207
    see also internal decision-making bodies
self-government rights 75–76, 76, 127
    see also self-determination, right to
self-hatred 21–22
self-representation 26
Senge, Peter M. 223
separatism 136
sexual orientation 60, 172–173
Sharia 65
Simmons, Beth 213–214
simpler rights 68–69
social interaction, communicative modes of 107–108
social minorities 71
    cultural minorities v. 71
    type of treatment 71
social services
    cross-cultural competency of 178
    elderly people and 182
societal cultures 72
South Asia, minority rights regime in 50
Southeast Asia, minority rights regime in 50, 52–54
South Korea, minority rights regime in 51

sovereignty, state 30
    in Asia 49
    definition 79
    popular sovereignty v. human rights 106, 108
    sovereign state v. cultural group 79–80
special representation rights 76
Stability Pact (Paris, 1995) 34
standard-setting in minority rights 27
state assistance see assistance, right to
state obligations 211
    commitment to international human rights regime 213–214
    division of duties between states and minority groups 200
    establishment of internal decision-making bodies for minority groups 187
    in ICCPR 9, 10
    language rights 22–23
    mentally incapacitated people 181
states
    approaches to right of self-determination 190, 192–196
        indifference and abandonment 195–196
        modernisation 194–195
        paternalism and welfare dependency 192–194
    cooperation with indigenous peoples 199–200
    enforcement of rights by 115
    ratification of international human rights instruments 213–214
    relation with NGOs 205–206
    see also rights against the State
subjective well-being 167–171, 172
substantive collective minority rights 124
    dialogical dimension 121–123
substantive rights 105
Sunder, Madhavi 172–173
Sunni Islam 62
Survival International 196
symbolic demands (category of group rights) 77, 127
Synergies in Minority Protection (Kirstin Henrard, Robert Dunbar) 30
Syria, minority rights regime in 63

Taking Rights Seriously (Ronald Dworkin) 164

taxonomies of group rights *see* classification/categorization of group rights
Taylor, Charles   100–101, 109
territorial integrity   16–17, 30
terrorism   5
Thailand, minority rights regime in   53
A Theory of Justice (John Rawls)   93, 163
third-generation human rights   110
  cost of   116–117
  legal status of   116
toleration   94, 95, 96, 97–99, 154, 219–220
  limitations/boundaries of   130–138, 143, 145
    group illiberalness and degrees of   130–136
    national interests   136
  normative value of   98
  passive v. active   102
Toleration and the Limits of Liberalism (Susan Mendes)   99
total exemptions (category of group rights)   76, 126
transitional rights   122, 123
Treaty Establishing the European Community (TEC), *Article 151* (culture)   32, 34
Treaty on European Union *see* Maastricht Treaty
Treaty on the Functioning of the European Union (TFEU), *Article 167* (culture)   32–33, 36
truth claims, absolute   149–151
Tyler, Tom   141
Tylor, Edward   72

UN Charter   2, 3
undernourishment   196
United Nations   7–8
  see also Declaration of Minority Rights; Declaration on the Rights of Indigenous Peoples; ICCPR; ICERD; ICESCR; Universal Declaration of Human Rights
United States   45
Universal Declaration of Cultural Diversity (UNESCO, 2001), *Article 5* (cultural rights enabling cultural diversity)   129
Universal Declaration of Human Rights   2, 8, 176
  Article 29(2) (limitations)   56
universal human rights
  cross-cultural legitimacy of   219
  in ICCPR   10, 12
  in United States   45

Van Cott, Donna Lee   46
veiling   183, 184, 215
Verstichel, Annelies   30
Vietnam, minority rights regime in   53

Wahhabism   174
Waldron, Jeremy   221–222
Walzer, Michael   130, 225
A Way of Life That Does Not Exist (Colin Samson)   196
welfare dependency (state approach to self-determination rights)   192, 197
welfare state   193n10
well-being
  definition   165, 167
  diagram   230*ill.*
  objective well-being   166–167
  responsibilities of internal decision-making bodies   202
  subjective well-being   167–171
Western conception of human rights   49, 66, 212, 219
will formation, influencing law-making   107
Williams, Melissa   142
'will theory' of rights   188–189, 206
women
  in anti-liberal/isolationist groups   175
  genital mutilation   184–185
  individual right to internal dialogue   182–185
women driven reform   182–183
Working Group of Indigenous Peoples (UN)   15, 194

Young, Iris Marion   193n10

Printed in the United States
By Bookmasters